SECOND EDITION

The Meaning of Life

Edited by

E. D. Klemke

New York   Oxford

OXFORD UNIVERSITY PRESS

2000

Oxford University Press

Oxford   New York
Athens   Auckland   Bangkok   Bogotá   Buenos Aires   Calcutta
Cape Town   Chennai   Dar es Salaam   Delhi   Florence   Hong Kong   Istanbul
Karachi   Kuala Lumpur   Madrid   Melbourne   Mexico City   Mumbai
Nairobi   Paris   São Paulo   Singapore   Taipei   Tokyo   Toronto   Warsaw

and associated companies in
Berlin   Ibadan

Published by Oxford University Press, Inc.,
198 Madison Avenue, New York, New York, 10016
http://www.oup-usa.org
1-800-334-4249

Library of Congress Cataloging-in-Publication Data

The meaning of life / [edited by] E.D. Klemke. — 2nd ed.
      p.   cm.
   Includes bibliographical references.
   ISBN 13: 978-0-19-512703-4
   ISBN: 019-512703-X
   1. Life. I. Klemke, E. D., 1926–   .
BD431.M4688 2000   98-47102
128—dc21   CIP

Printing (last digit): 9 8

Printed in the United States of America
on acid-free paper

To
DIRK J. SCHOLTEN

whose wise advise, encouragement,
and friendship have enriched my life
and made it more meaningful.

Contents

Contents

PART THREE

Questioning the Question   **207**

Preface

Viktor Frankl once wrote: "Man's concern about a meaning of life is the truest expression of the state of being human." Because I agree with this view, I was led some years ago to put together a collection of essays on the topic of the meaning of life. Since that time I have found many new essays on the topic as well as some that I overlooked in working on the first edition.

The selections contained in this revised edition are, I believe, the most important essays (or chapters) that have been written on the topic of the meaning of life. All but two of the selections are by twentieth-century writers, philosophers, theologians, and others. In some collections of essays, the editor provides a brief summary of all of the selections contained in the anthology. I shall not attempt to do that here, for I believe that the readers' delight and stimulation will be enhanced if they turn to the selections and let the authors speak for themselves.

I would like to express my gratitude to all those who have helped with regard to the planning and preparation of this book. Among those to whom I am especially grateful are Gary Comstock, John Donaghy, John Nerness, Edna Wiser, William D. Hein, and Charles K. Benton.

I would also like to express my appreciation to Robert B. Miller, Jeffrey Broesche, and all of the staff at Oxford University Press.

Finally, I would like to express my unfailing gratitude to some friends who have helped me find meaning and purpose in my own life. Among these I must especially acknowledge Dirk Scholten, Bruce Hardy, Bryan Graveline, Robert Gitchell, Bryan Walker, Steve and Pattie Stamy, David Hauser, William Hein, Robert and Karen Ridgway, and finally, Tom Zmolek, Jim Moran, Matt Schulte, and all of the great employees at Peoples.

Ames, Iowa   E. D. K.
February 1999

INTRODUCTION

The Question of the Meaning of Life

E. D. Klemke

In his work "A Confession," Tolstoy gives an account of how, when he was 50 years old and at the height of his career, he became deeply distressed by the conviction that life was meaningless:

> Five years ago, something very strange began to happen with me; I was overcome by minutes at first of perplexity and then an arrest of life, as though I did not know how to live or what to do, and I lost myself and was dejected. But that passed and I continued to live as before. Then those moments of perplexity were repeated oftener and oftener, and always in one and the same form. These arrests of life found their expression in ever the same question: "Why? Well, and then?"
>
> At first I thought that those were simply aimless, inappropriate questions. It seemed to me that that was all well known and that if I wanted to busy myself with their solution, it would not cost me much labour,—that now I had not time to attend to them, but that if I wanted to I should find the proper answers. But the questions began to repeat themselves oftener and oftener, answers were demanded more and more persistently, and like dots that fall on the same spot, these questions, without any answers, thickened into one black blotch. . . .
>
> I felt that what I was standing on had given way, that I had no foundation to stand on, that that which I lived by no longer existed, and that I had nothing to live by. . . .
>
> "Well, I know," I said to myself, "all which science wants to persistently to know, but there is no answer to the question about the meaning of life."[1]

Perhaps almost every sensitive and reflective person has had at least some moments when similar fears and questions have arisen in his or her life. Perhaps the experiences were not as extreme as Tolstoy's, but they have nevertheless been troublesome. And surely almost everyone has at some time asked: What is the meaning of life? Is there any meaning at all? What is it all about? What is the point of it all? It seems evident, then, that the question of the meaning of life is one of the most important questions. Also it is important for all persons, not merely for philosophers.

At least one writer has maintained that it is the most urgent question. In *The Myth of Sisyphus*, Camus writes:

> There is but one truly serious philosophical problem, and that is suicide. Judging whether life is or is not worth living amounts to answering the fundamental question of philosophy. All the rest—whether the world has three dimensions, whether the mind has nine or twelve categories—come afterward. These are games; one must first answer. . . . If I ask myself how to judge that this question is more urgent than that, I reply that one judges by the actions it entails. I have never seen anyone die for the ontological argument [for the existence of a god]. Galileo, who held a scientific truth of great importance, abjured it with the greatest of ease as soon as it endangered his life. In a certain sense he did right. That truth was not worth the stake. Whether the earth or the sun revolved around the other is a matter of profound indifference. To tell the truth, it is a futile question. On the other hand, I see many people die because they judge that life is not worth living. I see others paradoxically getting killed for the ideas or illusions that give them a reason for living (what is called a reason for living is also an excellent reason for dying). I therefore conclude that the meaning of life is the most urgent of questions.[2]

However we may rank the question—as the most urgent of all or as one of the most urgent of all—most of us do find the question to be one that merits our serious attention. Part of its urgency stems from the fact that it is related to many other questions that face us in our daily lives. Many of the decisions we make with regard to careers, leisure time, moral dilemmas, and other matters depend on how we answer the question of the meaning of life.

However, the question may mean several things. Let us attempt to distinguish some of them. The question "What is the meaning of life?" may mean any of the following: (1) Why does the universe exist? Why is there something rather than nothing? Is there some plan for the whole universe? (2) Why do humans (in general) exist? Do they exist for some purpose? If so, what is it? (3) Why do *I* exist Do I exist for some purpose? If so, how am I to find what it is? If not, how can life have any significance or value?

I do not mean to suggest that these are rigidly distinct questions. They are obviously interrelated. Hence we many interpret the question "What is the meaning of life?" broadly so that it can include any one or any two or all three of these questions. In so doing, we will be following common usage. Perhaps most of those who are deeply concerned with the question interepret it mainly in terms of question (3). However, there are others who include either question (1) or (2) or both along with question (3). Again, we need not be concerned with specifying one of the interpretations as the "correct" one. Rather let us recognize that all of them are often involved when one asks about the meaning of life.

In turning to possible answers to the question of the meaning of life, we find different approaches or stances:

I. The theistic answer

II. The nontheistic alternative

III. The approach that questions the meaningfulness of the question

These three different approaches are represented by the readings found in Parts I, II, and III, respectively, of this volume. Perhaps a brief summary of each would be desirable at this point.

I. According to the theistic answer, the meaning of life is found in the existence of a god—a supremely benevolent and all-powerful being, transcendent to the natural universe, but who created the universe and fashioned man in his image and endowed him with a preordained purpose. In this view, without the existence of God, or at least without faith in God, life has no meaning or purpose and hence is not worth living. It is difficult to find many works in which this position is explicitly defended from a *philosophical* view. However, it is an answer that is held widely by religious believers, and it is apparent that in many cases it is a basis (or part of the basis) for religous belief. Apart from Tolstoy's *Confession*, the other essays found in Part I of this volume do provide a direct theological, existential defense of this view.

II. The nontheistic (or humanistic) alternative, of course, denies the claim that the meaning of life is dependent on the existence of a god. According to this alternative, since there is no good reason to believe in the existence of a transcendent god, there is no good reason to believe that life has any objective meaning or purpose—that is, any meaning that is dependent on anything outside of the natural universe. Rather, the meaning of life, if there is one, must be found within the natural universe. Some adherents of this view go on to claim that there is no good reason to think life has any meaning in *any* objective sense, but there is good reason to believe that it can nevertheless have meaning in a subjective sense. In other words, it is up to each individual to fashion or create his or her own meaning by virtue of his own consciousness and creative activity. A defense of this position is found in the editor's own essay and in other essays in Part II of this volume.

III. There is yet a third approach to the question of the meaning of life. According to this approach, the question "What is the meaning of life?" is a peculiar or at least an ambiguous one. What kind of question are we asking when we ask about the meaning of life? There are some who think that on analysis of terms such as "meaning," "purpose," and "value," the question of the meaning of life turns out to be cognitively meaningless. However, there are others who reject that claim and take the opposing view. According to them, the various questions that make up the larger question of the meaning of life can be given an interpretation that renders them to be intelligible and cognitively significant. Various aspects of and perspectives on this position are presented in the essays in Part III of this volume.

It is my view that the question of the meaning of life is a significant and important one and that it can be given an answer. I believe that the answer does not rest on any theistic or metaphysical assumptions. Since my defense of this position has been given in my essay "Living Without Appeal: An Affirmative Philosophy of Life," contained in this volume, I will not repeat what I have said there except to say this: It will be recalled that in the passage quoted above, Camus maintains that "Judging whether life is or is not worth living amounts to answering the fundamental question of philosophy." The answer I have given to that question is that there is no formula or recipe or slogan to guarantee that life will be worth living; but I believe that it can be worth living. I believe that I shall die, but that in the meantime, I can find a genuine meaning and purpose in life that makes it worth living.

There are some who will object: But how can life have any meaning or worth or value if it must come to an end? Sir Karl Popper has given the best answer I know of to that question. He writes: "There are those who think that life is valueless because it comes to an end. They fail to see that the opposite argument might also be proposed: that if there were no end to life, life would have no value; that it is, in part, the ever-present danger of losing it which helps to bring home to us the value of life."[3]

NOTES

1. From L. Tolstoy, *My Confession*, trans. Leo Weiner (London: J. M. Dent, 1905), passim.

2. A. Camus, *The Myth of Sisyphus*, trans. J. O'Brien (New York: Alfred A. Knopf, 1955), p. i.

3. Sir Karl Popper, "How I See Philosophy." In A. Mercier and M. Svilar (eds.), *Philosophers on Their Own Work*, Vol. 3 (Berne and Frankfurt am Main: Peter Lang, 1977), p. 148.

PROLOGUE

The Meaning of Life

Thomas Nagel

Perhaps you have had the thought that nothing really matters, because in two hundred years we'll all be dead. This is a peculiar thought, because it's not clear why the fact that we'll be dead in two hundred years should imply that nothing we do now really matters.

The idea seems to be that we are in some kind of rat race, struggling to achieve our goals and make something of our lives, but that this makes sense only if those achievements will be permanent. But they won't be. Even if you produce a great work of literature which continues to be read thousands of years from now, eventually the solar system will cool or the universe will wind down or collapse, and all trace of your efforts will vanish. In any case, we can't hope for even a fraction of this sort of immortality. If there's any point at all to what we do, we have to find it within our own lives.

Why is there any difficulty in that? You can explain the point of most of the things you do. You work to earn money to support yourself and perhaps your family. You eat because you're hungry, sleep because you're tired, go for a walk or call up a friend because you feel like it, read the newspaper to find out what's going on in the world. If you didn't do any of those things you'd be miserable; so what's the big problem?

The problem is that although there are justifications and explanations for most of the things, big and small, that we do *within* life, none of these explanations explain the point of your life as a whole—the whole of which all these activities, successes and failures, strivings and disappointments are parts. If you think about the whole thing, there seems to be no point to it at all. Looking at it from the outside, it wouldn't matter if you had never existed. And after you have gone out of existence, it won't matter that you did exist.

Of course your existence matters to other people—your parents and others who care about you—but taken as a whole, their lives have no point either, so it ultimately doesn't matter that you matter to them. You matter to them and they matter to you, and that may give your life a feeling of significance, but you're just taking in each other's washing, so to speak. Given that any person exists, he has needs and concerns which make particular things and people within his life matter to him. But the *whole thing* doesn't matter.

But does it matter that it doesn't matter? "So what?" you might say. "It's enough that it matters whether I get to the station before my train leaves, or whether I've remembered to feed the cat. I don't need more than that to keep going." This is a perfectly good reply. But it only works if you really can avoid setting your sights higher, and asking what the point of the whole thing is. For once you do that, you open yourself to the possibility that your life is meaningless.

The thought that you'll be dead in two hundred years is just a way of seeing your life embedded in a larger context, so that the point of smaller things inside it seems not to be enough—seems to leave a larger question unanswered. But what if your life as a whole did have a point in relation to something larger? Would that mean that it wasn't meaningless after all?

There are various ways your life could have a larger meaning. You might be part of a political or social movement which changed the world for the better, to the benefit of future generations. Or you might just help provide a good life for your own children and their descendants. Or your life might be thought to have meaning in a religious context, so that your time on Earth was just a preparation for an eternity in direct contact with God.

About the types of meaning that depend on relations to other people, even people in the distant future, I've already indicated what the problem is. If one's life has a point as a part of something larger, it is still possible to ask about that larger thing, what is the point of *it?* Either there's an answer in terms of something still larger or there isn't. If there is, we simply repeat the question. If there isn't, then our search for a point has come to an end with something which has no point. But if that pointlessness is acceptable for the larger thing of which our life is a part, why shouldn't it be acceptable already for our life taken as a whole? Why isn't it all right for your life to be pointless? And if it isn't acceptable there, why should it be acceptable when we get to the larger context? Why don't we have to go on to ask, "But what is the point of all *that?*" (human history, the succession of the generations, or whatever).

The appeal to a religious meaning to life is a bit different. If you believe that the meaning of your life comes from fulfilling the purpose of God, who loves you, and seeing Him in eternity, then it doesn't seem appropriate to ask, "And what is the point of *that?*" It's supposed to be something which is its own point, and can't have a purpose outside itself. But for this very reason it has its own problems.

The idea of God seems to be the idea of something that can explain everything else, without having to be explained itself. But it's very hard to understand how there could be such a thing. If we ask the question, "Why is the world like this?" and are offered a religious answer, how can we be prevented from asking again, "And why is *that* true?" What kind of answer would bring all of our "Why?" questions to a stop, once and for all? And if they can stop there, why couldn't they have stopped earlier?

The same problem seems to arise if God and His purposes are offered as the ultimate explanation of the value and meaning of our lives. The idea that our lives fulfil God's purpose is supposed to give them their point, in a way that doesn't require or admit of any further point. One isn't supposed to ask "What is the point of God?" any more than one is supposed to ask, "What is the explanation of God?"

But my problem here, as with the role of God as ultimate explanation, is that I'm not sure I understand the idea. Can there really be something which gives point to everything else by encompassing it, but which couldn't have, or need, any point itself? Something whose point can't be questioned from outside because there is no outside?

If God is supposed to give our lives a meaning that we can't understand, it's not much of a consolation. God as ultimate justification, like God as ultimate explanation, may be an incomprehensible answer to a question that we can't get rid of. On the other hand, maybe that's the whole point, and I am just failing to understand religious ideas. Perhaps the belief in God is the belief that the universe is intelligible, but not to us.

Leaving that issue aside, let me return to the smaller-scale dimensions of human life. Even if life as a whole is meaningless, perhaps that's nothing to worry about. Perhaps we can recognize it and just go on as before. The trick is to keep your eyes on what's in front of you, and allow justifications to come to an end inside your life, and inside the lives of others to whom you are connected. If you ever ask yourself the question, "But what's the point of being alive at all?"—leading the particular life of a student or bartender or whatever you happen to be—you'll answer "There's no point. It wouldn't matter if I didn't exist at all, or if I didn't care about anything. But I do. That's all there is to it."

Some people find this attitude perfectly satisfying. Others find it depressing, though unavoidable. Part of the problem is that some of us have an incurable tendency to take ourselves seriously. We want to matter to ourselves "from the outside." If our lives as a whole seem pointless, then a part of us is dissatisfied—the part that is always looking over our shoulders at what we are doing. Many human efforts, particularly those in the service of serious ambitions rather than just comfort and survival, get some of their energy from a sense of importance—a sense that what you are doing is not just important to you, but important in some larger sense: important, period. If we have to give this up, it may threaten to take the wind out of our sails. If life is not real, life is not earnest, and the grave is its goal, perhaps it's ridiculous to take ourselves so seriously. On the other hand, if we can't help taking ourselves so seriously, perhaps we just have to put up with being ridiculous. Life may be not only meaningless but absurd.

PART ONE   # The Theistic
Answer

CHAPTER 1   L E O   T O L S T O Y

My Confession

Although I regarded authorship as a waste of time, I continued to write during those fifteen years. I had tasted of the seduction of authorship, of the seduction of enormous monetary remunerations and applauses for my insignificant labour, and so I submitted to it, as being a means for improving my material condition and for stifling in my soul all questions about the meaning of my life and life in general.

In my writings I advocated, what to me was the only truth, that it was necessary to live in such a way as to derive the greatest comfort for oneself and one's family.

Thus I proceeded to live, but five years ago something very strange began to happen with me: I was overcome by minutes at first of perplexity and then of an arrest of life, as though I did not know how to live or what to do, and I lost myself and was dejected. But that passed, and I continued to live as before. Then those minutes of perplexity were repeated oftener and oftener, and always in one and the same form. These arrests of life found their expression in ever the same questions: "Why? Well, and then?"

At first I thought that those were simply aimless, inappropriate questions. It seemed to me that that was all well known and that if I ever wanted to busy myself with their solution, it would not cost me much labour,—that now I had no time to attend to them, but that if I wanted to I should find the proper answers. But the questions began to repeat themselves oftener and oftener, answers were demanded more and more persistently, and, like dots that fall on the same spot, these questions, without any answers, thickened into one black blotch.

There happened what happens with any person who falls ill with a mortal internal disease. At first there appear insignificant symptoms of indisposition, to which the patient pays no attention; then these symptoms are repeated more and more frequently and blend into one temporally indivisible suffering. The suffering keeps growing, and before the patient has had time to look around, he becomes conscious that what he took for an indisposition is the most significant thing in the world to him,—is death.

The same happened with me. I understood that it was not a passing indisposition, but something very important, and that, if the questions were going to repeat themselves, it would be necessary to find an answer for them. And I tried to answer them. The questions seemed to be so foolish, simple, and childish. But the moment I touched them and tried to solve them, I became convinced, in the first place, that they were not childish and foolish, but very important and profound questions in life, and, in the second, that, no matter how much I might try, I should not be able to answer them. Before attending to my Samára estate, to my son's education, or to the writing of a book, I ought to know why I should do that. So long as I did not know why, I could not do anything. I could not live. Amidst my thoughts of farming, which interested me very much during that time, there would suddenly pass through my head a question like this: "All right, you are going to have six thousand desyatínas of land in the Government of Samára, and three hundred horses,—and then?" And I completely lost my senses and did not know what to think farther. Or, when I thought of the education of my children, I said to myself: "Why?" Or, reflecting on the manner in which the masses might obtain their welfare, I suddenly said to myself: "What is that to me?" Or, thinking of the fame which my works would get me, I said to myself: "All right, you will be more famous than Gógol, Púshkin, Shakespeare, Molière, and all the writers in the world,—what of it?" And I was absolutely unable to make any reply. The questions were not waiting, and I had to answer them at once; if I did not answer them, I could not live.

I felt that what I was standing on had given way, that I had no foundation to stand on, that that which I lived by no longer existed, and that I had nothing to live by. . . .

All that happened with me when I was on every side surrounded by what is considered to be complete happiness. I had a good, loving, and beloved wife, good children, and a large estate, which grew and increased without any labour on my part. I was respected by my neighbours and friends, more than ever before, was praised by strangers, and, without any self-deception, could consider my name famous. With all that, I was not deranged or mentally unsound,—on the contrary, I was in full command of my mental and physical powers, such as I had rarely met with in people of my age: physically I could work in a field, mowing, without falling behind a peasant; mentally I could work from eight to ten hours in succession, without experiencing any consequences from the strain. And while in such condition I arrived at the conclusion that I could not live, and, fearing death, I had to use cunning against myself, in order that I might not take my life.

This mental condition expressed itself to me in this form: my life is a stupid, mean trick played on me by somebody. Although I did not recognize that "somebody" as having created me, the form of the conception that some one had played a mean, stupid trick on me by bringing me into the world was the most natural one that presented itself to me.

Involuntarily I imagined that there, somewhere, there was somebody who was now having fun as he looked down upon me and saw me, who had lived for thirty or forty years, learning, developing, growing in body and mind, now that I had become strengthened in mind and had reached that summit of life from which it lay all before me, standing as a complete fool on that summit and seeing clearly that there was nothing in life and never would be. And that was fun to him—

But whether there was or was not that somebody who made fun of me, did not make it easier for me. I could not ascribe any sensible meaning to a single act, or to my whole life. I was only surprised that I had not understood that from the start. All that had long ago been known to everybody. Sooner or later there would come diseases and death (they had come already) to my dear ones and to me, and there would be nothing left but stench and worms. All my affairs, no matter what they might be, would sooner or later be forgotten, and I myself should not exist. So why should I worry about all these things? How could a man fail to see that and live,—that was surprising! A person could live only so long as he was drunk; but the moment he sobered up, he could not help seeing that all that was only a deception, and a stupid deception at that! Really, there was nothing funny and ingenious about it, but only something cruel and stupid.

Long ago has been told the Eastern story about the traveller who in the steppe is overtaken by an infuriated beast. Trying to save himself from the animal, the traveller jumps into a waterless well, but at its bottom he sees a dragon who opens his jaws in order to swallow him. And the unfortunate man does not dare climb out, lest he perish from the infuriated beast, and does not dare jump down to the bottom of the well, lest he be devoured by the dragon, and so clutches the twig of a wild bush growing in a cleft of the well and holds on to it. His hands grow weak and he feels that soon he shall have to surrender to the peril which awaits him at either side; but he still holds on and sees two mice, one white, the other black, in even measure making a circle around the main trunk of the bush to which he is clinging, and nibbling at it on all sides. Now, at any moment, the bush will break and tear off, and he will fall into the dragon's jaws. The traveller sees that and knows that he will inevitably perish; but while he is still clinging, he sees some drops of honey hanging on the leaves of the bush, and so reaches out for them with his tongue and licks the leaves. Just so I hold on to the branch of life, knowing that the dragon of death is waiting inevitably for me, ready to tear me to pieces, and I cannot understand why I have fallen on such suffering. And I try to lick that honey which used to give me pleasure; but now it no longer gives me joy, and the white and the black mouse day and night nibble at the branch to which I am holding on. I clearly see the dragon, and the honey is no longer sweet to me. I see only the inevitable dragon and the mice, and am unable to turn my glance away from them. That is not a fable, but a veritable, indisputable, comprehensible truth.

The former deception of the pleasures of life, which stifled the terror of the dragon, no longer deceives me. No matter how much one should say to me, "You cannot understand the meaning of life, do not think, live!" I am unable to do so, because I have been doing it too long before. Now I cannot help seeing day and night, which run and lead me up to death. I see that alone, because that alone is the truth. Everything else is a lie.

The two drops of honey that have longest turned my eyes away from the cruel truth, the love of family and of authorship, which I have called an art, are no longer sweet to me.

"My family—" I said to myself, "but my family, my wife and children, they are also human beings. They are in precisely the same condition that I am in: they must either live in the lie or see the terrible truth. Why should they live? Why should I love them, why guard, raise, and watch them? Is it for the same despair which is in me, or for dulness of perception? Since I love them, I cannot conceal the truth from them,—every step in cognition leads them up to this truth. And the truth is death."

"Art, poetry?" For a long time, under the influence of the success of human praise, I tried to persuade myself that that was a thing which could be done, even though death should come and destroy everything, my deeds, as well as my memory of them; but soon I came to see that that, too, was a deception. It was clear to me that art was an adornment of life, a decoy of life. But life lost all its attractiveness for me. How, then, could I entrap others? So long as I did not live my own life, and a strange life bore me on its waves; so long as I believed that life had some sense, although I was not able to express it,—the reflections of life of every description in poetry and in the arts afforded me pleasure, and I was delighted to look at life through this little mirror of art; but when I began to look for the meaning of life, when I experienced the necessity of living myself, that little mirror became either useless, superfluous, and ridiculous, or painful to me. I could no longer console myself with what I saw in the mirror, namely, that my situation was stupid and desperate. It was all right for me to rejoice so long as I believed in the depth of my soul that life had some sense. At that time the play of lights—of the comical, the tragical, the touching, the beautiful, the terrible in life— afforded me amusement. But when I knew that life was meaningless and terrible, the play in the little mirror could no longer amuse me. No sweetness of honey could be sweet to me, when I saw the dragon and the mice that were nibbling down my support. . . .

In my search after the question of life I experienced the same feeling which a man who has lost his way in the forest may experience.

He comes to a clearing, climbs a tree, and clearly sees an unlimited space before him; at the same time he sees that there are no houses there, and that there can be none; he goes back to the forest, into the darkness, and he sees darkness, and again there are no houses.

Thus I blundered in this forest of human knowledge, between the clearings of the mathematical and experimental sciences, which disclosed to me clear horizons, but such in the direction of which there could be no house, and between the darkness of the speculative sciences, where I sunk into a deeper darkness, the farther I proceeded, and I convinced myself at last that there was no way out and could not be.

By abandoning myself to the bright side of knowledge I saw that I only turned my eyes away from the question. No matter how enticing and clear the horizons were that were disclosed to me, no matter how enticing it was to bury myself in the infinitude of this knowledge, I comprehended that these sciences were the more clear, the less I needed them, the less they answered my question.

"Well, I know," I said to myself, "all which science wants so persistently to know, but there is no answer to the question about the meaning of my life." But in the speculative sphere I saw that, in spite of the fact that the aim of the knowledge was directed straight to the answer of my question, or because of that fact, there could be no other answer than what I was giving to myself: "What is the meaning of my life?"—"None." Or, "What will come of my life?"—"Nothing." Or, "Why does everything which exists exist, and why do I exist?"—"Because it exists."

Putting the question to the one side of human knowledge, I received an endless quantity of exact answers about what I did not ask: about the chemical composition of the stars, about the movement of the sun toward the constellation of Hercules, about the origin of species and of man, about the forms of infinitely small, imponderable particles of ether; but the answer in this sphere of knowledge to my question what the meaning of my life was, was always: "You are what you call your life; you are a temporal, accidental conglomeration of particles. The interrelation, the change of these particles, produces in you that which you call life. This congeries will last for some time; then the interaction of these particles will cease, and that which you call life and all your questions will come to an end. You are an accidentally cohering globule of something. The globule is fermenting. This fermentation the globule calls its life. The globule falls to pieces, and all fermentation and all questions will come to an end." Thus the clear side of knowledge answers, and it cannot say anything else, if only it strictly follows its principles.

With such an answer it appears that the answer is not a reply to the question. I want to know the meaning of my life, but the fact that it is a particle of the infinite not only gives it no meaning, but even destroys every possible meaning.

Those obscure transactions, which this side of the experimental, exact science has with speculation, when it says that the meaning of life consists in evolution and the coöperation with this evolution, because of their obscurity and inexactness cannot be regarded as answers.

The other side of knowledge, the speculative, so long as it sticks strictly to its fundamental principles in giving a direct answer to the question, everywhere and at all times has answered one and the same: "The world is something infinite and incomprehensible. Human life is an incomprehensible part of this incomprehensible *all*. . . ."

I lived for a long time in this madness, which, not in words, but in deeds, is particularly characteristic of us, the most liberal and learned of men. But, thanks either to my strange, physical love for the real working class, which made me understand it and see that it is not so stupid as we suppose, or to the sincerity of my conviction, which was that I could know nothing and that the best that I could do was to hang myself,—I felt that if I wanted to live and understand the meaning of life, I ought naturally to look for it, not among those who had lost the meaning of life and wanted to kill themselves, but among those billions departed and living men who had been carrying their own lives and ours upon their shoulders. And I looked around at the enormous masses of deceased and living men,—not learned and wealthy, but simple men,—and I saw something quite different. I saw that all these billions of men that lived or had lived, all, with rare exceptions, did not fit into my subdivisions,[1] and that I could not recognize them as not understanding the question, because they themselves put it and answered it with surprising clearness. Nor could I recognize them as Epicureans, because their lives were composed rather of privations and suffering than of enjoyment. Still less could I recognize them as senselessly living out their meaningless lives, because every act of theirs and death itself was explained by them. They regarded it as the greatest evil to kill themselves. It appeared, then, that all humanity was in possession of a knowledge of the meaning of life, which I did not recognize and which I condemned. It turned out that rational knowledge did not give any meaning to life, excluded life, while the meaning which by billions of people, by all humanity, was ascribed to life was based on some despised, false knowledge.

The rational knowledge in the person of the learned and the wise denied the meaning of life, but the enormous masses of men, all humanity, recognized this meaning in an irrational knowledge. This irrational knowledge was faith, the same that I could not help but reject. That was God as one and three, the creation in six days, devils and angels, and all that which I could not accept so long as I had not lost my senses.

My situation was a terrible one. I knew that I should not find anything on the path of rational knowledge but the negation of life, and there, in faith, nothing but the negation of reason, which was still more impossible than the negation of life. From the rational knowledge it followed that life was an evil and men knew it,—it depended on men whether they should cease living, and yet they lived and continued to live, and I myself lived, though I had known long ago that life was meaningless and an evil. From faith it followed that, in order to understand life, I must renounce reason, for which alone a meaning was needed.

There resulted a contradiction, from which there were two ways out: either what I called rational was not so rational as I had thought; or that which to me appeared irrational was not so irrational as I had thought. And I began to verify the train of thoughts of my rational knowledge.

In verifying the train of thoughts of my rational knowledge, I found that it was quite correct. The deduction that life was nothing was inevitable; but I saw a mistake. The mistake was that I had not reasoned in conformity with the question put by me. The question was, "Why should I live?" that is, "What real, indestructible essence will come from my phantasmal, destructible life? What meaning has my finite existence in this infinite world?" And in order to answer this question, I studied life.

The solutions of all possible questions of life apparently could not satisfy me, because my question, no matter how simple it appeared in the beginning, included the necessity of explaining the finite through the infinite, and vice versa.

I asked, "What is the extra-temporal, extra-causal, extra-spatial meaning of life?" But I gave an answer to the question, "What is the temporal, causal, spatial meaning of my life?" The result was that after a long labour of mind I answered, "None."

In my reflections I constantly equated, nor could I do otherwise, the finite with the finite, the infinite with the infinite, and so from that resulted precisely what had to result: force was force, matter was matter, will was will, infinity was infinity, nothing was nothing,—and nothing else could come from it.

There happened something like what at times takes place in mathematics: you think you are solving an equation, when you have only an identity. The reasoning is correct, but you receive as a result the answer: $a = a$, or $x = x$, or $o = o$. The same happened with my reflection in respect to the question about the meaning of my life. The answers given by all science to that question are only identities.

Indeed, the strictly scientific knowledge, that knowledge which, as Descartes did, begins with a full doubt in everything, rejects all knowledge which has been taken on trust, and builds everything anew on the laws of reason and experience, cannot give any other answer to the question of life than what I received,—an indefinite answer. It only seemed to me at first that science gave me a positive answer,—Schopenhauer's answer: "Life has no meaning, it is an evil." But when I analyzed the matter, I saw that the answer was not a positive one, but that it was only my feeling which expressed it as such. The answer, strictly expressed, as it is expressed by the Brahmins, by Solomon, and by Schopenhauer, is only an indefinite answer, or an identity, $o = o$, life is nothing. Thus the philosophical knowledge does not negate anything, but only answers that the question cannot be solved by it, that for philosophy the solution remains insoluble.

When I saw that, I understood that it was not right for me to look for an answer to my question in rational knowledge, and that the answer given by rational knowledge was only an indication that the answer might be got if the question were differently put, but only when into the discussion of the question should be introduced the question of the relation of the finite to the infinite. I also understood that, no matter how irrational and monstrous the answers might be that faith gave, they had this advantage that they introduced into each answer the relation of the finite to the infinite, without which there could be no answer.

No matter how I may put the question, "How must I live?" the answer is, "According to God's law." "What real result will there be from my life?"—"Eternal torment or eternal bliss." "What is the meaning which is not destroyed by death?"—"The union with infinite God, paradise."

Thus, outside the rational knowledge, which had to me appeared as the only one, I was inevitably led to recognize that all living humanity had a certain other irrational knowledge, faith, which made it possible to live.

All the irrationality of faith remained the same for me, but I could not help recognizing that it alone gave to humanity answers to the questions of life, and, in consequence of them, the possibility of living.

The rational knowledge brought me to the recognition that life was meaningless,—my life stopped, and I wanted to destroy myself. When I looked around at people, at all humanity, I saw that people lived and asserted that they knew the meaning of life. I looked back at myself: I lived so long as I knew the meaning of life. As to other people, so even to me, did faith give the meaning of life and the possibility of living.

Looking again at the people of other countries, contemporaries of mine and those passed away, I saw again the same. Where life had been, there faith, ever since humanity had existed, had given the possibility of living, and the chief features of faith were everywhere one and the same.

No matter what answers faith may give, its every answer gives to the finite existence of man the sense of the infinite,—a sense which is not destroyed by suffering, privation, and death. Consequently in faith alone could we find the meaning and possibility of life. What, then, was faith? I understood that faith was not merely an evidence of things not seen, and so forth, not revelation (that is only the description of one of the symptoms of faith), not the relation of man to man (faith has to be defined, and then God, and not first God, and faith through him), not merely an agreement with what a man was told, as faith was generally understood,—that faith was the knowledge of the meaning of human life, in consequence of which man did not destroy himself, but lived. Faith is the power of life. If a man lives he believes in something. If he did not believe that he ought to live for some purpose, he would not live. If he does not see and understand the phantasm of the finite, he believes in that finite; if he understands the phantasm of the finite, he must believe in the infinite. Without faith one cannot live. . . .

In order that all humanity may be able to live, in order that they may continue living, giving a meaning to life, they, those billions, must have another, a real knowledge of faith, for not the fact that I, with Solomon and Schopenhauer, did not kill myself convinced me of the existence of faith, but that these billions had lived and had borne us, me and Solomon, on the waves of life.

Then I began to cultivate the acquaintance of the believers from among the poor, the simple and unlettered folk, of pilgrims, monks, dissenters, peasants. The doctrine of these people from among the masses was also the Christian doctrine that the quasi-believers of our circle professed. With the Christian truths were also mixed in very many superstitions, but there was this difference: the superstitions of our circle were quite unnecessary to them, had no connection with their lives, were only a kind of an Epicurean amusement, while the superstitions of the believers from among the labouring classes were to such an extent blended with their life that it would have been impossible to imagine it without these superstitions,—it was a necessary condition of that life. I began to examine closely the lives and beliefs of these people, and the more I examined them, the more did I become convinced that they had the real faith, that their faith was necessary for them, and that it alone gave them a meaning and possibility of life. In contradistinction to what I saw in our circle, where life without faith was possible, and where hardly one in a thousand professed to be a believer, among them there was hardly one in a thousand who was not a believer. In contradistinction to what I saw in our circle, where all life passed in idleness, amusements, and tedium of life, I saw that the whole life of these people was passed in hard work, and that they were satisfied with life. In contradistinction to the people of our circle, who struggled and murmured against fate because of their privations and their suffering, these people accepted diseases and sorrows without any perplexity or opposition, but with the calm and firm conviction that it was all for good. In contradistinction to the fact that the more intelligent we are, the less do we understand the meaning of life and the more do we see a kind of a bad joke in our suffering and death, these people live, suffer, and approach death, and suffer in peace and more often in joy. In contradistinction to the fact that a calm death, a death without terror or despair, is the greatest exception in our circle, a restless, insubmissive, joyless death is one of the greatest exceptions among the masses. And of such people, who are deprived of everything which for Solomon and for me constitutes the only good of life, and who withal experience the greatest happiness, there is an enormous number. I cast a broader glance about me. I examined the life of past and present vast masses of men, and I saw people who in like manner had understood the meaning of life, who had known how to live and die, not two, not three, not ten, but hundreds, thousands, millions. All of them, infinitely diversified as to habits, intellect, culture, situation, all equally and quite contrary to my ignorance knew the meaning of life and of death, worked calmly, bore privations and suffering, lived and died, seeing in that not vanity, but good.

I began to love those people. The more I penetrated into their life, the life of the men now living, and the life of men departed, of whom I had read and heard, the more did I love them, and the easier it became for me to live. Thus I lived for about two years, and within me took place a transformation, which had long been working within me, and the germ of which had always been in me. What happened with me was that the life of our circle,—of the rich and the learned,—not only disgusted me, but even lost all its meaning. All our acts, reflections, sciences, arts,—all that appeared to me in a new light. I saw that all that was mere pampering of the appetites, and that no meaning could be found in it; but the life of all the working masses, of all humanity, which created life, presented itself to me in its real significance. I saw that that was life itself and that the meaning given to this life was truth, and I accepted it.

NOTES

1. In a passage omitted here, Tolstoy characterized four attitudes that people have toward life: living in ignorance of the problem of the meaning of life; ignoring it and trying to attain as much pleasure as possible; admitting that life is meaningless and committing suicide; admitting that life is meaningless but continuing to live aimlessly. (Ed.)

CHAPTER 2

DAVID F. SWENSON

The Dignity of Human Life

Man lives forward, but he thinks backward. As an active being, his task is to press forward to the things that are before, toward the goal where is the prize of the high calling. But as a thinking, active being, his forward movement is conditioned by a retrospect. If there were no past for a man, there could be no future; and if there were no future and no past, but only such an immersion in the present as is characteristic of the brute which perisheth, then there would be nothing eternal in human life, and everything distinctively and essentially human would disappear from our existence.

As a preparation for an existence in the present, the youth of a nation are trained in various skills and along devious lines, according to their capacities and circumstances, for the parts they are to play in existence; their natural talents are developed, some by extended periods of intellectual training, others for participation in various forms of business or technical training; but whatever be the ultimate end of the training, its purpose is to develop those latent powers they possess which will eventually prove of benefit to themselves or to others. But, in addition to this, which we may call a preparation for the external life, a something else is urgently needed, a something so fundamentally important that in its absence every other form of preparation is revealed as imperfect and incomplete, even ineffective and futile.

This so particularly indispensable something is a view of life, and a view of life is not acquired as a direct and immediate result of a course of study, the reading of books, or a communication of results. It is wholly a product of the individual's own knowledge of himself as an individual, of his individual capabilities and aspirations. A view of life is a principle of living, a spirit and an attitude capable of maintaining its unity and identity with itself in all of life's complexities and varying vicissitudes; and yet also capable of being declined, to use the terminology of the grammatical sciences, in all the infinite variety of cases that the language of life affords. Without this preparation the individual life is like a ship without a rudder, a bit of wreckage floating with the current to an uncomprehended destiny. A view of life is not objective knowledge, but subjective conviction. It is a part of a man's own self, the source whence the stream of his life issues. It is the dominant attitude of the spirit which gives to life its direction and its goal. This is why it cannot be directly communicated or conveyed, like an article of commerce, from one person to another. If a view of life were a body of knowledge about life, or a direct and immediate implication from such knowledge, it would be subject to objective communication and systematic instruction. But it is rather a personal expression of what a man essentially is in his own inmost self, and this cannot be learned by rote, or accepted at the hands of some external authority. Knowledge is the answer or answers that things give to the questions we ask of them; a view of life is the reply a person gives to the question that life asks of him. We begin life by scrutinizing our environment, ourselves playing the role of questioners and examiners and critics; but at a later moment, when the soul comes of age and is about to enter upon its majority, it learns that the tables have been turned and the roles reversed; from that moment it confronts a question, a searching and imperative question, in relation to which no evasion can avail, and to which no shifting of responsibility is possible.

In discussing the problem of a view of life which can give it meaning and dignity and worth, I am well aware that no one can acquire a view of life by listening to a speech. Nevertheless, a speech may serve the more modest purpose of stimulating a search, perhaps a more earnest search; and may render more articulate possibly the convictions of those who have already won some such conception, having made it their own by a heart-felt and spontaneous choice.

All men are endowed by nature with a desire for happiness—a principle so obvious as scarcely to need any explanation, and certainly no defense. A human life without happiness or hope of happiness is not a life, but rather a death in life. Happiness is life's vital fluid and the very breath of its nostrils. Happiness and life are so much one and the same thing that the more profoundly any life discovers happiness, the more significant and abundant is that life itself. This is also the principle of the Christian religion, which even dares to formulate the task of life as the duty of being happy; for does not the Apostle Paul say, "Rejoice . . . always: again I will say, Rejoice"? So deeply grounded in human nature is the need for happiness, that the desire for it is not only universal and instinctive, but ineradicable and imperative. Man is made for happiness; an essentially unhappy man has missed his goal, and has failed to realize his humanity.

But for a thinking human being—and God made every man a thinker, whatever may be our estimate of that which men make of themselves—for a thinking human being, happiness cannot consist in the satisfaction of momentary impulse, of blind feeling, of brute immediacy. A pleasant absorption in the present, oblivious of prospect or retrospect, careless of the wider relations or the deeper truth of life, can be called happiness only on the basis of frivolity and thoughtlessness. Just as life is not life unless it is happy, so happiness is not happiness unless it can be justified. In order really to be happiness it requires to be interpenetrated with a sense of meaning, reason, and worth.

For the quest for happiness, like every other human quest, faces a danger. The danger that confronts it is the possibility of error: the error of permitting oneself to be lured into promising paths that lead to no goal, and the error of coming to rest in hollow satisfactions and empty joys. It is possible to believe oneself happy, to seem happy to oneself and to others, and yet in reality to be plunged in the deepest misery; just as, on the other hand, it is possible to stand possessed of the greatest treasure, and yet, in thoughtlessness, to imagine oneself destitute, and through that very thoughtlessness not only neglect and ignore but actually deprive oneself of what one already has. The basic problem of life, the question in response to which a view of life seeks to propound an answer, may therefore be formulated as follows: What is that happiness which is also a genuine and lasting good? In what does it consist, and how may it be attained?

There exists an ancient handbook, an *Art of Rhetoric,* compiled for the guidance and information of orators and other public speakers, written by one of the greatest of Greek philosophers. In this handbook the author formulates the commonly prevailing conceptions of happiness as among the things useful for public speakers to know. This textbook is almost twenty-five hundred years old, and the views it presents on this subject may therefore be expected to seem childish in the light of our greater insight and extraordinary progress in all things. Nevertheless, let us note them in passing, if only for the sake of seeing how far we have advanced beyond them. Happiness is said to be commonly defined as independence of life, as prosperity with virtue, as comfortable circumstances with security, or as the enjoyment of many possessions, together with the power to keep and defend them. Its constituent elements are noble birth, wealth, many good and influential friends, bodily health and beauty, talents and capacities, good fortune, honors, and lastly virtue. We readily perceive how strange and old-fashioned these conceptions are, how foreign to all our modern and enlightened notions. I shall therefore subjoin a more up-to-date consideration of the same subject, derived from a very modern author writing in a journal of today. The author raises the question as to what circumstances and conditions have the power to make him feel really alive, tingling with vitality, instinct with the joy of living. He submits a long list including a variety of things, of which I shall quote the chief: the sense of health; successful creative work, like writing books; good food and drink; pleasant surroundings; praise, not spread on too thick; friends and their company; beautiful things, books, music; athletic exercises and sports; daydreaming; a good fight in a tolerably decent cause; the sense of bodily danger escaped; the consciousness of being a few steps ahead of the wolf of poverty. His social ideal is a community where beauty abounds, where the fear of want is absent, where a man may dress as he pleases, do the work that suits him best; a community where arts and letters flourish, where abundant leisure breaks the remorseless pace of ceaseless work, and, lastly, for those who value religion, a church is provided, with a great nave and a great organ and the sound of vespers across the evening fields. So speaks our modern writer. And now that I have juxtaposed these two accounts, I have to confess to the strange feeling that, despite the interval of more than two thousand years between them, they sound unexpectedly alike, even to the generous inclusion of a place for morality and religion as not an entirely negligible factor in promoting the good and happy life. How strange to find such a similarity! Can it be that after all that has been said and written about the revolutionary and radical changes introduced into life by modern science, modern invention, and modern industry, the influence of the steam engine and the printing press, the telegraph and the radio, the automobile and the airplane, together with the absolutely devastating discoveries of astronomers—can it be, in spite of all this, that the current conceptions of life and its meaning have remained essentially unchanged? Is not this a remarkable testimony to the profound inner resemblance to one another, despite all changes of form and circumstance, exhibited by the countless generations of men, both in their wisdom and in their folly?

However that may be, I do not think that anyone will deny that such views as these are widely held, and constitute the view of life perhaps of the majority of men. The testimony to their prevalence is not merely the articulate confession of the tongue, but the no less revealing though inarticulate direction of the life. I hope not to be misunderstood. The present speaker is human enough to find these objectives, or the majority of them, not only natural but inviting; he finds them desirable, and is by no means schooled in any heroic or stoic indifference to the goods that have rightly been called external, rooted as they are in fortunate circumstances and special privilege. But there are serious difficulties in the way of constructing a view of life out of such considerations.

The constituents of happiness are in both cases a multiplicity of things. As Aristotle so simply says, virtue alone will not make a man happy, but he needs also goods and friends. But the self which sets its heart upon any such multiplicity of external goods, which lives in them and by them and for them, dependent upon them for the only happiness it knows—such a self is captive to the diverse world of its desires. It belongs to the world and does not own itself. It is not in the deepest sense a self, since it is not free and is not a unity. The manifold conditions of its happiness split the self asunder; no ruling passion dominates its life; no concentration gives unity to the personality and single-mindedness to the will. Its name is legion, and its nature is double-mindedness. And if some one thing, like wealth or power, is made the single ambition of an exceptional life, it still remains true that such things are only apparently single; in reality they are various and manifold. The soul that lives in them is torn by diverse impulses, is drawn in many different directions at once, and cannot find the peace which comes only from single-minded devotion, from the pursuit of an end which is intrinsically and genuinely one.

Reflection discovers yet another difficulty in connection with such views of life. Whoever seeks his happiness in external conditions, of whatever sort, seeks it in that which is in its essential nature precarious. He presumes upon the realization of conditions which are not intrinsic to him, or within his control. This happiness is subject to the law of uncertainty, to the qualification of an unyielding, mysterious *perhaps.* Here lurks the possibility of despair. Give a man the full satisfaction of his wishes and ambitions, and he deems himself happy; withdraw from him the smile of fortune's favor, and disappoint his expectation and his hope, and he will be plunged into despair. The shift from happiness to unhappiness in such a life is every moment imminent. And therefore its despair is latent even in its happiness, and discord lurks imminent in the soul's most beautiful music; its presence is masked only by a brutish self-satisfaction, the habit of thoughtlessness, breathless haste in trifling errands, and darkness in the soul's deepest ground, each and all miserable defenses indeed against the enemy within the gates.

A third consideration. Wealth and power and the like, even bodily health and beauty of person, are not in the strictest sense intrinsic values, but rather representative and comparative, conditional and hypothetical. Money is good—if I have learned how to use it; and so with power and influence, health and strength. But in themselves these things are abstract and neutral, and no man can truthfully say whether the acquirement of them in any individual case will work more good than harm. This is a consideration which applies to nearly every item of what we call progress. A new discovery or invention, like the printing press, promises radically to improve life, to secure for us a hitherto undreamed-of happiness and well-being. We hail it with enthusiasm as inaugurating a new era, and in the distance we descry the dawn of a millennial day. A century or so passes. What then? Why, all the old difficulties and problems, all the old dissatisfactions and complaints, the very difficulties and problems that were to be solved by the new invention, are seen to be still with us, having but slightly changed their outward form and habitat. In addition, the new improvement that was to usher in the millennium, is seen to be the source of so many and so serious abuses (consider the abuse of the printing press!) that the best minds of the race have to be concentrated upon the problem of finding a remedy for these abuses, and keeping them under some sort of control. And so also in the individual life. Every access of power and prosperity, and of outward comfort, brings with it its own griefs and dangers. Every such improvement is only potentially a good, as it is also potentially an evil. It is a mere quantity whose qualitative meaning is indeterminate, awaiting the seal of something else, something from within the soul itself, in order to determine its final significance for weal or woe, for happiness or unhappiness.

Lastly, it must be pointed out that the conditions of happiness as conceived in all such views of life, inevitably imply a privileged status for the happy individual. They rest upon differential capabilities and exceptionally fortunate circumstances. To choose them as the end and aim of life constitutes an injury to the mass of men who are not so privileged. This one thought alone is of so arresting a quality as to give the deepest concern to every man who has the least trace of human sympathy and human feeling. I hope I have a soul not entirely a stranger to happy admiration; I know I feel moved to bend low in respect before exceptional talent and performance, and that I am eager to honor greatness and genius wherever I have the gift to understand it. And I am not so unfeeling as to refuse a tribute of sympathetic joy to those who rejoice in fortune's favors and bask in the smiles of outward success. But as the fundamental source of inspiration of my life, I need something that is not exclusive and differential, but inclusive and universal. I require to drink from a spring at which all men may refresh themselves; I need an aim that reconciles me to high and low, rich and poor, cultured and uncultured, sophisticated and simple; to the countless generations of the past as well as to the men and women of the future. I need a spiritual bond that binds me to all human beings in a common understanding of that which is fundamental and essential to human life. To have my life and happiness in that which is inaccessible to the many or to the few, seems to me an act of treason to humanity, a cowardly and pusillanimous attack upon the brotherhood of man; for without the inner spiritual tie of an essential aim which all can reach and all can understand, the concept of the human race as a spiritual unity is destroyed, and nothing is left of mankind but a biological species, only slightly better equipped than the other animals to cope with the present state of their physical environment. The differences between man and man are indeed inseparable from this our imperfect temporal existence; but I cannot and will not believe that their development constitutes the perfection of life itself. Rather is this to be found in the discovery and expectation of something underlying and absolute, something that can be found by all who seek it in earnest, something to which our lives may give expression, subordinating to its unifying principle the infinite multitude of ends, reducing them to their own relative measure and proportion, and refusing to permit the unimportant to become important, the relative to become absolute. The possibility of making this discovery and of giving it expression is, so it seems to me, the fundamental meaning of life, the source of its dignity and worth. The happiness that is found with this discovery is not invidious and divisive, but unifying and reconciling; it does not abrogate the differences, but it destroys their power to wound and to harm, the fortunate through being puffed up in arrogance and pride, the unfortunate through being depressed in envy and disappointment. For this happiness is not denied to any man, no matter how insignificant and humble.

Our criticism has brought us to the threshold of an ethical view of life. That the essence of life and its happiness is to be sought in the moral consciousness alone is the conviction that animates this address, and gives it its reason for being. This view holds that the individual human self has an infinite worth, that the personality has an eternal validity, that the bringing of this validity to expression in the manifold relations and complications of life is the true task of the self, that this task gives to the individual's historical development an infinite significance, because it is a process through which the personality in its truth and depth comes to its own. "Find your self," says the moral consciousness; "reclaim it in its total and in so far unworthy submergence in relative ends; dare to think the nothingness, the hollowness, the relativity, the precariousness, the lack of intrinsic meaning of that which constitutes the entire realm of the external and the manifold; liberate yourself from slavery to finite ends; have the courage to substitute the one thing needful for the many things wished for, and perhaps desirable, making first things first, and all other things secondary—and you will find that these other things will be added unto you in the measure in which you require them and can use them as servants and ministers of your highest good."

So speaks the voice within us, a still small voice, a soft whisper easily overwhelmed by the noise and traffic of life, but a voice, nevertheless, which no one can permit to be silenced except at the cost of acquiring restlessness instead of peace, anxiety instead of trust and confidence, a distracted spirit instead of harmony with one's self. The moral spirit finds the meaning of life in choice. It finds it in that which proceeds from man and remains with him as his inner essence rather than in the accidents of circumstance and turns of external fortune. The individual has his end in himself. He is no mere instrument in the service of something external, nor is he the slave of some powerful master; nor of a class, a group, or party; nor of the state or nation; nor even of humanity itself, as an abstraction solely external to the individual. Essentially and absolutely he is an end; only accidentally and relatively is he a means. And this is true of the meanest wage slave, so called, in industry's impersonal machine—precisely as true of him as it is of the greatest genius or the most powerful ruler.

Is there anyone so little stout-hearted, so effeminately tender, so extravagantly in love with an illusory and arbitrary freedom, as to feel that the glorious promise of such a view of life is ruined, its majestic grandeur shriveled into cramped pettiness, because the task which it offers the individual is not only an invitation, but also an obligation as well? Shall we confess that we cannot endure this "Thou must" spoken to ourselves,[1] even when the voice proceeds from no external power but from our in-most self, there where the human strikes its roots into the divine? Truly, it is this "Thou must" that is the eternal guarantee of our calling, the savior of our hope, the inspirer of our energy, the preserver of our aim against the shiftings of feeling and the vicissitudes of circumstance. It steels the will and makes it fast; it gives courage to begin after failure; it is the triumph over despondency and despair. For duty is the eternal in a man, or that by which he lays hold of the eternal; and only through the eternal can a man become a conqueror of the life of time. It is in the moral consciousness that a man begins truly to sense the presence of God; and every religion that has omitted the ethical is in so far a misunderstanding of religion, reducing it to myth and poetry, having significance only for the imagination, but not for the whole nature of man as concrete reality. The moral consciousness is a lamp, a wonderful lamp; but not like the famous lamp of Aladdin,[2] which when rubbed had the power to summon a spirit, a willing servant ready and able to fulfill every wish. But whenever a human being rubs the lamp of his moral consciousness with moral passion, a Spirit does appear. This Spirit is God, and the Spirit is master and lord, and man becomes his servant. But this service is man's true freedom, for a derivative spirit like man, who certainly has not made himself, or given himself his own powers, cannot in truth impose upon himself the law of his own being. It is in the "Thou must" of God and man's "I can" that the divine image of God in human life is contained, to which an ancient book refers when it asserts that God made man in his own image. That is the inner glory, the spiritual garb of man, which transcends the wonderful raiment with which the Author of the universe has clothed the lilies of the field, raiment which in its turn puts to shame the royal purple of Solomon. The lilies of the field[3] cannot hear the voice of duty or obey its call; hence they cannot bring their will into harmony with the divine will. In the capacity to do this lies man's unique distinction among all creatures; here is his self, his independence, his glory and his crown.

I know that all men do not share this conviction. Youth is often too sure of its future. The imagination paints the vision of success and fortune in the rosiest tints; the sufferings and disappointments of which one hears are for youth but the exception that proves the rule; the instinctive and blind faith of youth is in the relative happiness of some form of external success. Maturity, on the other hand, has often learned to be content with scraps and fragments, wretched crumbs saved out of the disasters on which its early hopes suffered shipwreck. Youth pursues an ideal that is illusory; age has learned, O wretched wisdom! to do without an ideal altogether. But the ideal is there, implanted in the heart and mind of man by his Maker, and no mirages of happiness or clouds of disappointment, not the stupor of habit or the frivolity of thoughtlessness, can entirely erase the sense of it from the depths of the soul. The present generation of men—particularly in the circles of the cultured and the sophisticated, those who are often called "intellectuals" and who perhaps also think of themselves as constituting a special class, characterized by a particularly acute awareness of life—the present generation exhibits in marked degree a loss of faith and enthusiasm, which it is pleased to call "disillusionment," and which perhaps also is disillusionment. They think of themselves, these moderns, as beset with despair;[4] the values that formerly seemed to be unquestionable have somehow gone dead, and many of them find nothing by which they are enabled to see life as dignified and serious. By and large, this despair is an aesthetic despair, an imperfect despair, which has not yet reached the ethical, or grasped the boundless meaning of the moral realm in its truth. Morality is for them not an infinite spontaneity, an inner life, an emancipation and an ennoblement of the self; it is for them mainly a system of conventions and traditional rules, an arbitrary burden imposed from without by social forces that have been outlived; or it is a mere device for reaching finite ends, whose worth has become doubtful. In so far as this despair is an aesthetic despair, it is all to the good; for this is the road which the spirit of man must take in order to find itself. Let us but learn to perceive that no differential talent, no privileged status, no fortunate eventuality, can at bottom be worth while as a consummation; that all such things are quite incapable of dignifying life; and when the misunderstandings with respect to the nature of a moral consciousness have been cleared away, the road will be open to the discovery of man as man. A preoccupation with the secondary thoughts and interests of life is always exhausting and trivializing, and in the end bewildering. Our true refreshment and invigoration will come through going back to the first and simplest thoughts, the primary and indispensable interests. We have too long lost ourselves in anxious considerations of what it may mean to be a shoemaker or a philosopher, a poet or a millionaire; in order to find ourselves, it is needful that we concentrate our energies upon the infinitely significant problem of what it means simply to be a man, without any transiently qualifying adjectives. When Frederick the Great asked his Court preacher if he knew anything about the future life, the preacher answered, "Yes, Your Majesty, it is absolutely certain that in the future life Your Highness will not be king of Prussia." And so it is; we were men before we became whatever of relative value we became in life, and we shall doubtless be human beings long after what we thus became or acquired will have lost its significance for us. On the stage some actors have roles in which they are royal and important personages; others are simple folk, beggars, workingmen, and the like. But when the play is over and the curtain is rolled down, the actors cast aside their disguises, the differences vanish, and all are once more simply actors. So, when the play of life is over, and the curtain is rolled down upon the scene, the differences and relativities which have disguised the men and women who have taken part will vanish, and all will be simply human beings. But there is this difference between the actors of the stage and the actors of life. On the stage it is imperative that the illusion be maintained to the highest degree possible; an actor who plays the role of king as if he was an actor, or who too often reminds us that he is assuming a role, is precisely a poor actor. But on the stage of life, the reverse is the case. There it is the task, not to preserve, but to expose, the illusion; to win free from it while still retaining one's disguise. The disguising garment ought to flutter loosely about us, so loosely that the least wind of human feeling that blows may reveal the royal purple of humanity beneath. This revelation is the moral task; the moral consciousness is the consciousness of the dignity that invests human life when the personality has discovered itself, and is happy in the will to be itself.

Such is the view of life to which the present speaker is committed. He has sought to make it seem inviting, but not for a moment has he wished to deny that it sets a difficult task for him who would express it in the daily intercourse of life. Perhaps it has long since captured our imaginations; for it is no new gospel worked out to satisfy the imaginary requirements of the most recent fashions in human desire and feeling; on the contrary, it is an old, old view. But it is not enough that the truth of the significance inherent in having such a view of life should be grasped by the imagination, or by the elevated mood of a solemn hour; only the heart's profound movement, the will's decisive commitment,[5] can make that which is truth in general also a truth for me.

NOTES

1. Suggested by Emerson's "So nigh is grandeur to our dust." *Voluntaries.*
2. S. Kierkegaard, *Postscript*, p. 124.
3. S. Kierkegaard, *The Gospel of Suffering*, pp. 174–177.
4. *Postscript*, pp. 327, 328.
5. *Postscript*, p. 226.

CHAPTER 3

DAVID F. SWENSON

The Transforming Power of Otherworldliness

The modern spirit exerts two powerful pressures on the religious address. On the theoretical side it insists on placing in the foreground of attention the problem of assimilating modern knowledge. The religious address is tempted either to defend religion against a possible attack from this quarter or to seek support for religious ideas in the results of recent scientific research or in recent philosophical speculation. On the practical side there is a tendency to seek a justification for religion in the eyes of common sense, to enroll religion in the service of the wisdom of experience, and to show how valuable it is as an instrument of efficiency. The promise of godliness for the life to come retreats into the background; its promise for the life that now is monopolizes the attention; and—what is more significant still—the latter promise tends more and more to be so interpreted as to bring it into complete accord with that natural desire for success which is so deep-rooted in human beings.

These influences exert their pressure upon the present speaker as upon others. Nor have I any wish to condemn them unqualifiedly as temptations to be shunned or evils to be resisted. The search for intellectual clarity has its obvious and genuine significance, and much that may be said about the contributions of religion to efficiency and energy in the business of life seems to me just and sound. But the tendency to an exclusive preoccupation with such considerations is another matter. This cannot but tend to obscure the distinctiveness of the religious message, and the qualitative heterogeneity of the religious principles.

Religion claims a place in human life, but the place it claims is not one of tolerance, but of supremacy. True religion does not borrow significance from other forms of human culture; it does not ask to be supported either by science or by art, although it makes free to utilize both for its own distinctive ends. It does not wish to be impressed into the service of a kind of well-being or happiness external to its own spirit; it seeks to vivify and transform these conceptions themselves, and thus to be the arbiter of human valuations. It is, in brief, the master passion. It seeks control of "all thoughts, all passions, all delights, whatever stirs this mortal frame"; it strives to make all human activities its ministers—servants that feed the sacred flame of faith.

To speak otherwise of religion is to rob it of its spirit of aggressiveness. But the aggressiveness of religion is so much its very heart and soul that it cannot be defended or patronized without suffering betrayal. And yet it happens, strangely enough, that its representatives sometimes appear in the role of insinuating beggars, seeking the crumbs that fall from the table of the scientist or the philosopher or the worldly-wise man. In its truth, however, the religious spirit is a bestowing spirit, capable of making all rich, both rich and poor.

In this conviction I have chosen to speak this evening on the power exerted in human life by the spirit of otherworldliness. I do not mean to deny the significance of this-worldliness, or that religion has a this-worldly aspect. On the contrary, I claim for religion an inclusiveness, a suppleness, a quality of penetration, an absolute commensurability, which makes it at home in every situation. But it is my conviction that these two aspects of life, this-worldliness on the one side and otherworldliness on the other, are in their truth to be valued as the relative is to the absolute, the subordinate to the dominant, the many things useful to the one thing needful. Take away from life every relation to the absolute, and the relative itself is puffed up into the semblance of an importance that it cannot sustain. Take away from life every relation to the absolute, and the relativities of life lose their adequate ordering principle; life tends to become an anarchic chaos, or "a tale . . . full of sound and fury, signifying nothing."

Before proceeding with this talk, I wish to acknowledge my indebtedness to one of the great religious thinkers of all time, the Danish philosopher Søren Kierkegaard, whose name, although he has been dead three quarters of a century, is still practically unknown to English-speaking people, nor have any of his numerous works as yet found their way into English.* Because he created a new religious philosophy which stressed the category of the individual and his relation to God, and showed that truth can exist only in subjectivity, I feel that he is destined to exert a powerful ethical and religious influence upon future thinking, and I am therefore glad to afford you a brief introduction to some phases of his thought by drawing freely upon the ideas he set forth in one of his edifying discourses, entitled, "The Expectation of an Eternal Happiness," published in 1844; and by paraphrasing certain passages I shall try to give you some idea of the clarity, the simplicity, and the earnestness with which Kierkegaard appealed "to that individual" whom he was happy to call "my reader." Hence, employing the same text as did Kierkegaard, I call your attention to certain moving words of the Apostle Paul, which you will find in his Second Letter to the Corinthians, words that express the conviction embodied in my theme:

*This was true when Swenson wrote this essay; it no longer is. [Ed.]

Wherefore we faint not; but though our outward man is decaying, yet our inward man is renewed day by day. For our light affliction, which is for the moment, worketh for us more and more exceedingly an eternal weight of glory; while we look not at the things which are seen, but at the things which are not seen: for the things which are seen are temporal; but the things which are not seen are eternal.

These words of Paul testify to a conviction which his life gloriously interprets. The principle of this conviction is the thoroughgoing interpenetration of life with the consciousness of the eternal, the bringing of the invisible everywhere to bear upon the visible, finding in the eternal the ultimate ground and the final clarification of human life.

The modern spirit is not indisposed to admire the boldness of Paul's faith, but it hesitates to follow in his footsteps. Its reasons are multifarious, but chief among them is the lurking fear that such faith is, after all, a retreat from life into the realm of fancy. It must be admitted that we are all of us confronted with this danger, a danger that presents itself not in one form only but in many, not only when life is professedly religious, but also when life is thoroughly secularized. Imaginary compensations for actual weakness, the selfish and cowardly indulgence in daydreams that but increase that weakness more and more, sapping the soul's vitality—these are a sickness of the soul which may threaten to become a sickness unto death. The spirit of otherworldliness in religion is not only intolerant of this weakness but is an actual cure for it. The hope of eternal bliss is for Paul not a refuge from life; it is a challenge to live yet more deeply and intensely. The essence of daydreaming is the separation of the imagination from the will, its development in isolation from the rest of life. The essence of a religious faith in an external order is its transforming power over the rest of life, an influence that dares ignore no single detail as too small or unimportant. The eternal presses instantly upon the will; its motto is: "Work . . . while it is day"; "Now is the acceptable time." If the expectation of the eternal does not work this result upon the life, it is a counterfeit expectation and not a genuine faith, a credulous superstition, an unclarified yearning, an affectation, an insincerity, a sick soul's flight from life, not a sound soul's sincere presence in the temporal.

Those who do not share the enthusiasm of this faith naturally regard it as an illusion. Nevertheless, it must not be forgotten that faith in the eternal arises like the phoenix out of the ashes of all the soul's previous illusions. It supersedes not only the happy illusions of childhood and the beautiful illusions of youth, the illusion of a romantic love that is happiness without responsibility; the illusions of maturity, which center about fame and money, power and success; but also the most persistent and deepseated of all illusions, the illusion of self-adequacy and self-righteousness. This supersession is that dying away from the world of which religion speaks, a dying that conditions the life that is life indeed; the pain of this dying is mingled with the joy of this living; and this most significant of all the struggles that life affords is the supreme test of the reality of the soul's thoughts and aims and feelings.

Human life sometimes affords us a glimpse of an aesthetic perfection from which this deeper struggle seems to be excluded. The life of creative art, for example, appears to have a perfection of unity that knows nothing of the deep cleft between preparation and consummation. Each step or phase of such an activity seems both an end in itself, yielding its own immanent satisfaction, as well as a transition to the equally significant next step or stage. But such experiences are fortunate episodes in life, not expressive of its essential structure. They are imperfect analogues, foreshadowing dimly that deeper harmony which can enter into the present life only by anticipation and faith. Man is a duality;[1] such is the testimony of one of the greatest thinkers of antiquity, whose mythical genealogy of Eros as the child of Poverty and Plenty, who because of his participation in this double nature is always striving, desiring, seeking for that which in its fullness is beyond the present self, is an imaginative fancy meant as an essential picture of human life.

Such is also the testimony of Paul, who makes human life a synthesis of the temporal and the eternal, faith the anticipation that knits them together, eternity the true fulfillment. Time separates the way from the goal to which it leads; it separates means from ends, preparation from consummation. Every more earnest view of life acknowledges the significance of this separation; only frivolity expects to reap its harvest the instant it has sown. The more ambitious the view of life, the more remote the consummation that it proposes; this principle is, in general, the measure both of the worth of the striving and of the significance of the reward sought. The religious view of life is the most ambitious of all; it is charged with a demand upon life that makes even the most beautiful temporal consummation seem a sorry imperfection, if it is to be *the* consummation. It disposes of an enthusiasm that is content to make, not a longer or shorter period within time, but the entire earthly life a state of striving and of preparation. The religious man confesses to the view that life is a way, that a man is, in his true character, a pilgrim; he looks toward an unseen city, "a house not made with hands, eternal, in the heavens." In testimony of this he calls himself a believer, which means in his mouth what the staff signifies in the wayfarer's hands, namely, "What I seek is not yet here."

Let us now consider this view of life from a variety of aspects in order that we may be enabled to grasp more clearly the part that it plays in human life; the difference that is made, the power that is exerted, by the expectation of an eternal life and an eternal joy.

First, let us note that this expectancy gives to our lives their greatest possible tension, since it evokes the maximum interest. To bestow an infinite interest upon a finite value is the torturing self-contradiction of the mere worldly life. It is not only hope that is found to be precarious, but experience teaches us that the things hoped for deceive us even though they be attained. The fulfillment at hand, we ask ourselves, "Is *this* the consummation I so devoutly wished?" The eternal alone can furnish the true objective for that infinite interest which God has implanted as a potentiality in the heart of man. And, conversely, it is the evocation of this interest which constitutes the core of the true belief in immortality. Where this passion is atrophied or suppressed, the idea of immortality is a mere luxury, an unmeaning decorative addition to the surface of life, an affectation and a fancy. It is this deep and vital interest that is the oil in the lamps of all those who wait the coming of the bridegroom, the neglect of which excludes one from participation in the marriage feast; for an infinite personal interest is the subjective form for an indwelling of the eternal. When once the possibility of such an interest has dawned upon man's horizon, he is confronted with a challenge which he cannot evade or deny without doing violence to his deeper self; this glimpse of immortality makes a belief in it morally necessary, in the same sense that a philosopher once said of God that if God is possible,[2] then he is also necessary.

Let us also note that the consciousness of immortality removes the last vestige of abstractness, of casualness, of the possibility of subterfuge and evasion from man's relationship to God, and reveals life in its absolute earnestness. A transitory relation has in it the seeds of unreality. God's immanence in the world and in the human consciousness is an invisible presence; it does not have the immediately obvious or compelling character of an external or sensible reality. His omnipresence is therefore a seeking, a questioning, a solicitation—a courting, if you will, of man's free spirit; and this unobtrusive courtship is the most tremendous concession conceivable to man's independence. But lest this concession become a mere weakness on the part of God, a sheer madness, it must be permeated by the condition of an inescapable responsibility on the part of man. But if, after a lifetime of evasion and neglect, I can end all by simply tucking myself away in a grave, and be as if neither I nor God had ever been, then God has permitted himself to be mocked, and life is not real and earnest to the last degree. But God is not mocked, and it is for this reason also that he is not the God of the dead, but of the living. The true faith in immortality is thus nurtured in fear and trembling.

The expectation of immortality presents to the individual an ideal goal in which he can be concretely present, because it is a goal in whose attainment he himself participates. There are views of life that seek to enhance its ideal significance by setting the individual a task whose realization is placed beyond the individual life, in some future period of mankind or of the world. This view makes all the preceding generations of men mere instruments, not ends in themselves; it arbitrarily selects a particular generation, or a group of generations, to be the fortunate beneficiaries of an effort which they have not shared, and permits them to reap where they have not sown. The concept of the progress of the race doubtless has its relative meaning and justification; but alone and by itself as the highest good, it is a mere abstraction. If, on the other hand, every human being has his ideal goal in himself, and if this self is no mere particularistic entity but a true individual, at one and the same time itself and the human race, so that men cannot without humanity be made perfect, then there is established an immanent end for man, which makes him no mere instrument, and makes of his life something higher than slavery in the service of external ends. And the human race too becomes something more than an intellectual abstraction, as it is in the historical process; in the relationship of each and every man to the eternal, the human race as such becomes a concrete reality.

The expectation of immortality has the power to reconcile every human being to his neighbor, his friend, and his foe, in a common understanding of the essential in life. It unites him to his fellow men in the most profound of all sympathies, and in the only thinkable universal goal. Every other goal is to a greater or less extent divisive, depends upon differences, and establishes invidious distinctions, not forgetting the invidious distinction between those who are privileged to give and those who are foredoomed merely to receive. But the expectation of immortality is not relevant to differential talent or fortunate circumstances; it establishes itself upon the basis of our common humanity, and no one is excluded who does not exclude himself. It cultivates no stoic insensibility; it acknowledges the genuineness of relative goods, but it denies that they constitute the perfection of life. It looks, therefore, toward a more perfect life, in which all men will have all things; in which God, who is all in all, will by the miracle of his love be present whole and entire in every single human heart. To believe something like this, so it seems to me, is to be human. And believing this, one may learn to wear his differences lightly, as if they were but the disguising cloak for the royal purple of humanity beneath.

The expectation of an eternal issue for human life will also help to liberate a man from the ruinous illusion that the quality of the means he chooses is of less importance than the ends he seeks. It is of the essence of the eternal, as the goal of life, that method and end are always in exact and perfect harmony. The methods, on the contrary, by which any temporal end may be attained, are diverse and incommensurable, and the choice of means becomes more or less a matter of indifference. He who stakes everything upon his success in attaining such ends will in the last analysis succumb to necessity that knows no law. Every ethical principle will tend to become for him vacillating and uncertain. Honesty is the best policy—aye, in most circumstances perhaps—at any rate the appearance of honesty, if not the reality, and a certain degree of honesty, if not its utmost perfection. And so with every other ethical principle; it must not be applied too severely, lest it defeat its own ends and fail to be justified by the results. The maxim of a worldly prudence is therefore always *ne quid nimis,* to carry nothing to extremes. It has no sympathy with that divine madness, the transcendent enthusiasm, which breaks through the confines of a petty calculation, because it derives its strength from the eternal and the unchanging. The statesman permits himself an appeal to the lower levels of character and intelligence, and thus abdicates his leadership before he enters upon it, because he fears that any other course would jeopardize an immediate success. All who make it their highest aim to secure for themselves any form of external power—kings and emperors and statesmen and demagogues and ecclesiastics and sophists—have not scrupled to exploit and foster human weakness and illusions, its prejudices, and its basest passions. They boast of taking the world as they find it; it cannot escape a thoughtful contemplation that they also leave the world in essentially the same situation. Not so the saints, the apostles, the prophets, and the martyrs, the men and women who have yielded allegiance to an eternal order, and have dedicated their lives to bear witness for the truth. Concession and distortion might have brought them a tremendous success; but they lived for eternity, and hence chose rather the threat of failure and the certainty of opposition. And eternity knows them, and acknowledges them for its own. In the perspective of the moment, success is everything, and failure is failure; in the longer perspective of history, the immediate success is already of lesser importance, and the failure of the moment is sometimes the success of the future; in the perspective of eternity, success is nothing and failure is nothing, but the spirit of endurance in suffering and loyalty in striving for a good cause is everything. The expectation of the eternal will help a man to be steadfast and true to his cause; it will help him to understand the difference between the devotion that serves a cause and the calculation that attaches itself to a cause in order to be served by it; and it will habituate in him the search for the most glorious harmony of human life, the harmony of the means with their corresponding end.

The expectation of the eternal will help a man to be contemporary with himself in time, and wean him from the paralyzing effort of trying to shoulder the vaguely looming burden of tomorrow, or of all the tomorrows, in place of a concentration of effort and attention upon the definitely restricted burden of today. The power to concern himself with the future is a mark of man's kinship with the divine. For if there were no future, there would be no past, and if there were no past and no future, man would be hidebound in his instincts and a child of the moment, his horizon no broader and his head no higher than that of the beast that perishes. The struggle with the future is therefore an ennobling struggle, and no man can conquer the present who has not first conquered the future. But how can a man conquer the future before he has fought with the present? Only through that expectation of victory which is of the essence of faith in the eternal. This expectation is no mere youthful buoyancy, no mere confident self-appraisal. It is an expectation of a victory that transcends both success and defeat, both happiness and sorrow. It is the assurance that all things work together for good to them that love God. When the future has been conquered in this sense and in this sign, then and only then can the individual soberly and without illusion be wholly present in the present task, in each successive moment contemporary with himself.

Finally, let us note that the expectation of an eternal happiness gives a man a measuring rod, a standard of estimation, which will help him to understand himself in time, as over against the extremes of stress and strain, of fortune and misfortune. The wisdom of experience yields some such standard, and is useful in estimating the individual moments of life, mediating an adjustment to them that lends to man some degree of poise and equanimity. But this wisdom is based upon the individual and the particular, upon the partial and the discrete; the measure that it yields is a restricted and finite measure, the application of its standard confined within a limited compass and sphere. Whenever a man's soul is pregnant with the expectation of the eternal, this measure becomes for him too small and petty; he may thus, unwisely, be tempted to reject its relative aid. But neither can he fall back upon the romantic standards of youth. Whoever has only a finite standard of evaluations has a life that is wholly a child of time, and cannot even be assured of his ability to cope with the finite, since it is always possible that events will break that his experience cannot help him to surmount. If this happens, he becomes the prey of despair. Whoever has experienced this has learned from experience that experience is not enough. But he who cherishes in his soul the lively expectation of an eternal joy has in that expectation a measure that is always adequate and always valid. By means of this standard he will be enabled to understand himself in times of stress and strain, when life's demands exceed the measure of a finite understanding, and the wisdom of experience breaks under a pressure it cannot bear. He will not permit success or happiness to rob him of this eternally valid standard, and substitute in its place the false and transient standards of vanity and conceit; he will not permit sorrow and suffering to impose upon him their false standards, and teach him the despairing grief that knows no hope.

"For our light affliction, which is for the moment, worketh for us more and more exceedingly an eternal weight of glory." Let us imagine for a moment that we know nothing more about the author of these words than the fact that he had said them. And let us assume that we tried, as well as we knew how, to infer from these words what sort of life must have fallen to his lot—to the lot of one who could give this earthly life and the life to come such a testimony. Doubtless we should conclude, should we not, that this man's life must have been relatively quiet and uneventful, a life in honorable obscurity, far from the turmoil and stress of great crises, not perhaps entirely unaware of that secret wisdom which suffering bestows upon its initiates, but nevertheless not tried in the extremes of physical danger and mental anguish. We should perhaps be reminded of another saying of apparently similar purport and background, namely, "that the earth is beautiful enough as a country to travel through, but not so beautiful as to make the wayfarer forget that he is on his way." And, having drawn this or a similar conclusion, let us suppose that someone then outlines for us, as if for the first time, the story of Paul's life. He tells us of Paul's spiritual trial on the road to Damascus, when he was made to reverse his whole concept of right and wrong, and hence evidently was a man not without experience of the soul's supreme crisis; he tells us of Paul's mystical exaltation and rapture, his being lifted up into the third heaven—and so we see that Paul was doubtless tempted to conceive a distaste for the ordinary humdrum course of life; he tells us that Paul was often heard to testify with an enthusiasm that made him seem a madman; that for the many years of an active life he was without home and without security, a scandal in the eyes of his compatriots, a fool to the Greeks, an outcast from the world, often in danger to life, experienced in hunger and nakedness, often in prison, and at last executed as a criminal.

Would not this narration tend to shake us out of ourselves, our poise and our equanimity, and extort from our lips the exclamation that such a life was not to be endured—an everlasting strain and the heaviest affliction? The standards of our experience would break down under the attempt to compass and to estimate such a life. But Paul had an eternal goal, and an eternally valid measure; hence it is that where we speak of a heavy and unendurable burden, he spoke of "a light affliction, which is for the moment." When the storms of life threatened to overwhelm him, Paul looked toward his goal, and measured the storms with his standard, and behold, they became light and momentary afflictions! When experience failed to help him, when its wisdom fell short of the demands of life, then his faith leaped to the rescue, laying hold of a joy and peace beyond all understanding.

When the stress of life transcends the measure of experience, and plunges worldly wisdom into the depths of despair, human life becomes a chaotic turmoil, without comfort and without hope, unless the hope of an eternal weight of glory brings into our lives its order and its calm. This is that genuine transvaluation of all values which religion through its otherworldliness brings to life: not the fantastic transvaluation of an imaginary superman, but the simple faith of common men and women, a faith, however, from which no genius need be excluded unless he excludes himself.

NOTES

1. Plato, *Symposium;* S. Kierkegaard, *Postscript,* p. 54.
2. Voltaire.

CHAPTER 4

WILLIAM LANE CRAIG

The Absurdity of Life Without God

THE NECESSITY OF GOD AND IMMORTALITY

Man, writes Loren Eiseley, is the Cosmic Orphan. He is the only creature in the universe who asks, "Why?" Other animals have instincts to guide them, but man has learned to ask questions.

"Who am I?" man asks. "Why am I here? Where am I going?" Since the Enlightenment, when he threw off the shackles of religion, man has tried to answer these questions without reference to God. But the answers that came back were not exhilarating, but dark and terrible. "You are the accidental by-product of nature, a result of matter plus time plus chance. There is no reason for your existence. All you face is death."

Modern man thought that when he had gotten rid of God, he had freed himself from all that repressed and stifled him. Instead, he discovered that in killing God, he had also killed himself.

For if there is no God, then man's life becomes absurd.

If God does not exist, then both man and the universe are inevitably doomed to death. Man, like all biological organisms, must die. With no hope of immortality, man's life leads only to the grave. His life is but a spark in the infinite blackness, a spark that appears, flickers, and dies forever. Compared to the infinite stretch of time, the span of man's life is but an infinitesimal moment; and yet this is all the life he will ever know. Therefore, everyone must come face to face with what theologian Paul Tillich has called "the threat of non-being." For though I know now that I exist, that I am alive, I also know that someday I will no longer exist, that I will no longer be, that I will die. This thought is staggering and threatening: to think that the person I call "myself" will cease to exist, that I will be no more!

I remember vividly the first time my father told me that someday I would die. Somehow as a child the thought had just never occurred to me. When he told me, I was filled with fear and unbearable sadness. And though he tried repeatedly to reassure me that this was a long way off, that did not seem to matter. Whether sooner or later, the undeniable fact was that I would die and be no more, and the thought overwhelmed me. Eventually, like all of us, I grew to simply accept the fact. We all learn to live with the inevitable. But the child's insight remains true. As the French existentialist Jean-Paul Sartre observed, several hours or several years make no difference once you have lost eternity.

Whether it comes sooner or later, the prospect of death and the threat of non-being is a terrible horror. But I met a student once who did not feel this threat. He said he had been raised on the farm and was used to seeing the animals being born and dying. Death was for him simply natural—a part of life, so to speak. I was puzzled by how different our two perspectives on death were and found it difficult to understand why he did not feel the threat of non-being. Years later, I think I found my answer in reading Sartre. Sartre observed that death is not threatening so long as we view it as the death of the other, from a third-person standpoint, so to speak. It is only when we internalize it and look at it from the first-person perspective—"*my* death: *I* am going to die"—that the threat of non-being becomes real. As Sartre points out, many people never assume this first-person perspective in the midst of life; one can even look at one's own death from the third-person standpoint, as if it were the death of another or even of an animal, as did my friend. But the true existential significance of *my death* can only be appreciated from the first-person perspective, as I realize that I am going to die and forever cease to exist. My life is just a momentary transition out of oblivion into oblivion.

And the universe, too, faces death. Scientists tell us that the universe is expanding, and everything in it is growing farther and farther apart. As it does so, it grows colder and colder, and its energy is used up. Eventually all the stars will burn out and all matter will collapse into dead stars and black holes. There will be no light at all; there will be no heat; there will be no life; only the corpses of dead stars and galaxies, ever expanding into the endless darkness and the cold recesses of space—a universe in ruins. The entire universe marches irreversibly toward its grave. So not only is the life of each individual person doomed; the entire human race is doomed. The universe is plunging toward inevitable extinction—death is written throughout its structure. There is no escape. There is no hope.

THE ABSURDITY OF LIFE WITHOUT GOD AND IMMORTALITY

If there is no God, then man and the universe are doomed. Like prisoners condemned to death, we await our unavoidable execution. There is no God, and there is no immortality. And what is the consequence of this? It means that life itself is absurd. It means that the life we have is without ultimate significance, value, or purpose. Let's look at each of these.

No Ultimate Meaning without Immortality and God

If each individual person passes out of existence when he dies, then what ultimate meaning can be given to his life? Does it really matter whether he ever existed at all? It might be said that his life was important because it influenced others or affected the course of history. But this only shows a relative significance to his life, not an ultimate significance. His life may be important relative to certain other events, but what is the ultimate significance of any of those events? If all the events are meaningless, then what can be the ultimate meaning of influencing any of them? Ultimately it makes no difference.

Look at it from another perspective: Scientists say that the universe originated in an explosion called the "Big Bang" about 15 billion years ago. Suppose the Big Bang had never occurred. Suppose the universe had never existed. What ultimate difference would it make? The universe is doomed to die anyway. In the end it makes no difference whether the universe ever existed or not. Therefore, it is without ultimate significance.

The same is true of the human race. Mankind is a doomed race in a dying universe. Because the human race will eventually cease to exist, it makes no ultimate difference whether it ever did exist. Mankind is thus no more significant than a swarm of mosquitos or a barnyard of pigs, for their end is all the same. The same blind cosmic process that coughed them up in the first place will eventually swallow them all again.

And the same is true of each individual person. The contributions of the scientist to the advance of human knowledge, the researches of the doctor to alleviate pain and suffering, the efforts of the diplomat to secure peace in the world, the sacrifices of good men everywhere to better the lot of the human race—all these come to nothing. In the end they don't make one bit of difference, not one bit. Each person's life is therefore without ultimate significance. And because our lives are ultimately meaningless, the activities we fill our lives with are also meaningless. The long hours spent in study at the university, our jobs, our interests, our friendships—all these are, in the final analysis, utterly meaningless. This is the horror of modern man: because he ends in nothing, he is nothing.

But it is important to see that it is not just immortality that man needs if life is to be meaningful. Mere duration of existence does not make that existence meaningful. If man and the universe could exist forever, but if there were no God, their existence would still have no ultimate significance. To illustrate: I once read a science-fiction story in which an astronaut was marooned on a barren chunk of rock lost in outer space. He had with him two vials: one containing poison and the other a potion that would make him live forever. Realizing his predicament, he gulped down the poison. But then to his horror, he discovered he had swallowed the wrong vial—he had drunk the potion for immortality. And that meant that he was cursed to exist forever—a meaningless, unending life. Now if God does not exist, our lives are just like that. They could go on and on and still be utterly without meaning. We could still ask of life, "So what?" So it is not just immortality man needs if life is to be ultimately significant; he needs God and immortality. And if God does not exist, then he has neither.

Twentieth-century man came to understand this. Read *Waiting for Godot* by Samuel Beckett. During this entire play two men carry on trivial conversation while waiting for a third man to arrive, who never does. Our lives are like that, Beckett is saying; we just kill time waiting—for what, we don't know. In a tragic portrayal of man, Beckett wrote another play in which the curtain opens revealing a stage littered with junk. For thirty long seconds, the audience sits and stares in silence at that junk. Then the curtain closes. That's all.

One of the most devastating novels I've ever read was *Steppenwolf*, by Hermann Hesse. At the novel's end, Harry Haller stands looking at himself in a mirror. During the course of his life he had experienced all the world offers. And now he stands looking at himself, and he mutters, "Ah, the bitter taste of life!" He spits at himself in the looking-glass, and then he kicks it to pieces. His life has been futile and meaningless.

French existentialists Jean-Paul Sartre and Albert Camus understood this, too. Sartre portrayed life in his play *No Exit* as hell—the final line of the play are the words of resignation, "Well, let's get on with it." Hence, Sartre writes elsewhere of the "nausea" of existence. Camus, too, saw life as absurd. At the end of his brief novel *The Stranger*, Camus's hero discovers in a flash of insight that the universe has no meaning and there is no God to give it one. The French biochemist Jacques Monod seemed to echo those sentiments when he wrote in his work *Chance and Necessity*, "Man finally knows he is alone in the indifferent immensity of the universe."

Thus, if there is no God, then life itself becomes meaningless. Man and the universe are without ultimate significance.

No Ultimate Value without Immortality and God

If life ends at the grave, then it makes no difference whether one has lived as a Stalin or as a saint. Since one's destiny is ultimately unrelated to one's behavior, you may as well just live as you please. As Dostoyevsky put it: "If there is no immortality then all things are permitted." On this basis, a writer like Ayn Rand is absolutely correct to praise the virtues of selfishness. Live totally for self; no one holds you accountable! Indeed, it would be foolish to do anything else, for life is too short to jeopardize it by acting out of anything but pure self-interest. Sacrifice for another person would be stupid. Kai Nielsen, an atheist philosopher who attempts to defend the viability of ethics without God, in the end admits,

> We have not been able to show that reason requires the moral point of view, or that all really rational persons, unhoodwinked by myth or ideology, need not be individual egoists or classical amoralists. Reason doesn't decide here. The

picture I have painted for you is not a pleasant one. Reflection on it depresses me. . . . Pure practical reason, even with a good knowledge of the facts, will not take you to morality.[1]

But the problem becomes even worse. For, regardless of immortality, if there is no God, then there can be no objective standards of right and wrong. All we are confronted with is, in Jean-Paul Sartre's words, the bare, valueless fact of existence. Moral values are either just expressions of personal taste or the by-products of socio-biological evolution and conditioning. In the words of one humanist philosopher, "The moral principles that govern our behavior are rooted in habit and custom, feeling and fashion."[2] In a world without God, who is to say which values are right and which are wrong? Who is to judge that the values of Adolf Hitler are inferior to those of a saint? The concept of morality loses all meaning in a universe without God. As one contemporary atheistic ethicist points out, "to say that something is wrong because . . . it is forbidden by God, is . . . perfectly understandable to anyone who believes in a law-giving God. But to say that something is wrong . . . even though no God exists to forbid it, is *not* understandable. . . ." "The concept of moral obligation [is] unintelligible apart from the idea of God. The words remain but their meaning is gone."[3] In a world without God, there can be no objective right and wrong, only our culturally and personally relative, subjective judgments. This means that it is impossible to condemn war, oppression, or crime as evil. Nor can one praise brotherhood, equality, and love as good. For in a universe without God, good and evil do not exist—there is only the bare valueless fact of existence, and there is no one to say you are right and I am wrong.

No Ultimate Purpose without Immortality and God

If death stands with open arms at the end of life's trail, then what is the goal of life? To what end has life been lived? Is it all for nothing? Is there no reason for life? And what of the universe? Is it utterly pointless? If its destiny is a cold grave in the recesses of outer space, the answer must be yes—it is pointless. There is no goal, no purpose, for the universe. The litter of a dead universe will just go on expanding and expanding—forever.

And what of man? Is there no purpose at all for the human race? Or will it simply peter out someday lost in the oblivion of an indifferent universe? The English writer H. G. Wells foresaw such a prospect. In his novel *The Time Machine* Wells's time traveler journeys far into the future to discover the destiny of man. All he finds is a dead earth, save for a few lichens and moss, orbiting a gigantic red sun. The only sounds are the rush of the wind and the gentle ripple of the sea. "Beyond these lifeless sounds," writes Wells, "the world was silent. Silent? It would be hard to convey the stillness of it. All the sounds of man, the bleating of sheep, the cries of birds, the hum of insects, the stir that makes the background of our lives—all that was over."[4] And so Wells's time traveler returned. But to what?—to merely an earlier point on the purposeless rush toward oblivion. When as a non-Christian I first read Wells's book, I thought, "No, no! It can't end that way!" But if there is no God, it will end that way, like it or not. This is reality in a universe without God: there is no hope; there is no purpose. It reminds me of T.S. Eliot's haunting lines:

This is the way the world ends
This is the way the world ends
This is the way the world ends
Not with a bang but a whimper.[5]

What is true of mankind as a whole is true of each of us individually: we are here to no purpose. If there is no God, then our life is not qualitatively different from that of a dog. I know that's harsh, but it's true. As the ancient writer of Ecclesiastes put it: "The fate of the sons of men and the fate of beasts is the same. As one dies so dies the other; indeed, they all have the same breath and there is no advantage for man over beast, for all is vanity. All go to the same place. All come from the dust and all return to the dust" (Ecclesiastes 3:19–20). In this book, which reads more like a piece of modern existentialist literature than a book of the Bible, the writer shows the futility of pleasure, wealth, education, political fame, and honor in a life doomed to end in death. His verdict? "Vanity of vanities! All is vanity" (1:2). If life ends at the grave, then we have no ultimate purpose for living.

But more than that: even if it did not end in death, without God life would still be without purpose. For man and the universe would then be simple accidents of chance, thrust into existence for no reason. Without God the universe is the result of a cosmic accident, a chance explosion. There is no reason for which it exists. As for man, he is a freak of nature—a blind product of matter plus time plus chance. Man is just a lump of slime that evolved into rationality. There is no more purpose in life for the human race than for a species of insect; for both are the result of the blind interaction of chance and necessity. As one philosopher has put it: "Human life is mounted upon a subhuman pedestal and must shift for itself alone in the heart of a silent and mindless universe."[6]

What is true of the universe and of the human race is also true of us as individuals. Insofar as we are individual human beings, we are the results of certain combinations of heredity and environment. We are victims of a kind of genetic and environmental roulette. Psychologists following Sigmund Freud tell us our actions are the result of various repressed sexual tendencies. Sociologists following B. F. Skinner argue that all our choices are determined by conditioning, so that freedom is an illusion. Biologists like Francis Crick regard man as an electro-chemical machine that can be controlled by altering its genetic code. If God does not exist, then you are just a miscarriage of nature, thrust into a purposeless universe to live a purposeless life.

So if God does not exist, that means that man and the universe exist to no purpose—since the end of everything is death—and that they came to be for no purpose, since they are only blind products of chance. In short, life is utterly without reason.

Do you understand the gravity of the alternatives before us? For if God exists, then there is hope for man. But if God does not exist, then all we are left with is despair. Do you understand why the question of God's existence is so vital to man? As one writer has aptly put it, "If God is dead, then man is dead, too."

Unfortunately, the mass of mankind do not realize this fact. They continue on as though nothing has changed. I'm reminded of Nietzsche's story of the madman who in the early morning hours burst into the marketplace, lantern in hand, crying, "I seek God! I seek God!" Since many of those standing about did not believe in God, he provoked much laughter. "Did God get lost?" they taunted him. "Or is he hiding? Or maybe he has gone on a voyage or emigrated!" Thus they yelled and laughed. Then, writes Nietzsche, the madman turned in their midst and pierced them with his eyes.

> 'Whither is God?' he cried, 'I shall tell you. *We have killed him*—you and I. All of us are his murderers. But how have we done this? How were we able to drink up the sea? Who gave us the sponge to wipe away the entire horizon? What did we do when we unchained this earth from its sun? Whither is it moving now? Away from all suns? Are we not plunging continually? Backward, sideward, forward, in all directions? Is there any up or down left? Are we not straying as through an infinite nothing? Do we not feel the breath of empty space? Has it not become colder? Is not night and more night coming on all the while? Must not lanterns be lit in the morning? Do we not hear anything yet of the noise of the gravediggers who are burying God? . . . God is dead. . . . And we have killed him. How shall we, the murderers of all murderers, comfort ourselves?'[7]

The crowd stared at the madman in silence and astonishment. At last he dashed his lantern to the ground. "I have come too early," he said. "This tremendous event is still on its way—it has not yet reached the ears of man." Men did not yet truly comprehend the consequences of what they had done in killing God. But Nietzsche predicted that someday people would realize the implications of their atheism; and this realization would usher in an age of nihilism—the destruction of all meaning and value in life. The end of Christianity, wrote Nietzsche, means the advent of nihilism. This most gruesome of guests is standing already at the door. "Our whole European culture is moving for some time now," wrote Nietzsche, "with a tortured tension that is growing from decade to decade, as toward a catastrophe: restlessly, violently, headlong, like a river that wants to reach the end, that no longer reflects, that is afraid to reflect."[8]

Most people still do not reflect on the consequences of atheism and so, like the crowd in the marketplace, go unknowingly on their way. But when we realize, as did Nietzsche, what atheism implies, then his question presses hard upon us: how *shall* we, the murderers of all murderers, comfort ourselves?

THE PRACTICAL IMPOSSIBILITY OF ATHEISM

About the only solution the atheist can offer is that we face the absurdity of life and live bravely. Bertrand Russell, for example, wrote that we must build our lives upon "the firm foundation of unyielding despair."[9] Only by recognizing that the world really is a terrible place can we successfully come to terms with life. Camus said that we should honestly recognize life's absurdity and then live in love for one another.

The fundamental problem with this solution, however, is that it is impossible to live consistently and happily within such a world view. If one lives consistently, he will not be happy; if one lives happily, it is only because he is not consistent. Francis Schaeffer has explained this point well. Modern man, says Schaeffer, resides in a two-story universe. In the lower story is the finite world without God; here life is absurd, as we have seen. In the upper story are meaning, value, and purpose. Now modern man lives in the lower story because he believes there is no God. But he cannot live happily in such an absurd world; therefore, he continually makes leaps of faith into the upper story to affirm meaning, value, and purpose, even though he has no right to, since he does not believe in God. Modern man is totally inconsistent when he makes this leap, because these values cannot exist without God, and man in his lower story does not have God.

Let's look again, then, at each of the three areas in which we saw life was absurd without God, to show how man cannot live consistently and happily with his atheism.

Meaning of Life

First, the area of meaning. We saw that without God, life has no meaning. Yet philosophers continue to live as though life does have meaning. For example, Sartre argued that one may create meaning for his life by freely choosing to follow a certain course of action. Sartre himself chose Marxism.

Now this is utterly inconsistent. It is inconsistent to say life is objectively absurd and then to say one may create meaning for his life. If life is really absurd, then man is trapped in the lower story. To try to create meaning in life represents a leap to the upper story. But Sartre has no basis for this leap. Without God, there can be no objective meaning in life. Sartre's program is actually an exercise in self-delusion. For the universe does not really acquire meaning just because *I* give it one. This is easy to see: for suppose I give the universe one meaning, and you give it another. Who is right? The answer, of course, is neither one. For the universe without God remains objectively meaningless, no matter how *we* regard it. Sartre is really saying, "Let's *pretend* the universe has meaning." And this is just fooling ourselves.

The point is this: if God does not exist, then life is objectively meaningless; but man cannot live consistently and happily knowing that life is meaningless; so in order to be happy he pretends life has meaning. But this is, of course, entirely inconsistent—for without God, man and the universe are without any real significance.

Value of Life

Turn now to the problem of value. Here is where the most blatant inconsistencies occur. First of all, atheistic humanists are totally inconsistent in affirming the traditional values of love and brotherhood. Camus has been rightly criticized for inconsistently holding both to the absurdity of life and the ethics of human love and brotherhood. The two are logically incompatible. Bertrand Russell, too, was inconsistent. For though he was an atheist, he was an outspoken social critic, denouncing war and restrictions on sexual freedom. Russell admitted that he could not live as though ethical values were simply a matter of personal taste, and that he therefore found his own views "incredible." "I do not know the solution," he confessed.[10] The point is that if there is no God, then objective right and wrong cannot exist. As Dostoyevsky said, "All things are permitted."

But Dostoyevsky also showed that man cannot live this way. He cannot live as though it is perfectly all right for soldiers to slaughter innocent children. He cannot live as though it is all right for dictatorial regimes to follow a systematic program of physical torture of political prisoners. He cannot live as though it is all right for dictators like Pol Pot to exterminate millions of their own countrymen. Everything in him cries out to say these acts are wrong—really wrong. But if there is no God, he cannot. So he makes a leap of faith and affirms values anyway. And when he does so, he reveals the inadequacy of a world without God.

The horror of a world devoid of value was brought home to me with new intensity a few years ago as I viewed a BBC television documentary called "The Gathering." It concerned the reunion of survivors of the Holocaust in Jerusalem, where they rediscovered lost friendships and shared their experiences. Now, I had heard stories of the Holocaust before and had even visited Dachau and Buchenwald, and I thought I was beyond shocking by further tales of horror. But I found that I was not. Perhaps I had been made more sensitive by the recent birth of our beautiful baby girl, so that I applied the situations to her as they were related on the television. In any case, one woman prisoner, a nurse, told of how she was made the gynecologist at Auschwitz. She observed that pregnant women were grouped together by the soldiers under the direction of Dr. Mengele and housed in the same barracks. Some time passed, and she noted that she no longer saw any of these women. She made inquiries. "Where are the pregnant women who were housed in that barracks?" "Haven't you heard?" came the reply. "*Dr. Mengele used them for vivisection.*"

Another woman told of how Mengele had bound up her breasts so that she could not suckle her infant. The doctor wanted to learn how long an infant could survive without nourishment. Desperately this poor woman tried to keep her baby alive by giving it pieces of bread soaked in coffee, but to no avail. Each day the baby lost weight, a fact that was eagerly monitored by Dr. Mengele. A nurse then came secretly to this woman and told her, "I have arranged a way for you to get out of here, but you cannot take your baby with you. I have brought a morphine injection that you can give to your child to end its life." When the woman protested, the nurse was insistent: "Look, your baby is going to die anyway. At least save yourself." And so *this mother took the life of her own baby*. Dr. Mengele was furious when he learned of it because he had lost his experimental specimen, and he searched among the dead to find the baby's discarded corpse so that he could have one last weighing.

My heart was torn by these stories. One rabbi who survived the camp summed it up well when he said that at Auschwitz it was as though there existed a world in which all the Ten Commandments were reversed. Mankind had never seen such a hell.

And yet, if God does not exist, then in a sense, our world *is* Auschwitz: there is no absolute right and wrong; *all things* are permitted. But no atheist, no agnostic, can live consistently with such a view. Nietzsche himself, who proclaimed the necessity of living "beyond good and evil," broke with his mentor Richard Wagner precisely over the issue of the composer's anti-Semitism and strident German nationalism. Similarly Sartre, writing in the aftermath of the Second World War, condemned anti-Semitism, declaring that a doctrine that leads to extermination is not merely an opinion or matter of personal taste, of equal value with its opposite.[11] In his important essay "Existentialism Is a Humanism," Sartre struggles vainly to elude the contradiction between his denial of divinely pre-established values and his urgent desire to affirm the value of human persons. Like Russell, he could not live with the implications of his own denial of ethical absolutes.

A second problem is that if God does not exist and there is no immortality, then all the evil acts of men go unpunished and all the sacrifices of good men go unrewarded. But who can live with such a view? Richard Wurmbrand, who has been tortured for his faith in communist prisons, says,

> The cruelty of atheism is hard to believe when man has no faith in the reward of good or the punishment of evil. There is no reason to be human. There is no restraint from the depths of evil which is in man. The communist torturers often said, 'There is no God, no Hereafter, no punishment for evil. We can do what we wish.' I have heard one torturer even say, 'I thank God, in whom I don't believe, that I have lived to this hour when I can express all the evil in my heart.' He expressed it in unbelievable brutality and torture inflicted on prisoners.[12]

The English theologian Cardinal Newman once said that if he believed that all evils and injustices of life throughout history were not to be made right by God in the afterlife, "Why I think I should go mad." Rightly so.

And the same applies to acts of self-sacrifice. A number of years ago, a terrible mid-winter air disaster occurred in which a plane leaving the Washington, D.C. airport smashed into a bridge spanning the Potomac River, plunging its passengers into the icy waters. As the rescue helicopters came, attention was focused on one man who again and again pushed the dangling rope ladder to other passengers rather than be pulled to safety himself. Six times he passed the ladder by. When they came again, he was gone. He had freely given his life that others might live. The whole nation turned its eyes to this man in respect and admiration for the selfless and good act he had performed. And yet, if the atheist is right, that man was not noble—he did the stupidest thing possible. He should have gone for the ladder first, pushed others away if necessary in order to survive. But to die for others he did not even know, to give up all the brief existence he would ever have—what for? For the atheist there can be no reason. And yet the atheist, like the rest of us, instinctively reacts with praise for this man's selfless action. Indeed, one will probably never find an atheist who lives consistently with his system. For a universe without moral accountability and devoid of value is unimaginably terrible.

Purpose of Life

Finally, let's look at the problem of purpose in life. The only way most people who deny purpose in life live happily is either by making up some purpose, which amounts to self-delusion as we saw with Sartre, or by not carrying their view to its logical conclusions. Take the problem of death, for example. According to Ernst Bloch, the only way modern man lives in the face of death is by subconsciously borrowing the belief in immortality that his forefathers held to, even though he himself has no basis for this belief, since he does not believe in God. Bloch states that the belief that life ends in nothing is hardly, in his words, "sufficient to keep the head high and to work as if there were no end." By borrowing the remnants of a belief in immortality, writes Bloch, "modern man does not feel the chasm that unceasingly surrounds him and that will certainly engulf him at last. Through these remnants, he saves his sense of self-identity. Through them the impression arises that man is not perishing, but only that one day the world has the whim no longer to appear to him." Bloch concludes, "This quite shallow courage feasts on a borrowed credit card. It lives from earlier hopes and the support that they once had provided."[13] Modern man no longer has any right to that support, since he rejects God. But in order to live purposefully, he makes a leap of faith to affirm a reason for living.

We often find the same inconsistency among those who say that man and the universe came to exist for no reason or purpose, but just by chance. Unable to live in an impersonal universe in which everything is the product of blind chance, these persons begin to ascribe personality and motives to the physical processes themselves. It is a bizarre way of speaking and represents a leap from the lower to the upper story. For example, the brilliant Russian physicists Zeldovich and Novikov, in contemplating the properties of the universe, ask, Why did "Nature" choose to create this sort of universe instead of another? "Nature" has obviously become a sort of God-substitute, filling the role and function of God. Francis Crick halfway through his book *The Origin of the Genetic Code* begins to spell nature with a capital "N" and elsewhere speaks of natural selection as being "clever" and as "thinking" of what it will do. Fred Hoyle, the English astronomer, attributes to the universe itself the qualities of God. For Carl Sagan the "Cosmos," which he always spells with a capital letter, obviously fills the role of a God-substitute. Though all these men profess not to believe in God, they smuggle in a God-substitute through the back door because they cannot bear to live in a universe in which everything is the chance result of impersonal forces.

And it's interesting to see many thinkers betray their views when they're pushed to their logical conclusions. For example, certain feminists have raised a storm of protest over Freudian sexual psychology because it is chauvinistic and degrading to women. And some psychologists have knuckled under and revised their theories. Now this is totally inconsistent. If Freudian psychology is really true, then it doesn't matter if it's degrading to women. You can't change the truth because you don't like what it leads to. But people cannot live consistently and happily in a world where other persons are devalued. Yet if God does not exist, then nobody has any value. Only if God exists can a person consistently support women's rights. For if God does not exist, then natural selection dictates that the male of the species is the dominant and aggressive one. Women would no more have rights than a female goat or chicken have rights. In nature whatever is, is right. But who can live with such a view? Apparently not even Freudian psychologists, who betray their theories when pushed to their logical conclusions.

Or take the sociological behaviorism of a man like B. F. Skinner. This view leads to the sort of society envisioned in George Orwell's *1984,* where the government controls and programs the thoughts of everybody. If Pavlov's dog can be made to salivate when a bell rings, so can a human being. If Skinner's theories are right, then there can be no objection to treating people like the rats in Skinner's rat-box as they run through their mazes, coaxed on by food and electric shocks. According to Skinner, all our actions are determined anyway. And if God does not exist, then no moral objection can be raised against this kind of programming, for man is not qualitatively different from a rat, since both are just matter plus time plus chance. But again, who can live with such a dehumanizing view?

Or finally, take the biological determinism of a man like Francis Crick. The logical conclusion is that man is like any other laboratory specimen. The world was horrified when it learned that at camps like Dachau the Nazis had used prisoners for medical experiments on living humans. But why not? If God does not exist, there can be no objection to using people as human guinea pigs. A memorial at Dachau says *Nie Wieder*—"Never Again"—but this sort of thing is still going on. It was revealed a few years ago that in the United States several people had been injected, unknown to them, with a sterilization drug by medical researchers. Must we not protest that this is wrong—that man is more than an electro-chemical machine? The end of this view is population control in which the weak and unwanted are killed off to make room for the strong. But the only way we can consistently protest this view is if God exists. Only if God exists can there be purpose in life.

The dilemma of modern man is thus truly terrible. And insofar as he denies the existence of God and the objectivity of value and purpose, this dilemma remains unrelieved for "post-modern" man as well. Indeed, it is precisely the awareness that modernism issues inevitably in absurdity and despair that constitutes the anguish of post-modernism. In some respects, post-modernism just *is* the awareness of the bankruptcy of modernity. The atheistic world view is insufficient to maintain a happy and consistent life. Man cannot live consistently and happily as though life were ultimately without meaning, value, or purpose. If we try to live consistently within the atheistic world view, we shall find ourselves profoundly unhappy. If instead we manage to live happily, it is only by giving the lie to our world view.

Confronted with this dilemma, man flounders pathetically for some means of escape. In a remarkable address to the American Academy for the Advancement of Science in 1991, Dr. L. D. Rue, confronted with the predicament of modern man, boldly advocated that we deceive ourselves by means of some "Noble Lie" into thinking that we and the universe still have value.[14] Claiming that "The lesson of the past two centuries is that intellectual and moral relativism is profoundly the case," Dr. Rue muses that the consequence of such a realization is that one's quest for personal wholeness (or self-fulfillment) and the quest for social coherence become independent from one another. This is because on the view of relativism the search for self-fulfillment becomes radically privatized: each person chooses his own set of values and meaning. "There is no final, objective reading on the world or the self. There is no universal vocabulary for integrating cosmology and morality." If we are to avoid "the madhouse option," where self-fulfillment is pursued regardless of social coherence, and "the totalitarian option," where social coherence is imposed at the expense of personal wholeness, then we have no choice but to embrace some Noble Lie that will inspire us to live beyond selfish interests and so achieve social coherence. A Noble Lie "is one that deceives us, tricks us, compels us beyond self-interest, beyond ego, beyond family, nation, [and] race." It is a lie, because it tells us that the universe is infused with value (which is a great fiction), because it makes a claim to universal truth (when there is none), and because it tells me not to live for self-interest (which is evidently false). "But without such lies, we cannot live."

This is the dreadful verdict pronounced over modern man. In order to survive, he must live in self-deception. But even the Noble Lie option is in the end unworkable. For if what I have said thus far is correct, belief in a Noble Lie would not only be necessary to achieve social coherence and personal wholeness for the masses, but it would also be necessary to achieve one's *own* personal wholeness. For one cannot live happily and consistently on an atheistic world view. In order to be happy, one must believe in objective meaning, value, and purpose. But how can one believe in those Noble Lies while at the same time believing in atheism and relativism? The more convinced you are of the necessity of a Noble Lie, the less you are able to believe in it. Like a placebo, a Noble Lie works only on those who believe it is the truth. Once we have seen through the fiction, then the Lie has lost its power over us. Thus, ironically, the Noble Lie cannot solve the human predicament for anyone who has come to see that predicament.

The Noble Lie option therefore leads at best to a society in which an elitist group of *illuminati* deceive the masses for their own good by perpetuating the Noble Lie. But then why should those of us who are enlightened follow the masses in their deception? Why should we sacrifice self-interest for a fiction? If the great lesson of the past two centuries is moral and intellectual relativism, then why (if we could) pretend that we do not know this truth and live a lie instead? If one answers, "for the sake of social coherence," one may legitimately ask why I should sacrifice my self-interest for the sake of social coherence? The only answer the relativist can give is that social coherence is in my self-interest—but the problem with this answer is that self-interest and the interest of the herd do not always coincide. Besides, if (out of self-interest) I do care about social coherence, the totalitarian option is always open to me: forget the Noble Lie and maintain social coherence (as well as my self-fulfillment) at the expense of the personal wholeness of the masses. Generations of Soviet leaders who extolled proletarian virtues while they rode in limousines and dined on caviar in their country *dachas* found this alternative quite workable. Rue would undoubtedly regard such an option as repugnant. But therein lies the rub. Rue's dilemma is that he obviously values deeply both social coherence and personal wholeness for their own sakes; in other words, they are objective values, which according to his philosophy do not exist. He has already leapt to the upper story. The Noble Lie option thus affirms what it denies and so refutes itself.

THE SUCCESS OF BIBLICAL CHRISTIANITY

But if atheism fails in this regard, what about biblical Christianity? According to the Christian world view, God does exist, and man's life does not end at the grave. In the resurrection body man may enjoy eternal life and fellowship with God. Biblical Christianity therefore provides the two conditions necessary for a meaningful, valuable, and purposeful life for man: God and immortality. Because of this, we can live consistently and happily. Thus, biblical Christianity succeeds precisely where atheism breaks down.

CONCLUSION

Now I want to make it clear that I have not yet shown biblical Christianity to be true. But what I have done is clearly spell out the alternatives. If God does not exist, then life is futile. If the God of the Bible does exist, then life is meaningful. Only the second of these two alternatives enables us to live happily and consistently. Therefore, it seems to me that even if the evidence for these two options were absolutely equal, a rational person ought to choose biblical Christianity. It seems to me positively irrational to prefer death, futility, and destruction to life, meaningfulness, and happiness. As Pascal said, we have nothing to lose and infinity to gain.

The foregoing discussion makes clear the role I conceive cultural apologetics to play: it is not one's whole apologetic but rather an introduction to positive argumentation. It serves to lay out in a dramatic way the alternatives facing the unbeliever in order to create a felt need in him. When he realizes the predicament he is in, he will see why the gospel is so important to him; and many a non-Christian will be impelled by these considerations alone to give his life to Christ.

In sharing this material with an unbeliever, we need to push him to the logical conclusions of his position. If I am right, no atheist or agnostic really lives consistently with his world view. In some way he affirms meaning, value, or purpose without an adequate basis. It is our job to discover those areas and lovingly show him where those beliefs are groundless. We need not attack his values themselves—for they are probably largely correct—but we may agree with him concerning them, and then point out only that he lacks any foundation for those values, whereas the Christian has such a foundation. Thus, we need not make him defensive by a frontal attack on his personal values; rather we offer him a foundation for the values he already possesses.

I have found the material on the absence of objective moral value in an atheistic world view to be an especially powerful apologetic to university students. Although students may give lip-service to relativism, my experience is that 95% can be very quickly convinced that objective moral values do exist after all. All you have to do is produce a few illustrations and let them decide for themselves. Ask what they think of the Hindu practice of *suttee* (burning widows alive on the funeral pyres of their husbands) or the ancient Chinese custom of crippling women for life by tightly binding their feet from childhood to resemble lotus-blossoms. Point out that without God to provide a trans-cultural basis for moral values, we're left with sociocultural relativism, so that such practices are morally unobjectionable—which scarcely anyone can sincerely accept.

Of course, sometimes you find some hard-liners, but usually their position is seen to be so extreme that others are repulsed by it. For example, at a recent meeting of the Society of Biblical Literature, I attended a panel discussion on "Biblical Authority and Homosexuality," in which all the panelists endorsed the legitimacy of homosexual activity. One panelist dismissed scriptural prohibitions against such activity on the grounds that they reflect the cultural milieu in which they were written. Since this is the case for all of Scripture's commands (it wasn't written in a vacuum), he concluded that "there are no timeless, normative, moral truths in Scripture." In discussion from the floor, I pointed out that such a view leads to sociocultural relativism, which makes it impossible to criticize *any* society's moral values, including those of a society which persecutes homosexuals. He responded with a fog of theological double-talk and claimed that there's no place outside Scripture where we can find timeless moral values either. "But that just *is* what we mean by moral relativism," I said. "In fact, on your view there's no content to the notion of the goodness of God. He might as well be dead. And Nietzsche recognized that the death of God leads to nihilism." At this point another panelist came in with that knockdown refutation: "Well, if you're going to get pejorative, we might as well not discuss it."

I sat down, but the point wasn't lost on the audience. The next man who stood up said, "Wait a minute. I'm rather confused. I'm a pastor and people are always coming to me, asking if something they have done is wrong and if they need forgiveness. For example, isn't it always wrong to abuse a child?" I couldn't believe the panelist's response. She replied: "What counts as abuse differs from society to society, so we can't really use the word 'abuse' without tying it to a historical context." "Call it whatever you like," the pastor insisted, "but child abuse is damaging to children. Isn't it wrong to damage children?" And still she wouldn't admit it! This sort of hardness of heart ultimately backfires on the moral relativist and exposes in the minds of most people the bankruptcy of such a world view.

In sharing this material with unbelievers, it's important also to ask ourselves exactly what part of our case his objections are meant to refute. Thus, if he says that values are merely social conventions pragmatically adopted to ensure mutual survival, what does this purport to refute? Not that life without God really is without value, for this the objection admits. Therefore, it would be a mistake to react by arguing that values are not social conventions but are grounded in God. Rather the objection is really aimed at the claim that one cannot live as though values do not exist; it holds that one may live by social conventions alone.

Seen in this light, however, the objection is entirely implausible, for we have argued precisely that man cannot live as though morality were merely a matter of social convention. We believe certain acts to be genuinely wrong or right. Therefore, one ought to respond to the unbeliever on this score by saying, "You're exactly right: if God does not exist, then values are merely social conventions. But the point I'm trying to make is that it is impossible to live consistently and happily with such a world view." Push him on the Holocaust or some issue of popular concern like ethnic cleansing, apartheid, or child abuse. Bring it home to him personally and if he's honest and you are not threatening, I think he will admit that he does hold to some absolutes. Thus, it's very important to analyze exactly what the unbeliever's objection actually attacks before we answer.

I believe that this mode of apologetics can be very effective in helping to bring people to Christ because it does not concern neutral matters but cuts to the heart of the unbeliever's own existential situation. I remember that once, when I was delivering a series of talks at the University of Birmingham in England, the audience the first night was very hostile and aggressive. The second night I spoke on the absurdity of life without God. This time the largely same audience was utterly subdued: the lions had turned to lambs, and now their questions were no longer attacking but sincere and searching. The remarkable transformation was due to the fact that the message had penetrated their intellectual facade and struck at the core of their existence. I would encourage you to employ this material in evangelistic dorm meetings and fraternity/sorority meetings, where you can compel people to really *think* about the desperate human predicament in which we all find ourselves.

NOTES

1. Kai Nielsen, "Why Should I Be Moral?" *American Philosophical Quarterly* 21 (1984): 90.

2. Paul Kurtz, *Forbidden Fruit* (Buffalo, NY: Prometheus, 1988), p. 73.

3. Richard Taylor, *Ethics, Faith, and Reason* (Englewood Cliffs, NJ: Prentice Hall, 1985), pp. 90, 84.

4. H. G. Wells, *The Time Machine* (New York: Berkeley, 1957), chap. 11.

5. T.S. Eliot, "The Hollow Men," in *Collected Poems 1909–1962* (New York: Harcourt, Brace, Jovanovich, Inc., 1934). Reprinted by permission of the publisher.

6. W. E. Hocking, *Types of Philosophy* (New York: Scribner's, 1959), p. 27.

7. Friedrich Nietzsche, "The Gay Science," in *The Portable Nietzsche,* ed. and trans. W. Kaufmann (New York: Viking, 1954), p. 95.

8. Friedrich Nietzsche, "The Will to Power," trans. W. Kaufmann, in *Existentialism from Dostoyevsky to Sartre,* 2nd. ed., ed. with an Introduction by W. Kaufmann (New York: New American Library, Meridian, 1975), pp. 130–131.

9. Bertrand Russell, "A Free Man's Worship," in *Why I Am Not a Christian,* ed. P. Edwards (New York: Simon & Schuster, 1957), p. 107.

10. Bertrand Russell, Letter to the *Observer,* 6 October 1957.

11. Jean Paul Sartre, "Portrait of the Antisemite," trans. M. Guiggenheim, in *Existentialism,* p. 330.

12. Richard Wurmbrand, *Tortured for Christ* (London: Hodder & Stoughton, 1967), p. 34.

13. Ernst Bloch, *Das Prinzip Hoffnung,* 2nd. ed., 2 vols. (Frankfurt am Main: Suhrkamp Verlag, 1959), 2: 360–361.

14. Loyal D. Rue, "The Saving Grace of Noble Lies," address to the American Academy for the Advancement of Science, February 1991.

CHAPTER 5

PHILIP L. QUINN

The Meaning of Life According to Christianity

In the heyday of logical positivism, philosophical discussion of the meaning of life fell under a cloud of suspicion. When I was younger, more than once I heard the reason for suspicion put this way. The bearers of meaning are linguistic entities such as texts or utterances. But a human life is not a linguistic entity. Hence attributing meaning to a human life involves a category mistake. To ask what a human life means is therefore to ask a pseudoquestion.

In our own postpositivistic and postmodern era, this argument is apt to seem too quick and dirty to produce conviction. It is possible to define with tolerable clarity and precision several concepts of the meaning a human life might possess. Two such definitions are of particular importance in the discussion of religious views of the meaning of life, for reasons I have detailed in the article from which this chapter is extrapolated. They are as follows:

(AM)   A human life has positive axiological meaning if and only if (i) it has positive intrinsic value, and (ii) it is on the whole good for the person who leads it; and

(TM)   A human life has positive teleological meaning if and only if (i) it contains some purposes the person who lives it takes to be non-trivial and achievable, (ii) these purposes have positive value, and (iii) it also contains actions that are directed toward achieving these purposes and are performed with zest.

Though I do not know how to prove it, I think the axiological and the teleological are logically independent kinds of meaning, and so I hold that a human life can have more than one sort of meaning. To me it seems possible

From "How Christianity Secures Life's Meaning," forthcoming in the *Proceedings of the 1997 Chapman University Conference on The Meaning of Life in the World Religions*, edited by Joseph Runzo and Nancy M. Martin. This essay is a lightly revised version of the third section of that paper.

that a premortem human life should have positive axiological meaning and lack positive teleological meaning and possible that a premortem human life should lack positive axiological meaning and have positive teleological meaning; it also seems possible that a human life should lack both sorts of meaning and possible that a human life should have both sorts of meaning. To explicate the last of these possibilities, I propose the following definition:

> (CM)   A human life has positive complete meaning if and only if it has
>   both positive axiological meaning and positive teleological meaning.

In this essay, I propose to discuss some Christian views of the meaning of life in these three senses.

What is more, though a human life is not itself a text or an utterance, the events of which it is composed can be narrated, and narratives of human lives are meaningful linguistic entities. The history of the human race is also at least the potential subject of a meaningful linguistic metanarrative. Of course, not all narratives of human lives exhibit them as having positive meaning in any of the senses previously defined. A narrative might, for example, portray a human life in terms of "a tale, told by an idiot, full of sound and fury, signifying nothing."[1] Or a narrative might depict a human life as lacking positive meaning of the three kinds previously enumerated. Nevertheless, some narratives do present human lives that have these three kinds of meanings. Because Christianity is a religion in which history is important, narratives loom large in its traditions. The gospel stories of the life of Jesus are, for instance, narratives of a human life that has special significance for Christians.

Adopting a suggestion recently made by Nicholas Wolterstorff, I think the gospel narratives "are best understood as *portraits* of Jesus, designed to reveal who he really was and what was really happening in his life, death and resurrection."[2] And like the part of Simon Schama's recent *Dead Certainties* about the death of General James Wolfe on the plains of Abraham, what they assert at some points is "not that things *did go* thus and so but that, whether or not they did, they *might well have gone* thus and so."[3] The importance of the portrait of Jesus thus narrated for his Christian followers is that it furnishes them with a paradigm to which the narratives of their own lives should be made to conform as closely as circumstances permit. The idea that the lives of Christians should imitate the life of Jesus is, of course, a familiar theme in Christian spirituality; it is developed with particular cogency in Thomas à Kempis's *The Imitation of Christ*. Søren Kierkegaard discusses it in terms of a striking contrast between admiring Christ and imitating Christ in his *Practice in Christianity*.

According to Anti-Climacus, the pseudonymous author of *Practice*, "Christ's life here on earth is the paradigm; I and every Christian are to strive to model our lives in likeness to it."[4] The demand is stringent because the likeness is to be as close as possible. "To be an imitator," he tells us, "means that your life has as much similarity to his as is possible for a human life to have."[5] The Christ who is to be imitated is not the glorious Christ of the second coming but is instead the crucified Christ of human history. Hence the imitator of Christ must come to terms with Christ in his lowliness and abasement.

One thing this means is being prepared to suffer as Christ suffered. Anti-Climacus says that Christ freely willed to be the lowly one because he "wanted to express what *the truth* would have to suffer and what the truth must suffer in every generation."[6] Imitators of Christ must therefore be willing to endure suffering akin to his suffering. Anti-Climacus explains what this involves: "To suffer in a way akin to Christ's suffering is not to put up patiently with the inescapable, but it is to suffer evil at the hands of people because as a Christian or in being a Christian one wills and endeavors to do the good: thus one could avoid this suffering by giving up willing the good."[7] Since the Christian is not supposed to give up willing the good, however, he or she must willingly suffer evil precisely because of the endeavor to do the good.

Coming to terms with Christ in his lowliness and abasement also means being "halted by the possibility of offense."[8] Anti-Climacus wittily describes how respectable people of various sorts might have been offended if they had been Christ's contemporaries. A sagacious and sensible person might have said: "What has he done about his future? Nothing. Does he have a permanent job? No. What are his prospects? None."[9] A clergyman might have denounced him as "an impostor and demagogue."[10] A philosopher might have criticized him for lacking a system and having only "a few aphorisms, some maxims, and a couple of parables, which he goes on repeating or revising, whereby he blinds the masses."[11] And others might have scoffed at him and reviled him in other ways. Yet Anti-Climacus insists that no one can arrive at mature Christian faith without first confronting the possibility of offense. He says that "from the possibility of offense, one turns either to offense or to faith, but one never comes to faith except from the possibility of offense."[12] Thus imitators of Christ can also count on being found offensive by those who have chosen to turn to offense rather than to faith.

Imitators of Christ should, therefore, anticipate suffering evils for trying to do good and expect to be found offensive. To join Christ as a follower, it is necessary to have a realistic awareness of the conditions on which discipleship is offered. According to Anti-Climacus, they are "to become just as poor, despised, insulted, mocked, and if possible even a little more, considering that in addition one was an adherent of such a despised individual, whom every sensible person shunned."[13] If any imitators of Christ are not subject to such treatment, it must be the result of good fortune they cannot count on or expect. No mere admirer would want to join Christ on these conditions.

What is the difference between an imitator and a mere admirer? "An imitator *is* or strives *to be* what he admires," Anti-Climacus says, "and an admirer keeps himself personally detached, consciously or unconsciously does not discover that what is admired involves a claim upon him, to be or at least to strive to be what is admired."[14] The difference is to be seen most clearly in their contrasting responses to the stringent practical demands of discipleship. The mere admirer is only willing to pay them lip-service. According to Anti-Climacus, "the admirer will make no sacrifices, renounce nothing, give up nothing earthly, will not transform his life, will not be what is admired, will not let his life express it—but in words, phrases, assurances he is inexhaustible about how highly he prizes Christianity."[15] Unlike the mere admirer, the imitator, who also acknowledges in words the truth of Christianity, acts decisively to obey "Christian teaching about ethics and obligation, Christianity's requirement to die to the world, to surrender the earthly, its requirement of self-denial."[16] And, Anti-Climacus adds wryly, mere admirers are sure to become exasperated with a genuine imitator.

Not all Christians will accept this radical Kierkegaardian view of the demands of discipleship. There is, however, a lesson to be learned about the meanings of a distinctively Christian life if we take it to approximate the most demanding interpretation of what is involved in the call to Christians to conform the narratives of their lives to the portrait of Jesus embedded in the gospel narratives. There seems to be no difficulty in supposing that the life of a successful Kierkegaardian imitator of Christ, devoted to willing and endeavoring to do the good, will have positive teleological meaning, despite the suffering it is likely to contain. But there is a problem in supposing that every such life will also have positive axiological meaning if it terminates in bodily death, because some of these lives appear not to be good on the whole for those who lead them. But, of course, the earthly life of Jesus, which ended in horrible suffering and ignominious death, gives rise to the very same problem. It is part of traditional Christian faith, however, that the life of Jesus did not terminate in bodily death but continued after his resurrection and will continue until he comes again in glory; hence it is on the whole a good life for him. Like the life of Jesus himself, the lives of at least some successful Kierkegaardian imitators of Christ will on the whole be good for them only if they extend beyond death into an afterlife of some sort. Hence survival of bodily death seems required to secure positive axiological meaning and thus positive complete meaning for the lives of all those whose narratives conform as closely as is humanly possible, as Kierkegaard understands what is involved in such conformity, to the paradigm or prototype presented in the gospel narratives of the life of Jesus.

Christianity also tells a tale of the destiny of the human race through the cosmic metanarrative of salvation history. It begins with the creation of humans in God's image and likeness. The Incarnation, in which God the Son becomes fully human and redeems sinful humanity, is a crucial episode. It will culminate with the promised coming of the Kingdom of God. Christians have been divided over some questions about the details of salvation history. Will all humans ultimately be saved? If some will not, did God predestine them to reprobation? But the broad outlines of the story make manifest God's loving concern for humanity and the providential care in which it is expressed. The story's emphasis on what God has done for humans also makes it clear that they are important from a God's eye point of view.

The narrative of salvation history reveals some of God's purposes both for individual humans and for humanity as a whole. Christians are expected to align themselves with these purposes and to act to further them to the extent that their circumstances permit. Such purposes can thus be among those that give positive teleological meaning and thereby contribute to giving positive complete meaning to a Christian's life. We may safely assume that every Christian and, indeed, every human being has a meaningful role to play in the great drama of salvation history if Christianity's view of its shape is even approximately correct.

But what are we to say about those who refuse to align themselves with God's purposes? Mark 14:21 quotes Jesus as saying, "For the Son of Man goes as it is written of him, but woe to that one by whom the Son of Man is betrayed! It would have been better for that one not to have been born." If it would have been better for Judas not to have been born, then his life is not on the whole good for him and so lacks positive axiological meaning. This will be true of Judas on the traditional assumption that he dies fixed in his rejection of God's purposes and so suffers everlastingly in hell. On the universalist assumption, however, even Judas will eventually turn to God, align himself with God's purposes, and be saved. Were this to happen, even the life of Judas would ultimately have both positive axiological meaning and positive teleological meaning. In that case, it would not be true that it would be better for Judas not to have been born.

In a stimulating discussion of the meaning of life, Thomas Nagel argues that from a detached, objective point of view human lives lack importance or significance. He says: "When you look at your struggles as if from a great height, in abstraction from the engagement you have with this life because it is yours—perhaps even in abstraction from your identification with the human race—you may feel a certain sympathy for the poor beggar, a pale pleasure in his triumphs and a mild concern for his disappointments."[17] But, he continues, "it wouldn't matter all that much if he failed, and it would matter perhaps even less if he didn't exist at all."[18] Christians would do well, I think, to resist the seductions of this picture of the objective standpoint. For them, the objective standpoint is the point of view of an omniscient and perfectly good God. Their faith informs them humanity is so important to such a God that he freely chose to become incarnate and to suffer and die for its sake.

The snare Christians need to avoid is assuming that humanity is the most important thing or the only important thing from a God's eye point of view. Such assumptions would bespeak a prideful cosmic anthropocentrism. Nagel claims that "the most general effect of the objective stance ought to be a form of humility: the recognition that you are no more important than you are, and that the fact that something is of importance to you, or that it would be good or bad if you did or suffered something, is a fact of purely local significance."[19] Christians have reasons to believe that facts of the sorts Nagel mentions are of more than purely local significance, but they should have the humility to recognize that such facts may well have less cosmic significance than other facts of which God is aware. Within a balanced Christian perspective, in other words, facts about what it is good or bad for humans to do or suffer have some cosmic importance because God cares about them, but Christians would be unwarranted if they supposed that God cares more about such facts than about anything else that transpires in the created cosmos. Human lives and human life generally are objectively important. Their importance should, however, not be exaggerated.

Nor should Christians exaggerate the certainty about life's meanings to be derived from their narratives. The gospel narratives permit, and historically have received, diverse and often conflicting interpretations. When reasonable interpretations clash, confidence in the exclusive rightness of any one of them should diminish. What is more, other religions have reasonable stories to tell about life's meanings, as do some nonreligious worldviews. Confronted with the twin challenges of reasonable intra-Christian pluralism and reasonable interreligious pluralism, Christians ought to adopt an attitude of epistemic modesty when making claims about life's meanings. They can be, I think, entitled to believe that Christian narratives provide the best story we have about life's meanings. But claims to furnish the complete story should, I believe, be advanced only with fear and trembling. When Christianity secures life's meanings, it should not offer Christians so much security that they acquire the arrogant tendency to set their story apart from and above all other sources of insight into life's meanings.[20]

NOTES

1. William Shakespeare, *Macbeth* V. v. 26–28.
2. Nicholas Wolterstorff, *Divine Discourse* (Cambridge: Cambridge University Press, 1995), p. 259.
3. *Ibid.*, p. 257.
4. Søren Kierkegaard, *Practice in Christianity,* ed. trans. Howard V. Hong and Edna H. Hong (Princeton: Princeton University Press, 1991), p. 107.
5. *Ibid.*, p. 106.
6. *Ibid.*, pp. 34–35.
7. *Ibid.*, p. 173.
8. *Ibid.*, p. 39.
9. *Ibid.*, p. 43.
10. *Ibid.*, p. 46.
11. *Ibid.*, p. 48.
12. *Ibid.*, p. 81.
13. *Ibid.*, p. 241.
14. *Ibid.*
15. *Ibid.*, p. 252.
16. *Ibid.*

17. Thomas Nagel, *The View from Nowhere* (New York and Oxford: Oxford University Press, 1986), p. 216.

18. *Ibid.*, p. 216.

19. *Ibid.*, p. 222.

20. I am grateful to Bill Wainwright and Kate McCarthy for helpful comments on the material in this essay.

PART TWO   The Non-Theistic
Alternative

CHAPTER 6   ARTHUR SCHOPENHAUER

On the Vanity of Existence

1

The vanity of existence is revealed in the whole form existence assumes: in the infiniteness of time and space contrasted with the finiteness of the individual in both; in the fleeting present as the sole form in which actuality exists; in the contingency and relativity of all things; in continual becoming without being; in continual desire without satisfaction; in the continual frustration of striving of which life consists. *Time* and that *perishability* of all things existing in time that time itself brings about is simply the form under which the will to live, which as thing in itself is imperishable, reveals to itself the vanity of its striving. Time is that by virtue of which everything becomes nothingness in our hands and loses all real value.

2

That which *has been* no longer *is*; it as little exists as does that which has *never* been. But everything that *is* in the next moment *has been*. Thus the most insignificant present has over the most significant past the advantage of *actuality*, which means that the former bears to the latter the relation of something to nothing.

To our amazement we suddenly exist, after having for countless millennia not existed; in a short while we will again not exist, also for countless millennia. That cannot be right, says the heart: and even upon the crudest intelligence there must, when it considers such an idea, dawn a presentiment of the ideality of time. This however, together with that of space, is the key to all true metaphysics, because it makes room for a quite different order of things than that of nature. That is why Kant is so great.

Every moment of our life belongs to the present only for a moment; then it belongs forever to the past. Every evening we are poorer by a day. We would perhaps grow frantic at the sight of this ebbing away of our short span of time were we not secretly conscious in the profoundest depths of our being that we share in the inexhaustible well of eternity, out of which we can for ever draw new life and renewed time.

You could, to be sure, base on considerations of this kind a theory that the greatest *wisdom* consists in enjoying the present and making this enjoyment the goal of life, because the present is all that is real and everything else merely imaginary. But you could just as well call this mode of life the greatest *folly:* for that which in a moment ceases to exist, which vanishes as completely as a dream, cannot be worth any serious effort.

3

Our existence has no foundation on which to rest except the transient present. Thus its form is essentially unceasing *motion,* without any possibility of that repose which we continually strive after. It resembles the course of a man running down a mountain who would fall over if he tried to stop and can stay on his feet only by running on; or a pole balanced on the tip of the finger; or a planet which would fall into its sun if it ever ceased to plunge irresistibly forward. Thus existence is typified by unrest.

In such a world, where no stability of any kind, no enduring state is possible, where everything is involved in restless change and confusion and keeps itself on its tightrope only by continually striding forward—in such a world, happiness is not so much as to be thought of. It cannot dwell where nothing occurs but Plato's "continual becoming and never being." In the first place, no man is happy but strives his whole life long after a supposed happiness which he seldom attains, and even if he does it is only to be disappointed with it; as a rule, however, he finally enters harbour ship-wrecked and dismasted. In the second place, however, it is all one whether he has been happy or not in a life which has consisted merely of a succession of transient present moments and is now at an end.

4

The scenes of our life resemble pictures in rough mosaic; they are ineffective from close up, and have to be viewed from a distance if they are to seem beautiful. That is why to attain something desired is to discover how vain it is; and why, though we live all our lives in expectation of better things, we often at the same time long regretfully for what is past. The present, on the other hand, is regarded as something quite temporary and serving only as the road to our goal. That is why most men discover when they look back on their life that they have the whole time been living *ad interim*, and are surprised to see that which they let go by so unregarded and unenjoyed was precisely their life, was precisely that in expectation of which they lived.

5

Life presents itself first and foremost as a task: the task of maintaining itself, *de gagner sa vie*. If this task is accomplished, what has been gained is a burden, and there then appears a second task: that of doing something with it so as to ward off boredom, which hovers over every secure life like a bird of prey. Thus the first task is to gain something and the second to become unconscious of what has been gained, which is otherwise a burden.

That human life must be some kind of mistake is sufficiently proved by the simple observation that man is a compound of needs which are hard to satisfy; that their satisfaction achieves nothing but a painless condition in which he is only given over to boredom; and that boredom is a direct proof that existence is in itself valueless, for boredom is nothing other than the sensation of the emptiness of existence. For if life, in the desire for which our essence and existence consists, possessed in itself a positive value and real content, there would be no such thing as boredom: mere existence would fulfil and satisfy us. As things are, we take no pleasure in existence except when we are striving after something—in which case distance and difficulties make our goal look as if it would satisfy us (an illusion which fades when we reach it)—or when engaged in purely intellectual activity, in which case we are really stepping out of life so as to regard it from outside, like spectators at a play. Even sensual pleasure itself consists in a continual striving and ceases as soon as its goal is reached. Whenever we are not involved in one or other of these things but directed back to existence itself we are overtaken by its worthlessness and vanity and this is the sensation called boredom.

6

That the most perfect manifestation of the will to live represented by the human organism, with its incomparably ingenious and complicated machinery, must crumble to dust and its whole essence and all its striving be palpably given over at last to annihilation—this is nature's unambiguous declaration that all the striving of this will is essentially vain. If it were something possessing value in itself, something which ought unconditionally to exist, it would not have non-being as its goal.

Yet what a difference there is between our beginning and our end! We begin in the madness of carnal desire and the transport of voluptuousness, we end in the dissolution of all our parts and the musty stench of corpses. And the road from the one to the other too goes, in regard to our well-being and enjoyment of life, steadily downhill: happily dreaming childhood, exultant youth, toil-filled years of manhood, infirm and often wretched old age, the torment of the last illness and finally the throes of death—does it not look as if existence were an error the consequences of which gradually grow more and more manifest?

We shall do best to think of life as a *desengaño*, as a process of disillusionment: since this is, clearly enough, what everything that happens to us is calculated to produce.

CHAPTER 7　　　　　　B E R T R A N D　R U S S E L L

A Free Man's Worship

To Dr. Faustus in his study Mephistophelis told the history of the Creation, saying,

> The endless praises of the choirs of angels had begun to grow wearisome; for, after all, did he not deserve their praise? Had he not given them endless joy? Would it not be more amusing to obtain undeserved praise, to be worshiped by beings whom he tortured? He smiled inwardly, and resolved that the great drama should be performed.
>
> For countless ages the hot nebula whirled aimlessly through space. At length it began to take shape, the central mass threw off planets, the planets cooled, boiling seas and burning mountains heaved and tossed, from black masses of cloud hot sheets of rain deluged the barely solid crust. And now the first germ of life grew in the depths of the ocean and developed rapidly in the fructifying warmth into vast forest trees, huge ferns springing from the damp mold, sea monsters breeding, fighting, devouring, and passing away. And from the monsters, as the play unfolded itself, Man was born, with the power of thought, the knowledge of good and evil, and the cruel thirst for worship. And Man saw that all is passing in this mad, monstrous world, that all is struggling to snatch, at any cost, a few brief moments of life before Death's inexorable decree. And Man said, "There is a hidden purpose, could we but fathom it, and the purpose is good; for we must reverence something, and in the visible world there is nothing worthy of reverence." And Man stood aside from the struggle, resolving that God intended harmony to come out of chaos by human efforts. And when he followed the instincts which God had transmitted to him from his ancestry of beasts of prey, he called it Sin, and asked God to forgive him. But he doubted whether he could be justly forgiven, until he invented a divine Plan by which God's wrath was to have been appeased. And seeing the present was bad, he made it yet worse, that thereby the future might

be better. And he gave God thanks for the strength that enabled him to forgo even the joys that were possible. And God smiled; and when he saw that Man had become perfect in renunciation and worship, he sent another sun through the sky, which crashed into Man's sun; and all returned again to nebula.

"Yes," he murmured, "it was a good play; I will have it performed again."

Such, in outline, but even more purposeless, more void of meaning, is the world which science presents for our belief. Amid such a world, if anywhere, our ideals henceforward must find a home. That man is the product of causes which had no prevision of the end they were achieving; that his origin, his growth, his hopes and fears, his loves and his beliefs, are but the outcome of accidental collocations of atoms; that no fire, no heroism, no intensity of thought and feeling, can preserve an individual life beyond the grave; that all the labors of the ages, all the devotion, all the inspiration, all the noonday brightness of human genius, are destined to extinction in the vast death of the solar system, and that the whole temple of man's achievement must inevitably be buried beneath the debris of a universe in ruins—all these things, if not quite beyond dispute, are yet so nearly certain that no philosophy which rejects them can hope to stand. Only within the scaffolding of these truths, only in the firm foundation of unyielding despair, can the soul's habitation henceforth be safely built.

How, in such an alien and inhuman world, can so powerless a creature as man preserve his aspirations untarnished? A strange mystery it is that nature, omnipotent but blind, in the revolutions of her secular hurryings through the abysses of space, has brought forth at last a child, subject still to her power, but gifted with sight, with knowledge of good and evil, with the capacity of judging all the works of his unthinking mother. In spite of death, the mark and seal of the parental control, man is yet free, during his brief years, to examine, to criticize, to know, and in imagination to create. To him alone, in the world with which he is acquainted, this freedom belongs; and in this lies his superiority to the resistless forces that control his outward life.

The savage, like ourselves, feels the oppression of his impotence before the powers of nature; but having in himself nothing that he respects more than power, he is willing to prostrate himself before his gods, without inquiring whether they are worthy of his worship. Pathetic and very terrible is the long history of cruelty and torture, of degradation and human sacrifice, endured in the hope of placating the jealous gods: surely, the trembling believer thinks, when what is most precious has been freely given, their lust for blood must be appeased, and more will not be required. The religion of Moloch—as such creeds may be generically called—is in essence the cringing submission of the slave, who dare not, even in his heart, allow the thought that his master deserves no adulation. Since the independence of ideals is not yet acknowledged, power may be freely worshiped and receive an unlimited respect, despite its wanton infliction of pain.

But gradually, as morality grows bolder, the claim of the ideal world begins to be felt; and worship, if it is not to cease, must be given to gods of another kind than those created by the savage. Some, though they feel the demands of the ideal, will still consciously reject them, still urging that naked power is worthy of worship. Such is the attitude inculcated in God's answer to Job out of the whirlwind: the divine power and knowledge are paraded, but of the divine goodness there is not hint. Such also is the attitude of those who, in our own day, base their morality upon the struggle for survival, maintaining that the survivors are necessarily the fittest. But others, not content with an answer so repugnant to the moral sense, will adopt the position which we have become accustomed to regard as specially religious, maintaining that, in some hidden manner, the world of fact is really harmonious with the world of ideals. Thus man created God, all-powerful and all-good, the mystic unity of what is and what should be.

But the world of fact, after all, is not good; and, in submitting our judgment to it, there is an element of slavishness from which our thoughts must be purged. For in all things it is well to exalt the dignity of man, by freeing him as far as possible from the tyranny of nonhuman power. When we have realized that power is largely bad, that man, with his knowledge of good and evil, is but a helpless atom in a world which has no such knowledge, the choice is again presented to us: Shall we worship force, or shall we worship goodness? Shall our God exist and be evil, or shall he be recognized as the creation of our own conscience?

The answer to this question is very momentous and affects profoundly our whole morality. The worship of force, to which Carlyle and Nietzsche and the creed of militarism have accustomed us, is the result of failure to maintain our own ideals against a hostile universe: it is itself a prostrate submission to evil, a sacrifice of our best to Moloch. If strength indeed is to be respected, let us respect rather the strength of those who refuse that false "recognition of facts" which fails to recognize that facts are often bad. Let us admit that, in the world we know, there are many things that would be better otherwise, and that the ideals to which we do and must adhere are not realized in the realm of matter. Let us preserve our respect for truth, for beauty, for beauty, for the ideal of perfection which life does not permit us to attain, though none of these things meets with the approval of the unconscious universe. If power is bad, as it seems to be, let us reject it from our hearts. In this lies man's true freedom: in determination to worship only the God created by our own love of the good, to respect only the heaven which inspires the insight of our best moments. In action, in desire, we must submit perpetually to the tyranny of outside forces; but in thought, in aspiration, we are free, free from our fellow men, free from the petty planet on which our bodies impotently crawl, free even, while we live, from the tyranny of death. Let us learn, then, that energy of faith which enables us to live constantly in the vision of the good; and let us descend, in action, into the world of fact, with that vision always before us.

When first the opposition of fact and ideal grows fully visible, a spirit of fiery revolt, of fierce hatred of the gods, seems necessary to the assertion of freedom. To defy with Promethean constancy a hostile universe, to keep its evil always in view, always actively hated, to refuse no pain that the malice of power can invent, appears to be the duty of all who will not bow before the inevitable. But indignation is still a bondage, for it compels our thoughts to be occupied with an evil world; and in the fierceness of desire from which rebellion springs there is a kind of self-assertion which it is necessary for the wise to overcome. Indignation is a submission of our thoughts but not of our desires; the Stoic freedom in which wisdom consists is found in the submission of our desires but not of our thoughts. From the submission of our desires springs the virtue of resignation; from the freedom of our thoughts springs the whole world of art and philosophy, and the vision of beauty by which, at last, we half reconquer the reluctant world. But the vision of beauty is possible only to unfettered contemplation, to thoughts not weighted by the load of eager wishes; and thus freedom comes only to those who no longer ask of life that it shall yield them any of those personal goods that are subject to the mutations of time.

Although the necessity of renunciation is evidence of the existence of evil, yet Christianity, in preaching it, has shown a wisdom exceeding that of the Promethean philosophy of rebellion. It must be admitted that, of the things we desire, some, though they prove impossible, are yet real goods; others, however, as ardently longed for, do not form part of a fully purified ideal. The belief that what must be renounced is bad, though sometimes false, is far less often false than untamed passion supposes; and the creed of religion, by providing a reason for proving that it is never false, has been the means of purifying our hopes by the discovery of many austere truths.

But there is in resignation a further good element: even real goods, when they are unattainable, ought not to be fretfully desired. To every man comes, sooner or later, the great renunciation. For the young, there is nothing unattainable; a good thing desired with the whole force of a passionate will, and yet impossible, is to them not credible. Yet, by death, by illness, by poverty, or by the voice of duty, we must learn, each one of us, that the world was not made for us, and that, however beautiful may be the things we crave, Fate may nevertheless forbid them. It is the part of courage, when misfortune comes, to bear without repining the ruin of our hopes, to turn away our thoughts from vain regrets. This degree of submission to power is not only just and right: it is the very gate of wisdom.

But passive renunciation is not the whole of wisdom; for not by renunciation alone can we build a temple for the worship of our own ideals. Haunting foreshadowings of the temple appear in the realm of imagination, in music, in architecture, in the untroubled kingdom of reason, and in the golden sunset magic of lyrics, where beauty shines and glows, remote from the touch of sorrow, remote from the fear of change, remote from the failures and disenchantments of the world of fact. In the contemplation of these things the vision of heaven will shape itself in our hearts, giving at once a touchstone to judge the world about us and an inspiration by which to fashion to our needs whatever is not incapable of serving as a stone in the sacred temple.

Except for those rare spirits that are born without sin, there is a cavern of darkness to be traversed before that temple can be entered. The gate of the cavern is despair, and its floor is paved with the gravestones of abandoned hopes. There self must die; there the eagerness, the greed of untamed desire, must be slain, for only so can the soul be freed from the empire of Fate. But out of the cavern, the Gate of Renunciation leads again to the daylight of wisdom, by whose radiance a new insight, a new joy, a new tenderness, shine forth to gladden the pilgrim's heart.

When, without the bitterness of impotent rebellion, we have learned both to resign ourselves to the outward rule of Fate and to recognize that the nonhuman world is unworthy of our worship, it becomes possible at last so to transform and refashion the unconscious universe, so to transmute it in the crucible of imagination, that a new image of shining gold replaces the old idol of clay. In all the multiform facts of the world—in the visual shapes of trees and mountains and clouds, in the events of the life of man, even in the very omnipotence of death—the insight of creative idealism can find the reflection of a beauty which its own thoughts first made. In this way mind asserts its subtle mastery over the thoughtless forces of nature. The more evil the material with which it deals, the more thwarting to untrained desire, the greater is its achievement in inducing the reluctant rock to yield up its hidden treasures, the prouder its victory in compelling the opposing forces to swell the pageant of its triumph. Of all the arts, tragedy is the proudest, the most triumphant; for it builds its shining citadel in the very center of the enemy's country, on the very summit of his highest mountain; from its impregnable watchtowers, his camps and arsenals, his columns and forts, are all revealed; within its walls the free life continues, while the legions of death and pain and despair, and all the servile captains of tyrant Fate, afford the burghers of that dauntless city new spectacles of beauty. Happy those sacred ramparts, thrice happy the dwellers on that all-seeing eminence. Honor to those brave warriors who, through countless ages of warfare, have preserved for us the priceless heritage of liberty and have kept undefiled by sacrilegious invaders the home of the unsubdued.

But the beauty of tragedy does but make visible a quality which, in more or less obvious shapes, is present always and everywhere in life. In the spectacle of death, in the endurance of intolerable pain, and in the irrevocableness of a vanished past, there is a sacredness, an overpowering awe, a feeling of the vastness, the depth, the inexhaustible mystery of existence, in which, as by some strange marriage of pain, the sufferer is bound to the world by bonds of sorrow. In these moments of insight, we lose all eagerness of temporary desire, all struggling and striving for petty ends, all care for the little trivial things that, to a superficial view, make up the common life of day by day; we see, surrounding the narrow raft illumined by the flickering light of human comradeship, the dark ocean on whose rolling waves we toss for a brief hour; from the great night without, a chill blast breaks in upon our refuge; all the loneliness of humanity amid hostile forces is concentrated upon the individual soul, which must struggle alone, with what of courage it can command, against the whole weight of a universe that cares nothing for its hopes and fears. Victory, in this struggle with the powers of darkness, is the true baptism into the glorious company of heroes, the true initiation into the overmastering beauty of human existence. From that awful encounter of the soul with the outer world, renunciation, wisdom, and charity are born; and with their birth a new life begins. To take into the inmost shrine of the soul the irresistible forces whose puppets we seem to be—death and change, the irrevocableness of the past, and the powerlessness of man before the blind hurry of the universe from vanity to vanity—to feel these things and know them is to conquer them.

This is the reason why the past has such magical power. The beauty of its motionless and silent pictures is like the enchanted purity of late autumn, when the leaves, though one breath would make them fall, still glow against the sky in golden glory. The past does not change or strive; like Duncan, after life's fitful fever it sleeps well; what was eager and grasping, what was petty and transitory, has faded away; the things that were beautiful and eternal shine out of it like stars in the night. Its beauty, to a soul not worthy of it, is unendurable; but to a soul which has conquered Fate it is the key of religion.

The life of man, viewed outwardly, is but a small thing in comparison with the forces of nature. The slave is doomed to worship Time and Fate and Death, because they are greater than anything he finds in himself, and because all his thoughts are of things which they devour. But, great as they are, to think of them greatly, to feel their passionless splendor, is greater still. And such thought makes us free men; we no longer bow before the inevitable in Oriental subjection, but we absorb it and make it a part of ourselves. To abandon the struggle for private happiness, to expel all eagerness of temporary desire, to burn with passion for eternal things—this is emancipation, and this is the free man's worship. And this liberation is effected by contemplation of Fate; for Fate itself is subdued by the mind which leaves nothing to be purged by the purifying fire of time.

United with his fellow men by the strongest of all ties, the tie of a common doom, the free man finds that a new vision is with him always, shedding over every daily task the light of love. The life of man is a long march through the night, surrounded by invisible foes, tortured by weariness and pain, toward a goal that few can hope to reach, and where none may tarry long. One by one, as they march, our comrades vanish from our sight, seized by the silent orders of omnipotent death. Very brief is the time in which we can help them, in which their happiness or misery is decided. Be it ours to shed sunshine on their path, to lighten their sorrows by the balm of sympathy, to give them the pure joy of a never-tiring affection, to strengthen failing courage, to instill faith in hours of despair. Let us not weigh in grudging scales their merits and demerits, but let us think only of their need—of the sorrows, the difficulties, perhaps the blindness, that make the misery of their lives; let us remember that they are fellow sufferers in the same darkness, actors in the same tragedy with ourselves. And so, when their day is over, when their good and their evil have become eternal by the immortality of the past, be it ours to feel that, where they suffered, where they failed, no deed of ours was the cause; but wherever a spark of the divine fire kindled in their hearts, we were ready with encouragement, with sympathy, with brave words in which high courage glowed.

Brief and powerless is man's life; on him and all his race the slow, sure doom falls pitiless and dark. Blind to good and evil, reckless of destruction, omnipotent matter rolls on its relentless way; for man, condemned today to lose his dearest, tomorrow himself to pass through the gate of darkness, it remains only to cherish, ere yet the blow fall, the lofty thoughts that ennoble his little day; disdaining the coward terrors of the slave of Fate, to worship at the shrine that his own hands have built; undismayed by the empire of chance, to preserve a mind free from the wanton tyranny that rules his out-ward life; proudly defiant of the irresistible forces that tolerate, for a moment, his knowledge and his condemnation, to sustain alone, a weary but unyield-ing Atlas, the world that his own ideals have fashioned despite the trampling march of unconscious power.

CHAPTER 8

JULIAN HUXLEY

The Creed of a Scientific Humanist

I believe that life can be worth living. I believe this in spite of pain, squalor, cruelty, unhappiness, and death. I do not believe that it is necessarily worth living, but only that for most people it can be.

I also believe that man, as individual, as group, and collectively as mankind, can achieve a satisfying purpose in existence. I believe this in spite of frustration, aimlessness, frivolity, boredom, sloth, and failure. Again I do not believe that a purpose inevitably inheres in the universe or in our existence, or that mankind is bound to achieve a satisfying purpose, but only that such a purpose can be found.

I believe that there exists a scale or hierarchy of values, ranging from simple physical comforts up to the highest satisfactions of love, esthetic enjoyment, intellect, creative achievement, virtue. I do not believe that these are absolute, or transcendental in the sense of being vouchsafed by some external power or divinity: they are the product of human nature interacting with the outer world. Nor do I suppose that we can grade every valuable experience into an accepted order, any more than I can say whether a beetle is a higher organism than a cuttlefish or a herring. But just as it can unhesitatingly be stated that there are general grades of biological organization, and that a beetle *is* a higher organism than a sponge, or a human being than a frog, so I can assert, with the general consensus of civilized human beings, that there is a higher value in Dante's *Divine Comedy* than in a popular hymn, in the scientific activity of Newton or Darwin than in solving a crossword puzzle, in the fullness of love than in sexual gratification, in selfless than in purely self-regarding activities—although each and all can have their value of a sort.

I do not believe that there is any absolute of truth, beauty, morality, or virtue, whether emanating from an external power or imposed by an internal standard. But this does not drive me to the curious conclusion, fashionable in certain quarters, that truth and beauty and goodness do not exist, or that there is no force or value in them.

I believe that there are a number of questions that it is no use our asking, because they can never be answered. Nothing but waste, worry, or unhappiness is caused by trying to solve insoluble problems. Yet some people seem determined to try. I recall the story of the philosopher and the theologian. The two were engaged in disputation and the theologian used the old quip about a philosopher resembling a blind man, in a dark room, looking for a black cat—which wasn't there. "That may be," said the philosopher: "but a theologian would have found it."

Even in matters of science, we must learn to ask the right questions. It seemed an obvious question to ask how animals inherit the result of their parents' experience, and enormous amounts of time and energy have been spent on trying to give an answer to it. It is, however, no good asking the question, for the simple reason that no such inheritance of acquired characters exists. The chemists of the eighteenth century, because they asked themselves the question, "What substance is involved in the process of burning?" became involved in the mazes of the phlogiston theory; they had to ask, "What sort of process is burning?" before they could see that it did not involve a special substance, but was merely a particular case of chemical combination.

When we come to what are usually referred to as fundamentals, the difficulty of not asking the wrong kind of question is much increased. Among most African tribes, if a person dies, the only question asked is, "Who caused his death, and by what form of magic?" The idea of death from natural causes is unknown. Indeed, the life of the less civilized half of mankind is largely based on trying to find an answer to a wrong question, "What magical forces or powers are responsible for good or bad fortune, and how can they be circumvented or propitiated?"

I do not believe in the existence of a god or gods. The conception of divinity seems to me, though built up out of a number of real elements of experience, to be a false one, based on the quite unjustifiable postulate that there must be some more or less personal power in control of the world. We are confronted with forces beyond our control, with incomprehensible disasters, with death; and also with ecstasy, with a mystical sense of union with something greater than our ordinary selves, with sudden conversion to a new way of life, with the burden of guilt and sin and of ways in which these burdens may be lifted. In theistic religions, all these elements of actual experience have been woven into a unified body of belief and practice, in relation to the fundamental postulate of the existence of a god or gods.

I believe this fundamental postulate to be nothing more than the result of asking a wrong question, "Who or what rules the universe?" So far as we can see, it rules itself, and indeed the whole analogy with a country and its ruler is false. Even if a god does exist behind or above the universe as we experience it, we can have no knowledge of such a power: the actual gods of historical religions are only the personifications of impersonal facts of nature and of facts of our inner mental life. Though we can answer the question, "What are the Gods of actual religions?" we can only do so by dissecting them into their components and showing their divinity to be a figment of human imagination, emotion, and rationalization. The question, "What is the nature of God?" we cannot answer, since we have no means of knowing whether such a being exists or not.

Similarly with immortality. With our present faculties, we have no means of giving a categorical answer to the question whether we survive death, much less the question of what any such life after death will be like. That being so, it is a waste of time and energy to devote ourselves to the problem of achieving salvation in the life to come. However, just as the idea of God is built out of bricks of real experience, so too is the idea of salvation. If we translate salvation into terms of this world, we find that it means achieving harmony between different parts of our nature, including its subconscious depths and its rarely touched heights, and also achieving some satisfactory relation of adjustment between ourselves and the outer world, including not only the world of nature, but the social world of man. I believe it to be possible to "achieve salvation" in this sense, and right to aim at doing so, just as I believe it possible and valuable to achieve a sense of union with something bigger than our ordinary selves, even if that something be not a god but an extension of our narrow core to include in a single grasp ranges of outer experience and inner nature on which we do not ordinarily draw.

But if God and immortality be repudiated, what is left? That is the question usually thrown at the atheist's head. The orthodox believer likes to think that nothing is left. That, however, is because he has only been accustomed to think in terms of his orthodoxy.

In point of fact, a great deal is left.

That is immediately obvious from the fact that many men and women have led active, or self-sacrificing, or noble, or devoted lives without any belief in God or immortality. Buddhism in its uncorrupted form has no such belief, nor did the great nineteenth-century agnostics, nor do the orthodox Russian Communists, nor did the Stoics. Of course, the unbelievers have often been guilty of selfish or wicked actions; but so have the believers. And in any case that is not the fundamental point. The point is that without these beliefs men and women may yet possess the mainspring of full and purposive living, and just as strong a sense that existence can be worth while as is possible to the most devout believers.

I would say that this is much more readily possible today than in any previous age. The reason lies in the advances of science.

No longer are we forced to accept the external catastrophes and miseries of existence as inevitable or mysterious; no longer are we obliged to live in a world without history, where change is only meaningless. Our ancestors saw an epidemic as an act of divine punishment: to us it is a challenge to be overcome, since we know its causes and that it could be controlled or prevented. The understanding of infectious disease is entirely due to scientific advance.

So, to take a very recent happening, is our understanding of the basis of nutrition, which holds out new possibilities of health and energy to the human race. So is our understanding of earthquakes and storms: if we cannot control them, we at least do not have to fear them as evidence of God's anger.

Some, at least, of our internal miseries can be lightened in the same way. Through knowledge derived from psychology, children can be prevented from growing up with an abnormal sense of guilt, and so making life a burden both to themselves and to those with whom they come into contact. We are beginning to understand the psychological roots of irrational fear and irrational cruelty: some day we shall be able to make the world a brighter place by preventing their appearance.

The ancients had no history worth mentioning. Human existence in the present was regarded as a degradation from that of the original Golden Age. Down even to the nineteenth century, what was known of human history was regarded by the nations of the West as an essentially meaningless series of episodes sandwiched into the brief space between the Creation and the Fall, a few thousand years ago, and the Second Coming and the Last Judgment, which might be on us at any moment, and in any case could not be pushed back for more than a few thousand years into the future. In this perspective, a millennium was almost an eternity. With such an outlook, no wonder life seemed, to the great mass of humanity, "nasty, brutish and short," its miseries and shortcomings merely bewildering unless illuminated by the illusory light of religion.

Today, human history merges back into prehistory, and prehistory again into biological evolution. Our time-scale is profoundly altered. A thousand years is a short time for prehistory, which thinks in terms of hundreds of thousands of years, and an insignificant time for evolution, which deals in ten-million-year periods. The future is extended equally with the past: if it took over a thousand million years for primeval life to generate man, man and his descendents have at least an equal allowance of time before them.

Most important of all, the new history has a basis of hope. Biological evolution has been appallingly slow and appallingly wasteful. It has been cruel, it has generated the parasites and the pests as well as the more agreeable types. It has led life up innumerable blind alleys. But in spite of this, it has achieved progress. In a few lines, whose number has steadily diminished with time, it has avoided the cul-de-sac of mere specialization and arrived at a new level of organization, more harmonious and more efficient, from which it could again launch out toward greater control, greater knowledge, and greater independence. Progress is, if you will, all-round specialization. Finally, but one line was left which was able to achieve further progress: all the others had led up blind alleys. This was the line leading to the evolution of the human brain.

This at one bound altered the perspective of evolution. Experience could now be handed down from generation to generation; deliberate purpose could be substituted for the blind sifting of selection; change could be speeded up ten-thousandfold. In man evolution could become conscious.

Admittedly it is far from conscious yet, but the possibility is there, and it has at least been consciously envisaged.

Seen in this perspective, human history represents but the tiniest portion of the time man has before him; it is only the first ignorant and clumsy gropings of the new type, born heir to so much biological history. Attempts at a general philosophy of history are seen in all their futility—as if someone whose acquaintance with man as a species were limited to a baby one year old should attempt a general account of the human mind and soul. The constant setbacks, the lack of improvement in certain respects for over two thousand years, are seen to be phenomena as natural as the tumbles of a child learning to walk, or the deflection of a sensitive boy's attention by the need of making a living.

The broad facts remain. Life had progressed, even before man was first evolved. Life progressed further by evolving man. Man has progressed during the half million or so years from the first Hominidae, even during the ten thousand years since the final amelioration of climate after the Ice Age. And the potentialities of progress which are revealed, once his eyes have been opened to the evolutionary vista, are unlimited.

At last we have an optimistic, instead of a pessimistic, theory of this world and our life upon it. Admittedly the optimism cannot be facile, and must be tempered with reflection on the length of time involved, on the hard work that will be necessary, on the inevitable residuum of accident and unhappiness that will remain. Perhaps we had better call it a melioristic rather than an optimistic view: but at least it preaches hope and inspires to action.

I believe very definitely that it is among human personalities that there exist the highest and most valuable achievements of the universe—or at least the highest and most valuable achievements of which we have or, apparently, can have knowledge. That means that I believe that the State exists for the development of individual lives, not individuals for the development of the State.

But I also believe that the individual is not an isolated, separate thing. An individual is a transformer of matter and experience: it is a system of relations between its own basis and the universe, including other individuals. An individual may believe that he should devote himself entirely to a cause, even sacrifice himself to it—his country, truth, art, love. It is in the devotion or the sacrifice that he becomes most himself, it is because of the devotion or sacrifice of individuals that causes become of value. But of course the individual must in many ways subordinate himself to the community—only not to the extent of believing that in the community resides any virtue higher than that of the individuals which compose it.

The community provides the machinery for the existence and development of individuals. There are those who deny the importance of social machinery, who assert that the only important thing is a change of heart, and that the right machinery is merely a natural consequence of the right inner attitude. This appears to me mere solipsism. Different kinds of social machinery predispose to different inner attitudes. The most admirable machinery is useless if the inner life is unchanged: but social machinery *can* affect the fullness and quality of life. Social machinery can be devised to make war more difficult, to promote health, to add interest to life. Let us not despise machinery in our zeal for fullness of life, any more than we should dream that machinery can ever automatically grind out perfection of living.

I believe in diversity. Every biologist knows that human beings differ in their hereditary outfits, and therefore in the possibilities that they can realize. Psychology is showing us how different are the types that jostle each other on the world's streets. No amount of persuasion or education can make the extravert really understand the introvert, the verbalist understand the lover of handicraft, the nonmathematical or nonmusical person understand the passion of the mathematician or the musician. We can try to forbid certain attitudes of mind. We could theoretically breed out much of human variety. But this would be a sacrifice. Diversity is not only the salt of life, but the basis of collective achievement. And the complement of diversity is tolerance and understanding. This does not mean rating all values alike. We must protect society against criminals: we must struggle against what we think wrong. But just as in our handling of the criminal we should try to reform rather than merely to punish, so we must try to understand why we judge others' actions as wrong, which implies trying to understand the workings of our own minds, and discounting our own prejudices.

Finally, I believe that we can never reduce our principles to any few simple terms. Existence is always too various and too complicated. We must supplement principles with faith. And the only faith that is both concrete and comprehensive is in life, its abundance and its progress. My final belief is in life.

CHAPTER 9   W A L T E R   T .   S T A C E

Man Against Darkness

The Catholic bishops of America once issued a statement in which they said that the chaotic and bewildered state of the modern world is due to man's loss of faith, his abandonment of God and religion. I agree with this statement though I do not accept the religious beliefs of most bishops. It is no doubt an oversimplification to speak of *the* cause of so complex a state of affairs as the tortured condition of the world today. Its causes are doubtless multitudinous. Yet allowing for some element of oversimplification, I say that the bishops' assertion is substantially true.

M. Jean-Paul Sartre, the French existentialist philosopher, labels himself an atheist. Yet his views seem to me plainly to support the statement of the bishops. So long as there was believed to be a God in the sky, he says, men could regard him as the source of their moral ideals. The universe, created and governed by a fatherly God, was a friendly habitation for man. We could be sure that, however great the evil in the world, good in the end would triumph and the forces of evil would be routed. With the disappearance of God from the sky all this has changed. Since the world is not ruled by a spiritual being, but rather by blind forces, there cannot be any ideals, moral or otherwise, in the universe outside us. Our ideals, therefore, must proceed only from our own minds; they are our own inventions. Thus the world which surrounds us is nothing but an immense spiritual emptiness. It is a dead universe. We do not live in a universe which is on the side of our values. It is completely indifferent to them.

Years ago Mr. Bertrand Russell, in his essay "A Free Man's Worship," said much the same thing.

> Such in outline, but even more purposeless, more void of meaning, is the
> world which Science presents for our belief. Amid such a world, if anywhere,

From *The Atlantic Monthly*, September 1948. Copyright © 1948, ® 1976, by The Atlantic Monthly Company, Boston, Massachusetts. Used by permission of Mrs. Walter T. Stace and The Atlantic Monthly Company.

our ideals henceforward must find a home. . . . Blind to good and evil, reckless of destruction, omnipotent matter rolls on its relentless way; for man, condemned today to lose his dearest, tomorrow himself to pass through the gate of darkness, it remains only to cherish, ere yet the blow falls, the lofty thoughts that ennoble his little day; . . . to worship at the shrine his own hands have built; . . . to sustain alone, a weary but unyielding Atlas, the world that his own ideals have fashioned despite the trampling march of unconscious power.

It is true that Mr. Russell's personal attitude to the disappearance of religion is quite different from either that of M. Sartre or the bishops or myself. The bishops think it a calamity. So do I. M. Sartre finds it "very distressing." And he berates as shallow the attitude of those who think that without God the world can go on just the same as before, as if nothing had happened. This creates for mankind, he thinks, a terrible crisis. And in this I agree with him. Mr. Russell, on the other hand, seems to believe that religion has done more harm than good in the world, and that its disappearance will be a blessing. But his picture of the world, and of the modern mind, is the same as that of M. Sartre. He stresses the *purposelessness* of the universe, the facts that man's ideals are his own creations, that the universe outside him in no way supports them, that man is alone and friendless in the world.

Mr. Russell notes that it is science which has produced this situation. There is no doubt that this is correct. But the way in which it has come about is not generally understood. There is a popular belief that some particular scientific discoveries or theories, such as the Darwinian theory of evolution, or the views of geologists about the age of the earth, or a series of such discoveries, have done the damage. It would be foolish to deny that these discoveries have had a great effect in undermining religious dogmas. But this account does not at all go to the root of the matter. Religion can probably outlive any scientific discoveries which could be made. It can accommodate itself to them. The root cause of the decay of faith has not been any particular discovery of science, but rather the general spirit of science and certain basic assumptions upon which modern science, from the seventeenth century onwards, has proceeded.

It was Galileo and Newton—notwithstanding that Newton himself was a deeply religious man—who destroyed the old comfortable picture of a friendly universe governed by spiritual values. And this was effected, not by Newton's discovery of the law of gravitation nor by any of Galileo's brilliant investigations, but by the general picture of the world which these men and others of their time made the basis of the science, not only of their own day, but of all succeeding generations down to the present. That is why the century immediately following Newton, the eighteenth century, was notoriously an age of religious skepticism. Skepticism did not have to wait for the discoveries of Darwin and the geologists in the nineteenth century. It flooded the world immediately after the age of the rise of science. Neither the Copernican hypothesis nor any of Newton's or Galileo's particular discoveries were the real causes. Religious faith might well have accommodated itself to the new astronomy. The real turning point between the medieval age of faith and the modern age of unfaith came when the scientists of the seventeenth century turned their backs upon what used to be called "final causes." The final cause of a thing or event meant the purpose which it was supposed to serve in the universe, its cosmic purpose. What lay back of this was the presupposition that there is a cosmic order or plan and that everything which exists could in the last analysis be explained in terms of its place in this cosmic plan, that is, in terms of its purpose.

Plato and Aristotle believed this, and so did the whole medieval Christian world. For instance, if it were true that the sun and the moon were created and exist for the purpose of giving light to man, then this fact would explain why the sun and the moon exist. We might not be able to discover the purpose of everything, but everything must have a purpose. Belief in final causes thus amounted to a belief that the world is governed by purposes, presumably the purposes of some overruling mind. This belief was not the invention of Christianity. It was basic to the whole of Western civilization, whether in the ancient pagan world or in Christendom, from the time of Socrates to the rise of science in the seventeenth century.

The founders of modern science—for instance, Galileo, Kepler, and Newton—were mostly pious men who did not doubt God's purposes. Nevertheless they took the revolutionary step of consciously and deliberately expelling the idea of purpose as controlling nature from their new science of nature. They did this on the ground that inquiry into purposes is useless for what science aims at: namely, the prediction and control of events. To predict an eclipse, what you have to know is not its purpose but its causes. Hence science from the seventeenth century onwards became exclusively an inquiry into causes. The conception of purpose in the world was ignored and frowned on. This, though silent and almost unnoticed, was the greatest revolution in human history, far outweighing in importance any of the political revolutions whose thunder has reverberated through the world.

For it came about in this way that for the past three hundred years there has been growing up in men's minds, dominated as they are by science, a new imaginative picture of the world. The world, according to this new picture, is purposeless, senseless, meaningless. Nature is nothing but matter in motion. The motions of matter are governed, not by any purpose, but by blind forces and laws. Nature in this view, says Whitehead—to whose writings I am indebted in this part of my essay—is "merely the hurrying of material, endlessly, meaninglessly." You can draw a sharp line across the history of Europe dividing it into two epochs of very unequal length. The line passes through the lifetime of Galileo. European man before Galileo—whether ancient pagan or more recent Christian—thought of the world as controlled by plan and purpose. After Galileo European man thinks of it as utterly purposeless. This is the great revolution of which I spoke.

It is this which has killed religion. Religion could survive the discoveries that the sun, not the earth, is the center; that men are descended from simian ancestors; that the earth is hundreds of millions of years old. These discoveries may render out of date some of the details of older theological dogmas, may force their restatement in new intellectual frameworks. But they do not touch the essence of the religious vision itself, which is the faith that there is plan and purpose in the world, that the world is a moral order, that in the end all things are for the best. This faith may express itself through many different intellectual dogmas, those of Christianity, of Hinduism, of Islam. All and any of these intellectual dogmas may be destroyed without destroying the essential religious spirit. But that spirit cannot survive destruction of belief in a plan and purpose of the world, for that is the very heart of it. Religion can get on with any sort of astronomy, geology, biology, physics. But it cannot get on with a purposeless and meaningless universe. If the scheme of things is purposeless and meaningless, then the life of man is purposeless and meaningless too. Everything is futile, all effort is in the end worthless. A man may, of course, still pursue disconnected ends, money, fame, art, science, and may gain pleasure from them. But his life is hollow at the center. Hence the dissatisfied, disillusioned, restless, spirit of modern man.

The picture of a meaningless world, and a meaningless human life is, I think, the basic theme of much modern art and literature. Certainly it is the basic theme of modern philosophy. According to the most characteristic philosophies of the modern period from Hume in the eighteenth century to the so-called positivists of today, the world is just what it is, and that is the end of all inquiry. There is no *reason* for its being what it is. Everything might just as well have been quite different, and there would have been no reason for that either. When you have stated what things are, what things the world contains, there is nothing more which could be said, even by an omniscient being. To ask any question about *why* things are thus, or what purpose their being so serves, is to ask a senseless question, because they serve no purpose at all. For instance, there is for modern philosophy no such thing as the ancient problem of evil. For this once famous question presupposes that pain and misery, though they seem so inexplicable and irrational to us, must ultimately subserve some rational purpose, must have their places in the cosmic plan. But this is nonsense. There is no such overruling rationality in the universe. Belief in the ultimate irrationality of everything is the quintessence of what is called the modern mind.

It is true that, parallel with these philosophies which are typical of the modern mind, preaching the meaninglessness of the world, there has run a line of idealistic philosophies whose contention is that the world is after all spiritual in nature and that moral ideals and values are inherent in its structure. But most of these idealisms were simply philosophical expressions of romanticism, which was itself no more than an unsuccessful counterattack of the religious against the scientific view of things. They perished, along with romanticism in literature and art, about the beginning of the present century, though of course they still have a few adherents. At the bottom these idealistic systems of thought were rationalizations of man's wishful thinking. They were born of the refusal of men to admit the cosmic darkness. They were comforting illusions within the warm glow of which the more tender-minded intellectuals sought to shelter themselves from the icy winds of the universe. They lasted a little while. But they are shattered now, and we return once more to the vision of a purposeless world.

Along with the ruin of the religious vision there went the ruin of moral principles and indeed of all values. If there is a cosmic purpose, if there is in the nature of things a drive towards goodness, then our moral systems will derive their validity from this. But if our moral rules do not proceed from something outside us in the nature of the universe—whether we say it is God or simply the universe itself—then they must be our own inventions. Thus it came to be believed that moral rules must be merely an expression of our own likes and dislikes. But likes and dislikes are notoriously variable. What pleases one man, people, or culture displeases another. Therefore morals are wholly relative. This obvious conclusion from the idea of a purposeless world made its appearance in Europe immediately after the rise of science, for instance in the philosophy of Hobbes. Hobbes saw at once that if there is no purpose in the world there are no values either. "Good and evil," he writes, "are names that signify our appetites and aversions; which in different tempers, customs, and doctrines of men are different. . . . Every man calleth that which pleaseth him, good; and that which displeaseth him, evil."

This doctrine of the relativity of morals, though it has recently received an impetus from the studies of anthropologists, was thus really implicit in the whole scientific mentality. It is disastrous for morals because it destroys their entire traditional foundation. That is why philosophers who see the danger signals, from the time at least of Kant, have been trying to give to morals a new foundation, that is, a secular or non-religious foundation. This attempt may very well be intellectually successful. Such a foundation, independent of the religious view of the world, might well be found. But the question is whether it can ever be a *practical* success, that is, whether apart from its logical validity and its influence with intellectuals, it can ever replace among the masses of men the lost religious foundation. On that question hangs perhaps the future of civilization. But meanwhile disaster is overtaking us.

The widespread belief in "ethical relativity" among philosophers, psychologists, ethnologists, and sociologists is the theoretical counterpart of the repudiation of principle which we see all around us, especially in international affairs, the field in which morals have always had the weakest foothold. No one any longer effectively believes in moral principles except as the private prejudices either of individual men or of nations or cultures. This is the inevitable consequence of the doctrine of ethical relativity, which in turn is the inevitable consequence of believing in a purposeless world.

Another characteristic of our spiritual state is loss of belief in the freedom of the will. This also is a fruit of the scientific spirit, though not of any particular scientific discovery. Science has been built up on the basis of determinism, which is the belief that every event is completely determined by a chain of causes and is therefore theoretically predictable beforehand. It is true that recent physics seems to challenge this. But so far as its practical consequences are concerned, the damage has long ago been done. A man's actions, it was argued, are as much events in the natural world as is an eclipse of the sun. It follows that men's actions are as theoretically predictable as an eclipse. But if it is certain now that John Smith will murder Joseph Jones at 2:15 P.M. on January 1, 2000 A.D., what possible meaning can it have to say that when that time comes John Smith will be *free* to choose whether he will commit the murder or not? And if he is not free, how can he be held responsible?

It is true that the whole of this argument can be shown by a competent philosopher to be a tissue of fallacies—or at least I claim that it can. But the point is that the analysis required to show this is much too subtle to be understood by the average entirely unphilosophical man. Because of this, the argument against free will is generally swallowed whole by the unphilosophical. Hence the thought that man is not free, that he is the helpless plaything of forces over which he has no control, has deeply penetrated the modern mind. We hear of economic determinism, cultural determinism, historical determinism. We are not responsible for what we do because our glands control us, or because we are the products of environment or heredity. Not moral self-control, but the doctor, the psychiatrist, the educationist, must save us from doing evil. Pills and injections in the future are to do what Christ and the prophets have failed to do. Of course I do not mean to deny that doctors and educationists can and must help. And I do not mean in any way to belittle their efforts. But I do wish to draw attention to the weakening of moral controls, the greater or less repudiation of personal responsibility which, in the popular thinking of the day, result from these tendencies of thought.

What, then, is to be done? Where are we to look for salvation from the evils of our time? All the remedies I have seen suggested so far are, in my opinion, useless: Let us look at some of them.

Philosophers and intellectuals generally can, I believe, genuinely do something to help. But it is extremely little. What philosophers can do is to show that neither the relativity of morals nor the denial of free will really follows from the grounds which have been supposed to support them. They can also try to discover a genuine secular basis for morals to replace the religious basis which has disappeared. Some of us are trying to do these things. But in the first place philosophers unfortunately are not agreed about these matters, and their disputes are utterly confusing to the non-philosophers. And in the second place their influence is practically negligible because their analyses necessarily take place at a level on which the masses are totally unable to follow them.

The bishops, of course, propose as remedy a return to belief in God and in the doctrines of the Christian religion. Others think that a new religion is what is needed. Those who make these proposals fail to realize that the crisis in man's spiritual condition is something unique in history for which there is no sort of analogy in the past. They are thinking perhaps of the collapse of the ancient Greek and Roman religions. The vacuum then created was easily filled by Christianity, and it might have been filled by Mithraism if Christianity had not appeared. By analogy they think that Christianity might now be replaced by a new religion, or even that Christianity itself, if revivified, might bring back health to men's lives.

But I believe that there is no analogy at all between our present state and that of the European peoples at the time of the fall of paganism. Men had at that time lost their belief only in particular dogmas, particular embodiments of the religious view of the world. It had no doubt become incredible that Zeus and the other gods were living on the top of Mount Olympus. You could go to the top and find no trace of them. But the imaginative picture of a world governed by purpose, a world driving towards the good—which is the inner spirit of religion—had at that time received no serious shock. It had merely to re-embody itself in new dogmas, those of Christianity or some other religion. Religion itself was not dead in the world, only a particular form of it.

But now the situation is quite different. It is not merely that particular dogmas, like that of the virgin birth, are unacceptable to the modern mind. That is true, but it constitutes a very superficial diagnosis of the present situation of religion. Modern skepticism is of a wholly different order from that of the intellectuals of the ancient world. It has attacked and destroyed not merely the outward forms of the religious spirit, its particularized dogmas, but the very essence of that spirit itself, belief in a meaningful and purposeful world. For the founding of a new religion a new Jesus Christ or Buddha would have to appear, in itself a most unlikely event and one for which in any case we cannot afford to sit and wait. But even if a new prophet and a new religion did appear, we may predict that they would fail in the modern world. No one for long would believe in them, for modern men have lost the vision, basic to all religion, of an ordered plan and purpose of the world. They have before their minds the picture of a purposeless universe, and such a world-picture must be fatal to any religion at all, not merely to Christianity.

We must not be misled by occasional appearances of a revival of the religious spirit. Men, we are told, in their disgust and disillusionment at the emptiness of their lives, are turning once more to religion, or are searching for a new message. It may be so. We must expect such wistful yearnings of the spirit. We must expect men to wish back again the light that is gone, and to try to bring it back. But however they may wish and try, the light will not shine again—not at least in the civilization to which we belong.

Another remedy commonly proposed is that we should turn to science itself, or the scientific spirit, for our salvation. Mr. Russell and Professor Dewey both made this proposal, though in somewhat different ways. Professor Dewey seemed to believe that discoveries in sociology, the application of scientific method to social and political problems, will rescue us. This seems to me to be utterly naive. It is not likely that science, which is basically the cause of our spiritual troubles, is likely also to produce the cure for them. Also it lies in the nature of science that, though it can teach us the best means for achieving our ends, it can never tell us what ends to pursue. It cannot give us any ideals. And our trouble is about ideals and ends, not about the means for reaching them.

No civilization can live without ideals, or to put it in another way, without a firm faith in moral ideas. Our ideals and moral ideas have in the past been rooted in religion. But the religious basis of our ideals has been undermined, and the superstructure of ideals is plainly tottering. None of the commonly suggested remedies on examination seems likely to succeed. It would therefore look as if the early death of our civilization were inevitable.

Of course we know that it is perfectly possible for individual men, very highly educated men, philosophers, scientists, intellectuals in general, to live moral lives without any religious convictions. But the question is whether a whole civilization, a whole family of peoples, composed almost entirely of relatively uneducated men and women, can do this. It follows, of course, that if we could make the vast majority of men as highly educated as the very few are now, we might save the situation. And we are already moving slowly in that direction through the techniques of mass education. But the critical question seems to concern the time-lag. Perhaps in a hundred years most of the population will, at the present rate, be sufficiently highly educated and civilized to combine high ideals with an absence of religion. But long before we reach any such stage, the collapse of our civilization may have come about. How are we to live through the intervening period?

I am sure that the first thing we have to do is to face the truth, however bleak it may be, and then next we have to learn to live with it. Let me say a word about each of these two points. What I am urging as regards the first is complete honesty. Those who wish to resurrect Christian dogmas are not, of course, consciously dishonest. But they have that kind of unconscious dishonesty which consists in lulling oneself with opiates and dreams. Those who talk of a new religion are merely hoping for a new opiate. Both alike refuse to face the truth that there is, in the universe outside man, no spirituality, no regard for values, no friend in the sky, no help or comfort for man of any sort. To be perfectly honest in the admission of this fact, not to seek shelter in new or old illusions, not to indulge in wishful dreams about this matter, this is the first thing we shall have to do.

I do not urge this course out of any special regard for the sanctity of truth in the abstract. It is not self-evident to me that truth is the supreme value to which all else must be sacrificed. Might not the discoverer of a truth which would be fatal to mankind be justified in suppressing it, even in teaching men a falsehood? Is truth more valuable than goodness and beauty and happiness? To think so is to invent yet another absolute, another religious delusion in which Truth with a capital T is substituted for God. The reason why we must now boldly and honestly face the truth that the universe is non-spiritual and indifferent to goodness, beauty, happiness, or truth is not that it would be wicked to suppress it, but simply that it is too late to do so, so that in the end we cannot do anything else but face it. Yet we stand on the brink, dreading the icy plunge. We need courage. We need honesty.

Now about the other point, the necessity of learning to live with the truth. This means learning to live virtuously and happily, or at least contentedly, without illusions. And this is going to be extremely difficult because what we have now begun dimly to perceive is that human life in the past, or at least human happiness, has almost wholly depended upon illusions. It has been said that man lives by truth, and that the truth will make us free. Nearly the opposite seems to me to be the case. Mankind has managed to live only by means of lies, and the truth may very well destroy us. If one were a Bergsonian one might believe that nature deliberately puts illusions into our souls in order to induce us to go on living.

The illusions by which men have lived seem to be of two kinds. First, there is what one may perhaps call the Great Illusion—I mean the religious illusion that the universe is moral and good, that it follows a wise and noble plan, that it is gradually generating some supreme value, that goodness is bound to triumph in it. Secondly, there is a whole host of minor illusions on which human happiness nourishes itself. How much of human happiness notoriously comes from the illusions of the lover about his beloved? Then again we work and strive because of the illusions connected with fame, glory, power, or money. Banners of all kinds, flags, emblems, insignia, ceremonials, and rituals are invariably symbols of some illusion or other. The British Empire, the connection between mother country and dominions, used to be partly kept going by illusions surrounding the notion of kingship. Or think of the vast amount of human happiness which is derived from the illusion of supposing that if some nonsense syllable, such as "sir" or "count" or "lord" is pronounced in conjunction with our names, we belong to a superior order of people.

There is plenty of evidence that human happiness is almost wholly based upon illusions of one kind or another. But the scientific spirit, or the spirit of truth, is the enemy of illusions and therefore the enemy of human happiness. That is why it is going to be so difficult to live with the truth. There is no reason why we should have to give up the host of minor illusions which render life supportable. There is no reason why the lover should be scientific about the loved one. Even the illusions of fame and glory may persist. But without the Great Illusion, the illusion of a good, kindly, and purposeful universe, we shall *have* to learn to live. And to ask this is really no more than to ask that we become genuinely civilized beings and not merely sham civilized beings.

I can best explain the difference by a reminiscence. I remember a fellow student in my college days, an ardent Christian, who told me that if he did not believe in a future life, in heaven and hell, he would rape, murder, steal and be a drunkard. That is what I call being a sham civilized being. On the other hand, not only could a Huxley, a John Stuart Mill, a David Hume, live great and fine lives without any religion, but a great many others of us, quite obscure persons, can at least live decent lives without it. To be genuinely civilized means to be able to walk straightly and to live honorably without the props and crutches of one or another of the childish dreams which have so far supported men. That such a life is likely to be ecstatically happy I will not claim. But that it can be lived in quiet content, accepting resignedly what cannot be helped, not expecting the impossible, and being thankful for small mercies, this I would maintain. That it will be difficult for men in general to learn this lesson I do not deny. But that it will be impossible I would not admit since so many have learned it already.

Man has not yet grown up. He is not adult. Like a child he cries for the moon and lives in a world of fantasies. And the race as a whole has perhaps reached the great crisis of its life. Can it grow up as a race in the same sense as individual men grow up? Can man put away childish things and adolescent dreams? Can he grasp the real world as it actually is, stark and bleak, without its romantic or religious halo, and still retain his ideals, striving for great ends and noble achievements? If he can, all may yet be well. If he cannot, he will probably sink back into the savagery and brutality from which he came, taking a humble place once more among the lower animals.

CHAPTER 10 ALBERT CAMUS

The Absurdity of
Human Existence

ABSURDITY AND SUICIDE

There is but one truly serious philosophical problem, and that is suicide.
Judging whether life is or is not worth living amounts to answering the fundamental question of philosophy. All the rest—whether or not the world has
three dimensions, whether the mind has nine or twelve categories—comes
afterwards. These are games; one must first answer. And if it is true, as Nietzsche claims, that a philosopher, to deserve our respect, must preach by
example, you can appreciate the importance of that reply, for it will precede
the definitive act. These are facts the heart can feel; yet they call for careful
study before they become clear to the intellect.

If I ask myself how to judge that this question is more urgent than that, I
reply that one judges by the actions it entails. I have never seen anyone die for
the ontological argument. Galileo, who held a scientific truth of great importance, abjured it with the greatest of ease as soon as it endangered his life. In
a certain sense, he did right.[1] That truth was not worth the stake. Whether the
earth or the sun revolves around the other is a matter of profound indifference. To tell the truth, it is a futile question. On the other hand, I see many
people die because they judge that life is not worth living. I see others para-
doxically getting killed for the ideas or illusions that give them a reason for
living (what is called a reason for living is also an excellent reason for dying).
I therefore conclude that the meaning of life is the most urgent of questions.
How to answer it? On all essential problems (I mean thereby those that run
the risk of leading to death or those that intensify the passion of living) there
are probably but two methods of thought: the method of La Palisse and the
method of Don Quixote. Solely the balance between evidence and lyricism

can allow us to achieve simultaneously emotion and lucidity. In a subject at once so humble and so heavy with emotion, the learned and classical dialectic must yield, one can see, to a more modest attitude of mind deriving at one and the same time from common sense and understanding.

Suicide has never been dealt with except as a social phenomenon. On the contrary, we are concerned here, at the outset, with the relationship between individual thought and suicide. An act like this is prepared within the silence of the heart, as is a great work of art. The man himself is ignorant of it. One evening he pulls the trigger or jumps. Of an apartment-building manager who had killed himself I was told that he had lost his daughter five years before, that he had changed greatly since, and that that experience had "undermined" him. A more exact word cannot be imagined. Beginning to think is beginning to be undermined. Society has but little connection with such beginnings. The worm is in man's heart. That is where it must be sought. One must follow and understand this fatal game that leads from lucidity in the face of existence to flight from light. . . .

But if it is hard to fix the precise instant, the subtle step when the mind opted for death, it is easier to deduce from the act itself the consequences it implies. In a sense, and as in melodrama, killing yourself amounts to confessing. It is confessing that life is too much for you or that you do not understand it. Let's not go too far in such analogies, however, but rather return to everyday words. It is merely confessing that that "is not worth the trouble." Living, naturally, is never easy. You continue making the gestures commanded by existence for many reasons, the first of which is habit. Dying voluntarily implies that you have recognized, even instinctively, the ridiculous character of that habit, the absence of any profound reason for living, the insane character of that daily agitation, and the uselessness of suffering.

What, then, is that incalculable feeling that deprives the mind of the sleep necessary to life? A world that can be explained even with bad reasons is a familiar world. But, on the other hand, in a universe suddenly divested of illusions and lights, man feels an alien, a stranger. His exile is without remedy since he is deprived of the memory of a lost home or the hope of a promised land. This divorce between man and his life, the actor and his setting, is properly the feeling of absurdity. All healthy men having thought of their own suicide, it can be seen, without further explanation, that there is a direct connection between this feeling and the longing for death.

The subject of this essay is precisely this relationship between the absurd and suicide, the exact degree to which suicide is a solution to the absurd. The principle can be established that for a man who does not cheat, what he believes to be true must determine his action. Belief in the absurdity of existence must then dictate his conduct. It is legitimate to wonder, clearly and without false pathos, whether a conclusion of this importance requires forsaking as rapidly as possible an incomprehensible condition. I am speaking, of course, of men inclined to be in harmony with themselves.

Stated clearly, this problem may seem both simple and insoluble. But it is wrongly assumed that simple questions involve answers that are no less simple and that evidence implies evidence. *A priori* and reversing the terms of the problem, just as one does or does not kill oneself, it seems that there are but two philosophical solutions, either yes or no. This would be too easy. But allowance must be made for those who, without concluding, continue questioning. Here I am only slightly indulging in irony: this is the majority. I notice also that those who answer "no" act as if they thought "yes." As a matter of fact, if I accept the Nietzschean criterion, they think "yes" in one way or another. On the other hand, it often happens that those who commit suicide were assured of the meaning of life. These contradictions are constant. It may even be said that they have never been so keen as on this point where, on the contrary, logic seems so desirable. It is a commonplace to compare philosophical theories and the behavior of those who profess them. . . . Schopenhauer is often cited, as a fit subject for laughter, because he praised suicide while seated at a well-set table. This is no subject for joking. That way of not taking the tragic seriously is not so grievous, but it helps to judge a man.

In the face of such contradictions and obscurities must we conclude that there is no relationship between the opinion one has about life and the act one commits to leave it? Let us not exaggerate in this direction. In a man's attachment to life there is something stronger than all the ills in the world. The body's judgment is as good as the mind's, and the body shrinks from annihilation. We get into the habit of living before acquiring the habit of thinking. In that race which daily hastens us toward death, the body maintains its irreparable lead. In short, the essence of that contradiction lies in what I shall call the act of eluding because it is both less and more than diversion in the Pascalian sense. Eluding is the invariable game. The typical act of eluding, the fatal evasion that constitutes the third theme of this essay, is hope. Hope for another life one must "deserve" or trickery of those who live not for life itself but for some great idea that will transcend it, refine it, give it a meaning, and betray it. . . .

ABSURDITY AND MEANING

All great deeds and all great thoughts have a ridiculous beginning. Great works are often born on a street-corner or in a restaurant's revolving door. So it is with absurdity. The absurd world more than others derives its nobility from that abject birth. In certain situations, replying "nothing" when asked what one is thinking about may be pretense in a man. Those who are loved are well aware of this. But if that reply is sincere, if it symbolizes that odd state of soul in which the void becomes eloquent, in which the chain of daily gestures is broken, in which the heart vainly seeks the link that will connect it again, then it is as it were the first sign of absurdity.

It happens that the stage sets collapse. Rising, streetcar, four hours in the office or the factory, meal, streetcar, four hours of work, meal, sleep, and

Monday Tuesday Wednesday Thursday Friday and Saturday according to the same rhythm—this path is easily followed most of the time. But one day the "why" arises and everything begins in that weariness tinged with amazement. "Begins"—this is important. Weariness comes at the end of the acts of a mechanical life, but at the same time it inaugurates the impulse of consciousness. It awakens consciousness and provokes what follows. What follows is the gradual return into the chain or it is the definitive awakening. At the end of the awakening comes, in time, the consequence: suicide or recovery. In itself weariness has something sickening about it. Here, I must conclude that it is good. For everything begins with consciousness and nothing is worth anything except through it. . . .

At the heart of all beauty lies something inhuman, and these hills, the softness of the sky, the outline of these trees at this very minute lose the illusory meaning with which we had clothed them, henceforth more remote than a lost paradise. The primitive hostility of the world rises up to face us across millennia. For a second we cease to understand it because for centuries we have understood it in solely the images and designs that we had attributed to it beforehand, because henceforth we lack the power to make use of that artifice. The world evades us because it becomes itself again. That stage scenery masked by habit becomes again what it is. It withdraws at a distance from us. Just as there are days when under the familiar face of a woman, we see as a stranger her we had loved months or years ago, perhaps we shall come even to desire what suddenly leaves us so alone. But the time has not yet come. Just one thing: that denseness and that strangeness of the world is the absurd.

Men, too, secrete the inhuman. At certain moments of lucidity, the mechanical aspect of their gestures, their meaningless pantomine makes silly everything that surrounds them. A man is talking on the telephone behind a glass partition; you cannot hear him, but you see his incomprehensible dumb show: you wonder why he is alive. This discomfort in the face of man's own inhumanity, this incalculable tumble before the image of what we are, this "nausea," as a writer of today calls it, is also the absurd. Likewise, the stranger who at certain seconds comes to meet us in a mirror, the familiar and yet alarming brother we encounter in our own photographs is also the absurd.

I come at last to death and to the attitude we have toward it. On this point everything has been said and it is only proper to avoid pathos. Yet one will never be sufficiently surprised that everyone lives as if no one "knew." This is because in reality there is no experience of death. Properly speaking, nothing has been experienced but what has been lived and made conscious. Here, it is barely possible to speak of the experience of others' deaths. It is a substitute, an illusion, and it never quite convinces us. That melancholy convention cannot be persuasive. The horror comes in reality from the mathematical aspect of the event. If time frightens us, this is because it works out the problem and the solution comes afterward. All the pretty speeches about the soul will have their contrary convincingly proved, at least for a time. From this inert body on which a slap makes no mark the soul has disappeared. This elementary and definitive aspect of the adventure constitutes the absurd feeling. Under the fatal lighting of that destiny, its uselessness becomes evident. No code of ethics and no effort are justifiable a priori in the face of the cruel mathematics that command our condition. . . .

Understanding the world for a man is reducing it to the human, stamping it with his seal. The cat's universe is not the universe of the anthill. The truism "All thought is anthropomorphic" has no other meaning. Likewise, the mind that aims to understand reality can consider itself satisfied only by reducing it to terms of thought. If man realized that the universe like him can love and suffer, he would be reconciled. If thought discovered in the shimmering mirrors of phenomena eternal relations capable of summing them up and summing themselves up in a single principle, then would be seen an intellectual joy of which the myth of the blessed would be but a ridiculous imitation. That nostalgia for unity, that appetite for the absolute illustrates the essential impulse of the human drama. But the fact of that nostalgia's existence does not imply that it is to be immediately satisfied. . . .

With the exception of professional rationalists, today people despair of true knowledge. If the only significant history of human thought were to be written, it would have to be the history of its successive regrets and its impotences.

Of whom and of what indeed can I say: "I know that!" This heart within me I can feel, and I judge that it exists. This world I can touch, and I likewise judge that it exists. There ends all my knowledge, and the rest is construction. For if I try to seize this self of which I feel sure, if I try to define and to summarize it, it is nothing but water slipping through my fingers. I can sketch one by one all the aspects it is able to assume, all those likewise that have been attributed to it, this upbringing, this origin, this ardor of these silences, this nobility or this vileness. But aspects cannot be added up. This very heart which is mine will forever remain indefinable to me. Between the certainty I have of my existence and the content I try to give to that assurance, the gap will never be filled. Forever I shall be a stranger to myself. . . .

Hence the intelligence, too, tells me in its way that this world is absurd. . . . In this unintelligible and limited universe, man's fate hence-forth assumes its meaning. A horde of irrationals has sprung up and surrounds him until his ultimate end. In his recovered and now studied lucidity, the feeling of the absurd becomes clear and definite. I said that the world is absurd, but I was too hasty. This world in itself is not reasonable, that is all that can be said. But what is absurd is the confrontation of this irrational and the wild longing for clarity whose call echoes in the human heart. The absurd depends as much on man as on the world. . . .

I don't know whether this world has a meaning that transcends it. But I know that I do not know that meaning and that it is impossible for me just now to know it. What can a meaning outside my condition mean to me? I can understand only in human terms. What I touch, what resists me—that is what I understand. And these two certainties—my appetite for the absolute and for unity and the impossibility of reducing this world to a rational and reasonable principle—I also know that I cannot reconcile them. What other truth can I admit without lying, without bringing in a hope I lack and which means nothing within the limits of my condition?

If I were a tree among trees, a cat among animals, this life would have a meaning, or rather this problem would not rise, for I should belong to this world. I should *be* this world to which I am now opposed by my whole consciousness and my whole insistence upon familiarity. This ridiculous reason is what sets me in opposition to all creation. I cannot cross it out with a stroke of the pen. What I believe to be true I must therefore preserve. What seems to me so obvious, even against me, I must support. And what constitutes the basis of that conflict, of that break between the world and my mind, but the awareness of it? If therefore I want to preserve it, I can through a constant awareness, ever revived, ever alert. This is what, for the moment, I must remember. . . .

Let us insist again on the method: it is a matter of persisting. At a certain point on his path the absurd man is tempted. History is not lacking in either religions or prophets, even without gods. He is asked to leap. All he can reply is that he doesn't fully understand, that it is not obvious. Indeed, he does not want to do anything but what he fully understands. He is assured that this is the sin of pride, but he does not understand the notion of sin; that perhaps hell is in store, but he has not enough imagination to visualize that strange future; that he is losing immortal life, but that seems to him an idle consideration. An attempt is made to get him to admit his guilt. He feels innocent. To tell the truth, that is all he feels—his irreparable innocence. This is what allows him everything. Hence, what he demands of himself is to live *solely* with what he knows, to accommodate himself to what is, and to bring in nothing that is not certain. He is told that nothing is. But this at least is a certainty. And it is with this that he is concerned: he wants to find out if it is possible to live *without appeal*. . . .

Before encountering the absurd, the everyday man lives with aims, a concern for the future or for justification (with regard to whom or what is not the question). He weighs his chances, he counts on "someday," his retirement or the labor of his sons. He still thinks that something in his life can be directed. In truth, he acts as if he were free, even if all the facts make a point of contradicting that liberty. But after the absurd, everything is upset. That idea that "I am," my way of acting as if everything has a meaning (even if, on occasion, I said that nothing has)—all that is given the lie in vertiginous fashion by the absurdity of a possible death. Thinking of the future, establishing aims for oneself, having preferences—all this presupposes a belief in freedom, even if one occasionally ascertains that one doesn't feel it. But at that moment I am well aware that that higher liberty, that freedom *to be*, which alone can serve as basis for a truth, does not exist. Death is there as the only reality. . . .

But at the same time the absurd man realizes that hitherto he was bound to that postulate of freedom on the illusion of which he was living. In a certain sense, that hampered him. To the extent to which he imagined a purpose to his life, he adapted himself to the demands of a purpose to be achieved and became the slave of his liberty. Thus I could not act otherwise than as the father (or the engineer or the leader of a nation, or the post-office subclerk) that I am preparing to be. . . .

The absurd enlightens me on this point: there is no future. Henceforth, this is the reason for my inner freedom. . . .

But what does life mean in such a universe? Nothing else for the moment but indifference to the future and a desire to use up everything that is given. Belief in the meaning of life always implies a scale of values, a choice, our preferences. Belief in the absurd, according to our definitions, teaches the contrary. But this is worth examining.

Knowing whether or not one can live *without appeal* is all that interests me. I do not want to get out of my depth. This aspect of life being given me, can I adapt myself to it? Now, faced with this particular concern, belief in the absurd is tantamount to substituting the quantity of experiences for the quality. If I convince myself that this life has no other aspect than that of the absurd, if I feel that its whole equilibrium depends on that perpetual opposition between my conscious revolt and the darkness in which it struggles, if I admit that my freedom has no meaning except in relation to its limited fate, then I must say that what counts is not the best of living but the most living. . . .

On the one hand the absurd teaches that all experiences are unimportant, and on the other it urges toward the greatest quantity of experiences. How, then, can one fail to do as so many of those men I was speaking of earlier—choose the form of life that brings us the most possible of that human matter, thereby introducing a scale of values that on the other hand one claims to reject?

But again it is the absurd and its contradictory life that teaches us. For the mistake is thinking that that quantity of experiences depends on the circumstances of our life when it depends solely on us. Here we have to be over-simple. To two men living the same number of years, the world always provides the same sum of experiences. It is up to us to be conscious of them. Being aware of one's life, one's revolt, one's freedom, and to the maximum, is living, and to the maximum. Where lucidity dominates, the scale of values becomes unless. . . .

NOTE

1. From the point of view of the relative value of truth. On the other hand, from the point of view of virile behavior, this scholar's fragility may well make us smile.

CHAPTER 11   K U R T   B A I E R

The Meaning of Life

Tolstoy, in his autobiographical work, "A Confession," reports how, when he was fifty and at the height of his literary success, he came to be obsessed by the fear that life was meaningless.

> At first I experienced moments of perplexity and arrest of life, as though I did not know what to do or how to live; and I felt lost and became dejected. But this passed, and I went on living as before. Then these moments of perplexity began to recur oftener and oftener, and always in the same form. They were always expressed by the questions: What is it for? What does it lead to? At first it seemed to me that these were aimless and irrelevant questions. I thought that it was all well known, and that if I should ever wish to deal with the solution it would not cost me much effort; just at present I had no time for it, but when I wanted to, I should be able to find the answer. The questions however began to repeat themselves frequently, and to demand replies more and more insistently; and like drops of ink always falling on one place they ran together into one black blot.[1]

A Christian living in the Middle Ages would not have felt any serious doubts about Tolstoy's questions. To him it would have seemed quite certain that life had a meaning and quite clear what it was. The medieval Christian world picture assigned to man a highly significant, indeed the central part in the grand scheme of things. The universe was made for the express purpose of providing a stage on which to enact a drama starring Man in the title role.

To be exact, the world was created by God in the year 4004 B.C. Man was the last and the crown of this creation, made in the likeness of God, placed in the Garden of Eden on earth, the fixed centre of the universe, round which revolved the nine heavens of the sun, the moon, the planets and the fixed stars, producing as they revolved in their orbits the heavenly harmony of the

Inaugural Lecture delivered at the Canberra University College, 1957. Copyright © 1957 by Kurt Baier. Used by permission of the author.

spheres. And this gigantic universe was created for the enjoyment of man, who was originally put in control of it. Pain and death were unknown in paradise. But this state of bliss was not to last. Adam and Eve ate of the forbidden tree of knowledge, and life on this earth turned into a death-march through a vale of tears. Then, with the birth of Jesus, new hope came into the world. After He had died on the cross, it became at least possible to wash away with the purifying water of baptism some of the effects of Original Sin and to achieve salvation. That is to say, on condition of obedience to the law of God, man could now enter heaven and regain the state of everlasting, deathless bliss, from which he had been excluded because of the sin of Adam and Eve.

To the medieval Christian the meaning of human life was therefore perfectly clear. The stretch on earth is only a short interlude, a temporary incarceration of the soul in the prison of the body, a brief trial and test, fated to end in death, the release from pain and suffering. What really matters, is the life after the death of the body. One's existence acquires meaning not by gaining what this life can offer but by saving one's immortal soul from death and eternal torture, by gaining eternal life and everlasting bliss.

The scientific world picture which has found ever more general acceptance from the beginning of the modern era onwards is in profound conflict with all this. At first, the Christian conception of the world was discovered to be erroneous in various important details. The Copernican theory showed up the earth as merely one of several planets revolving round the sun, and the sun itself was later seen to be merely one of many fixed stars each of which is itself the nucleus of a solar system similar to our own. Man, instead of occupying the centre of creation, proved to be merely the inhabitant of a celestial body no different from millions of others. Furthermore, geological investigations revealed that the universe was not created a few thousand years ago, but was probably millions of years old.

Disagreements over details of the world picture, however, are only superficial aspects of a much deeper conflict. The appropriateness of the whole Christian outlook is at issue. For Christianity, the world must be regarded as the "creation" of a kind of Superman, a person possessing all the human excellences to an infinite degree and none of the human weaknesses, Who has made man in His image, a feeble, mortal, foolish copy of Himself. In creating the universe, God acts as a sort of playwright-cum-legislator-cum-judge-cum-executioner. In the capacity of playwright, He creates the historical world process, including man. He erects the stage and writes, in outline, the plot. He creates the *dramatis personae* and watches over them with the eye partly of a father, partly of the law. While on stage, the actors are free to extemporise, but if they infringe the divine commandments, they are later dealt with by their creator in His capacity of judge and executioner.

Within such a framework, the Christian attitudes towards the world are natural and sound: it is natural and sound to think that all is arranged for the best even if appearances belie it; to resign oneself cheerfully to one's lot; to be filled with awe and veneration in regard to anything and everything that happens; to want to fall on one's knees and worship and praise the Lord. These are wholly fitting attitudes within the framework of the world view just outlined. And this world view must have seemed wholly sound and acceptable because it offered the best explanation which was then available of all the observed phenomena of nature.

As the natural sciences developed, however, more and more things in the universe came to be explained without the assumption of a supernatural creator. Science, moreover, could explain them better, that is, more accurately and more reliably. The Christian hypothesis of a supernatural maker, whatever other needs it was capable of satisfying, was at any rate no longer indispensable for the purpose of explaining the existence or occurrence of anything. In fact, scientific explanations do not seem to leave any room for this hypothesis. The scientific approach demands that we look for a natural explanation of anything and everything. The scientific way of looking at and explaining things has yielded an immensely greater measure of understanding of, and control over, the universe than any other way. And when one looks at the world in this scientific way, there seems to be no room for a personal relationship between human beings and a supernatural perfect being ruling and guiding men. Hence many scientists and educated men have come to feel that the Christian attitudes towards the world and human existence are inappropriate. They have become convinced that the universe and human existence in it are without a purpose and therefore devoid of meaning.[2]

1. THE EXPLANATION OF THE UNIVERSE

Such beliefs are disheartening and unplausible. It is natural to keep looking for the error that must have crept into our arguments. And if an error has crept in, then it is most likely to have crept in with science. For before the rise of science, people did not entertain such melancholy beliefs, while the scientific world picture seems literally to force them on us.

There is one argument which seems to offer the desired way out. It runs somewhat as follows. Science and religion are not really in conflict. They are, on the contrary, mutually complementary, each doing an entirely different job. Science gives provisional, if precise, explanations of small parts of the universe, religion gives final and over-all, if comparatively vague, explanations of the universe as a whole. The objectionable conclusion, that human existence is devoid of meaning, follows only if we use scientific explanations where they do not apply, namely, where total explanations of the whole universe are concerned.[3]

After all, the argument continues, the scientific world picture is the inevitable outcome of rigid adherence to scientific method and explanation, but scientific, that is, causal explanations from their very nature are incapable of producing real illumination. They can at best tell us *how* things are or have come about, but never *why*. They are incapable of making the universe intelligible, comprehensible, meaningful to us. They represent the universe as meaningless, not because it *is* meaningless, but because scientific explanations are not designed to yield answers to investigations into the why and wherefore, into the meaning, purpose, or point of things. Scientific explanations (this argument continues) began, harmlessly enough, as partial and provisional explanations of the movement of material bodies, in particular the planets, within the general framework of the medieval world picture. Newton thought of the universe as a clock made, originally wound up, and occasionally set right by God. His laws of motion only revealed the ways in which the heavenly machinery worked. Explaining the movement of the planets by these laws was analogous to explaining the machinery of a watch. Such explanations showed *how* the thing worked, but not *what it was for* or *why* it existed. Just as the explanation of how a watch works can help our understanding of the watch only if, in addition, we assume that there is a watchmaker who has designed it for a purpose, made it, and wound it up, so the Newtonian explanation of the solar system helps our understanding of it only on the similar assumption that there is some divine artificer who has designed and made this heavenly clockwork for some purpose, has wound it up, and perhaps even occasionally sets it right, when it is out of order.

Socrates, in the Phaedo complained that only explanations of a thing showing the good or purpose for which it existed could offer a *real* explanation of it. He rejected the kind of explanation we now call "causal" as no more than mentioning "that without which a cause could not be a cause," that is, as merely a necessary condition, but not the *real* cause, the real explanation.[4] In other words, Socrates held that *all* things can be explained in two different ways: either by mentioning merely a necessary condition, or by giving the *real* cause. The former is not an elucidation of the explicandum, not really a help in understanding it, in grasping its "why" and "wherefore."

This Socratic view, however, is wrong. It is not the case that there are two kinds of explanation for everything, one partial, preliminary, and not really clarifying, the other full, final, and illuminating. The truth is that these two kinds of explanation are equally explanatory, equally illuminating, and equally full and final, but that they are appropriate for different kinds of explicanda.

When in an uninhabited forest we find what looks like houses, paved streets, temples, cooking utensils, and the like, it is no great risk to say that these things are the ruins of a deserted city, that is to say, of something man-made. In such a case, the appropriate explanation is teleological, that is, in terms of the purposes of the builders of that city. On the other hand, when a comet approaches the earth, it is similarly a safe bet that, unlike the city in the forest, it was not manufactured by intelligent creatures and that, therefore, a teleological explanation would be out of place, whereas a causal one is suitable.

It is easy to see that in some cases causal, and in others teleological explanations are appropriate. A small satellite circling the earth may or may not have been made by man. We may never know which is the true explanation, but either hypothesis is equally explanatory. It would be wrong to say that only a teleological explanation can *really* explain it. Either explanation would yield complete clarity although, of course, only one can be true. Teleological explanation is only one of several that are possible.

It may indeed be strictly correct to say that the question *"Why* is there a satellite circling the earth?" can only be answered by a teleological explanation. It may be true that "Why?"—questions can really be used properly only in order to elicit *someone's reasons for* doing something. If this is so, it would explain our dissatisfaction with causal answers to "Why?"—questions. But even if it is so, it does not show that "Why is the satellite there?" *must be answered by a teleological explanation.* It shows only that either it must be so answered or it must not be asked. The question "Why have you stopped beating your wife?" can be answered only by a teleological explanation, but if you have never beaten her, it is an improper question. Similarly, if the satellite is not man-made, "Why is there a satellite?" is improper since it implies an origin it did not have. Natural science can indeed only tell us *how* things in nature have come about and not *why,* but this is so not because something else can tell us the *why* and *wherefore,* but because there is none.

There is, however, another point which has not yet been answered. The objection just stated was that causal explanations did not even set out to answer the crucial question. We ask the question "Why?" but science returns an answer to the question "How?" It might now be conceded that this is no ground for a complaint, but perhaps it will instead be said that causal explanations do not give complete or full answers even to that latter question. In causal explanations, it will be objected, the existence of one thing is explained by reference to its cause, but this involves asking for the cause of that cause, and so on, ad infinitum. There is no resting place which is not as much in need of explanation as what has already been explained. Nothing at all is ever fully and completely explained by this sort of explanation.

Leibniz has made this point very persuasively. "Let us suppose a book of the elements of geometry to have been eternal, one copy always having been taken down from an earlier one; it is evident that, even though a reason can be given for the present book out of a past one, nevertheless, out of any number of books, taken in order, going backwards, we shall never come upon *a full* reason; though we might well always wonder why there should have been such books from all time—why there were books at all, and why they were written in this manner. What is true of books is true also of the different states of the world; for what follows is in some way copied from what precedes ... And so, however far you go back to earlier states, you will never find in those states *a full reason* why there should be any world rather than none, and why it should be such as it is."[5]

However, a moment's reflection will show that if any type of explanation is merely preliminary and provisional, it is teleological explanation, since it presupposes a background which itself stands in need of explanation. If I account for the existence of the man-made satellite by saying that it was made by some scientists for a certain purpose, then such an explanation can clarify the existence of the satellite only if I assume that there existed materials out of which the satellite was made, and scientists who made it for some purpose. It therefore does not matter what type of explanation we give, whether causal or teleological: either type, any type of explanation, will imply the existence of something by reference to which the explicandum can be explained. And this in turn must be accounted for in the same way, and so on for ever.

But is not God a necessary being? Do we not escape the infinite regress as soon as we reach God? It is often maintained that, unlike ordinary intelligent beings, God is eternal and necessary; hence His existence, unlike theirs, is not in need of explanation. For what is it that creates the vicious regress just mentioned? It is that, if we accept the principle of sufficient reason (that there must be an explanation for the existence of anything and everything the existence of which is not logically necessary, but merely contingent[6]), the existence of all the things referred to in any explanation requires itself to be explained. If, however, God is a logically necessary being, then His existence requires no explanation. Hence the vicious regress comes to an end with God.

Now, it need not be denied that God is a necessary being in some sense of that expression. In one of these senses, I, for instance, am a necessary being: it is impossible that I should not exist, because it is self-refuting to say "I do not exist." The same is true of the English language and of the universe. It is self-refuting to say "There is no such thing as the English language" because this sentence is in the English language, or "There is no such thing as the universe" because whatever there is, *is* the universe. It is impossible that these things should not in fact exist since it is impossible that we should be mistaken in thinking that they exist. For what possible occurrence could even throw doubt on our being right on these matters, let alone show that we are wrong? I, the English language, and the universe, are necessary beings, simply in the sense in which all is necessarily true which has been *proved* to be true. The occurrence of utterances such as "I exist," "The English language exists" and "The universe exists" is in itself sufficient proof of their truth. These remarks are therefore necessarily true, hence the things asserted to exist are necessary things.

But this sort of necessity will not satisfy the principle of sufficient reason, because it is only hypothetical or consequential necessity.[7] *Given that* someone says "I exist," then it is logically impossible that *he* should not exist. Given the evidence we have, the English language and the universe most certainly do exist. But there is no necessity about the evidence. On the principle of sufficient reason, we must explain the existence of the evidence, for its existence is not logically necessary.

In other words, the only sense of "necessary being" capable of terminating the vicious regress is "logically necessary being," but it is no longer seriously in dispute that the notion of a logically necessary being is self-contradictory.[8] Whatever can be conceived of as existing can equally be conceived of as not existing.

However, even if per impossible, there were such a thing as a logically necessary being, we could still not make out a case for the superiority of teleological over causal explanation. The existence of the universe cannot be explained in accordance with the familiar model of manufacture by a craftsman. For that model presupposes the existence of materials out of which the product is fashioned. God, on the other hand, must create the materials as well. Moreover, although we have a simple model of "creation out of nothing," for composers create tunes out of nothing, yet this is a great difference between creating *something to be sung,* and making the sounds which are a singing of it, or producing the piano on which to play it. Let us, however, waive all these objections and admit, for argument's sake, that creation out of nothing is conceivable. Surely, even so, no one can claim that it is the kind of explanation which yields the clearest and fullest understanding. Surely, to round off scientific explanations of the origin of the universe with creation out of nothing, does not add anything to our *understanding.* There may be merit of some sort in this way of speaking, but whatever it is, it is not greater clarity or explanatory power.[9]

What then, does all this amount to? Merely to the claim that scientific explanations are no worse than any other. All that has been shown is that all explanations suffer from the same defect: all involve a vicious infinite regress. In other words, no type of human explanation can help us to unravel the ultimate, unanswerable mystery. Christian ways of looking at things may not be able to render the world any more lucid than science can, but at least they do not pretend that there are no impenetrable mysteries. On the contrary, they point out untiringly that the claims of science to be able to elucidate everything are hollow. They remind us that science is not merely limited to the exploration of a tiny corner of the universe but that, however far out probing instruments may eventually reach, we can never even approach the answers to the last questions: "Why is there a world at all rather than nothing?" and "Why is the world such as it is and not different?" Here our finite human intellect bumps against its own boundary walls.

Is it true that scientific explanations involve an infinite vicious regress? Are scientific explanations really only provisional and incomplete? The crucial point will be this. Do *all* contingent truths call for explanation? Is the principle of sufficient reason sound? Can scientific explanations never come to a definite end? It will be seen that with a clear grasp of the nature and purpose of explanation we can answer these questions.[10]

Explaining something to someone is making him understand it. This involves bringing together in his mind two things, a model which is accepted as already simple and clear, and that which is to be explained, the explicandum, which is not so. Understanding the explicandum is seeing that it belongs to a range of things which could legitimately have been expected by anyone familiar with the model and with certain facts.

There are, however, two fundamentally different positions which a person may occupy relative to some explicandum. He may not be familiar with any model capable of leading him to expect the phenomenon to be explained. Most of us, for instance, are in that position in relation to the phenomena occurring in a good seance. With regard to other things people will differ. Someone who can play chess, already understands chess, already has such a model. Someone who has never seen a game of chess has not. He sees the moves on the board but he cannot understand, cannot follow, cannot make sense of what is happening. Explaining the game to him is giving him an explanation, is making him understand. He can understand or follow chess moves only if he can see them as conforming to a model of a chess game. In order to acquire such a model, he will, of course, need to know the constitutive rules of chess, that is, the permissible moves. But that is not all. He must know that a normal game of chess is a competition (not all games are) between two people, each trying to win, and he must know what it is to win at chess: to manoeuvre the opponent's king into a position of check-mate. Finally, he must acquire some knowledge of what is and what is not conducive to winning: the tactical rules or canons of the game.

A person who has been given such an explanation and who has mastered it—which may take quite a long time—has now reached understanding, in the sense of the ability to follow each move. A person cannot in that sense understand merely one single move of chess and no other. If he does not understand any other moves, we must say that he has not yet mastered the explanation, that he does not really understand the single move either. If he has mastered the explanation, then he understands all those moves which he can see as being in accordance with the model of the game inculcated in him during the explanation.

However, even though a person who has mastered such an explanation will understand many, perhaps most, moves of any game of chess he cares to watch, he will not necessarily understand them all, as some moves of a player may not be in accordance with his model of the game. White, let us say, at his fifteenth move, exposes his queen to capture by Black's knight. Though in accordance with the constitutive rules of the game, this move is nevertheless perplexing and calls for explanation, because it is not conducive to the achievement by White of what must be assumed to be his aim: to win the game. The queen is a much more valuable piece than the knight against which he is offering to exchange.

An onlooker who has mastered chess may fail to understand this move, be perplexed by it, and wish for an explanation. Of course he may fail to be perplexed, for if he is a very inexperienced player he may not *see* the disadvantageousness of the move. But there is such a need whether anyone sees it or not. The move *calls for* explanation because to anyone who knows the game it must appear to be incompatible with the model which we have learnt during the explanation of the game, and by reference to which we all explain and understand normal games.

However, the required explanation of White's 15th move is of a very different kind. What is needed now is not the acquisition of an explanatory model, but the removal of the real or apparent incompatibility between the player's move and the model of explanation he has already acquired. In such a case the perplexity can be removed only on the assumption that the incompatibility between the model and the game is merely apparent. As our model includes a presumed aim of both players, there are the following three possibilities: (a) White has made a mistake: he has over-looked the threat to his queen. In that case, the explanation is that White thought his move conducive to his end, but it was not. (b) Black has made a mistake: White set a trap for him. In that case, the explanation is that Black thought White's move was not conducive to White's end, but it was. (c) White is not pursuing the end which any chess player may be presumed to pursue: he is not trying to win his game. In that case, the explanation is that White has made a move which he knows is not conducive to the end of winning his game because, let us say, he wishes to please Black who is his boss.

Let us now set out the differences and similarities between the two types of understanding involved in these two kinds of explanation. I shall call the first kind "model"—understanding and explaining, respectively, because both involve the use of a model by reference to which understanding and explaining is effected. The second kind I shall call "unvexing," because the need for this type of explanation and understanding arises only when there is a perplexity arising out of the incompatibility of the model and the facts to be explained.

The first point is that unvexing presupposes model-understanding, but not vice versa. A person can neither have nor fail to have unvexing-understanding of White's fifteenth move at chess, if he does not already have model-understanding of chess. Obviously, if I don't know how to play chess, I shall fail to have model-understanding of White's fifteenth move. But I can neither fail to have nor, of course, can I have unvexing-understanding of it, for I cannot be perplexed by it. I merely fail to have model-understanding of this move as, indeed, of any other move of chess. On the other hand, I may well have model-understanding of chess without having unvexing-understanding of every move. That is to say, I may well know how to play chess without understanding White's fifteenth move. A person cannot fail to have unvexing-understanding of the move unless he is vexed or perplexed by it, hence he cannot even fail to have unvexing-understanding unless he already has model-understanding. It is not true that one either understands or fails to understand. On certain occasions, one neither understands nor fails to understand.

The second point is that there are certain things which cannot call for unvexing-explanations. No one can for instance call for an unvexing-explanation of White's first move, which is Pawn to King's Four. For no one can be perplexed or vexed by this move. Either a person knows how to play chess or he does not. If he does, then he must understand this move, for if he does not understand it, he has not yet mastered the game. And if he does not know how to play chess, then he cannot yet have, or fail to have, unvexing-understanding, he cannot therefore need an unvexing-explanation. Intellectual problems do not arise out of ignorance, but out of insufficient knowledge. An ignoramus is puzzled by very little. Once a student can see problems, he is already well into the subject.

The third point is that model-understanding implies being able, without further thought, to have model-understanding of a good many other things, unvexing-understanding does not. A person who knows chess and therefore has model-understanding of it, must understand a good many chess moves, in fact all except those that call for unvexing-explanations. If he claims that he can understand White's first move, but no others, then he is either lying or deceiving himself or he really does not understand any move. On the other hand, a person who, after an unvexing-explanation, understands White's fifteenth move, need not be able, without further explanation, to understand Black's or any other further move which calls for unvexing-explanation.

What is true of explaining deliberate and highly stylized human behaviour such as playing a game of chess is also true of explaining natural phenomena. For what is characteristic of natural phenomena, that they recur in essentially the same way, that they are, so to speak, repeatable, is also true of chess games, as it is not of games of tennis or cricket. There is only one important difference: man himself has invented and laid down the rules of chess, as he has not invented or laid down the "rules or laws governing the behaviour of things." This difference between chess and phenomena is important, for it adds another way to the three already mentioned,[11] in which a perplexity can be removed by an unvexing-explanation, namely, by abandoning the original explanatory model. This is, of course, not possible in the case of games of chess, because the model for chess is not a "construction" on the basis of the already existing phenomena of chess, but an invention. The person who first thought up the model of chess could not have been mistaken. The person who first thought of a model explaining some phenomenon could have been mistaken.

Consider an example. We may think that the following phenomena belong together: the horizon seems to recede however far we walk towards it; we seem to be able to see further the higher the mountain we climb; the sun and moon seem every day to fall into the sea on one side but to come back from behind the mountains on the other side without being any the worse for it. We may explain these phenomena by two alternative models: (a) that the earth is a large disc; (b) that it is a large sphere. However, to a believer in the first theory there arises the following perplexity: how is it that when we travel long enough towards the horizon in any one direction, we do eventually come back to our starting point without ever coming to the edge of the earth? We may at first attempt to "save" the model by saying that there is only an apparent contradiction. We may say either that the model does not require us to come to an edge, for it may be possible only to walk round and round on the flat surface. Or we may say that the person must have walked over the edge without noticing it, or perhaps that the travellers are all lying. Alternatively, the fact that our model is "constructed" and not invented or laid down enables us to say, what we could not do in the case of chess, that the model is inadequate or unsuitable. We can choose another model which fits all the facts, for instance, that the earth is round. Of course, then we have to give an unvexing-explanation for why it *looks* flat, but we are able to do that.

We can now return to our original question, "Are scientific explanations true and full explanations or do they involve an infinite regress, leaving them for ever incomplete?"

Our distinction between model- and unvexing-explanations will help here. It is obvious that only those things which are perplexing *call for* and *can be given* unvexing-explanations. We have already seen that in disposing of one perplexity, we do not necessarily raise another. On the contrary, unvexing-explanations truly and completely explain what they set out to explain, namely, how something is possible which, on our explanatory model, seemed to be impossible. There can therefore be no infinite regress here. Unvexing-explanations are real and complete explanations.

Can there be an infinite regress, then, in the case of model-explanations? Take the following example. European children are puzzled by the fact that their antipodean counterparts do not drop into empty space. This perplexity can be removed by substituting for their explanatory model another one. The European children imagine that throughout space there is an all-pervasive force operating in the same direction as the force that pulls them to the ground. We must, in our revised model, substitute for this force another acting everywhere in the direction of the centre of the earth. Having thus removed their perlexity by giving them an adequate model, we can, however, go on to ask *why* there should be such a force as the force of gravity, why bodies should "naturally," in the absence of forces acting on them, behave in the way stated in Newton's laws. And we might be able to give such an explanation. We might for instance construct a model of space which would exhibit as derivable from it what in Newton's theory are "brute facts." Here we would have a case of the brute facts of one theory being explained within the framework of another, more general theory. And it is a sound methodological principle that we should continue to look for more and more general theories.

Note two points, however. The first is that we must distinguish, as we have seen, between *the possibility* and *the necessity* of giving an explanation. Particular occurrences can be explained by being exhibited as instances of regularities, and regularities can be explained by being exhibited as instances of more general regularities. Such explanations make things clearer. They organize the material before us. They introduce order where previously there was disorder. But absence of this sort of explanation (model-explanation) does not leave us with a puzzle or perplexity, an intellectual restlessness or cramp. The unexplained things are not unintelligible, incomprehensible, or irrational. Some things, on the other hand, call for, require, demand an explanation. As long as we are without such an explanation, we are perplexed, puzzled, intellectually perturbed. We need an unvexing-explanation.

Now, it must be admitted that we may be able to construct a more general theory, from which, let us say, Newton's theory can be derived. This would further clarify the phenomena of motion and would be intellectually satisfying. But failure to do so would not leave us with an intellectual cramp. The facts stated in Newton's theory do not require, or stand in need of, unvexing-explanations. They could do so only if we already had another theory or model with which Newton's theory was incompatible. They could not do so, by themselves, prior to the establishment of such another model.

The second point is that there is an objective limit to which such explanations tend, and beyond which they are pointless. There is a very good reason for wishing to explain a less general by a more general theory. Usually, such a unification goes hand in hand with greater precision in measuring the phenomena which both theories explain. Moreover, the more general theory, because of its greater generality, can explain a wider range of phenomena including not only phenomena already explained by some other theories but also newly discovered phenomena, which the less general theory cannot explain. Now, the ideal limit to which such expansions of theories tend is an all-embracing theory which unifies all theories and explains all phenomena. Of course, such a limit can never be reached, since new phenomena are constantly discovered. Nevertheless, theories may be tending towards it. It will be remembered that the contention made against scientific theories was that there is no such limit because they involve an infinite regress. On that view, which I reject, there is no conceivable point at which scientific theories could be said to have explained the whole universe. On the view I am defending, there is such a limit, and it is the limit towards which scientific theories are actually tending. I claim that the nearer we come to this limit, the closer we are to a full and complete explanation of everything. For if we were to reach the limit, then though we could, of course, be left with a model which is itself unexplained and could be yet further explained by derivation from another model, there would be no need for, and no point in, such a further explanation. There would be no need for it, because any clearly defined model permitting us to expect the phenomena it is designed to explain offers full and complete explanations of these phenomena, however narrow the range. And while, at lower levels of generality, there is a good reason for providing more general models, since they further simplify, systematize, and organize the phenomena, this, which is the only reason for building more general theories, no longer applies once we reach the ideal limit of an all-embracing explanation.

It might be said that there is another reason for using different models: that they might enable us to discover new phenomena. Theories are not only instruments of explanation, but also of discovery. With this I agree, but it is irrelevant to my point: that *the needs of explanation* do not require us to go on for ever deriving one explanatory model from another.

It must be admitted, then, that in the case of model-explanations there is a regress, but it is neither vicious nor infinite. It is not vicious because, in order to explain a group of explicanda, a model-explanation *need* not itself be derived from another more general one. It gives a perfectly full and consistent explanation by itself. And the regress is not infinite, for there is a natural limit, an all-embracing model, which can explain all phenomena, beyond which it would be pointless to derive model-explanations from yet others.

What about our most serious question, "Why is there anything at all?" Sometimes, when we think about how one thing has developed out of another and that one out of a third, and so on back throughout all time, we are driven to ask the same question about the universe as a whole. We want to add up all things and refer to them by the name, "the world," and we want to know why the world exists and why there is not nothing instead. In such moments, the world seems to us a kind of bubble floating on an ocean of nothingness. Why should such flotsam be adrift in empty space? Surely, its emergence from the hyaline billows of nothingness is more mysterious even than Aphrodite's emergence from the sea. Wittgenstein expressed in these words the mystification we all feel: "Not *how* the world is, is the mystical, but *that* it is. The contemplation of the world *sub specie aeterni* is the contemplation of it as a limited whole. The feeling of the world as a limited whole is the mystical feeling."[12]

Professor J. J. C. Smart expresses his own mystification in these moving words:

"That anything should exist at all does seem to me a matter for the deepest awe. But whether other people feel this sort of awe, and whether they or I ought to is another question. I think we ought to. If so, the question arises: If 'Why should anything exist at all?' cannot be interpreted after the manner of the cosmological argument, that is, as an absurd request for the non-sensical postulation of a logically necessary being, what sort of question is it? What sort of question is this question 'Why should anything exist at all?' All I can say is that I do not yet know."[13]

It is undeniable that the magnitude and perhaps the very existence of the universe is awe-inspiring. It is probably true that it gives many people "the mystical feeling." It is also undeniable that our awe, our mystical feeling, aroused by contemplating the vastness of the world, is justified, in the same sense in which our fear is justified when we realize we are in danger. There is no more appropriate object for our awe or for the mystical feeling than the magnitude and perhaps the existence of the universe, just as there is no more appropriate object for our fear than a situation of personal peril. However, it does not follow from this that it is a good thing to cultivate, or indulge in, awe or mystical feelings, any more than it is necessarily a good thing to cultivate, or indulge in, fear in the presence of danger.

In any case, whether or not we ought to have or are justified in having a mystical feeling or a feeling of awe when contemplating the universe, having such a feeling is not the same as asking a meaningful question, although having it may well *incline us* to utter certain forms of words. Our question "Why is there anything at all?" may be no more than the expression of our feeling of awe or mystification, and not a meaningful question at all. Just as the feeling of fear may naturally but illegitimately give rise to the question "What sin have I committed?" so the feeling of awe or mystification may naturally but illegitimately lead to the question "Why is there anything at all?" What we have to discover, then, is whether this question makes sense or is meaningless.

Yes, of course, it will be said, it makes perfectly good sense. There is an undeniable fact and it calls for explanation. The fact is that the universe exists. In the light of our experience, there can be no possible doubt that something or other exists, and the claim that the universe exists commits us to no more than that. And surely this calls for explanation, because the universe must have originated somehow. Everything has an origin and the universe is no exception. Since the universe is the totality of things, it must have originated out of nothing. If it had originated out of something, even something as small as one single hydrogen atom, what has so originated could not be the whole universe, but only the universe minus the atom. And then the atom itself would call for explanation, for it too must have had an origin, and it must be *an origin out of nothing*. And how can anything originate out of nothing? Surely that calls for explanation.

However, let us be quite clear what is to be explained. There are two facts here, not one. The first is that the universe exists, which is undeniable. The second is that the universe must have originated out of nothing, and that is not undeniable. It is true that, *if it has originated at all*, then it must have originated out of nothing, or else it is not the universe that has originated. But need it have originated? Could it not have existed for ever?[14] It might be argued that nothing exists for ever, that everything has originated out of something else. That may well be true, but it is perfectly compatible with the fact that the universe is everlasting. We may well be able to trace the origin of any thing to the time when, by some transformation, it has developed out of some other thing, and yet it may be the case that no thing has its origin in nothing, and the universe has existed for ever. For even if every *thing* has a beginning and an end, the total of mass and energy may well remain constant.

Moreover, the hypothesis that the universe originated out of nothing is, empirically speaking, completely empty. Suppose, for argument's sake, that the annihilation of an object without remainder is conceivable. It would still not be possible for any hypothetical observer to ascertain whether space was empty or not. Let us suppose that *within the range of observation of our observer* one object after another is annihilated without remainder and that only one is left. Our observer could not then tell whether in remote parts of the universe, beyond his range of observation, objects are coming into being or passing out of existence. What, moreover, are we to say of the observer himself? Is he to count for nothing? Must we not postulate him away as well, if the universe is to have arisen out of nothing?

Let us, however, ignore all these difficulties and assume that the universe really has originated out of nothing. Even that does not prove that the universe has not existed for ever. If the universe can conceivably develop out of nothing, then it can conceivably vanish without remainder. And it can arise out of nothing again and subside into nothingness once more, and so on ad infinitum. Of course, "again" and "once more" are not quite the right words. The concept of time hardly applies to such universes. It does not make sense to ask whether one of them is earlier or later than, or perhaps simultaneous with, the other because we cannot ask whether they occupy the same or different spaces. Being separated from one another by "nothing," they are not separated from one another by "anything." We cannot therefore make any statements about their mutual spatio-temporal relations. It is impossible to distinguish between one long continuous universe and two universes separated by nothing. How, for instance, can we tell whether the universe including ourselves is not frequently annihilated and "again" reconstituted just as it was?

Let us now waive these difficulties as well. Let us suppose for a moment that we understand what is meant by saying that the universe originated out of nothing and that this has happened only once. Let us accept this as a fact. Does this fact call for explanation?

It does not call for an unvexing-explanation. That would be called for only if there were a perplexity due to the incompatibility of an accepted model with some fact. In our case, the fact to be explained is the origination of the universe out of nothing, hence there could not be such a perplexity, for we need not employ a model incompatible with this. If we had a model incompatible with our "fact," then that would be the wrong model and we would simply have to substitute another for it. The model we employ to explain the origin of the universe out of nothing could not be based on the similar origins of other things for, of course, there is nothing else with a similar origin.

All the same, it seems very surprising that something should have come out of nothing. It is contrary to the principle that every thing has an origin, that is, has developed out of something else. It must be admitted that there is this incompatibility. However, it does not arise because a well-established model does not square with an undeniable fact; it arises because a well-established model does not square with *an assumption* of which it is hard even to make sense and for which there is no evidence whatsoever. In fact, the only reason we have for making this assumption, is a simple logical howler: that because every thing has an origin, the universe must have an origin, too, except, that, being the universe, it must have originated out of nothing. This is a howler, because it conceives of the universe as a big thing, whereas in fact it is the totality of things, that is, not a thing. That every thing has an origin does not entail that the totality of things has an origin. On the contrary, it strongly suggests that it has not. For to say that every thing has an origin implies that any given thing must have developed out of something else which in turn, being a thing, must have developed out of something else, and so forth. If we assume that every thing has an origin, we need not, indeed it is hard to see how we can, assume that the totality of things has an origin as well. There is therefore no perplexity, because we need not and should not assume that the universe has originated out of nothing.

If, however, in spite of all that has been said just now, someone still wishes to assume, contrary to all reason, that the universe has originated out of nothing, there would still be no perplexity, for then he would simply have to give up the principle which is incompatible with this assumption, namely, that no thing can originate out of nothing. After all, this principle *could* allow for exceptions. We have no proof that it does not. Again, there is no perplexity, because no incompatibility between our assumption and an inescapable principle.

But, it might be asked, do we not need a model-explanation of our supposed fact? The answer is No. We do not need such an explanation, for there could not possibly be a model for this origin other than this origin itself. We cannot say that origination out of nothing is like birth, or emergence, or evolution, or anything else we know for it is not like anything we know. In all these cases, there is *something* out of which the new thing has originated.

To sum up. The question, "Why is there anything at all?" looks like a perfectly sensible question modelled on "Why does *this* exist?" or "How has *this* originated?" It looks like a question about the origin of a thing. However, it is not such a question, for the universe is not a thing, but the totality of things. There is therefore no reason to assume that the universe has an origin. The very assumption that it has is fraught with contradictions and absurdities. If, nevertheless, it were true that the universe has originated out of nothing, then this would not call either for an unvexing or a model-explanation. It would not call for the latter, because there could be no model of it taken from another part of our experience, since there is nothing analogous in our experience to origination out of nothing. It would not call for the former, because there can be no perplexity due to the incompatibility of a well-established model and an undeniable fact, since there is no undeniable fact and no well-established model. If, on the other hand, as is more probable, the universe has not originated at all, but is eternal, then the question why or how it has originated simply does not arise. There can then be no question about why anything at all exists, for it could not mean how or why the universe had originated, since ex hypothesi it has no origin. And what else could it mean?

Lastly, we must bear in mind that the hypothesis that the universe was made by God out of nothing only brings us back to the question who made God or how God originated. And if we do not find it repugnant to say that God is eternal, we cannot find it repugnant to say that the universe is eternal. The only difference is that we know for certain that the universe exists, while we have the greatest difficulty in even making sense of the claim that God exists.

To sum up. According to the argument examined, we must reject the scientific world picture because it is the outcome of scientific types of explanation which do not really and fully explain the world around us, but only tell us *how* things have come about, not *why*, and can give no answer to the ultimate question, why there is anything at all rather than nothing. Against this, I have argued that scientific explanations are real and full, just like the explanations of everyday life and of the traditional religions. They differ from those latter only in that they are more precise and more easily disprovable by the observation of facts.

My main points dealt with the question why scientific explanations were thought to be merely provisional and partial. The first main reason is the misunderstanding of the difference between teleological and causal explanations. It is first, and rightly, maintained that teleological explanations are answers to "Why?" questions, while causal explanations are answers to "How?" questions. It is further, and wrongly, maintained that, in order to obtain real and full explanations of anything, one must answer both "Why?" and "How?" questions. In other words, it is thought that all matters can and must be explained by both teleological and causal types of explanation. Causal explanations, it is believed, are merely provisional and partial, waiting to be completed by teleological explanations. Until a teleological explanation has been given, so the story goes, we have not *really* understood the explicandum. However, I have shown that both types are equally real and full explanations. The difference between them is merely that they are appropriate to different types of explicanda.

It should, moreover, be borne in mind that teleological explanations are not, in any sense, unscientific. They are rightly rejected in the natural sciences, not however because they are unscientific, but because no intelligences or purposes are found to be involved there. On the other hand, teleological explanations are very much in place in psychology, for we find intelligence and purpose involved in a good deal of human behaviour. It is not only not unscientific to give teleological explanations of deliberate human behaviour, but it would be quite unscientific to exclude them.

The second reason why scientific explanations are thought to be merely provisional and partial, is that they are believed to involve a vicious infinite regress. Two misconceptions have led to this important error. The first is the general misunderstanding of the nature of explanation, and in particular the failure to distinguish between the two types which I have called model- and unvexing-explanations, respectively. If one does not draw this distinction, it is natural to conclude that scientific explanations lead to a vicious infinite regress. For while it is true of those perplexing matters which are elucidated by unvexing-explanations that they are incomprehensible and cry out for explanation, it is not true that after an unvexing-explanation has been given, this itself is again capable, let alone in need of, a yet further explanation of the same kind. Conversely, while it is true that model-explanations of regularities can themselves be further explained by more general model-explanations, it is not true that, in the absence of such more general explanations, the less general are incomplete, hang in the air, so to speak, leaving the explicandum incomprehensible and crying out for explanation. The distinction between the two types of explanation shows us that an explicandum is either perplexing and incomprehensible, in which case an explanation of it *is necessary* for clarification and, when given, *complete*, or it is a regularity capable of being subsumed under a model, in which case a further explanation *is possible* and often profitable, but *not necessary* for clarification.

The second misconception responsible for the belief in a vicious infinite regress is the misrepresentation of scientific explanation *as essentially causal*. It has generally been held that, in a scientific explanation, the explicandum is the effect of some event, the cause, temporally prior to the explicandum. Combined with the principle of sufficient reason (the principle that anything is in need of explanation which might conceivably have been different from what it is), this error generates the nightmare of determinism. Since any event might have been different from what it was, acceptance of this principle has the consequence that *every* event must have a reason or explanation. But if the reason is itself an event *prior in time,* then every reason must have a reason preceding it, and so the infinite regress of explanation is necessarily tied to the time scale stretching infinitely back into the endless past. It is, however, obvious from our account that science is not primarily concerned with the forging of such causal chains. The primary object of the natural sciences is not historical at all. Natural science claims to reveal, not the beginnings of things, but their underlying reality. It does not dig up the past, it digs down into the structure of things existing here and now. Some scientists do allow themselves to speculate, and rather precariously at that, about origins. But their hard work is done on the structure of what exists now. In particular those explanations which are themselves further explained are not explanations linking event to event in a gapless chain reaching back to creation day, but generalisations of theories tending towards a unified theory.

2. THE PURPOSE OF MAN'S EXISTENCE

Our conclusion in the previous section has been that science is in principle able to give complete and real explanations of every occurrence and thing in the universe. This has two important corollaries: (i) Acceptance of the scientific world picture cannot be *one's reason for* the belief that the universe is unintelligible and therefore meaningless, though coming to accept it, after having been taught the Christian world picture, may well have been, in the case of many individuals, *the only or the main cause* of their belief that the universe and human existence are meaningless. (ii) It is not in accordance with reason to reject this pessimistic belief on the grounds that scientific explanations are only provisional and incomplete and must be supplemented by religious ones.

In fact, it might be argued that the more clearly we understand the explanations given by science, the more we are driven to the conclusion that human life has no purpose and therefore no meaning. The science of astronomy teaches us that our earth was not specially created about 6,000 years ago, but evolved out of hot nebulae which previously had whirled aimlessly through space for countless ages. As they cooled, the sun and the planets formed. On one of these planets at a certain time the circumstances were propitious and life developed. But conditions will not remain favourable to life. When our solar system grows old, the sun will cool, our planet will be covered with ice, and all living creatures will eventually perish. Another theory has it that the sun will explode and that the heat generated will be so great that all organic life on earth will be destroyed. That is the comparatively short history and prospect of life on earth. Altogether it amounts to very little when compared with the endless history of the inanimate universe.

Biology teaches us that the species man was not specially created but is merely, in a long chain of evolutionary changes of forms of life, the last link, made in the likeness not of God but of nothing so much as an ape. The rest of the universe, whether animate or inanimate, instead of serving the ends of man, is at best indifferent, at worst savagely hostile. Evolution to whose operation the emergence of man is due is a ceaseless battle among members of different species, one species being gobbled up by another, only the fittest surviving. Far from being the gentlest and most highly moral, man is simply the creature best fitted to survive, the most efficient if not the most rapacious and insatiable killer. And in this unplanned, fortuitous, monstrous, savage world man is madly trying to snatch a few brief moments of joy, in the short intervals during which he is free from pain, sickness, persecution, war or famine until, finally, his life is snuffed out in death. Science has helped us to know and understand this world, but what purpose or meaning can it find in it?

Complaints such as these do not mean quite the same to everybody, but one thing, I think, they mean to most people: science shows life to be meaningless, because life is without purpose. The medieval world picture provided life with a purpose, hence medieval Christians could believe that life had a meaning. The scientific account of the world takes away life's purpose and with it its meaning.

There are, however, two quite different senses of "purpose." Which one is meant? Has science deprived human life of purpose in both senses? And if not, is it a harmless sense, in which human existence has been robbed of purpose? Could human existence still have meaning if it did not have a purpose in that sense?

What are the two senses? In the first and basic sense, purpose is normally attributed only to persons or their behaviour as in "Did you have a purpose in leaving the ignition on?" In the second sense, purpose is normally attributed only to things, as in "What is the purpose of that gadget you installed in the workshop?" The two uses are intimately connected. We cannot attribute a purpose to a thing without implying that someone did something, in the doing of which he had some purpose, namely, to bring about the thing with the purpose. Of course, *his* purpose is not identical with *its* purpose. In hiring labourers and engineers and buying materials and a site for a factory and the like, the entrepreneur's purpose, let us say, is to manufacture cars, but the purpose of cars is to serve as a means of transportation.

There are many things that a man may do, such as buying and selling, hiring labourers, ploughing, felling trees, and the like, which it is foolish, pointless, silly, perhaps crazy, to do if one has no purpose in doing them. A man who does these things without a purpose is engaging in inane, futile pursuits. Lives crammed full with such activities devoid of purpose are pointless, futile, worthless. Such lives may indeed be dismissed as meaningless. But it should also be perfectly clear that acceptance of the scientific world picture does not force us to regard our lives as being without a purpose in this sense. Science has not only not robbed us of any purpose which we had before, but it has furnished us with enormously greater power to achieve these purposes. Instead of praying for rain or a good harvest or offspring, we now use ice pellets, artificial manure, or artificial insemination.

By contrast, having or not having a purpose, in the other sense, is value neutral. We do not think more or less highly of a thing for having or not having a purpose. "Having a purpose," in this sense, confers no kudos, "being purposeless" carries no stigma. A row of trees growing near a farm may or may not have a purpose: it may or may not be a windbreak, may or may not have been planted or deliberately left standing there in order to prevent the wind from sweeping across the fields. We do not in any way disparage the trees if we say they have no purpose, but have just grown that way. They are as beautiful, made of as good wood, as valuable, as if they had a purpose. And, of course, they break the wind just as well. The same is true of living creatures. We do not disparage a dog when we say that it has no purpose, is not a sheep dog or a watch dog or a rabbiting dog, but just a dog that hangs around the house and is fed by us.

Man is in a different category, however. To attribute to a human being a purpose in that sense is not neutral, let alone complimentary: it is offensive. It is degrading for a man to be regarded as merely serving a purpose. If, at a garden party, I ask a man in livery, "What is your purpose?" I am insulting him. I might as well have asked, "What are you *for?*" Such questions reduce him to the level of a gadget, a domestic animal, or perhaps a slave. I imply that *we* allot to *him* the tasks, the goals, the aims which he is to pursue; that *his* wishes and desires and aspirations and purposes are to count for little or nothing. We are treating him, in Kant's phrase, merely as a means to our ends, not as an end in himself.

The Christian and the scientific world pictures do indeed differ fundamentally on this point. The latter robs man of a purpose in this sense. It sees him as a being with no purpose allotted to him by anyone but himself. It robs him of any goal, purpose, or destiny appointed for him by any outside agency. The Christian world picture, on the other hand, sees man as a creature, a divine artefact, something halfway between a robot (manufactured) and an animal (alive), a homunculus, or perhaps Frankenstein, made in God's laboratory, with a purpose or task assigned him by his Maker.

However, lack of purpose in this sense does not in any way detract from the meaningfulness of life. I suspect that many who reject the scientific outlook because it involves the loss of purpose of life, and therefore meaning, are guilty of a confusion between the two senses of "purpose" just distinguished. They confusedly think that if the scientific world picture is true, then their lives must be futile because that picture implies that man has no purpose given him from without. But this is muddled thinking, for, as has already been shown, pointlessness, is implied only by purposelessness in the other sense, which is not at all implied by the scientific picture of the world. These people mistakenly conclude that there can be no purpose *in* life because there is no purpose *of* life; that *men* cannot themselves adopt and achieve purposes because *man*, unlike a robot or a watch dog, is not a creature with a purpose.[15]

However, not all people taking this view are guilty of the above confusion. Some really hanker after a purpose of life in this sense. To some people the greatest attraction of the medieval world picture is the belief in an omnipotent, omniscient, and all-good Father, the view of themselves as His children who worship Him, of their proper attitude to what befalls them as submission, humility, resignation in His will, and what is often described as the "creaturely feeling."[16] All these are attitudes and feelings appropriate to a being that stands to another in the same sort of relation, though of course on a higher plane, in which a helpless child stands to his progenitor. Many regard the scientific picture of the world as cold, unsympathetic, unhomely, frightening, because it does not provide for any appropriate object of this creaturely attitude. There is nothing and no one in the world, as science depicts it, in which we can have faith or trust, on whose guidance we can rely, to whom we can turn for consolation, whom we can worship or submit to— except other human beings. This may be felt as a keen disappointment, because it shows that the meaning of life cannot lie in submission to His will, in acceptance of whatever may come, and in worship. But it does not imply that life can have *no* meaning. It merely implies that it must have a different meaning from that which it was thought to have. Just as it is a great shock for a child to find that he must stand on his own feet, that his father and mother no longer provide for him, so a person who has lost his faith in God must reconcile himself to the idea that he has to stand on his own feet, alone in the world except for whatever friends he may succeed in making.

But is not this to miss the point of the Christian teaching? Surely, Christianity can tell us the meaning of life because it tells us the grand and noble end for which God has created the universe and man. No human life, however pointless it may seem, is meaningless because in being part of God's plan, every life is assured of significance.

This point is well taken. It brings to light a distinction of some importance: we call a person's life meaningful not only if it is worthwhile, but also if he has helped in the realization of some plan or purpose transcending his own concerns. A person who knows he must soon die a painful death, can give significance to the remainder of his doomed life by, say, allowing certain experiments to be performed on him which will be useful in the fight against cancer. In a similar way, only on a much more elevated plane, every man, however humble or plagued by suffering, is guaranteed significance by the knowledge that he is participating in God's purpose.

What, then, on the Christian view, is the grand and noble end for which God has created the world and man in it? We can immediately dismiss that still popular opinion that the smallness of our intellect prevents us from stating meaningfully God's design in all its imposing grandeur.[17] This view cannot possibly be a satisfactory answer to our question about the purpose of life. It is, rather, a confession of the impossibility of giving one. If anyone thinks that this "answer" can remove the sting from the impression of meaninglessness and insignificance in our lives, he cannot have been stung very hard.

If, then, we turn to those who are willing to state God's purpose in so many words, we encounter two insuperable difficulties. The first is to find a purpose grand and noble enough to explain and justify the great amount of undeserved suffering in this world. We are inevitably filled by a sense of bathos when we read statements such as this: ". . . history is the scene of a divine purpose, in which the whole history is included, and Jesus of Nazareth is the centre of that purpose, both as revelation and as achievement, as the fulfilment of all that was past, and the promise of all that was to come. . . . If God is God, and if He made all these things, why did He do it? . . . God created a universe, bounded by the categories of time, space, matter, and causality, because He desired to enjoy for ever the society of a fellowship of finite and redeemed spirits which have made to His love the response of free and voluntary love and service."[18] Surely this cannot be right? Could a God be called omniscient, omnipotent, *and* all-good who, for the sake of satisfying his desire to be loved and served, imposes (or has to impose) on his creatures the amount of undeserved suffering we find in the world?

There is, however, a much more serious difficulty still: God's purpose in making the universe must be stated in terms of a dramatic story many of whose key incidents symbolize religious conceptions and practices which we no longer find morally acceptable: the imposition of a taboo on the fruits of a certain tree, the sin and guilt incurred by Adam and Eve by violating the taboo, the wrath of God,[19] the curse of Adam and Eve and all their progeny, the expulsion from Paradise, the Atonement by Christ's bloody sacrifice on the cross which makes available by way of the sacraments God's Grace by which alone men can be saved (thereby, incidentally, establishing the valuable power of priests to forgive sins and thus alone make possible a man's entry to heaven[20]), Judgment Day on which the sheep are separated from the goats and the latter condemned to eternal torment in hell-fire.

Obviously it is much more difficult to formulate a purpose for creating the universe and man that will justify the enormous amount of undeserved suffering which we find around us, if that story has to be fitted in as well. For now we have to explain not only why an omnipotent, omniscient, and all-good God should create such a universe and such a man, but also why, foreseeing every move of the feeble, weak-willed, ignorant, and covetous creature to be created, He should nevertheless have created him and, having done so, should be incensed and outraged by man's sin, and why He should deem it necessary to sacrifice His own son on the cross to atone for this sin which was, after all, only a disobedience of one of his commands, and why this atonement and consequent redemption could not have been followed by man's return to Paradise—particularly of those innocent children who had not yet sinned—and why, on Judgment Day, this merciful God should condemn some to eternal torment.[21] It is not surprising that in the face of these and other difficulties, we find, again and again, a return to the first view: that God's purpose cannot meaningfully be stated.

It will perhaps be objected that no Christian to-day believes in the dramatic history of the world as I have presented it. But this is not so. It is the official doctrine of the Roman Catholic, the Greek Orthodox, and a large section of the Anglican Church.[22] Nor does Protestantism substantially alter this picture. In fact, by insisting on "Justification by Faith Alone" and by rejecting the ritualistic, magical character of the medieval Catholic interpretation of certain elements in the Christian religion, such as indulgences, the sacraments, and prayer, while at the same time insisting on the necessity of grace, Protestantism undermined the moral element in medieval Christianity expressed in the Catholics' emphasis on personal merit.[23] Protestantism, by harking back to St. Augustine, who clearly realized the incompatibility of grace and personal merit,[24] opened the way for Calvin's doctrine of Predestination (the intellectual parent of that form of rigid determinism which is usually blamed on science) and Salvation or Condemnation from all eternity.[25] Since Roman Catholics, Lutherans, Calvinists, Presbyterians and Baptists officially subscribe to the views just outlined, one can justifiably claim that the overwhelming majority of professing Christians hold or ought to hold them.

It might still be objected that the best and most modern views are wholly different. I have not the necessary knowledge to pronounce on the accuracy of this claim. It may well be true that the best and most modern views are such as Professor Braithwaite's who maintains that Christianity is, roughly speaking, "morality plus stories," where the stories are intended merely to make the strict moral teaching both more easily understandable and more palatable.[26] Or it may be that one or the other of the modern views on the nature and importance of the dramatic story told in the sacred Scriptures is the best. My reply is that even if it is true, it does not prove what I wish to disprove, that one can extract a sensible answer to our question, "What is the meaning of life?" from the kind of story subscribed to by the overwhelming majority of Christians, who would, moreover, reject any such modernist interpretation at least as indignantly as the scientific account. Moreover, though such views can perhaps avoid some of the worst absurdities of the traditional story, they are hardly in a much better position to state the purpose for which God has created the universe and man in it, because they cannot overcome the difficulty of finding a purpose grand and noble enough to justify the enormous amount of undeserved suffering in the world.

Let us, however, for argument's sake, waive all these objections. There remains one fundamental hurdle which no form of Christianity can overcome: the fact that it demands of man a morally repugnant attitude towards the universe. It is now very widely held[27] that the basic element of the Christian religion is an attitude of worship towards a being supremely worthy of being worshipped and that it is religious feelings and experiences which apprise their owner of such a being and which inspire in him the knowledge or the feeling of complete dependence, awe, worship, mystery, and self-abasement. There is, in other words, a bi-polarity (the famous "I-Thou relationship") in which the object, "the wholly-other," is exalted whereas the subject is abased to the limit. Rudolf Otto has called this the "creature-feeling"[28] and he quotes as an expression of it, Abraham's words when venturing to plead for the men of Sodom: "Behold now, I have taken upon me to speak unto the Lord, which am but dust and ashes" (Genesis XVIII.27). Christianity thus demands of men an attitude inconsistent with one of the presuppositions of morality: that man is not wholly dependent on something else, that man has free will, that man is in principle capable of responsibility. We have seen that the concept of grace is the Christian attempt to reconcile the claim of total dependence and the claim of individual responsibility (partial independence), and it is obvious that such attempts must fail. We may dismiss certain doctrines, such as the doctrine of original sin or the doctrine of eternal hellfire or the doctrine that there can be no salvation outside the Church as extravagant and peripheral, but we cannot reject the doctrine of total dependence without rejecting the characteristically Christian attitude as such.

3. THE MEANING OF LIFE

Perhaps some of you will have felt that I have been shirking the real problem. To many people the crux of the matter seems as follows. How can there be any meaning in our life if it ends in death? What meaning can there be in it that our inevitable death does not destroy? How can our existence be meaningful if there is no after-life in which perfect justice is meted out? How can life have any meaning if all it holds out to us are a few miserable earthly pleasures and even these to be enjoyed only rarely and for such a piteously short time?

I believe this is the point which exercises most people most deeply. Kirilov, in Dostoevsky's novel, *The Possessed*, claims, just before committing suicide, that as soon as we realize that there is no God, we cannot live any longer, we must put an end to our lives. One of the reasons which he gives is that when we discover that there is no paradise, we have nothing to live for.

". . . there was a day on earth, and in the middle of the earth were three crosses. One on the cross had such faith that He said to another, 'To-day thou shalt be with me in paradise.' The day came to an end, both died, and they went, but they found neither paradise nor resurrection. The saying did not come true. Listen: that man was the highest of all on earth. . . . There has never been any one like Him before or since, and never will be. . . . And if that is so, if the laws of Nature did not spare even *Him,* and made even Him live in the midst of lies and die for a lie, then the whole planet is a lie and is based on a lie and a stupid mockery. So the very laws of the planet are a lie and a farce of the devil. What, then, is there to live for?"[29] And Tolstoy, too, was nearly driven to suicide when he came to doubt the existence of God and an after-life.[30] And this is true of many.

What, then, is it that inclines us to think that if life is to have a meaning, there would be an after-life? It is this. The Christian world view contains the following three propositions. The first is that since the Fall, God's curse of Adam and Eve, and the expulsion from Paradise, life on earth for mankind has not been worth while, but a vale of tears, one long chain of misery, suffering, unhappiness, and injustice. The second is that a perfect after-life is awaiting us after the death of the body. The third is that we can enter this perfect life only on certain conditions, among which is also the condition of enduring our earthly existence to its bitter end. In this way, our earthly existence which, in itself, would not (at least for many people if not all) be worth living, acquires meaning and significance: only if we endure it, can we gain admission to the realm of the blessed.

It might be doubted whether this view is still held to-day. However, there can be no doubt that even to-day we all imbibe a good deal of this view with our earliest education. In sermons, the contrast between the perfect life of the blessed and our life of sorrow and drudgery is frequently driven home and we hear it again and again that Christianity has a message of hope and consolation for all those "who are weary and heavy laden."[31]

It is not surprising, then, that when the implications of the scientific world picture begin to sink in, when we come to have doubts about the existence of God and another life, we are bitterly disappointed. For if there is no afterlife, then all we are left is our earthly life which we have come to regard as a necessary evil, the painful fee of admission to the land of eternal bliss. But if there is no eternal bliss to come and if this hell on earth is all, why hang on till the horrible end?

Our disappointment therefore arises out of these two propositions, that the earthly life is not worth living, and that there is another perfect life of eternal happiness and joy which we may enter upon if we satisfy certain conditions. We can regard our lives as meaningful, if we believe both. We cannot regard them as meaningful if we believe merely the first and not the second. It seems to me inevitable that people who are taught something of the history of science, will have serious doubts about the second. If they cannot overcome these, as many will be unable to do, then they must either accept the sad view that their life is meaningless or they must abandon the first proposition: that this earthly life is not worth living. They must find the meaning of their life in this earthly existence. But is this possible?

A moment's examination will show us that the Christian evaluation of our earthly life as worthless, which we accept in our moments of pessimism and dissatisfaction, is not one that we normally accept. Consider only the question of murder and suicide. On the Christian view, other things being equal, the most kindly thing to do would be for every one of us to kill as many of our friends and dear ones as still have the misfortune to be alive, and then to commit suicide without delay, for every moment spent in this life is wasted. On the Christian view, God has not made it that easy for us. He has forbidden us to hasten others or ourselves into the next life. Our bodies are his private property and must be allowed to wear themselves out in the way decided by Him, however painful and horrible that may be. We are, as it were, driving a burning car. There is only one way out, to jump clear and let it hurtle to destruction. But the owner of the car has forbidden it on pain of eternal tortures worse than burning. And so we do better to burn to death inside.

On this view, murder is a less serious wrong than suicide. For murder can always be confessed and repented and therefore forgiven, suicide cannot–unless we allow the ingenious way out chosen by the heroine of Graham Greene's play, *The Living Room*, who swallows a slow but deadly poison and, while awaiting its taking effect, repents having taken it. Murder, on the other hand, is not so serious because, in the first place, it need not rob the victim of anything but the last lap of his march in the vale of tears, and, in the second place, it can always be forgiven. Hamlet, it will be remembered, refrains from killing his uncle during the latter's prayers because, as a true Christian, he believes that killing his uncle at that point, when the latter has purified his soul by repentance, would merely be doing him a good turn, for murder at such a time would simply despatch him to undeserved and everlasting happiness.

These views strike us as odd, to say the least. They are the logical consequence of the official medieval evaluation of this our earthly existence. If this life is not worth living, then taking it is not robbing the person concerned of much. The only thing wrong with it is the damage to God's property, which is the same both in the case of murder and suicide. We do not take this view at all. Our view, on the contrary, is that murder is the most serious wrong because it consists in taking away from some one else against his will his most precious possession, his life. For this reason, when a person suffering from an incurable disease asks to be killed, the mercy killing of such a person is regarded as a much less serious crime than murder because, in such a case, the killer is not robbing the other of a good against his will. Suicide is not regarded as a real crime at all, for we take the view that a person can do with his own possessions what he likes.

However, from the fact that these are our normal opinions, we can infer nothing about their truth. After all, we could easily be mistaken. Whether life is or is not worthwhile, is a value judgment. Perhaps all this is merely a matter of opinion or taste. Perhaps no objective answer can be given. Fortunately, we need not enter deeply into these difficult and controversial questions. It is quite easy to show that the medieval evaluation of earthly life is based on a misguided procedure.

Let us remind ourselves briefly of how we arrive at our value judgments. When we determine the merits of students, meals, tennis players, bulls, or bathing belles, we do so on the basis of some criteria and some standard or norm. Criteria and standards notoriously vary from field to field and even from case to case. But that does not mean that we have *no* idea about what are the appropriate criteria or standards to use. It would not be fitting to apply the criteria for judging bulls to the judgment of students or bathing belles. They score on quite different points. And even where the same criteria are appropriate as in the judgment of students enrolled in different schools and universities, the standards will vary from one institution to another. Pupils who would only just pass in one, would perhaps obtain honours in another. The higher the standard applied, the lower the marks, that is, the merit conceded to the candidate.

The same procedure is applicable also in the evaluation of a life. We examine it on the basis of certain criteria and standards. The medieval Christian view uses the criteria of the ordinary man: a life is judged by what the person concerned can get out of it: the balance of happiness over unhappiness, pleasure over pain, bliss over suffering. Our earthly life is judged not worthwhile because it contains much unhappiness, pain, and suffering, little happiness, pleasure, and bliss. The next life is judged worthwhile because it provides eternal bliss and no suffering.

Armed with these criteria, we can compare the life of this man and that, and judge which is more worthwhile, which has a greater balance of bliss over suffering. But criteria alone enable us merely to make comparative judgments of value, not absolute ones. We can say which is more and which is less worthwhile, but we cannot say which is worthwhile and which is not. In order to determine the latter, we must introduce a standard. But what standard ought we to choose?

Ordinarily, the standard we employ is the average of the kind. We call a man and a tree tall if they are well above the average of their kind. We do not say that Jones is a short man because he is shorter than a tree. We do not judge a boy a bad student because his answer to a question in the Leaving Examination is much worse than that given in reply to the same question by a young man sitting for his finals for the Bachelor's degree.

The same principles must apply to judging lives. When we ask whether a given life was or was not worthwhile, then we must take into consideration the range of worthwhileness which ordinary lives normally cover. Our end poles of the scale must be the best possible and the worst possible life that one finds. A good and worthwhile life is one that is well above average. A bad one is one well below.

The Christian evaluation of earthly lives is misguided because it adopts a quite unjustifiably high standard. Christianity singles out the major shortcomings of our earthly existence: there is not enough happiness; there is too much suffering; the good and bad points are quite unequally and unfairly distributed; the underprivileged and underendowed do not get adequate compensation; it lasts only a short time. It then quite accurately depicts the perfect or ideal life as that which does not have any of these shortcomings. Its next step is to promise the believer that he will be able to enjoy this perfect life later on. And then it adopts as its standard of judgment the perfect life, dismissing as inadequate anything that falls short of it. Having dismissed earthly life as miserable, it further damns it by characterizing most of the pleasures of which earthly existence allows as bestial, gross, vile, and sinful, or alternatively as not really pleasurable.

This procedure is as illegitimate as if I were to refuse to call anything tall unless it is infinitely tall, or anything beautiful unless it is perfectly flawless, or any one strong unless he is omnipotent. Even if it were true that there is available to us an after-life which is flawless and perfect, it would still not be legitimate to judge earthly lives by this standard. We do not fail every candidate who is not an Einstein. And if we do not believe in an after-life, we must of course use ordinary earthly standards.

I have so far only spoken of the worthwhileness, only of what a person can get out of a life. There are other kinds of appraisal. Clearly, we evaluate people's lives not merely from the point of view of what they yield to the persons that lead them, but also from that of other men on whom these lives have impinged. We judge a life more significant if the person has contributed to the happiness of others, whether directly by what he did for others, or by the plans, discoveries, inventions, and work he performed. Many lives that hold little in the way of pleasure or happiness for its owner are highly significant and valuable, deserve admiration and respect on account of the contributions made.

It is now quite clear that death is simply irrelevant. If life can be worthwhile at all, then it can be so even though it be short. And if it is not worthwhile at all, then an eternity of it is simply a nightmare. It may be sad that we have to leave this beautiful world, but it is so only if and because it is beautiful. And it is no less beautiful for coming to an end. I rather suspect that an eternity of it might make us less appreciative, and in the end it would be tedious.

It will perhaps be objected now that I have not really demonstrated that life has a meaning, but merely that it can be worthwhile or have value. It must be admitted that there is a perfectly natural interpretation of the question, "What is the meaning of life?" on which my view actually proves that life has no meaning. I mean the interpretation discussed in Section 2 of this lecture, where I attempted to show that, if we accept the explanations of natural science, we cannot believe that living organisms have appeared on earth in accordance with the deliberate plan of some intelligent being. Hence, on this view, life cannot be said to have a purpose, in the sense in which man-made things have a purpose. Hence it cannot be said to have a meaning or significance in that sense.

However, this conclusion is innocuous. People are disconcerted by the thought that *life as such* has no meaning in that sense only because they very naturally think it entails that no individual life can have meaning either. They naturally assume that *this* life or *that* can have meaning only if *life as such* has meaning. But it should by now be clear that your life and mine may or may not have meaning (in one sense) even if life as such has none (in the other). Of course, it follows from this that your life may have meaning while mine has not. The Christian view guarantees a meaning (in one sense) to every life, the scientific view does not (in any sense). By relating the question of the meaningfulness of life to the particular circumstances of an individual's existence, the scientific view leaves it an open question whether an individual's life has meaning or not. It is, however, clear that the latter is the important sense of "having a meaning." Christians, too, must feel that their life is wasted and meaningless if they have not achieved salvation. To know that even such lost lives have a meaning in another sense is no consolation to them: What matters is not that life should have a guaranteed meaning, whatever happens here or here-after, but that, by luck (Grace) or the right temperament and attitude (Faith) or a judicious life (Works) a person should make the most of his life.

"But here lies the rub," it will be said. "Surely, it makes all the difference whether there is an after-life. This is where morality comes in." It would be a mistake to believe that. Morality is not the meting out of punishment and reward. To be moral is to refrain from doing to others what, if they followed reason, they would not do to themselves, and to do for others what, if they followed reason, they would want to have done. It is, roughly speaking, to recognize that others, too, have a right to a worthwhile life. Being moral does not make one's own life worthwhile, it helps others to make theirs so.

4. CONCLUSION

I have tried to establish three points: (i) that scientific explanations render their explicanda as intelligible as pre-scientific explanations; they differ from the latter only in that, having testable implications and being more precisely formulated, their truth or falsity can be determined with a high degree of probability; (ii) that science does not rob human life of purpose, in the only sense that matters, but, on the contrary, renders many more of our purposes capable of realization; (iii) that common sense, the Christian world view, and the scientific approach agree on the criteria but differ on the standard to be employed in the evaluation of human lives; judging human lives by the standards of perfection, as Christians do, is unjustified; if we abandon this excessively high standard and replace it by an everyday one, we have no longer any reason for dismissing earthly existence as not worthwhile.

On the basis of these three points I have attempted to explain why so many people come to the conclusion that human existence is meaningless and to show that this conclusion is false. In my opinion, this pessimism rests on a combination of two beliefs, both partly true and partly false: the belief that the meaningfulness of life depends on the satisfaction of at least three conditions, and the belief that this universe satisfies none of them. The conditions are, first, that the universe is intelligible, second, that life has a purpose, and third, that all men's hopes and desires can ultimately be satisfied. It seemed to medieval Christians and it seems to many Christians today that Christianity offers a picture of the world which can meet these conditions. To many Christians and non-Christians alike it seems that the scientific world picture is incompatible with that of Christianity, therefore with the view that these three conditions are met, therefore with the view that life has a meaning. Hence they feel that they are confronted by the dilemma of accepting either a world picture incompatible with the discoveries of science or the view that life is meaningless.

I have attempted to show that the dilemma is unreal because life can be meaningful even if not all of these conditions are met. My main conclusion, therefore, is that acceptance of the scientific world picture provides no reason for saying that life is meaningless, but on the contrary every reason for saying that there are many lives which are meaningful and significant. My subsidiary conclusion is that one of the reasons frequently offered for retaining the Christian world picture, namely, that its acceptance gives us a guarantee of a meaning for human existence, is unsound. We can see that our lives can have a meaning even if we abandon it and adopt the scientific world picture instead. I have, moreover, mentioned several reasons for rejecting the Christian world picture: (i) the biblical explanations of the details of our universe are often simply false; (ii) the so-called explanations of the whole universe are incomprehensible or absurd; (iii) Christianity's low evaluation of earthly existence (which is the main cause of the belief in the meaninglessness of life) rests on the use of an unjustifiably high standard of judgment.

NOTES

1. Count Leo Tolstoy, "A Confession," reprinted in *A Confession, The Gospel in Brief, and What I Believe*, No. 229, The World's Classics (London: Geoffrey Cumberlege, 1940).

2. See, e.g., Edwyn Bevan, *Christianity*, pp. 211–227. See also H. J. Paton, *The Modern Predicament* (London: George Allen and Unwin Ltd., 1955), pp. 103–116, 374.

3. See for instance, L. E. Elliott-Binns, *The Development of English Theology in the Later Nineteenth Century* (London: Longmans, Green & Co., 1952), pp. 30–33.

4. See "Phaedo" (*Five Dialogues* by Plato, Everyman's Library No. 456), para. 99, p. 189.

5. "On the Ultimate Origination of Things" (*The Philosophical Writings of Leibniz*, Everyman's Library No. 905), p. 32.

6. See "Monadology" (*The Philosophical Writings of Leibniz*, Everyman's Library No. 905), para. 32–38, pp. 8–10.

7. To borrow the useful term coined by Professor D. A. T. Gasking of Melbourne University.

8. See, e.g., J. J. C. Smart, "The Existence of God," reprinted in *New Essays in Philosophical Theology*, ed. by A. Flew and A. MacIntyre (London: S.C.M. Press, 1957), pp. 35–39.

9. That creation out of nothing is not a clarificatory notion becomes obvious when we learn that "in the philosophical sense" it does not imply creation at a particular time. The universe could be regarded as a creation out of nothing even if it had no beginning. See, e.g., E. Gilson, *The Christian Philosophy of St. Thomas Aquinas* (London: Victor Gollancz Ltd. 1957), pp. 147–155 and E. L. Mascall, *Via Media* (London: Longmans, Green & Co., 1956), pp. 28 ff.

10. In what follows I have drawn heavily on the work of Ryle and Toulmin. See for instance G. Ryle, *The Concept of Mind* (London: Hutchinson's University Library, 1949), pp. 56–60 etc. and his article, "If, So, and Because," in *Philosophical Analysis* by Max Black, and S. E. Toulmin, *Introduction to the Philosophy of Science* (London: Hutchinson's University Library, 1953).

11. See above, p. 109 points (a)–(c).

12. L. Wittgenstein, *Tractatus Logico-Philosophicus* (London: Routledge & Kegan Paul Ltd., 1922), Sect. 6.44–6.45.

13. Op. cit. p. 46. See also Rudolf Otto, *The Idea of the Holy* (London: Geoffrey Cumberlege, 1952), esp. pp. 9–29.

14. Contemporary theologians would admit that it cannot be proved that the universe must have had a beginning. They would admit that we know it only through revelation. (See footnote No. 9.) I take it more or less for granted that Kant's attempted proof of the Thesis in his First Antinomy of Reason [Immanuel Kant's *Critique of Pure Reason*, trans. by Norman Kemp Smith (London: Macmillan and Co. Ltd., 1950), pp. 396–402] is invalid. It rests upon a premise which is false: that the completion of the infinite series of succession of states, which must have preceded the present state if the world has had no beginning, is logically impossible. We can persuade ourselves to think that this infinite series is logically impossible if we insist that it is a series which must, literally, be *completed*. For the verb "to complete," as normally used, implies an activity which, in turn, implies an agent who must have *begun* the activity at some time. If an infinite series is a whole that must be *completed* then, indeed, the world must have had a beginning. But that is precisely the question at issue. If we say, as Kant does at first, "that an eternity has elapsed," we do not feel the same impossibility. It is only when we take seriously the words "synthesis" and "completion," both of which suggest or imply "work" or "activity" and therefore "beginning," that it seems necessary that an infinity of successive states cannot have elapsed. [See also R. Crawshay-Williams, *Methods and Criteria of Reasoning* (London: Routledge & Kegan Paul, 1957), App. iv.]

15. See, e.g., "Is Life Worth Living?" B.B.C. Talk by the Rev. John Sutherland Bonnell in *Asking Them Questions*, Third Series, ed. by R. S. Wright (London: Geoffrey Cumberlege, 1950).

16. See, e.g., Rudolf Otto, *The Idea of the Holy*, pp. 9–11. See also C. A. Campbell, *On Selfhood and Godhood* (London: George Allen & Unwin Ltd., 1957), p. 246, and H. J. Paton, *The Modern Predicament*, pp. 69–71.

17. For a discussion of this issue, see the eighteenth century controversy between Deists and Theists, for instance, in Sir Leslie Stephen's *History of English Thought in the Eighteenth Century* (London: Smith, Elder & Co., 1902), pp. 112–119 and pp. 134–163. See also the attacks by Toland and Tindal on "the mysterious" in *Christianity not Mysterious and Christianity as Old as the Creation, or the Gospel a Republication of the Religion of Nature*, resp., parts of which are reprinted in Henry Bettenson's *Doctrines of the Christian Church*, pp. 426–431. For modern views maintaining that mysteriousness is an essential element in religion, see Rudolf Otto, *The Idea of the Holy*, esp. pp. 25–40, and most recently M. B. Foster, *Mystery and Philosophy* (London: S.C.M. Press, 1957), esp. Chs. IV. and VI. For the view that statements about God must be nonsensical or absurd, see, e.g., H. J. Paton, op. cit. pp. 119–120, 367–369. See also "Theology and Falsification" in *New Essays in Philosophical Theology*, ed. by A. Flew and A. MacIntyre (London: S.C.M. Press, 1955), pp. 96–131; also N. McPherson, "Religion as the Inexpressible," ibid., esp. pp. 137–143.

18. Stephen Neill, *Christian Faith To-day* (London: Penguin Books, 1955), pp. 240–241.

19. It is difficult to feel the magnitude of this first sin unless one takes seriously the words "Behold, the man has eaten of the fruit of the tree of knowledge of good and evil, and is become as one of us; and now, may he not put forth his hand, and take also of the tree of life, and eat, and live for ever?" Genesis iii, 22.

20. See in this connection the pastoral letter of 2nd February, 1905, by Johannes Katschtaler, Prince Bishop of Salzburg on the honour due to priests, contained in *Quellen zur Geschichte des Papsttums*, by Mirbt pp. 497–499, translated and reprinted in *The Protestant Tradition*, by J. S. Whale (Cambridge: University Press, 1955), pp. 259–262.

21. How impossible it is to make sense of this story has been demonstrated beyond any doubt by Tolstoy in his famous "Conclusion of A Criticism of Dogmatic Theology," reprinted in *A Confession, The Gospel in Brief, and What I Believe.*

22. See "The Nicene Creed," "The Tridentine Profession of Faith," "The Syllabus of Errors," reprinted in *Documents of the Christian Church*, pp. 34, 373, and 380 resp.

23. See, e.g., J. S. Whale, *The Protestant Tradition*, Ch. IV., esp. pp. 48–56.

24. See ibid., pp. 61 ff.

25. See "The Confession of Augsburg" esp. Articles II., IV., XVIII., XIX., XX.; "Christianae Religionis Institutio," "The Westminster Confession of Faith," esp. Articles III., VI., IX., X., XI., XVI., XVII.; "The Baptist Confession of Faith," esp. Articles III., XXI., XXIII., reprinted in *Documents of the Christian Church*, pp. 294 ff., 298 ff., 344 ff., 349 ff.

26. See, e.g., his *An Empiricist's View of the Nature of Religious Belief* (Eddington Memorial Lecture).

27. See, e.g., the two series of Gifford Lectures most recently published: *The Modern Predicament* by H. J. Paton (London: George Allen & Unwin Ltd., 1955), pp. 69 ff., and *On Selfhood and Godhood* by C. A. Campbell (London: George Allen & Unwin Ltd., 1957), pp. 231–250.

28. Rudolf Otto, *The Idea of the Holy*, p. 9.

29. Fyodor Dostoyevsky, *The Devils* (London: The Penguin Classics, 1953), pp. 613–614.

30. Leo Tolstoy, *A Confession, The Gospel in Brief, and What I Believe*, The World's Classics, p. 24.

31. See, for instance, J. S. Whale, *Christian Doctrine*, pp. 171, 176–178, etc. See also Stephen Neill, *Christian Faith To-day*, p. 241.

CHAPTER 12   PAUL EDWARDS

The Meaning and Value of Life

To the questions "Is human life ever worthwhile?" and "Does (or can) human life have any meaning?" many religious thinkers have offered affirmative answers with the proviso that these answers would not be justified unless two of the basic propositions of most Western religions were true—that human life is part of a divinely ordained cosmic scheme and that after death at least some human beings will be rewarded with eternal bliss. Thus, commenting on Bertrand Russell's statement that not only must each individual human life come to an end but that life in general will eventually die out, C. H. D. Clark contrasts this "doctrine of despair" with the beauty of the Christian scheme. "If we are asked to believe that all our striving is without final consequence," then "life is meaningless and it scarcely matters how we live if all will end in the dust of death." According to Christianity, on the other hand, "each action has vital significance." Clark assures us that "God's grand design is life eternal for those who walk in the steps of Christ. Here is the one grand incentive to good living. . . . As life is seen to have purpose and meaning, men find release from despair and the fear of death" (*Christianity and Bertrand Russell*, p. 30). In a similar vein, the Jewish existentialist Emil Fackenheim claims that "whatever meaning life acquires" is derived from the encounter between God and man. The meaning thus conferred upon human life "cannot be understood in terms of some finite human purpose, supposedly more ultimate than the meeting itself. For what could be more ultimate than the Presence of God?" It is true that God is not always "near," but "times of Divine farness" are by no means devoid of meaning. "Times of Divine nearness do not light up themselves alone. Their meaning extends over all of life." There is a "dialectic between Divine nearness and Divine farness," and it points to "an eschatological future in which it is overcome" ("Judaism and the Meaning of Life").

Among unbelievers not a few maintain that life can be worthwhile and have meaning in some humanly important sense even if the religious world view is rejected. Others, however, agree with the religious theorists that our two questions must be given negative answers if there is no God and if death means personal annihilation. Having rejected the claims of religion, they therefore conclude that life is not worthwhile and that it is devoid of meaning. These writers, to whom we shall refer here as "pessimists," do not present their judgments as being merely expressions of certain moods or feelings but as conclusions that are in some sense objectively warranted. They offer reasons for their conclusions and imply that anybody reaching a contradictory conclusion is mistaken or irrational. Most pessimists do not make any clear separation between the statements that life is not worthwhile and that life is without meaning. They usually speak of the "futility" or the "vanity" of life, and presumably they mean by this both that life is not worth living and that it has no meaning. For the time being we, too, shall treat these statements as if they were equivalent. However, later we shall see that in certain contexts it becomes important to distinguish between them.

Our main concern in this article will be to appraise pessimism as just defined. We shall not discuss either the question whether life is part of a divinely ordained plan or the question whether we survive our bodily death. Our question will be whether the pessimistic conclusions are justified if belief in God and immortality are rejected.

SCHOPENHAUER'S ARGUMENTS

Let us begin with a study of the arguments offered by the pessimists, remembering that many of these are indirectly endorsed by religious apologists. The most systematic and probably the most influential, though in fact not the gloomiest, of the pessimists was Schopenhauer. The world, he wrote, is something which ought not to exist: the truth is that "we have not to rejoice but rather to mourn at the existence of the world; that its non-existence would be preferable to its existence; that it is something which ought not to be." It is absurd to speak of life as a gift, as so many philosophers and thoughtless people have done. "It is evident that everyone would have declined such a gift if he could have seen it and tested it beforehand." To those who assure us that life is only a lesson, we are entitled to reply: "For this very reason I wish I had been left in the peace of the all-sufficient nothing, where I would have no need of lessons or of anything else" (*The World as Will and Idea*, Vol. III, p. 390).

Schopenhauer offers numerous arguments for his conclusion. Some of these are purely metaphysical and are based on his particular system. Others, however, are of a more empirical character and are logically independent of his brand of metaphysical voluntarism. Happiness, according to Schopenhauer, is unobtainable for the vast majority of mankind. "Everything in life shows that earthly happiness is destined to be frustrated or recognized as illusion." People either fail to achieve the ends they are striving for or else they do achieve them only to find them grossly disappointing. But as soon as a man discovers that a particular goal was not really worth pursuing, his eye is set on a new one and the same illusory quest begins all over again. Happiness, accordingly, always lies in the future or in the past, and "the present may be compared to a small dark cloud which the wind drives over the sunny plain: before and behind it all is bright, only it itself always casts a shadow. The present is therefore always insufficient; but the future is uncertain, and the past is irrevocable" (ibid., p. 383). Men in general, except for those sufficiently rational to become totally resigned, are constantly deluded—"now by hope, now by what was hoped for." They are taken in by "the enchantment of distance," which shows them "paradises." These paradises, however, vanish like "optical illusions when we have allowed ourselves to be mocked by them." The "fearful envy" excited in most men by the thought that somebody else is genuinely happy shows how unhappy they really are, whatever they pretend to others or to themselves. It is only "because they feel themselves unhappy" that "men cannot endure the sight of one whom they imagine happy."

On occasions Schopenhauer is ready to concede that some few human beings really do achieve "comparative" happiness, but this is not of any great consequence. For aside from being "rare exceptions," these happy people are really like "decoy birds"—they represent a possibility which must exist in order to lure the rest of mankind into a false sense of hope. Moreover, happiness, insofar as it exists at all, is a purely "negative" reality. We do not become aware of the greatest blessings of life—health, youth, and freedom—until we have lost them. What is called pleasure or satisfaction is merely the absence of craving or pain. But craving and pain are positive. As for the few happy days of our life—if there are any—we notice them only "after they have given place to unhappy ones."

Schopenhauer not infrequently lapsed from his doctrine of the "negative" nature of happiness and pleasure into the more common view that their status is just as "positive" as that of unhappiness and pain. But he had additional arguments which do not in any way depend on the theory that happiness and pleasure are negative. Perhaps the most important of these is the argument from the "perishableness" of all good things and the ultimate extinction of all our hopes and achievements in death. All our pleasures and joys "disappear in our hands, and we afterwards ask astonished where they have gone." Moreover, a joy which no longer exists does not "count"—it counts as little as if it had never been experienced at all:

> That which *has been* exists no more; it exists as little as that which has *never* been. But of everything that exists you may say, in the next moment, that it has been. Hence something of great importance in our past is inferior to something of little importance in our present, in that the latter is a *reality,* and related to the former as something to nothing. ("The Vanity of Existence," in *The Will to Live,* p. 229)

Some people have inferred from this that the enjoyment of the present should be "the supreme object of life." This is fallacious; for "that which in the next moment exists no more, and vanishes utterly, like a dream, can never be worth a serious effort."

The final "judgment of nature" is destruction by death. This is "the last proof" that life is a "false path," that all man's wishing is "a perversity," and that "nothing at all is worth our striving, our efforts and struggles." The conclusion is inescapable: "All good things are vanity, the world in all its ends bankrupt, and life a business which does not cover its expenses" (*The World as Will and Idea*, Vol. III, p. 383).

THE POINTLESSNESS OF IT ALL

Some of Schopenhauer's arguments can probably be dismissed as the fantasies of a lonely and embittered man who was filled with contempt for mankind and who was singularly incapable of either love or friendship. His own misery, it may be plausibly said, made Schopenhauer overestimate the unhappiness of human beings. It is frequently, but not universally, true that what is hoped for is found disappointing when it is attained, and while "fearful envy" of other people's successes is common enough, real sympathy and generosity are not quite so rare as Schopenhauer made them out to be. Furthermore, his doctrine that pleasure is negative while pain is positive, insofar as one can attach any clear meaning to it, seems glaringly false. To this it should be added, however, that some of Schopenhauer's arguments are far from idiosyncratic and that substantially the same conclusions have been endorsed by men who were neither lonely nor embittered and who did not, as far as one can judge, lack the gift of love or friendship.

Darrow

Clarence Darrow, one of the most compassionate men who ever lived, also concluded that life was an "awful joke." Like Schopenhauer, Darrow offered as one of his reasons the apparent aimlessness of all that happens. "This weary old world goes on, begetting, with birth and with living and with death," he remarked in his moving plea for the boy-murderers Loeb and Leopold, "and all of it is blind from the beginning to the end" (*Clarence Darrow—Attorney for the Damned*, A. Weinberg, ed., New York, 1957). Elsewhere he wrote: "Life is like a ship on the sea, tossed by every wave and by every wind; a ship headed for no port and no harbor, with no rudder, no compass, no pilot; simply floating for a time, then lost in the waves" ("Is Life Worth Living?," p. 43). In addition to the aimlessness of life and the universe, there is the fact of death. "I love my friends," wrote Darrow, "but they all must come to a tragic end." Death is more terrible the more one is attached to things in the world. Life, he concludes, is "not worth while," and he adds (somewhat inconsistently, in view of what he had said earlier) that "it is an unpleasant interruption of nothing, and the best thing you can say of it is that it does not last long" ("Is the Human Race Getting Anywhere?," p. 53).

Tolstoy

Tolstoy, unlike Darrow, eventually came to believe in Christianity, or at least in his own idiosyncratic version of Christianity, but for a number of years the only position for which he could see any rational justification was an extreme form of pessimism. During that period (and there is reason to believe that in spite of his later protestations to the contrary, his feelings on this subject never basically changed) Tolstoy was utterly overwhelmed by the thought of his death and the death of those he cared for and, generally, by the transitory nature of all human achievements. "Today or tomorrow," he wrote in "A Confession," "sickness and death will come to those I love or to me; nothing will remain but stench and worms. Sooner or later my affairs, whatever they may be, will be forgotten, and I shall not exist. Then why go on making any effort?" Tolstoy likened the fate of man to that of the traveler in the Eastern tale who, pursued by an enraged beast, seeks refuge in a dry well. At the bottom of the well he sees a dragon that has opened its jaws to swallow him. To escape the enraged beast above and the dragon below, he holds onto a twig that is growing in a crack in the well. As he looks around he notices that two mice are gnawing at the stem of the twig. He realizes that very soon the twig will snap and he will fall to his doom, but at the same time he sees some drops of honey on the leaves of the branch and reaches out with his tongue to lick them. "So I too clung to the twig of life, knowing that the dragon of death was inevitably awaiting me, ready to tear me to pieces. . . . I tried to lick the honey which formerly consoled me, but the honey no longer gave me pleasure. . . . I only saw the unescapable dragon and the mice, and I could not tear my gaze from them. And this is not a fable but the real unanswerable truth."

These considerations, according to Tolstoy, inevitably lead to the conclusion that life is a "stupid fraud," that no "reasonable meaning" can be given to a single action or to a whole life. To the questions "What is it for?" "What then?" "Why should I live?" the answer is "Nothing can come of it," "Nothing is worth doing," "Life is not worthwhile."

What ways out are available to a human being who finds himself in this "terrible position"? Judging by the conduct of the people he observed, Tolstoy relates that he could see only four possible "solutions." The first is the way of ignorance. People who adopt this solution (chiefly women and very young and very dull people) have simply not or not yet faced the questions that were tormenting him. Once a person has fully realized what death means, this solution is not available to him. The second way is that of "Epicureanism," which consists in admitting the "hopelessness of life" but seizing as many of life's pleasures as possible while they are within reach. It consists in "disregarding the dragon and the mice and licking the honey in the best way, especially if much of it is around." This, Tolstoy adds, is the solution adopted by the majority of the people belonging to his "circle," by which he presumably means the well-to-do intellectuals of his day. Tolstoy rejects this solution because the vast majority of human beings are not well-to-do and hence have little or no honey at their disposal and also because it is a matter of accident whether one is among those who have honey or those who have not. Moreover, Tolstoy observes, it requires a special "moral dullness," which he himself lacked, to enjoy the honey while knowing the truth about death and the deprivations of the great majority of men. The third solution is suicide. Tolstoy calls this the way of "strength and energy." It is chosen by a few "exceptionally strong and consistent people." After they realize that "it is better to be dead than to be alive, and that it is best of all not to exist," they promptly end the whole "stupid joke." The means for ending it are readily at hand for everybody, but most people are too cowardly or too irrational to avail themselves of them. Finally, there is the way of "weakness." This consists in seeing the dreadful truth and clinging to life nevertheless. People of this kind lack the strength to act rationally and Tolstoy adds that he belonged to this last category.

Strengths of the Pessimist Position

Is it possible for somebody who shares the pessimists' rejection of religion to reach different conclusions without being plainly irrational? Whatever reply may be possible, any intelligent and realistic person would surely have to concede that there is much truth in the pessimists' claims. That few people achieve real and lasting happiness, that the joys of life (where there are any) pass away much too soon, that totally unpredictable events frequently upset the best intentions and wreck the noblest plans—this and much more along the same lines is surely undeniable. Although one should not dogmatize that there will be no significant improvements in the future, the fate of past revolutions, undertaken to rid man of some of his apparently avoidable suffering, does not inspire great hope. The thought of death, too, even in those who are not so overwhelmed by it as Tolstoy, can be quite unendurable. Moreover, to many who have reflected on the implications of physical theory it seems plain that because of the constant increase of entropy in the universe all life anywhere will eventually die out. Forebodings of this kind moved Bertrand Russell to write his famous essay "A Free Man's Worship," in which he concluded that "all the labors of the ages, all the devotion, all the inspiration, all the noonday brightness of human genius, are destined to extinction in the vast death of the solar system, and the whole temple of man's achievement must inevitably be buried beneath the debris of a universe in ruins." Similarly, Wilhelm Ostwald observed that "in the longest run the sum of all human endeavor has no recognizable significance." Although it is disputed whether physical theory really has such gloomy implications, it would perhaps be wisest to assume that the position endorsed by Russell and Ostwald is well-founded.

COMPARATIVE VALUE JUDGMENTS
ABOUT LIFE AND DEATH

Granting the strong points in the pessimists' claims, it is still possible to detect certain confusions and dubious inferences in their arguments. To begin with, there is a very obvious inconsistency in the way writers like Darrow and Tolstoy arrive at the conclusion that death is better than life. They begin by telling us that death is something terrible because it terminates the possibility of any of the experiences we value. From this they infer that nothing is really worth doing and that death is better than life. Ignoring for the moment the claim that in view of our inevitable death nothing is "worth doing," there very plainly seems to be an inconsistency in first judging death to be such a horrible evil and in asserting later on that death is better than life. Why was death originally judged to be an evil? Surely because it is the termination of life. And if something, y, is bad because it is the termination of something, x, this can be so only if x is good or has positive value. If x were not good, the termination of x would not be bad. One cannot consistently have it both ways.

To this it may be answered that life did have positive value prior to one's realization of death but that once a person has become aware of the inevitability of his destruction life becomes unbearable and that this is the real issue. This point of view is well expressed in the following exchange between Cassius and Brutus in Shakespeare's *Julius Caesar* (III.i.102–105):

CASSIUS. Why he that cuts off twenty years of life
Cuts off so many years of fearing death.

BRUTUS. Grant that, and then is death a benefit:
So are we Caesar's friends that have abridged
His time of fearing death.

There is a very simple reply to this argument. Granting that some people after once realizing their doom cannot banish the thought of it from their minds, so much so that it interferes with all their other activities, this is neither inevitable nor at all common. It is, on the contrary, in the opinion of all except some existentialists, morbid and pathological. The realization that one will die does not in the case of most people prevent them from engaging in activities which they regard as valuable or from enjoying the things they used to enjoy. To be told that one is not living "authentically" if one does not brood about death day and night is simply to be insulted gratuitously. A person who knows that his talents are not as great as he would wish or that he is not as handsome as he would have liked to be is not usually judged to live "inauthentically," but on the contrary to be sensible if he does not constantly brood about his limitations and shortcomings and uses whatever talents he does possess to maximum advantage.

There is another and more basic objection to the claim that death is better than life. This objection applies equally to the claim that while death is better than life it would be better still not to have been born in the first place and to the judgment that life is better than death. It should be remembered that we are here concerned with such pronouncements when they are intended not merely as the expression of certain moods but as statements which are in some sense true or objectively warranted. It may be argued that a value comparison—any judgment to the effect that *A* is better or worse than *B* or as good as *B*—makes sense only if *both A* and *B* are, in the relevant respect, in principle open to inspection. If somebody says, for example, that Elizabeth Taylor is a better actress than Betty Grable, this seems quite intelligible. Or, again, if it is said that life for the Jews is better in the United States than it was in Germany under the Nazis, this also seems readily intelligible. In such cases the terms of the comparison are observable or at any rate describable. These conditions are fulfilled in some cases when value comparisons are made between life and death, but they are not fulfilled in the kind of case with which Tolstoy and the pessimists are concerned. If the conception of an afterlife is intelligible, then it would make sense for a believer or for somebody who has not made up his mind to say such things as "Death cannot be worse than this life" or "I wonder if it will be any better for me after I am dead." Achilles, in the *Iliad*, was not making a senseless comparison when he exclaimed that he would rather act

> ... as a serf of another,
> A man of little possessions, with scanty means of
>   subsistence,
> Than rule as a ghostly monarch the ghosts of all
>   the departed.

Again, the survivors can meaningfully say about a deceased individual "It is better (for the world) that he is dead" or the opposite. For the person himself, however, if there is no afterlife, death is not a possible object of observation or experience, and statements by him that his own life is better than, as good as, or worse than his own death, unless they are intended to be no more than expressions of certain wishes or moods, must be dismissed as senseless. At first sight the contention that in the circumstances under discussion value comparisons between life and death are senseless may seem implausible because of the widespread tendency to think of death as a shadowy kind of life—as sleep, rest, or some kind of homecoming. Such "descriptions" may be admirable as poetry or consolation, but taken literally they are simply false.

IRRELEVANCE OF THE DISTANT FUTURE

These considerations do not, however, carry us very far. They do not show either that life is worth living or that it "has meaning." Before tackling these problems directly, something should perhaps be said about the curious and totally arbitrary preference of the future to the present, to which writers like

Tolstoy and Darrow are committed without realizing it. Darrow implies that life would not be "futile" if it were not an endless cycle of the same kind of activities and if instead it were like a journey toward a destination. Tolstoy clearly implies that life would be worthwhile, that some of our actions at least would have a "reasonable meaning," if the present life were followed by eternal bliss. Presumably, what would make life no longer futile as far as Darrow is concerned is some feature of the destination, not merely the fact that it is a destination; and what would make life worthwhile in Tolstoy's opinion is not merely the eternity of the next life but the "bliss" which it would confer—eternal misery and torture would hardly do. About the bliss in the next life, if there is such a next life, Tolstoy shows no inclination to ask "What for?" or "So what?" But if bliss in the next life is not in need of any further justification, why should any bliss that there might be in the present life need justification?

The Logic of Value Judgments

Many of the pessimists appear to be confused about the logic of value judgments. It makes sense for a person to ask about something "Is it really worthwhile?" or "Is it really worth the trouble?" if he does not regard it as intrinsically valuable or if he is weighing it against another good with which it may be in conflict. It does not make sense to ask such a question about something he regards as valuable in its own right and where there is no conflict with the attainment of any other good. (This observation, it should be noted, is quite independent of what view one takes of the logical status of intrinsic value judgments.) A person driving to the beach on a crowded Sunday, may, upon finally getting there, reflect on whether the trip was really worthwhile. Or, after undertaking a series of medical treatments, somebody may ask whether it was worth the time and the money involved. Such questions make sense because the discomforts of a car ride and the time and money spent on medical treatments are not usually judged to be valuable for their own sake. Again, a woman who has given up a career as a physician in order to raise a family may ask herself whether it was worthwhile, and in this case the question would make sense not because she regards the raising of a family as no more than a means, but because she is weighing it against another good. However, if somebody is very happy, for any number of reasons—because he is in love, because he won the Nobel prize, because his child recovered from a serious illness—and if this happiness does not prevent him from doing or experiencing anything else he regards as valuable, it would not occur to him to ask "Is it worthwhile?" Indeed, this question would be incomprehensible to him, just as Tolstoy himself would presumably not have known what to make of the question had it been raised about the bliss in the hereafter.

It is worth recalling here that we live not in the distant future but in the present and also, in a sense, in the relatively near future. To bring the subject down to earth, let us consider some everyday occurrences: A man with a toothache goes to a dentist, and the dentist helps him so that the toothache disappears. A man is falsely accused of a crime and is faced with the possibility of a severe sentence as well as with the loss of his reputation; with the help of a devoted attorney his innocence is established, and he is acquitted. It is true that a hundred years later all of the participants in these events will be dead and none of them will *then* be able to enjoy the fruits of any of the efforts involved. But this most emphatically does not imply that the dentist's efforts were not worthwhile or that the attorney's work was not worth doing. To bring in considerations of what will or will not happen in the remote future is, in such and many other though certainly not in all human situations, totally irrelevant. Not only is the finality of death irrelevant here; equally irrelevant are the facts, if they are facts, that life is an endless cycle of the same kind of activities and that the history of the universe is not a drama with a happy ending.

This is, incidentally, also the answer to religious apologists like C. H. D. Clark who maintain that all striving is pointless if it is "without final consequence" and that "it scarcely matters how we live if all will end in the dust of death." Striving is not pointless if it achieves what it is intended to achieve even if it is without *final* consequence, and it matters a great deal how we live if we have certain standards and goals, although we cannot avoid "the dust of death."

The Vanished Past

In asserting the worthlessness of life Schopenhauer remarked that "what has been exists as little as what has never been" and that "something of great importance now past is inferior to something of little importance now present." Several comments are in order here. To begin with, if Schopenhauer is right, it must work both ways: if only the present counts, then past sorrows no less than past pleasures do not "count." Furthermore, the question whether "something of great importance now past is inferior to something of little importance now present" is not, as Schopenhauer supposed, a straightforward question of fact but rather one of valuation, and different answers, none of which can be said to be mistaken, will be given by different people according to their circumstances and interests. Viktor Frankl, the founder of "logotherapy," has compared the pessimist to a man who observes, with fear and sadness, how his wall calendar grows thinner and thinner as he removes a sheet from it every day. The kind of person whom Frankl admires, on the other hand, "files each successive leaf neatly away with its predecessors" and reflects "with pride and joy" on all the richness represented by the leaves removed from the calendar. Such a person will not in old age envy the young. "'No, thank you,' he will think. 'Instead of possibilities, I have realities in my past'" (*Man's Search for Meaning*, pp. 192–193). This passage is quoted not because it contains any great wisdom but because it illustrates that we are concerned here not with judgments of fact but with value judgments and that Schopenhauer's is not the only one that is possible. Nevertheless, his remarks are, perhaps, a healthy antidote to the cheap consolation and the attempts to cover up deep and inevitable misery that are the stock in trade of a great deal of popular psychology. Although Schopenhauer's judgments about the inferior value of the past cannot be treated as objectively true propositions, they express only too well what a great many human beings are bound to feel on certain occasions. To a man dying of cancer it is small consolation to reflect that there was a time when he was happy and flourishing; and while there are undoubtedly some old people who do not envy the young, it may be suspected that more often the kind of talk advocated by the prophets of positive thinking is a mask for envy and a defense against exceedingly painful feelings of regret and helplessness in the face of aging and death and the now-unalterable past.

THE MEANINGS OF THE "MEANING OF LIFE"

Let us now turn to the question whether, given the rejection of belief in God and immortality, life can nevertheless have any "meaning" or "significance." Kurt Baier has called attention to two very different senses in which people use these expressions and to the confusions that result when they are not kept apart. Sometimes when a person asks whether life has any meaning, what he wants to know is whether there is a superhuman intelligence that fashioned human beings along with other objects in the world to serve some end— whether their role is perhaps analogous to the part of an instrument (or its player) in a symphony. People who ask whether history has a meaning often use the word in the same sense. When Macbeth exclaimed that life "is a tale / Told by an idiot, full of sound and fury, / Signifying nothing," he was answering this cosmic question in the negative. His point evidently was not that human life is part of a scheme designed by a superhuman idiot but that it is not part of any design. Similarly, when Fred Hoyle, in his book *The Nature of the Universe* (rev. ed., New York, 1960), turns to what he calls "the deeper issues" and remarks that we find ourselves in a "dreadful situation" in which there is "scarcely a clue as to whether our existence has any real significance," he is using the word "significance" in this cosmic sense.

On the other hand, when we ask whether a *particular* person's life has or had any meaning, we are usually concerned not with cosmic issues but with the question whether certain purposes are to be found *in* his life. Thus, most of us would say without hesitation that a person's life had meaning if we knew that he devoted himself to a cause (such as the spread of Christianity or communism or the reform of mental institutions), or we would at least be ready to say that it "acquired meaning" once he became sufficiently attached to his cause. Whether we approve of what they did or not, most of us would be ready to admit—to take some random examples—that Dorothea Dix, Pasteur, Lenin, Margaret Sanger, Anthony Comstock, and Winston Churchill led meaningful lives. We seem to mean two things in characterizing such lives as meaningful: we assert, first, that the life in question had some dominant, over-all goal or goals which gave direction to a great many of the individual's actions and, second, that these actions and possibly others not immediately related to the overriding goal were performed with a special zest that was not present before the person became attached to his goal or that would not have been present if there had been no such goal in his life. It is not necessary, however, that a person should be devoted to a cause, in the sense just indicated, before we call his life meaningful. It is sufficient that he should have some attachments that are not too shallow. This last expression is of course rather vague, but so is the use of the word "meaning" when applied to human lives. Since the depth or shallowness of an attachment is a matter of degree, it makes perfectly good sense to speak of degrees of meaning in this context. Thus, C. G. Jung writes that in the lives of his patients there never was "sufficient meaning" (*Memories, Dreams, Reflections*, New York and Toronto, 1963, p. 140). There is nothing odd in such a locution, and there is equally nothing odd in saying about a man who has made a partial recovery from a deep depression that there is now again "some" meaning in his life.

Although frequently when people say about somebody that his life has or had meaning, they evidently regard this as a good thing, this is not invariably the case. One might express this point in the following way: saying that attachment to a certain goal has made a man's life meaningful is *not* tantamount to saying that the acts to which the goal has given direction are of positive value. A man might himself observe—and there would be nothing logically odd about it—"As long as I was a convinced Nazi (or communist or Christian or whatever) my life had meaning, my acts had a zest with which I have not been able to invest them since, and yet most of my actions were extremely harmful." Even while fully devoted to his cause or goal the person need not, and frequently does not, regard it as *intrinsically* valuable. If challenged he will usually justify the attachment to his goal by reference to more fundamental value judgments. Thus, somebody devoted to communism or to medical research or to the dissemination of birth-control information will in all likelihood justify his devotion in terms of the production of happiness and the reduction of suffering, and somebody devoted to Christianity will probably justify his devotion by reference to the will of God.

Let us refer to the first of the two senses we have been discussing as the "cosmic" sense and to the second as the "terrestrial" sense. (These are by no means the only senses in which philosophers and others have used the word "meaning" when they have spoken of the meaning or meaninglessness of life, but for our purposes it is sufficient to take account of these two senses.) Now if the theory of cosmic design is rejected it immediately follows that human life has no meaning in the first or cosmic sense. It does not follow in the least, however, that a particular human life is meaningless in the second, or terrestrial, sense. This conclusion has been very clearly summarized by Baier: "Your life or mine may or may not have meaning (in one sense)," he writes, "even if life as such has none (in the other). . . . The Christian view guarantees a meaning (in one sense) to every life, the scientific view [what we have simply been calling the unbeliever's position] does not in any sense" (*The Meaning of Life*, p. 28). In the terrestrial sense it will be an open question whether an individual's life has meaning or not, to be decided by the particular circumstances of his existence. It may indeed be the case that once a person comes to believe that life has no meaning in the cosmic sense his attachment to terrestrial goals will be undermined to such an extent that his life will cease to be meaningful in the other sense as well. However, it seems very plain that this is by no means what invariably happens, and even if it did invariably happen the meaninglessness of a given person's life in the terrestrial sense would not *logically* follow from the fact, if it is a fact, that life is meaningless in the cosmic sense.

This is perhaps the place to add a few words of protest against the rhetorical exaggerations of certain theological writers. Fackenheim's statement, quoted earlier, that "whatever meaning life acquires, it derives from the encounter between God and man" is typical of many theological pronouncements. Statements of this kind are objectionable on several grounds. Let us assume that there is a God and that meetings between God and certain human beings do take place; let us also grant that activities commanded by God in these meetings "acquire meaning" by being or becoming means to the end of pleasing or obeying God. Granting all this, it does not follow that obedience of God is the only possible unifying goal. It would be preposterous to maintain that the lives of *all* unbelievers have been lacking in such goals and almost as preposterous to maintain that the lives of believers never contain unifying goals other than obedience of God. There have been devout men who were also attached to the advance of science, to the practice of medicine, or to social reform and who regarded these ends as worth pursuing independently of any divine commandments. Furthermore, there is really no good reason to grant that the life of a particular person becomes meaningful in the terrestrial sense just because human life in general has meaning in the cosmic sense. If a superhuman being has a plan in which I am included, this fact will make (or help to make) my life meaningful in the terrestrial sense only if I know the plan and approve of it and of my place in it, so that working toward the realization of the plan gives direction to my actions.

IS HUMAN LIFE EVER WORTHWHILE?

Let us now turn to the question of whether life is ever worth living. This also appears to be denied by the pessimists when they speak of the vanity or the futility of human life. We shall see that in a sense it cannot be established that the pessimists are "mistaken," but it is also quite easy to show that in at least two senses which seem to be of importance to many people, human lives frequently are worth living. To this end, let us consider under what circumstances a person is likely to raise the question "Is my life (still) worthwhile?" and what is liable to provoke somebody into making a statement like "My life has ceased to be worth living." We saw in an earlier section that when we say of certain acts, such as the efforts of a dentist or a lawyer, that they were worthwhile we are claiming that they achieved certain goals. Something similar seems to be involved when we say that a person's life is (still) worthwhile or worth living. We seem to be making two assertions: first, that the person has some goals (other than merely to be dead or to have his pains eased) which do not seem to him to be trivial and, second, that there is some genuine possibility that he will attain these goals. These observations are confirmed by various systematic studies of people who contemplated suicide, of others who unsuccessfully attempted suicide, and of situations in which people did commit suicide. When the subjects of these studies declared that their lives were no longer worth living they generally meant either that there was nothing left in their lives about which they seriously cared or that there was no real likelihood of attaining any of the goals that mattered to them. It should be noted that in this sense an individual may well be mistaken in his assertion that his life is or is not worthwhile any longer: he may, for example, mistake a temporary indisposition for a more permanent loss of interest, or, more likely, he may falsely estimate his chances of achieving the ends he wishes to attain.

Different Senses of "Worthwhile"

According to the account given so far, one is saying much the same thing in declaring a life to be worthwhile and in asserting that it has meaning in the "terrestrial" sense of the word. There is, however, an interesting difference. When we say that a person's life has meaning (in the terrestrial sense) we are not committed to the claim that the goal or goals to which he is devoted have any positive value. (This is a slight oversimplification, assuming greater uniformity in the use of "meaning of life" than actually exists, but it will not seriously affect any of the controversial issues discussed here.) The question "As long as his life was dedicated to the spread of communism it had meaning *to him,* but was it really meaningful?" seems to be senseless. We are inclined to say, "If his life had meaning to him, then it had meaning—that's all there is to it." We are not inclined (or we are much less inclined) to say something of this kind when we speak of the worth of a person's life. We might say—for example, of someone like Eichmann—"While he was carrying out the extermination program, his life *seemed* worthwhile to him, but since his goal was so horrible, his life *was not* worthwhile." One might perhaps distinguish between a "subjective" and an "objective" sense of "worthwhile." In the subjective sense, saying that a person's life is worthwhile simply means that he is attached to some goals which he does not consider trivial and that these goals are attainable for him. In declaring that somebody's life is worthwhile in the objective sense, one is saying that he is attached to certain goals which are both attainable and of positive value.

It may be held that unless one accepts some kind of rationalist or intuitionist view of fundamental value judgments one would have to conclude that in the objective sense of "worthwhile" no human life (and indeed no human action) could ever be shown to be worthwhile. There is no need to enter here into a discussion of any controversial questions about the logical status of fundamental value judgments. But it may be pointed out that somebody who favors a subjectivist or emotivist account can quite consistently allow for the distinction between ends that only seem to have positive value and those that really do. To mention just one way in which this could be done: one may distinguish between ends that would be approved by rational and sympathetic human beings and those that do not carry such an endorsement. One may then argue that when we condemn such a life as Eichmann's as not being worthwhile we mean not that the ends to which he devoted himself possess some non-natural characteristic of badness but that no rational or sympathetic person would approve of them.

The Pessimists' Special Standards

The unexciting conclusion of this discussion is that some human lives are at certain times not worthwhile in either of the two senses we have distinguished, that some are worthwhile in the subjective but not in the objective sense, some in the objective but not in the subjective sense, and some are worthwhile in both senses. The unexcitingness of this conclusion is not a reason for rejecting it, but some readers may question whether it meets the challenge of the pessimists. The pessimist, it may be countered, surely does not deny the plain fact that human beings are on occasions attached to goals which do not seem to them trivial, and it is also not essential to his position to deny (and most pessimists do not in fact deny) that these goals are sometimes attainable. The pessimist may even allow that in a superficial ("immediate") sense the goals which people try to achieve are of positive value, but he would add that because our lives are not followed by eternal bliss they are not "really" or "ultimately" worthwhile. If this is so, then the situation may be characterized by saying that the ordinary man and the pessimist do not mean the same by "worthwhile," or that they do mean the same in that both use it as a positive value expression but that their standards are different: the standards of the pessimist are very much more demanding than those of most ordinary people.

Anybody who agrees that death is final will have to concede that the pessimist is not mistaken in his contention that judged by *his* standards, life is never worthwhile. However, the pessimist is mistaken if he concludes, as frequently happens, that life is not worthwhile by ordinary standards because it is not worthwhile by his standards. Furthermore, setting aside the objection mentioned earlier (that there is something arbitrary about maintaining that eternal bliss makes life worthwhile but not allowing this role to bliss in the present life), one may justifiably ask why one should abandon ordinary standards in favor of those of the pessimist. Ordinarily, when somebody changes standards (for example, when a school raises or lowers its standards of admission) such a change can be supported by reasons. But how can the pessimist justify his special standards? It should be pointed out here that our ordinary standards do something for us which the pessimist's standards do not: they guide our choices, and as long as we live we can hardly help making choices. It is true that in one type of situation the pessimist's standards also afford guidance—namely, in deciding whether to go on living. It is notorious, however, that whether or not they are, by their own standards, rational in this, most pessimists do not commit suicide. They are then faced with much the same choices as other people. In these situations their own demanding standards are of no use, and in fact they avail themselves of the ordinary standards. Schopenhauer, for example, believed that if he had hidden his antireligious views he would have had no difficulty in obtaining an academic appointment and other worldly honors. He may have been mistaken in this belief, but in any event his actions indicate that he regarded intellectual honesty as worthwhile in a sense in which worldly honors were not. Again, when Darrow had the choice between continuing as counsel for the Chicago and North Western Railway and taking on the defense of Eugene V. Debs and his harassed and persecuted American Railway Union, he did not hesitate to choose the latter, apparently regarding it as worthwhile to go to the assistance of the suppressed and not worthwhile to aid the suppressor. In other words, although no human action is worthwhile, some human actions and presumably some human lives are less unworthwhile than others.

IS THE UNIVERSE BETTER WITH HUMAN LIFE THAN WITHOUT IT?

We have not—at least not explicitly—discussed the claims of Schopenhauer, Eduard von Hartmann, and other pessimists that the nonexistence of the world would be better than its existence, by which they mean that a world without human life would be better than one with it.

Arguments of a Phenomenologist

Some writers do not think that life can be shown to have meaning in any philosophically significant sense unless an affirmative answer to this question can be justified. Thus, in his booklet *Der Sinn unseres Daseins* the German phenomenologist Hans Reiner distinguishes between the everyday question about what he calls the "need-conditioned" meaning of life, which arises only for a person who is already in existence and has certain needs and desires, and the question about the meaning of human life in general. The latter question arises in concrete form when a responsible person is faced with the *Zeugungsproblem*—the question whether he should bring a child into the world. Reiner allows that a person's life has meaning in the former or "merely subjective" sense as long as his ordinary goals (chiefly his desire for happiness) are attained. This, however, does not mean that his life has an "objective" or "existential" (*seinshaft*) meaning—a significance or meaning which "attaches to life as such" and which, unlike the need-conditioned meaning, cannot be destroyed by any accident of fate. The philosopher, according to Reiner, is primarily concerned with the question of whether life has meaning in this objective or existential sense. "Our search for the meaning of our life," Reiner writes, "is identical with the search for a logically compelling reason (*einen einsichtigen Grund*) why it is better for us to exist than not to exist" (*Der Sinn unseres Daseins*, p. 27). Again, the real question is "whether it is better that mankind should exist than that there should be a world without any human life" (ibid., p. 31). It may be questioned whether this is what anybody normally means when he asks whether life has any meaning, but Reiner certainly addresses himself to one of the questions raised by Schopenhauer and other pessimists that ought to be discussed here.

Reiner believes that he can provide a "logically compelling reason" why a world with human life is better than one without it. He begins by pointing out that men differ from animals by being, among other things, "moral individuals." To be a moral individual is to be part of the human community and to be actively concerned in the life of other human beings. It is indeed undeniable that people frequently fail to bring about the ends of morally inspired acts or wishes, but phenomenological analysis discloses that "the real moral value and meaning" of an act does not depend on the attainment of the "external goal." As Kant correctly pointed out, the decisive factor is "the good will," the moral intent or attitude. It is here that we find the existential meaning of life: "Since that which is morally good contains its meaning and value within itself, it follows that it is intrinsically worthwhile. The existence of what is morally good is therefore better than its nonexistence" (ibid., pp. 54–55). But the existence of what is morally good is essentially connected with the existence of free moral individuals, and hence it follows that the existence of human beings as moral agents is better than their nonexistence.

Unlike happiness, which constitutes the meaning of life in the everyday or need-conditioned sense, the morally good does not depend on the accidents of life. It is not within a person's power to be happy, but it is "essentially" (*grundsätzlich*) in everybody's power to do what is good. Furthermore, while all happiness is subjective and transitory, leaving behind it no more than a "melancholy echo," the good has eternal value. Nobody would dream of honoring and respecting a person for his happiness or prosperity. On the other hand, we honor every good deed and the expression of every moral attitude, even if it took place in a distant land and among a foreign people. If we discover a good act or a good attitude in an enemy we nevertheless respect it and cannot help deriving a certain satisfaction from its existence. The same is true of good deeds carried out in ages long past. In all this the essentially timeless nature of morality becomes evident. Good deeds cease to exist as historical events only; their value, on the other hand, has eternal reality and is collected as an indestructible "fund." This may be a metaphysical statement, but it is not a piece of "metaphysical speculation." It simply makes explicit what the experience of the morally good discloses to phenomenological analysis (ibid., pp. 55–57).

Paul Edwards

Replies To Reiner

There is a great deal in this presentation with which one could take issue. If one is not misled by the image of the ever-growing, indestructible "fund," one may wonder, for example, what could be meant by claiming that the value of a good deed is "eternal," other than that most human beings tend to approve of such an action regardless of when or where it took place. However, we are here concerned primarily with the question whether Reiner has met the challenge of the pessimists, and it seems clear that he has not. A pessimist like Schopenhauer or Darrow might provisionally grant the correctness of Reiner's phenomenological analysis of morality but still offer the following rejoinder: The inevitable misery of all or nearly all human beings is so great that even if in the course of their lives they have a chance to preserve their inner moral natures or their good will, the continued torture to which their lives condemn them would not be justified. Given the pessimist's estimate of human life, this is surely not an unreasonable rejoinder. Even without relying on the pessimist's description of human life, somebody while accepting Reiner's phenomenological analysis might reach the opposite conclusion. He might, for example, share the quietist strain of Schopenhauer's teachings and object to the whole hustle and bustle of life, concluding that the "peace of the all-sufficient nothing"—or, more literally, a universe without human life—was better in spite of the fact that moral deeds could not then be performed. Since he admits the "facts" of morality on which Reiner bases his case but considers the peace of the all-sufficient nothing more valuable than morality, it is not easy to see how an appeal to the latter would show him to be mistaken. What phenomenological analysis has not disclosed, to Reiner or, as far as is known, to anybody else, is that doing good is the only or necessarily the greatest value.

Why the Pessimist Cannot be Answered

The conclusion suggests itself that the pessimist cannot here be refuted, not because what he says is true or even because we do not know who is right and who is wrong but because the question whether a universe with human life is better than one without it does not have any clear meaning unless it is interpreted as a request for a statement of personal preference. The situation seems to be somewhat similar to what we found in the case of the question "Is my life better than my death?" when asked in certain circumstances. In some contexts indeed when we talk about human life in general, the word "better" has a reasonably clear meaning. Thus, if it is maintained that life for the human race will be better than it is now after cancer and mental illness have been conquered, or that human life will be better (or worse) after religion has disappeared, we understand fairly well what is meant, what facts would decide the issue either way. However, we do not really know what would count as evidence for or against the statement "The existence of human life as such is better than its nonexistence." Sometimes it is claimed that the question has a fairly clear meaning, namely, whether happiness outweighs unhappiness. Thus, von Hartmann supports his answer that the nonexistence of human life is better than its existence, that in fact an inanimate world would be better than one with life, with the argument that as we descend the scale of civilization and "sensitivity," we reach ever lower levels of misery. "The individuals of the lower and poorer classes and of ruder nations," he writes, "are happier than those of the elevated and wealthier classes and of civilized nations, not indeed because they are poorer and have to endure more want and privations, but because they are coarser and duller" (*Philosophy of the Unconscious*, Vol. III, p. 76). The "brutes," similarly, are "happier (i.e., less miserable)" than man, because "the excess of pain which an animal has to bear is less than that which a man has to bear." The same principle holds within the world of animals and plants:

> How much more painful is the life of the more finely-feeling horse compared with that of the obtuse pig, or with that of the proverbially happy fish in the water, its nervous system being of a grade so far inferior! As the life of a fish is more enviable than that of a horse, so is the life of an oyster than that of a fish, and the life of a plant than that of an oyster. (ibid.)

The conclusion is inevitable: the best or least undesirable form of existence is reached when, finally, we "descend beneath the threshold of consciousness"; for only there do we "see individual pain entirely disappear" (*Philosophy of the Unconscious*, Vol. III, pp. 76–77). Schopenhauer, also, addressing himself directly to the "*Zeugungsproblem*," reaches a negative answer on the ground that unhappiness usually or necessarily outweighs happiness. "Could the human race continue to exist," he asks (in *Parerga und Paralipomena*, Vol. II, pp. 321–322), if "the generative act were ... an affair of pure rational reflection? Would not rather everyone have so much compassion for the coming generation as to prefer to spare it the burden of existence, or at least be unwilling to take on himself the responsibility of imposing such a burden in cold blood?" In these passages Schopenhauer and von Hartmann assume that in the question "Is a world with human life better than one without human life?" the word "better" must be construed in a hedonistic or utilitarian sense—and the same is true of several other philosophers who do not adopt their pessimistic answer. However, while one may *stipulate* such a sense for "better" in this context, it is clear that this is *not* what is meant prior to the stipulation. Spinoza, for example, taught that the most miserable form of existence is preferable to nonexistence. Perhaps few who have directly observed the worst agonies and tortures that may be the lot of human beings or of animals would subscribe to this judgment, but Spinoza can hardly be accused of a self-contradictory error. Again, Nietzsche's philosophy is usually and quite accurately described as an affirmation of life, but Nietzsche was very careful not to play down the horrors of much of life. While he did not endorse Schopenhauer's value judgments, he thought that, by and large, Schopenhauer had not been far wrong in his description of the miseries of the human scene. In effect Nietzsche maintained that even though unhappiness is more prevalent than happiness, the existence of life is nevertheless better than its nonexistence, and this surely is not a self-contradiction.

It is important to point out what does not follow from the admission that in a nonarbitrary sense of "better," the existence of the human race cannot be shown to be better than its nonexistence: It does not follow that I or anybody else cannot or should not prefer the continued existence of the human race to its nonexistence or my own life to my death, and it does not follow that I or anybody else cannot or should not enjoy himself or that I or anybody else is "irrational" in any of these preferences. It is also impossible to prove that in some nonarbitrary sense of "better," coffee with cream is better than black coffee, but it does not follow that I cannot or should not prefer or enjoy it or that I am irrational in doing so. There is perhaps something a trifle absurd and obsessive in the need for a "proof" that the existence of life is better than its nonexistence. It resembles the demand to have it "established by argument" that love is better than hate.

Perhaps it would be helpful to summarize the main conclusions reached in this essay:

(1) In certain familiar senses of "meaning," which are not usually regarded as trivial, an action or a human life can have meaning quite independently of whether there is a God or whether we shall live forever.

(2) Writers like Tolstoy, who, because of the horror that death inspires, conclude that death is better than life, are plainly inconsistent. Moreover, the whole question of whether my life is better than my death, unless it is a question about my preference, seems to be devoid of sense.

(3) Those who argue that no human action can be worthwhile because we all must eventually die ignore what may be called the "short-term context" of much of our lives.

(4) Some human lives are worthwhile in one or both of the two senses in which "worthwhile" is commonly used, when people raise the question of whether a given person's life is worthwhile. The pessimists who judge human life by more demanding standards are not mistaken when they deny that by *their* standards no human life is ever worthwhile. However, they are guilty of a fallacious inference if they conclude that for this reason no human life can be worthwhile by the usual standards. Nor is it clear why anybody should embrace their standards in the place of those commonly adopted.

(5) It appears that the pessimists cannot be answered if in order to answer them one has to be able to prove that in some nonarbitrary sense of the word "better," the existence of life is better than its nonexistence. But this admission does not have any of the gloomy consequences which it is sometimes believed to entail.

CHAPTER 13

KAI NIELSEN

Death and the Meaning of Life

I

For intellectuals, at least, the effects of the posture of modernity is very pervasive. It characteristically leaves us with a fear of being caught out in trivialities and with a fear of saying the obvious.[1] This leads us to indirect discourse, to a penchant for being clever and, because of that very fear of saying the obvious, into triviality. Certainly on a topic such as our present one such anxieties readily surface and no doubt have a reasonable object. However, without any posturing at all, I shall simply brush them aside and plunge into my subject.

Most of what I say here I have said before and it has, as well, been said before by many others.[2] Moreover, it is my belief that most of the claims made here should be a series of commonplaces, but, given the direction of our popular culture, they are not. I repeat them because they seem to me to be true, to be truths which are repeatedly avoided and which need to be taken to heart.

J.M. Cameron, a distinguished Roman Catholic philosopher whose work I admire, has remarked that more and more people today think "that to die is to be annihilated."[3] Particularly for very many of us who are intellectuals and are touched by modernity and the swath of our secular culture, belief in the survival of bodily death is an impossibility. It seems to many of us at best a groundless bit of fantasy and at worst a conception which is through and through incoherent.[4] It is an interesting point, a point which I shall not pursue here, whether the philosophical arguments purporting to establish these thoroughly secular beliefs are sound or whether they simply reflect the *Weltbild*—itself without grounds—of the dominant secular culture with its deeply scientific orientation.[5] Whatever we should say about this, it remains the case that among the intelligentsia, and to a not inconsiderable degree else-

From *The Search for Absolute Values in a Changing World.* Proceedings of the Sixth International Conference of the Unity of Sciences. Copyright © 1978 by International Cultural Foundation. Used by permission of the International Conference of the Unity of the Sciences.

where as well, belief in the survival of death is either a very considerable stumbling block or something dismissed out of hand as something which is simply "beyond belief" for anyone who can look at the world non-evasively and think tolerably clearly.

Even Cameron, who presumably does believe in some form of the survival of the death of at least our present bodies, recognizes that for most men "the hypothesis of survival" is "impossibly difficult."[6] Annihilation seems plainly and evidently to be our end. Yet he thinks that the "full terror of death" and the need to give some significance to our lives will drive us, if we are honest with ourselves and probing, to such an at least seemingly implausible belief.[7]

I want to resist this. I shall argue that, even if death is, as I believe it to be, utter annihilation, we can still find significance in our lives and that, if we will think carefully and indeed humanly—from the emotions or existentially if you will—we need not, and indeed should not, feel death to be such a stark terror. Cameron, like Kierkegaard, seems to take it as almost true by definition that to be fully human is to so react to death. But why should we accept this conventional wisdom?

I shall, for a moment, as seems to me appropriate in this context, speak personally. Even though Tolstoy, Dostoevsky and Pascal have deeply touched my life, I do not feel terror when I dwell on death. Yet I know full well it must come and I firmly believe—believe without a shadow of doubt—that it will mean my utter annihilation. Yet I am without such a dread of death, though, of course, when I think of it, I feel regret that I must die, but, unlike Ivan Ilyitch, I do not feel that "before its face" all life is meaningless: nothing is worth experiencing or doing. As I am now in possession of the normal powers of life, with things I want to do and experience, with pleasure in life and with people I very much care for and who care for me, I certainly do not want to die. I should very much like, in such a state, to go on living forever. Yet plainly I cannot. In the face of this, it seems to me both a sane response and a human response to that inevitability to rather wistfully regret that fact about our common human lot and to want to make the most of the life one has. But I see no reason to make a mystery of death. And I see no reason why reflecting on my death should fill me with terror or dread or despair. One takes rational precautions against premature death and faces the rest stoically, as Freud did and as Samuel Johnson came to, and as I am confident countless others have as well. Death should only be dreadful if one's life has been a waste.

By a conventionalist's sulk such an attitude, as I have just evinced, is thought to be a shallow one devoid of the depth and the *angst* that Cameron evinces or that he finds in Ernest Becker's *The Denial of Death* or that we find in the existentialists. (I do not speak here of Nietzsche.) John Austin, when he was dying of cancer and knew that he was dying of cancer, but when others did not, was reported to have responded to a talk by Gabriel Marcel on death by remarking "Professor Marcel, we all know we have to die, but why do we have to sing songs about it?" The conventional wisdom would make this a shallow response, but, coupled with an understanding of the integrity and importance of Austin's work and with a knowledge of Austin's fierce determination to work right up to the end, it seems to me to be just the opposite. We know we must die; we would rather not, but why must we suffer *angst*, engage in theatrics and create myths for ourselves. Why not simply face it and get on with the living of our lives?

II

There is a tradition, finding its most persistent expression in Christianity, which contends that without life everlasting, without some survival of the death of one's present body and without the reality of God to ensure that such a life will have a certain character, life will be pointless and morality without significance. I shall now argue that these beliefs, common as they are, are not true.

It is indeed true that moral perplexity runs deep and moral ambivalence and anguish should be extensive. A recognition of this should be common ground between morally sensitive believers and sceptics. But there is no need to have the religious commitments of Christianity or its sister religions or any religious commitment at all to make sense of morality. Torturing human beings is vile; exploiting and degrading human beings is through-and-through evil; cruelty to human beings and animals is, morally speaking, unacceptable; and treating one's promises lightly or being careless about the truth is wrong. If we know anything to be wrong we know these things to be wrong and they would be wrong and just as wrong in a Godless world and in a world in which personal annihilation is inevitable as in a world with God and in which there is eternal life.

There is indeed a philosophical problem about how we know these things to be wrong, but this is as much a problem for the believer as for the sceptic. I would say that for anyone—for believer and sceptic alike—if he or she has an understanding of the concept of morality, has an understanding of what it is to take the moral point of view, he or she will, *eo ipso*, understand that it is wrong to harm others, that promises are to be kept and the truth to be told. This does not mean that he or she will be committed to the belief that a lie *never* can rightly be told, that a promise *never* can be broken or that a human being in *no circumstance* can rightly be harmed. But, if there is no understanding that such acts always require very special justification and that the presumption of morality is always against them, then there is no understanding of the concept of morality. But this understanding is not intrinsically or logically bound up with knowing God or knowing about God or the taking of a religious point of view or knowing or even believing that one will survive the death of one's "earthly body."

It might be responded that such an understanding does imply a knowledge of the reality of God because we *only* know these things to be wrong because we know they are against God's will and something is only good because God wills it and is only wrong because God prohibits it. Leaving aside sceptical questions about how we can know, or whether we can know, what God does and does not will, the old question arises whether something is good simply because God wills it or does God will it because it is good? What is plain—leaving aside God for a moment—is that something is not good simply because it is willed or commanded; indeed it is not even, morally speaking, a good thing to do simply because it is willed or commanded by an omnipotently powerful being, unless we want to reduce morality to power worship, as has one rather well known but (on this issue) confused philosopher.[8] But might—naked power—doesn't make right. And there is no implication that it will become right even when conjoined with faultless intelligence. There can be—and indeed are—thoroughly ruthless, exploitative, manipulative people who are very intelligent indeed. Neither omnipotence nor omniscience implies goodness.

However, it is still not implausible to say that it is *God's* willing it which makes all the difference, for God, after all, is the supreme, perfect good. But I in turn ask, how do we know that or do we know that? If we say we know it through studying the Scriptures and through the example of Jesus, then it should in turn be responded that it is only in virtue of our own quite independent moral understanding of the goodness of his behaviour and the behaviour of the characters in the Bible that we come to recognize this. Moral understanding is not grounded in a belief in God; just the reverse is the case: an understanding of the religious *significance* of Jesus and the Scriptures presupposes a moral understanding.

If, alternatively, we claim that we do not come to understand that God is the supreme and perfect good in that way but claim that it is a necessary truth—a proposition, like "Puppies are young dogs," which is true by definition—then we still should ask: how do we understand that putatively necessary proposition? But again we should recognize that it is only by having an understanding of what goodness is that we come to have some glimmering of the more complex and extremely perplexing notions of supreme goodness or perfect goodness. The crucial thing to see is that there are things which we can recognize on reflection to be wrong, God or no God, and that we can be far more confident that we are right in claiming that they are wrong, than we can be in claiming any knowledge of God or God's order.

Finally, someone might say that since God is the cause of everything, there could be no goodness or anything else if there were no God. But this confuses *causes* and *reasons*, confuses questions about causally bringing something into existence or sustaining its existence and justifying its existence. If there is the God of the Jews and the Christians everything causally depends on Him, but still, even if there were no God who made the world, it would still be wrong to torture little children, and even if there were no people to be kind, it would be timelessly true that human kindness would be a good thing and that the goodness of human kindness does not become good or cease to become good by God's fiat or anyone else's. And it is in no way dependent on whether we live out our fourscore years and ten or whether life is everlasting.

In terms of its fundamental rationale, morality is utterly independent of belief in God or a belief in immortality. To make sense of our lives as moral beings there is no need to make what may be an intellectually stultifying blind leap of religious faith or to in any way believe in an afterlife. Such a moral understanding, as well as a capacity for moral response and action, is available to us even if we are human beings who are utterly without religious faith.

Furthermore, it does not follow that our lives are pointless, empty or meaningless if there is no God and if death is unequivocally our lot. There is no good reason to believe that because of these things we are condemned to an Oblomov-like, senseless existence. There is no reason why we must despair if God is dead and if life must come to an end. If there is no God, it is indeed true that we are not blessed with the questionable blessing of being made for a purpose; furthermore, if there is neither God nor *Logos*, there is no purpose to life, no plan for the universe or providential ordering of things in accordance with which we must live our lives. Yet, from the fact, if it is a fact, that there is no purpose to life or no purposes for which we are made, it does not at all follow that there are no purposes *in* life that are worth achieving, doing or having, so that life in reality must be just one damn thing after another that finally senselessly terminates in death. "Purpose of life" is ambiguous: in talking of it we can, on the one hand, be talking of "purpose of life," or, on the other, of "purposes in life" in the sense of plans we form, ends we seek, etc. that result from our deliberate and intentional acts and our desires, including our reflective desires. The former require something like a god or a *Logos*, but the latter most certainly do not. Yet it is only the latter that are plainly necessary to make life meaningful in the sense that there are in our lives and our environment things worthwhile doing, having or experiencing, things that bring joy, understanding, exhilaration or contentment to ourselves or to others. That we will not have these things forever does not make them worthless any more than the inevitability of death and the probability of decay robs them, or our lives generally, of their sense. In a Godless world, in which death is inevitable, our lives are not robbed of meaning.

III

Some might concede all this and still respond that I am leaving out something crucial from the religious traditions. They could agree I have shown that life for an atheist can very well have meaning. But what I have not shown is that with the loss of the kind of hope and the kind of perspective that have gone with Judaism, Christianity and Islam something has not been irreparably taken from us, the loss of which is increasingly felt as the managed society of the Twentieth Century closes in on us.

Kai Nielsen

What I am alluding to can perhaps best be brought forward if I turn to a famous trio of questions of Kant's: "What can I know?," "What ought I to do?" and "What may I hope?"[9] Max Horkheimer, in commenting on them, remarks that an examination of the "third question leads to the idea of the highest good and absolute justice."[10] He then adds that the "moral conscience . . . rebels against the thought that the present state of reality is final. . . ."[11] In the struggles of our everyday life, in the world as we know it, our hopes for a realization, or even approximation, of a truly human society, a society of human brotherhood and sisterhood, a just society or even a rational society are constantly dashed, constantly defeated. This led Kant, Lessing and even Voltaire to postulate immortality in order to make some match between our aspirations and what is realizable. Such postulations are indeed easy to satirize and indeed it is folly to try to argue from such hopes to any likelihood at all that such a reality will obtain.[12] But one can understand it as a hope—a hope which a person who truly cares about his fellows and has lost all faith in anything like a Marxist humanist future, might well keep close to his heart. If we believe, as Horkheimer and Adorno do, that we live in a world where we grow lonelier, more isolated, more caught up in meaningless work routines, more passive, more and more incapable of seeing things as a whole and of having any believable sense of where we come from, who we are or where we are going, we may perhaps rightly become "knights of faith" and make such an otherwise absurd postulation.

Yet, if we can rightly live in hope here, can we not, even more rightly, live in accordance with the less intellectually stultifying hope that we humans can attain a certain rationality and come to see things whole and in time make real, through our struggles, a truly human society without exploitation and degradation in which all human beings will flourish? Even *if* this hope is utopian—another dream of the "dreamers of the absolute"—it is still far less utopian, and far less fantastical, than the hope for "another world" where we will go "by and by." Moreover, such secular hopes are in the various Marxisms (reified and otherwise) as alive in traditions as are the other-worldly conceptions of Christianity.

NOTES

1. The sense of this is very acute in Stanley Cavell's *Must We Mean What We Say* (New York: Charles Scribner's Sons, 1969) and this sense is further astutely conveyed in Francis Sparshott's discussion of it in *The Times Literary Supplement*. July 22, 1977, p. 899.

2. *My Ethics Without God* (London: Pemberton Books, 1973), *Scepticism* (London: Macmillan, 1973). "Linguistic Philosophy and 'The Meaning of Life,'" *Cross-Currents*, Vol. XIV (Summer 1964), "Linguistic Philosophy and Beliefs," *Philosophy Today*, No. 2, Jerry H. Gill (ed.) (London: Collier Macmillan Ltd., 1969), "An Examination of the Thomistic Theory of Natural Moral Law," *Natural Law Forum*, Vol. 4 (1959) and "God and the Good: Does Morality Need Religion," *Theology Today*, Vol. XXI (April 1964).

3. J.M. Cameron, "Surviving Death," *The New York Review of Books*, Vol. XXI, No. 17 (October 1974), pp. 6–11.

4. Antony Flew, "Is There a Case for Disembodied Survival?" *The Journal of the American Society For Psychical Research*, Vol. 66 (April 1972), pp. 129–144, part III of Antony Flew, *The Presumption of Atheism* (New York: Barnes & Noble, 1976), Terrence Penelhum, *Survival and Disembodied Existence* (London: Routledge & Kegan Paul, 1970) and my "Logic, Incoherence and Religion," *International Logic Review*, forthcoming.

5. Ludwig Wittgenstein, *On Certainty*, translated by Denis Paul and G.E.M. Anscombe (Oxford: Basil Blackwell, 1969) and G.H. von Wright, "Wittgenstein on Certainty," *Problems in the Theory of Knowledge*, ed. by G.H. von Wright (The Hague: Martinus Nijhoff, 1972), pp. 47–60.

6. J.M. Cameron, *op. cit.*, p. 11.

7. *Ibid.*

8. Peter Geach, *God and the Soul* (London: Routledge & Kegan Paul, 1969), pp. 117–129.

9. Immanuel Kant, *Critique of Pure Reason*, tr. by J.M.D. Meiklejohn (New York: Dutton, 1934), p. 457.

10. Max Horkheimer, *Critique of Instrumental Reason* (New York: The Seabury Press, 1974), p. 2.

11. *Ibid.*

12. J.L. Mackie, "Sidgwick's Pessimism," *Philosphical Quarterly* (1976), pp. 326–327.

CHAPTER 14

HAZEL E. BARNES

The Far Side of Despair

Among the accusing adjectives which hostile critics have attached to humanistic existentialism, one of the most frequently heard is "nihilistic." Existentialists, it appears, believe in *nothing*; hence nothing stands to block their destructive impulses, and we may expect *anything* from them. Whether spoken naively or formulated with philosophical sophistication, this attitude contains an important assumption: that there is a logical connection between what one believes about ultimate reality, one's sense of purpose, one's values, and one's concrete action. . . .

It is generally assumed that a lack of higher meaning or overall purpose in the Universe is a terribly bad thing. Even Sartre has remarked that it would be much better if God the Father existed. Our forlornness is due to our discovery that He is not there. It is worthwhile to ask ourselves just what this hypothesis of higher meaning and purpose really does and has meant to man and why he has felt the necessity to project it. Most of the time I believe it has been bound up with the hope for immortality. Certainly in traditional Christianity, as in any religion which promises a personal afterlife, the significant part of the idea of historical development is not that God and His Universe are infinitely good and eternal but that the individual shares in this destiny. Most important of all for our present selves is the thought that the specific role we play in this far future is determined by the way we conduct ourselves here and now. This life on earth is our trial and test, and the grade we receive indicates the eternal class we go into. The undeniable positive element here is the conviction that what we do matters forever. If taken literally—or as near to literally as today's fundamentalist is willing to take it—the pragmatic value of this doctrine is overwhelming. Meaning, purpose, and progress toward some definite destination are clearly defined and omnipresent. The catch is that the more concrete and specific the positive promise, the darker the negative side. The Medieval Heaven gains part of its shining light from the contrast with the smoky darkness of the Hell which lies below it. "Here pity or here piety must die," says Dante; and I, for one, would at this point bid piety a hasty adieu. A God who would for eternity subject even one person to horrors surpassing those of Buchenwald, a Creator who would create souls capable of deserving such punishment seems to me to echo man's ignoble desire for vengeance more than his aspirations for an understanding Justice. Of course very few people today believe in everlasting punishment, and it is easy to see why. Only the most hardened sinner could bear to live with this sort of anticipation for any of his acquaintances—let alone the fear of being condemned himself.

In a more acceptable form, Christianity for today's average believer stresses the mercy of God. Although it may not be put in quite this way, the idea seems to be that since God views each life from within, He sees each man's good intentions. *"Tout comprendre, c'est tout pardonner."* Hell isn't left quite empty, but like the Greeks' realm of Hades, it is reserved for the really great sinners—like Hitler, perhaps—who are condemned by almost everybody and sufficiently remote so as not to concern us. Heaven and Hell are less concrete and precisely located than they used to be. If one gets liberal enough in his Christian commitment, he may think of Heaven as simply the eternal consciousness of God's presence and Hell as the painful awareness of His absence. At this point, even if individual immortality is not lost, we are in danger of floating off into a vague pantheism which is no longer specifically Christian. In itself, this makes no difference for our present discussion. The issue is not specifically between existentialism and Christianity. Yet we may note that the more the old idea of Heaven and Hell is subjected to ethical purification and intellectual criticism, the feebler becomes any specific hypothesis as to the meaning and ultimate goal of the individual life. If Christianity reaches the point of no longer postulating any afterlife for the specific person, then we may well ask what remains of what centuries have found most valuable—the infinite value of every human soul, its eternal existence, and its freedom of choice to determine the quality of that existence.

Not all hypotheses of the existence of a higher meaning necessarily postulate eternal life for the individual consciousness, whether separate or absorbed in some ultimate Unity. Aristotelianism does not—despite the First Cause, the Unmoved Mover which thinks itself and by its very presence draws all other forms upward toward pure Thought. The Hebrew prophets, too, speak of no future life for man. It is in the present that man must walk humbly and righteously in the sight of the Just God, who will champion those whose cause is right. These interpretations of reality are not oriented toward any eternal Future, but they do serve as some sort of absolute guarantee and point of reference. If the Universe is rationally organized, whether ordered by a Deist Creator, or simply sustained by an Unmoved Mover, it at least serves as a mirror for man wherein he can find himself and his proper place. If the order of the Universe both corresponds to human reason and exists independently of it, one may conclude, at the very least, that Reason is our essence and guide, that to develop it to its greatest extent is our highest good. It is an easy step from there to the notion that Reason may discover absolutes in the ethical sphere as well and that the ultimate attainment of rationality will be a culmination of all that is best in ourselves and a steadfast bond between us and the outside world. Similarly, the belief that the structure of things is permeated with the spirit of Justice offers a sustenance and guarantee to man which come from outside himself. Not only will God reward the Just. He furnishes the assurance that we *ought* to be just and that we may know what Justice is.

Existentialism rejects all of these blandishments. In the early writing of French existentialists, man's recognition that he stood alone in an irrational world without God was expressed in an attitude in which revolt and despair were equally mingled. Things ought not to be this way, was the cry. We will never accept our fate with resignation, but we will live it—in our own way—against the Universe. At the end of *The Flies*, Orestes declares: "On the far side of despair, life begins." But the life which was to start involved no change in the view of things which precipitated Orestes' self-chosen exile. Camus said that his thought had gone beyond what he formulated early in *The Myth of Sisyphus*, but he added that he had never renounced the vision of the absurd which led him to ask, "Can I live without appeal? Can Thought live in this desert?" It is important not to forget this tragic vision of man against the Universe. Humanistic existentialism finds no divine presence, no ingrained higher meaning, no reassuring Absolute. At the same time, no humanistic existentialist will allow that the only alternative is despair and irresponsibility. Camus has pointed out the fallacy involved in leaping from the premise "The Universe has no higher meaning" to the conclusion, "Therefore my life is not worth living." The individual life may have an intrinsic value, both to the one who lives it and to those in the sphere of his influence, whether the Universe knows what it is doing or not.

Merleau Ponty has remarked, "Life makes no sense, but it is ours to make sense of." In a popular lecture, Sartre expressed somewhat the same idea, explaining in simple terms both what he means by creating or "inventing" values and by value itself.

> To say that we invent values means nothing except this: life has no meaning a priori. Before you live it, life is nothing, but it is for you to give it a meaning. Value is nothing other than this meaning which you choose.[1]

. . . In contrasting traditional and existentialist attitudes toward the question of the meaning of life, I should like to use a homely example as an illustration. Let us imagine reality to have the shape of a gigantic Chinese checkerboard—without even the logically arranged spacing of the regularly shaped holes as in the usual game board, and with various-sized marbles, only some of which will fit into the spaces provided. The traditional attitude of religion and philosophy has been that we faced two alternatives. Theological and rational positions have assumed that there exists some correct pattern, impressed into the board itself, which can be discovered and which will then show us how we may satisfactorily and correctly arrange the piles of marbles near us. They have assumed—and so have the Nihilists—that if there is no such pattern, then there is no reason to play at all. If there is no motive for making a particular pattern, they have concluded that one might as well destroy the patterns set up by others or commit suicide. Existentialism holds that there is a third possibility. There is no pre-existing pattern. No amount of delving into the structure of the board will reveal one inscribed there in matter. Nor is it sensible to hope for some nonmaterial force which might magnetically draw the marbles into their correct position if we put ourselves in touch with such a power by prayer or drugs or any other device which man might think of. But while this lack deprives man of guide and certain goal, it leaves him free to create his own pattern. It is true that there is no external model according to which one may pronounce the new pattern good or bad, better or worse. There are only the individual judgments by him who makes it and by those who behold it, and these need not agree. If the maker finds value in his own creation, if the process of making is satisfying, if the end result compares sufficiently favorably with the intention, then the pattern *has* value and the individual life has been worthwhile. I must quickly add that no such pattern exists alone. Although its unique form and color remain distinctly perceptible, it is intermeshed with the edges of the patterns of others— like the design of a paisley print. The satisfaction in a life may well result in large part from the sense that these intermeshings have positive significance for the individual pattern. There is another kind of satisfaction—that which comes from the knowledge that other persons have declared one's pattern good. Still a third derives from the realization that what one has done has helped make it easier for others to live patterns intrinsically satisfying to them.

That a positive value is present in experiencing a delight in what one has created and in the approval of others cannot be denied. For many people this is not enough. The sense that there is something missing is sufficient to undermine any quiet content with what one has. We hear most frequently three basic complaints, and these refer respectively to (1) the starting point, (2) the here and now, and (3) the farther on. First, there is the feeling that we need some sort of eternal archetype or measuring stick. Existentialism admits that there is nothing of the sort and that life is harder without it. Yet we may well ask whether the privilege of having such an authority would not come at too high a price, and cost more than it is worth. Pragmatically, the over-all destiny and purpose of the Universe play a small part in the daily projects of Western man—with the possible exception of those remaining fundamentalists who still take the promise of Heaven and Hell quite literally. Mostly it is there as a kind of consolation at moments of failure, cheering our discouragement with the idea that things may be better something in a way that we cannot begin to comprehend. I do not deny the psychic refreshment of such comfort. But if the belief in any such authority and plan is sufficiently specific to be more than a proud hope, it must be restrictive as well. If man can be sure that he is right by any nonhuman standard, then his humanity is strictly confined by the nonhuman. He is not free to bring anything new into the world. His possibilities are those of the slave or the well-bred child. Higher meaning is itself a limitation for a being-who-is-a-process. Such a future is not open but prescribed. Man as a tiny being in an impersonal world may be without importance from the theoretical but nonexistent point of view of an omniscient objective observer. Man in the theological framework of the medieval man-centered Universe has only the dignity of the child, who must regulate his life by the rules laid down by adults. The human adventure becomes a conducted tour. It is in this sense that I seriously question the sincerity or the wisdom of Sartre's statement that it would be better if God the Father existed. The time has come for man to leave his parents and to live in his own right by his own judgments.

The second disturbing aspect of a life of self-created patterns emerges when we compare ourselves with our fellow man. Obviously some people are satisfied with patterns which others regard as deplorable. Can we allow this chaos of judgments and still cling to the belief in the positive value of whatever patterns we ourselves have made? Is the result not such an anarchy of the arbitrary that to speak of pattern at all is nonsense? Here existentialism begins by saying that up to a point, arbitrariness, inconsistency, and the simultaneous existence of divergent value systems are not to be lamented but welcomed. The creative freedom to choose and structure one's own pattern would be worthless if we were to agree that we would all work in the same way toward the same end. Just as we expect persons to differ in their specific projects, so we should allow for those individual overall orientations which bestow upon the project its significance and which are, in turn, colored by it. Sartre has declared that the creation of a value system by which one is willing to live and to judge one's life is man's most important creative enterprise. This means more than the working out of standards of right and wrong and the regulation of one's own demands in the light of our relations with others. It involves the whole context of what we might call "the style" of a life—not just the moral but the aesthetic, the temperamental—everything which goes to make up the personality which continues, with varying degrees of modification, until death and which even then will leave behind it an objectified "Self for Others." Every such life is unique, no matter how hard the one who lives it may have tried to mold himself after the pattern of his contemporaries. Existentialism prizes this uniqueness and resists all attempts to reduce it to the lowest possible minimum. Existentialism recognizes and exults in the fact that since everyone is a point of view, there is no more possibility of all persons becoming the same than there is of reducing to one perspective the views of two people looking at a landscape from different spots. . . .

The absence of any discernible higher meaning in the Universe takes on a new and special significance when we confront the future, not merely my own but that of the world as a whole. What difference does it make, some will ask, whether I fashion one kind of pattern rather than another or none at all? All patterns will be blotted out as though they had never been. If this world is all, how can one attach any significance whatsoever to the individual life in the face of the immensity of space, the staggering infinity of Time? "We are sick with space!" cries Robert Frost. The French keep reminding us of the futility of all endeavor "from the point of view of Sirius." Again, I feel that we suffer still from Christianity's insistence that all of us together and the Universe with us are going somewhere definite and that the destination bestows its meaning on the present mile of the journey. Deprived of this forward voyaging, we find no delight in the nonpurposeful development of an impersonal cosmos which has no prearranged destination. Whether this drifting Universe will eventually become cold and lifeless, or whether there will occur once again—or many times—the coming together of organized matter and the appearance of other forms of consciousness, it seems unlikely that man will be remembered any more than we have reason to think that all of this present world of matter was put here for his express benefit.

Is there any reason *why* we should try to adopt the point of view of Sirius? We should realize that observation of a dead planet through a telescope is neither more nor less true as a vision of the Universe than is the examination of living organisms through a microscope. To see the big without the small is to exclude much of reality just as surely as to stay within the limits of the microscopic. If there is a falsification of boundaries at the one end, there is a blurring of details and elimination of foreground at the other. William James has commented that inasmuch as death comes at the end to cut off all human projects, every life is finally a failure. The point of view of Sirius reveals the same message on the cosmic scale. Yet if it were possible for one to stand on Sirius at the instant before the final disappearance of all life, that moment of conclusion would be no more real or significant than any one of the moments preceding it. If there is an absolute negative quality in the absence of what will not be, then there is a corresponding positive value in what will have been. This last awareness might just as well take pride in what had been there as despair in the knowledge that it will no longer be. One does not choose to eat something bitter today simply because tomorrow it will make no difference which food one has chosen. The addition of positive moments does not add up to zero even if the time arrives when nothing more is added to the series. One might say that there is never any adding up of the sum, but this is not quite true. The new digits carry the weight of those which have gone before.

It is illogical to conclude that human values and meanings are unreal and of no importance simply because they do not originate in the structure of the nonhuman Universe. It is enough that the world serves to support these subjective structures for the consciousness which lives them. At the same time it is only natural that an individual man, whose being is a self-projection, should rebel at the prospect of seeing his projects suddenly brought to a stop. If the patterns and meanings which a consciousness creates were restricted to those experiences which we can live directly, then despair would in truth seem to be our only proper response. But man's being is that of a creature who is always about-to-be. In a peculiar sense also, he is, in his being, always outside or beyond himself, out there in the objects of his intentions or—more accurately—in his projects in the world. An impersonal Universe cannot sustain these subjective structures. But we do not exist in an impersonal Universe. We live in a human world where multitudes of other consciousnesses are ceaselessly imposing their meanings upon Being-in-itself and confronting the projects which I have introduced. It is in the future of these intermeshed human activities that I most fully transcend myself. In so far as "I" have carved out my being in his human world, "I" go on existing in its future.

NOTE

1. Sartre, *L'Existentialisme est un humanisme*, pp. 89–90.

CHAPTER 15

RICHARD TAYLOR

The Meaning of Life

The question whether life has any meaning is difficult to interpret, and the more one concentrates his critical faculty on it the more it seems to elude him, or to evaporate as any intelligible question. One wants to turn it aside, as a source of embarrassment, as something that, if it cannot be abolished, should at least be decently covered. And yet I think any reflective person recognizes that the question it raises is important, and that it ought to have a significant answer.

If the idea of meaningfulness is difficult to grasp in this context, so that we are unsure what sort of thing would amount to answering the question, the idea of meaninglessness is perhaps less so. If, then, we can bring before our minds a clear image of meaningless existence, then perhaps we can take a step toward coping with our original question by seeing to what extent our lives, as we actually find them, resemble that image, and draw such lessons as we are able to from the comparison.

MEANINGLESS EXISTENCE

A perfect image of meaninglessness, of the kind we are seeking, is found in the ancient myth of Sisyphus. Sisyphus, it will be remembered, betrayed divine secrets to mortals, and for this he was condemned by the gods to roll a stone to the top of a hill, the stone then immediately to roll back down, again to be pushed to the top by Sisyphus, to roll down once more, and so on again and again, *forever*. Now in this we have the picture of meaningless, pointless toil, of a meaningless existence that is absolutely *never* redeemed. It is not even redeemed by a death that, if it were to accomplish nothing more, would at least bring this idiotic cycle to a close. If we were invited to imagine Sisyphus struggling for awhile and accomplishing nothing, perhaps eventually falling from exhaustion, so that we might suppose him then eventually turning to something having some sort of promise, then the meaninglessness of that chapter of his life would not be so stark. It would be a dark and dreadful dream, from which he eventually awakens to sunlight and reality. But he does not awaken, for there is nothing for him to awaken to. His repetitive toil is his life and reality, and it goes on forever, and it is without any meaning whatever. Nothing ever comes of what he is doing, except simply, more of the same. Not by one step, nor by a thousand, nor by ten thousand does he even expiate by the smallest token the sin against the gods that led him into this fate. Nothing comes of it, nothing at all.

This ancient myth has always enchanted men, for countless meanings can be read into it. Some of the ancients apparently thought it symbolized the perpetual rising and setting of the sun, and others the repetitious crashing of the waves upon the shore. Probably the commonest interpretation is that it symbolizes man's eternal struggle and unquenchable spirit, his determination always to try once more in the face of overwhelming discouragement. This interpretation is further supported by that version of the myth according to which Sisyphus was commanded to roll the stone *over* the hill, so that it would finally roll down the other side, but was never quite able to make it.

I am not concerned with rendering or defending any interpretation of this myth, however. I have cited it only for the one element it does unmistakably contain, namely, that of a repetitious, cyclic activity that never comes to anything. We could contrive other images of this that would serve just as well, and no myth-makers are needed to supply the materials of it. Thus, we can imagine two persons transporting a stone—or even a precious gem, it does not matter—back and forth, relay style. One carries it to a near or distant point where it is received by the other; it is returned to its starting point, there to be recovered by the first, and the process is repeated over and over. Except in this relay nothing counts as winning, and nothing brings the contest to any close, each step only leads to a repetition of itself. Or we can imagine two groups of prisoners, one of them engaged in digging a prodigious hole in the ground that is no sooner finished than it is filled in again by the other group, the latter then digging a new hole that is at once filled in by the first group, and so on and on endlessly.

Now what stands out in all such pictures as oppressive and dejecting is not that the beings who enact these roles suffer any torture or pain, for it need not be assumed that they do. Nor is it that their labors are great, for they are no greater than the labors commonly undertaken by most men most of the time. According to the original myth, the stone is so large that Sisyphus never quite gets it to the top and must groan under every step, so that his enormous labor is all for nought. But this is not what appalls. It is not that his great struggle comes to nothing, but that his existence itself is without meaning. Even if we suppose, for example, that the stone is but a pebble that can be carried effortlessly, or that the holes dug by the prisoners are but small ones, not the slightest meaning is introduced into their lives. The stone that Sisyphus moves to the top of the hill, whether we think of it as large or small, still rolls back every time, and the process is repeated forever. Nothing comes of it, and the work is simply pointless. That is the element of the myth that I wish to capture.

Again, it is not the fact that the labors of Sisyphus continue forever that deprives them of meaning. It is, rather, the implication of this: that they come to nothing. The image would not be changed by our supposing him to push a different stone up every time, each to roll down again. But if we supposed that these stones, instead of rolling back to their places as if they had never been moved, were assembled at the top of the hill and there incorporated, say, in a beautiful and enduring temple, then the aspect of meaninglessness would disappear. His labors would then have a point, something would come of them all, and although one could perhaps still say it was not worth it, one could not say that the life of Sisyphus was devoid of meaning altogether. Meaningfulness would at least have made an appearance, and we could see what it was.

That point will need remembering. But in the meantime, let us note another way in which the image of meaninglessness can be altered by making only a very slight change. Let us suppose that the gods, while condemning Sisyphus to the fate just described, at the same time, as an afterthought, waxed perversely merciful by implanting in him a strange and irrational impulse; namely, a compulsive impulse to roll stones. We may if we like, to make this more graphic, suppose they accomplish this by implanting in him some substance that has this effect on his character and drives. I call this perverse, because from our point of view there is clearly no reason why anyone should have a persistent and insatiable desire to do something so pointless as that. Nevertheless, suppose that is Sisyphus' condition. He has but one obsession, which is to roll stones, and it is an obsession that is only for the moment appeased by his rolling them—he no sooner gets a stone rolled to the top of the hill than he is restless to roll up another.

Now it can be seen why this little afterthought of the gods, which I called perverse, was also in fact merciful. For they have by this device managed to give Sisyphus precisely what he wants—by making him want precisely what they inflict on him. However it may appear to us, Sisyphus' fate now does not appear to him as a condemnation, but the very reverse. His one desire in life is to roll stones, and he is absolutely guaranteed its endless fulfillment. Where otherwise he might profoundly have wished surcease, and even welcomed the quiet of death to release him from endless boredom and meaninglessness, his life is now filled with mission and meaning, and he seems to himself to have been given an entry to heaven. Nor need he even fear death, for the gods have promised him an endless opportunity to indulge his single purpose, without concern or frustration. He will be able to roll stones *forever*.

What we need to mark most carefully at this point is that the picture with which we began has not really been changed in the least by adding this supposition. Exactly the same things happen as before. The only change is in Sisyphus' view of them. The picture before was the image of meaningless activity and existence. It was created precisely to be an image of that. It has not lost that meaninglessness, it has now gained not the least shred of meaningfulness. The stones still roll back as before, each phase of Sisyphus' life still exactly resembles all the others, the task is never completed, nothing comes of it, no temple ever begins to rise, and all this cycle of the same pointless thing over and over goes on forever in this picture as in the other. The *only* thing that has happened is this: Sisyphus has been reconciled to it, and indeed more, he has been led to embrace it. Not, however, by reason or persuasion, but by nothing more rational than the potency of a new substance in his veins.

THE MEANINGLESSNESS OF LIFE

I believe the foregoing provides a fairly clear content to the idea of meaninglessness and, through it, some hint of what meaningfulness, in this sense, might be. Meaninglessness is essentially endless pointlessness, and meaningfulness is therefore the opposite. Activity, and even long, drawnout and repetitive activity, has a meaning if it has some significant culmination, some more or less lasting end that can be considered to have been the direction and purpose of the activity. But the descriptions so far also provide something else; namely, the suggestion of how an existence that is objectively meaningless, in this sense, can nevertheless acquire a meaning for him whose existence it is.

Now let us ask: Which of these pictures does life in fact resemble? And let us not begin with our own lives, for here both our prejudices and wishes are great, but with the life in general that we share with the rest of creation. We shall find, I think, that it all has a certain pattern, and that this pattern is by now easily recognized.

We can begin anywhere, only saving human existence for our last consideration. We can, for example, begin with any animal. It does not matter where we begin, because the result is going to be exactly the same.

Thus, for example, there are caves in New Zealand, deep and dark, whose floors are quiet pools and whose walls and ceilings are covered with soft light. As one gazes in wonder in the stillness of these caves it seems that the Creator has reproduced there in microcosm the heavens themselves, until one scarcely remembers the enclosing presence of the walls. As one looks more closely, however, the scene is explained. Each dot of light identifies an ugly worm, whose luminous tail is meant to attract insects from the surrounding darkness. As from time to time one of these insects draws near it becomes entangled in a sticky thread lowered by the worm, and is eaten. This goes on month after month, the blind worm lying there in the barren stillness waiting to entrap an occasional bit of nourishment that will only sustain it to another bit of nourishment until. . . . Until what? What great thing awaits all this long and repetitive effort and makes it worthwhile? Really nothing. The larva just transforms itself finally to a tiny winged adult that lacks even mouth parts to feed and lives only a day or two. These adults, as soon as they have mated and laid eggs, are themselves caught in the threads and are devoured by the cannibalist worms, often without having ventured into the day, the only point to their existence having now been fulfilled. This has been going on for millions of years, and to no end other than that the same meaningless cycle may continue for another millions of years.

All living things present essentially the same spectacle. The larva of a certain cicada burrows in the darkness of the earth for seventeen years, through season after season, to emerge finally into the daylight for a brief flight, lay its eggs, and die—this all to repeat itself during the next seventeen years, and so on to eternity. We have already noted, in another connection, the struggles of fish, made only that others may do the same after them and that this cycle, having no other point than itself, may never cease. Some birds span an entire side of the globe each year and then return, only to insure that others may follow the same incredibly long path again and again. One is led to wonder what the point of it all is, with what great triumph this ceaseless effort, repeating itself through millions of years, might finally culminate, and why it should go on and on for so long, accomplishing nothing, getting nowhere. But then one realizes that there is no point to it at all, that it really culminates in nothing, that each of these cycles, so filled with toil, is to be followed only by more of the same. The point of any living thing's life is, evidently, nothing but life itself.

This life of the world thus presents itself to our eyes as a vast machine, feeding on itself, running on and on forever to nothing. And we are part of that life. To be sure, we are not just the same, but the differences are not so great as we like to think; many are merely invented, and none really cancels the kind of meaninglessness that we found in Sisyphus and that we find all around, wherever anything lives. We are conscious of our activity. Our goals, whether in any significant sense we choose them or not, are things of which we are at least partly aware and can therefore in some sense appraise. More significantly, perhaps, men have a history, as other animals do not, such that each generation does not precisely resemble all those before. Still, if we can in imagination disengage our wills from our lives and disregard the deep interest each man has in his own existence, we shall find that they do not so little resemble the existence of Sisyphus. We toil after goals, most of them—indeed every single one of them—of transitory significance and, having gained one of them, we immediately set forth for the next, as if that one had never been, with this next one being essentially more of the same. Look at a busy street any day, and observe the throng going hither and thither. To what? Some office or shop, where the same things will be done today as were done yesterday, and are done now so they may be repeated tomorrow. And if we think that, unlike Sisyphus, these labors do have a point, that they culminate in something lasting and, independently of our own deep interests in them, very worthwhile, then we simply have not considered the thing closely enough. Most such effort is directed only to the establishment and perpetuation of home and family; that is, to the begetting of others who will follow in our steps to do more of the same. Each man's life thus resembles one of Sisyphus' climbs to the summit of his hill, and each day of it one of his steps; the difference is that whereas Sisyphus himself returns to push the stone up again, we leave this to our children. We at one point imagined that the labors of Sisyphus finally culminated in the creation of a temple, but for this to make any difference it had to be a temple that would at least endure, adding beauty to the world for the remainder of time. Our achievements, even though they are often beautiful, are mostly bubbles; and those that do last, like the sand-swept pyramids, soon becomes mere curiosities while around them the rest of mankind continues its perpetual toting of rocks, only to see them roll down. Nations are built upon the bones of their founders and pioneers, but only to decay and crumble before long, their rubble then becoming the foundation for others directed to exactly the same fate. The picture of Sisyphus is the picture of existence of the individual man, great or unknown, of nations, of the race of men, and of the very life of the world.

On a country road one sometimes comes upon the ruined hulks of a house and once extensive buildings, all in collapse and spread over with weeds. A curious eye can in imagination reconstruct from what is left a once warm and thriving life, filled with purpose. There was the hearth, where a family once talked, sang, and made plans; there were the rooms, where people loved, and babes were born to a rejoicing mother; there are the musty remains of a sofa, infested with bugs, once bought at a dear price to enhance an ever-growing comfort, beauty, and warmth. Every small piece of junk fills the mind with what once, not long ago, was utterly real, with children's voices, plans made, and enterprises embarked upon. That is how these stones of Sisyphus were rolled up, and that is how they became incorporated into a beautiful temple, and that temple is what now lies before you. Meanwhile other buildings, institutions, nations, and civilizations spring up all around, only to share the same fate before long. And if the question "What for?" is now asked, the answer is clear: so that just this may go on forever.

The two pictures—of Sisyphus and of our own lives, if we look at them from a distance—are in outline the same and convey to the mind the same image. It is not surprising, then, that men invent ways of denying it, their religions proclaiming a heaven that does not crumble, their hymnals and prayer books declaring a significance to life of which our eyes provide no hint whatever.[1] Even our philosophies portray some permanent and lasting good at which all may aim, from the changeless forms invented by Plato to the beatific vision of St. Thomas and the ideals of permanence contrived by the moderns. When these fail to convince, then earthly ideals such as universal justice and brotherhood are conjured up to take their places and give meaning to man's seemingly endless pilgrimage, some final state that will be ushered in when the last obstacle is removed and the last stone pushed to the hilltop. No one believes, of course, that any such state will be final, or even wants it to be in case it means that human existence would then cease to be a struggle; but in the meantime such ideas serve a very real need.

THE MEANING OF LIFE

We noted that Sisyphus' existence would have meaning if there were some point to his labors, if his efforts ever culminated in something that was not just an occasion for fresh labors of the same kind. But that is precisely the meaning it lacks. And human existence resembles his in that respect. Men do achieve things—they scale their towers and raise their stones to their hill-tops—but every such accomplishment fades, providing only an occasion for renewed labors of the same kind.

But here we need to note something else that has been mentioned, but its significance not explored, and that is the state of mind and feeling with which such labors are undertaken. We noted that if Sisyphus had a keen and unap-peasable desire to be doing just what he found himself doing, then, although his life would in no way be changed, it would nevertheless have a meaning for him. It would be an irrational one, no doubt, because the desire itself would be only the product of the substance in his veins, and not any that rea-son could discover, but a meaning nevertheless.

And would it not, in fact, be a meaning incomparably better than the other? For let us examine again the first kind of meaning it could have. Let us suppose that, without having any interest in rolling stones, as such, and find-ing this, in fact, a galling toil, Sisyphus did nevertheless have a deep interest in raising a temple, one that would be beautiful and lasting. And let us sup-pose he succeeded in this, that after ages of dreadful toil, all directed at this final result, he did at last complete his temple, such that now he could say his work was done, and he could rest and forever enjoy the result. Now what? What picture now presents itself to our minds? It is precisely the picture of infinite boredom! Of Sisyphus doing nothing ever again, but contemplating what he has already wrought and can no longer add anything to, and con-templating it for an eternity! Now in this picture we have a meaning for Sisy-phus' existence, a point for his prodigious labor, because we have put it there; yet, at the same time, that which is really worthwhile seems to have slipped away entirely. Where before we were presented with the nightmare of eternal and pointless activity, we are now confronted with the hell of its eternal absence.

Our second picture, then, wherein we imagined Sisyphus to have had inflicted on him the irrational desire to be doing just what he found himself doing, should not have been dismissed so abruptly. The meaning that picture lacked was no meaning that he or anyone could crave, and the strange mean-ing it had was perhaps just what we were seeking.

At this point, then, we can reintroduce what has been until now, it is hoped, resolutely pushed aside in an effort to view our lives and human exis-tence with objectivity; namely, our own wills, our deep interest in what we find ourselves doing. If we do this we find that our lives do indeed still resemble that of Sisyphus, but that the meaningfulness they thus lack is pre-cisely the meaningfulness of infinite boredom. At the same time, the strange meaningfulness they possess is that of the inner compulsion to be doing just what we were put here to do, and to go on doing it forever. This is the nearest we may hope to get to heaven, but the redeeming side of that fact is that we do thereby avoid a genuine hell.

If the builders of a great and flourishing ancient civilization could somehow return now to see archaeologists unearthing the trivial remnants of what they had once accomplished with such effort—see the fragments of pots and vases, a few broken statues, and such tokens of another age and greatness—they could indeed ask themselves what the point of it all was, if this is all it finally came to. Yet, it did not seem so to them then, for it was just the building, and not what was finally built, that gave their life meaning. Similarly, if the builders of the ruined home and farm that I described a short while ago could be brought back to see what is left, they would have the same feelings. What we construct in our imaginations as we look over these decayed and rusting pieces would reconstruct itself in their very memories, and certainly with unspeakable sadness. The piece of a sled at our feet would revive in them a warm Christmas. And what rich memories would there be in the broken crib? And the weed-covered remains of a fence would reproduce the scene of a great herd of livestock, so laboriously built up over so many years. What was it all worth, if this is the final result? Yet, again, it did not seem so to them through those many years of struggle and toil, and they did not imagine they were building a Gibraltar. The things to which they bent their backs day after day, realizing one by one their ephemeral plans, were precisely the things in which their wills were deeply involved, precisely the things in which their interests lay, and there was no need then to ask questions. There is no more need of them now—the day was sufficient to itself, and so was the life.

This is surely the way to look at all of life—at one's own life, and each day and moment it contains; of the life of a nation; of the species; of the life of the world; and of everything that breathes. Even the glow worms I described, whose cycles of existence over the millions of years seem so pointless when looked at by us, will seem entirely different to us if we can somehow try to view their existence from within. Their endless activity, which gets nowhere, is just what it is their will to pursue. This is its whole justification and meaning. Nor would it be any salvation to the birds who span the globe every year, back and forth, to have a home made for them in a cage with plenty of food and protection, so that they would not have to migrate any more. It would be their condemnation, for it is the doing that counts for them, and not what they hope to win by it. Flying these prodigious distances, never ending, is what it is in their veins to do, exactly as it was in Sisyphus' veins to roll stones, without end, after the gods had waxed merciful and implanted this in him.

A human being no sooner draws his first breath than he responds to the will that is in him to live. He no more asks whether it will be worthwhile, or whether anything of significance will come of it, than the worms and the birds. The point of his living is simply to be living, in the manner that it is his nature to be living. He goes through his life building his castles, each of these beginning to fade into time as the next is begun; yet, it would be no salvation to rest from all this. It would be a condemnation, and one that would in no way be redeemed were he able to gaze upon the things he has done, even if these were beautiful and absolutely permanent, as they never are. What counts is that one should be able to begin a new task, a new castle, a new bubble. It counts only because it is there to be done and he has the will to do it. The same will be the life of his children, and of theirs; and if the philosopher is apt to see in this a pattern similar to the unending cycles of the existence of Sisyphus, and to despair, then it is indeed because the meaning and point he is seeking is not there—but mercifully so. The meaning of life is from within us, it is not bestowed from without, and it far exceeds in both its beauty and permanence any heaven of which men have ever dreamed or yearned for.

NOTE

1. A popular Christian hymn, sung often at funerals and typical of many hymns, expresses this thought:

> Swift to its close ebbs out life's little day;
> Earth's joys grow dim, its glories pass away;
> Change and decay in all around I see:
> O thou who changest not, abide with me.

CHAPTER 16

THOMAS NAGEL

The Absurd

Most people feel on occasion that life is absurd, and some feel it vividly and continually. Yet the reasons usually offered in defense of this conviction are patently inadequate: they *could* not really explain why life is absurd. Why then do they provide a natural expression for the sense that it is?

I

Consider some examples. It is often remarked that nothing we do now will matter in a million years. But if that is true, then by the same token, nothing that will be the case in a million years matters now. In particular, it does not matter now that in a million years nothing we do now will matter. Moreover, even if what we did now *were* going to matter in a million years, how could that keep our present concerns from being absurd? If their mattering now is not enough to accomplish that, how would it help if they mattered a million years from now?

Whether what we do now will matter in a million years could make the crucial difference only if its mattering in a million years depended on its mattering, period. But then to deny that whatever happens now will matter in a million years is to beg the question against its mattering, period; for in that sense one cannot know that it will not matter in a million years whether (for example) someone now is happy or miserable, without knowing that it does not matter, period.

What we say to convey the absurdity of our lives often has to do with

From *The Journal of Philosophy*, Vol. LXIII, No. 20, 1971. Used by permission of the journal and the author.

space or time: we are tiny specks in the infinite vastness of the universe; our lives are mere instants even on a geological time scale, let alone a cosmic one; we will all be dead any minute. But of course none of these evident facts can be what *makes* life absurd, if it is absurd. For suppose we lived forever; would not a life that is absurd if it lasts seventy years be infinitely absurd if it lasted through eternity? And if our lives are absurd given our present size, why would they be any less absurd if we filled the universe (either because we were larger or because the universe was smaller)? Reflection on our minuteness and brevity appears to be intimately connected with the sense that life is meaningless; but it is not clear what the connection is.

Another inadequate argument is that because we are going to die, all chains of justification must leave off in mid-air: one studies and works to earn money to pay for clothing, housing, entertainment, food, to sustain oneself from year to year, perhaps to support a family and pursue a career—but to what final end? All of it is an elaborate journey leading nowhere. (One will also have some effect on other people's lives, but that simply reproduces the problem, for they will die too.)

There are several replies to this argument. First, life does not consist of a sequence of activities each of which has as its purpose some later member of the sequence. Chains of justification come repeatedly to an end within life, and whether the process as a whole can be justified has no bearing on the finality of these end-points. No further justification is needed to make it reasonable to take aspirin for a headache, attend an exhibit of the work of a painter one admires, or stop a child from putting his hand on a hot stove. No larger context or further purpose is needed to prevent these acts from being pointless.

Even if someone wished to supply a further justification for pursuing all the things in life that are commonly regarded as self-justifying, that justification would have to end somewhere too. If *nothing* can justify unless it is justified in terms of something outside itself, which is also justified, then an infinite regress results, and no chain of justification can be complete. Moreover, if a finite chain of reasons cannot justify anything, what could be accomplished by an infinite chain, each link of which must be justified by something outside itself?

Since justifications must come to an end somewhere, nothing is gained by denying that they end where they appear to, within life—or by trying to subsume the multiple, often trivial ordinary justifications of action under a single, controlling life scheme. We can be satisfied more easily than that. In fact, through its misrepresentation of the process of justification, the argument makes a vacuous demand. It insists that the reasons available within life are incomplete, but suggests thereby that all reasons that come to an end are incomplete. This makes it impossible to supply any reasons at all.

The standard arguments for absurdity appear therefore to fail as arguments. Yet I believe they attempt to express something that is difficult to state, but fundamentally correct.

II

In ordinary life a situation is absurd when it includes a conspicuous discrepancy between pretension or aspiration and reality: someone gives a complicated speech in support of a motion that has already been passed; a notorious criminal is made president of a major philanthropic foundation; you declare your love over the telephone to a recorded announcement; as you are being knighted, your pants fall down.

When a person finds himself in an absurd situation, he will usually attempt to change it, by modifying his aspirations, or by trying to bring reality into better accord with them, or by removing himself from the situation entirely. We are not always willing or able to extricate ourselves from a position whose absurdity has become clear to us. Nevertheless, it is usually possible to imagine some change that would remove the absurdity—whether or not we can or will implement it. The sense that life as a whole is absurd arises when we perceive, perhaps dimly, an inflated pretension or aspiration which is inseparable from the continuation of human life and which makes its absurdity inescapable, short of escape from life itself.

Many people's lives are absurd, temporarily or permanently, for conventional reasons having to do with their particular ambitions, circumstances, and personal relations. If there is a philosophical sense of absurdity, however, it must arise from the perception of something universal—some respect in which pretension and reality inevitably clash for us all. This condition is supplied, I shall argue, by the collision between the seriousness with which we take our lives and the perpetual possibility of regarding everything about which we are serious as arbitrary, or open to doubt.

We cannot live human lives without energy and attention, nor without making choices which show that we take some things more seriously than others. Yet we have always available a point of view outside the particular form of our lives, from which the seriousness appears gratuitous. These two inescapable viewpoints collide in us, and that is what makes life absurd. It is absurd because we ignore the doubts that we know cannot be settled, continuing to live with nearly undiminished seriousness in spite of them.

This analysis requires defense in two respects: first as regards the unavoidability of seriousness; second as regards the inescapability of doubt.

We take ourselves seriously whether we lead serious lives or not and whether we are concerned primarily with fame, pleasure, virtue, luxury, triumph, beauty, justice, knowledge, salvation, or mere survival. If we take other people seriously and devote ourselves to them, that only multiplies the problem. Human life is full of effort, plans, calculation, success and failure: we *pursue* our lives, with varying degrees of sloth and energy.

It would be different if we could not step back and reflect on the process, but were merely led from impulse to impulse without self-consciousness. But human beings do not act solely on impulse. They are prudent, they reflect, they weigh consequences, they ask whether what they are doing is worth while. Not only are their lives full of particular choices that hang together in larger activities with temporal structure: they also decide in the broadest terms what to pursue and what to avoid, what the priorities among their various aims should be, and what kind of people they want to be or become. Some men are faced with such choices by the large decisions they make from time to time; some merely by reflection on the course their lives are taking as the product of countless small decisions. They decide whom to marry, what profession to follow, whether to join the Country Club, or the Resistance; or they may just wonder why they go on being salesmen or academics or taxi drivers, and then stop thinking about it after a certain period of inconclusive reflection.

Although they may be motivated from act to act by those immediate needs with which life presents them, they allow the process to continue by adhering to the general system of habits and the form of life in which such motives have their place—or perhaps only by clinging to life itself. They spend enormous quantities of energy, risk, and calculation on the details. Think of how an ordinary individual sweats over his appearance, his health, his sex life, his emotional honesty, his social utility, his self-knowledge, the quality of his ties with family, colleagues, and friends, how well he does his job, whether he understands the world and what is going on in it. Leading a human life is a full-time occupation, to which everyone devotes decades of intense concern.

This fact is so obvious that it is hard to find it extraordinary and important. Each of us lives his own life—lives with himself twenty-four hours a day. What else is he supposed to do—live someone else's life? Yet humans have the special capacity to step back and survey themselves, and the lives to which they are committed, with that detached amazement which comes from watching an ant struggle up a heap of sand. Without developing the illusion that they are able to escape from their highly specific and idiosyncratic position, they can view it *sub specie aeternitatis*—and the view is at once sobering and comical.

The crucial backward step is not taken by asking for still another justification in the chain, and failing to get it. The objections to that line of attack have already been stated; justifications come to an end. But this is precisely what provides universal doubt with its object. We step back to find that the whole system of justification and criticism, which controls our choices and supports our claims to rationality, rests on responses and habits that we never question, that we should not know how to defend without circularity, and to which we shall continue to adhere even after they are called into question.

The things we do or want without reasons, and without requiring reasons—the things that define what is a reason for us and what is not—are the starting points of our skepticism. We see ourselves from outside, and all the contingency and specificity of our aims and pursuits become clear. Yet when we take this view and recognize what we do as arbitrary, it does not disengage us from life, and there lies our absurdity: not in the fact that such an external view can be taken of us, but in the fact that we ourselves can take it, without ceasing to be the persons whose ultimate concerns are so coolly regarded.

III

One may try to escape the position by seeking broader ultimate concerns, from which it is impossible to step back—the idea being that absurdity results because what we take seriously is something small and insignificant and individual. Those seeking to supply their lives with meaning usually envision a role or function in something larger than themselves. They therefore seek fulfillment in service to society, the state, the revolution, the progress of history, the advance of science, or religion and the glory of God.

But a role in some larger enterprise cannot confer significance unless that enterprise is itself significant. And its significance must come back to what we can understand, or it will not even appear to give us what we are seeking. If we learned that we were being raised to provide food for other creatures fond of human flesh, who planned to turn us into cutlets before we got too stringy—even if we learned that the human race had been developed by animal breeders precisely for this purpose—that would still not give our lives meaning, for two reasons. First, we would still be in the dark as to the significance of the lives of those other beings; second, although we might acknowledge that this culinary role would make our lives meaningful to them, it is not clear how it would make them meaningful to us.

Admittedly, the usual form of service to a higher being is different from this. One is supposed to behold and partake of the glory of God, for example, in a way in which chickens do not share in the glory of coq au vin. The same is true of service to a state, a movement, or a revolution. People can come to feel, when they are part of something bigger, that it is part of them too. They worry less about what is peculiar to themselves, but identify enough with the larger enterprise to find their role in it fulfilling.

However, any such larger purpose can be put in doubt in the same way that the aims of an individual life can be, and for the same reasons. It is as legitimate to find ultimate justification there as to find it earlier, among the details of individual life. But this does not alter the fact that justifications come to an end when we are content to have them end—when we do not find it necessary to look any further. If we can step back from the purposes of individual life and doubt their point, we can step back also from the progress of human history, or of science, or the success of a society, or the kingdom, power, and glory of God,[1] and put all these things into question in the same way. What seems to us to confer meaning, justification, significance, does so in virtue of the fact that we need no more reasons after a certain point.

What makes doubt inescapable with regard to the limited aims of individual life also makes it inescapable with regard to any larger purpose that encourages the sense that life is meaningful. Once the fundamental doubt has begun, it cannot be laid to rest.

Camus maintains in *The Myth of Sisyphus* that the absurd arises because the world fails to meet our demands for meaning. This suggests that the world might satisfy those demands if it were different. But now we can see that this is not the case. There does not appear to be any conceivable world (containing us) about which unsettlable doubts could not arise. Consequently the absurdity of our situation derives not from a collision between our expectations and the world, but from a collision within ourselves.

IV

It may be objected that the standpoint from which these doubts are supposed to be felt does not exist—that if we take the recommended backward step we will land on thin air, without any basis for judgment about the natural responses we are supposed to be surveying. If we retain our usual standards of what is important, then questions about the significance of what we are doing with our lives will be answerable in the usual way. But if we do not, then those questions can mean nothing to us, since there is no longer any content to the idea of what matters, and hence no content to the idea that nothing does.

But this objection misconceives the nature of the backward step. It is not supposed to give us an understanding of what is *really* important, so that we see by contrast that our lives are insignificant. We never, in the course of these reflections, abandon the ordinary standards that guide our lives. We merely observe them in operation, and recognize that if they are called into question we can justify them only by reference to themselves, uselessly. We adhere to them because of the way we are put together; what seems to us important or serious or valuable would not seem so if we were differently constituted.

In ordinary life, to be sure, we do not judge a situation absurd unless we have in mind some standards of seriousness, significance, or harmony with which the absurd can be contrasted. This contrast is not implied by the philosophical judgment of absurdity, and that might be thought to make the concept unsuitable for the expression of such judgments. This is not so, however, for the philosophical judgment depends on another contrast which makes it a natural extension from more ordinary cases. It departs from them only in contrasting the pretensions of life with a larger context in which *no* standards can be discovered, rather than with a context from which alternative, overriding standards may be applied.

V

In this respect, as in others, philosophical perception of the absurd resembles epistemological skepticism. In both cases the final, philosophical doubt is not contrasted with any unchallenged certainties, though it is arrived at by extrapolation from examples of doubt within the system of evidence or justification, where a contrast with other certainties *is* implied. In both cases our limitedness joins with a capacity to transcend those limitations in thought (thus seeing them as limitations, and as inescapable).

Skepticism begins when we include ourselves in the world about which we claim knowledge. We notice that certain types of evidence convince us, that we are content to allow justifications of belief to come to an end at certain points, that we feel we know many things even without knowing or having grounds for believing the denial of others which, if true, would make what we claim to know false.

For example, I know that I am looking at a piece of paper, although I have no adequate grounds to claim I know that I am not dreaming; and if I am dreaming then I am not looking at a piece of paper. Here an ordinary conception of how appearance may diverge from reality is employed to show that we take our world largely for granted; the certainty that we are not dreaming cannot be justified except circularly, in terms of those very appearances which are being put in doubt. It is somewhat farfetched to suggest I may be dreaming; but the possibility is only illustrative. It reveals that our claim to knowledge depend on our not feeling it necessary to exclude certain incompatible alternatives, and the dreaming possibility or the total-hallucination possibility are just representatives for limitless possibilities most of which we cannot even conceive.[2]

Once we have taken the backward step to an abstract view of our whole system of beliefs, evidence, and justification, and seen that it works only, despite its pretensions, by taking the world largely for granted, we are *not* in a position to contrast all these appearances with an alternative reality. We cannot shed our ordinary responses, and if we could it would leave us with no means of conceiving a reality of any kind.

It is the same in the practical domain. We do not step outside our lives to a new vantage point from which we see what is really, objectively significant. We continue to take life largely for granted while seeing that all our decisions and certainties are possible only because there is a great deal we do not bother to rule out.

Both epistemological skepticism and a sense of the absurd can be reached via initial doubts posed within systems of evidence and justification that we accept, and can be stated without violence to our ordinary concepts. We can ask not only why we should believe there is a floor under us, but also why we should believe the evidence of our senses at all—and at some point the framable questions will have outlasted the answers. Similarly, we can ask not only why we should take aspirin, but why we should take trouble over our own comfort at all. The fact that we shall take the aspirin without waiting for an answer to this last question does not show that it is an unreal question. We shall also continue to believe there is a floor under us without waiting for an answer to the other question. In both cases it is this unsupported natural confidence that generates skeptical doubts; so it cannot be used to settle them.

Philosophical skepticism does not cause us to abandon our ordinary beliefs, but it lends them a peculiar flavor. After acknowledging that their truth is incompatible with possibilities that we have no grounds for believing do not obtain—apart from grounds in those very beliefs which we have called into question—we return to our familiar convictions with a certain irony and resignation. Unable to abandon the natural responses on which they depend, we take them back, like a spouse who has run off with someone else and then decided to return; but we regard them differently (not that the new attitude is necessarily inferior to the old, in either case).

The same situation obtains after we have put in question the seriousness with which we take our lives and human life in general and have looked at ourselves without presuppositions. We then return to our lives, as we must, but our seriousness is laced with irony. Not that irony enables us to escape the absurd. It is useless to mutter: "Life is meaningless; life is meaningless ..." as an accompaniment to everything we do. In continuing to live and work and strive, we take ourselves seriously in action no matter what we say.

What sustains us, in belief as in action, is not reason or justification, but something more basic than these—for we go on in the same way even after we are convinced that the reasons have given out.[3] If we tried to rely entirely on reason, and pressed it hard, our lives and beliefs would collapse—a form of madness that may actually occur if the inertial force of taking the world and life for granted is somehow lost. If we lose our grip on that, reason will not give it back to us.

VI

In viewing ourselves from a perspective broader than we can occupy in the flesh, we become spectators of our own lives. We cannot do very much as pure spectators of our own lives, so we continue to lead them, and devote ourselves to what we are able at the same time to view as no more than a curiosity, like the ritual of an alien religion.

This explains why the sense of absurdity finds its natural expression in those bad arguments with which the discussion began. Reference to our small size and short lifespan and to the fact that all of mankind will eventually vanish without a trace are metaphors for the backward step which permits us to regard ourselves from without and to find the particular form of our lives curious and slightly surprising. By feigning a nebula's-eye view, we illustrate the capacity to see ourselves without presuppositions, as arbitrary, idiosyncratic, highly specific occupants of the world, one of countless possible forms of life.

Before turning to the question whether the absurdity of our lives is something to be regretted and if possible escaped, let me consider what would have to be given up in order to avoid it.

Why is the life of a mouse not absurd? The orbit of the moon is not absurd either, but that involves no strivings or aims at all. A mouse, however, has to work to stay alive. Yet he is not absurd, because he lacks the capacities for self-consciousness and self-transcendence that would enable him to see that he is only a mouse. If that *did* happen, his life would become absurd, since self-awareness would not make him cease to be a mouse and would not enable him to rise above his mousely strivings. Bringing his new-found self-consciousness with him, he would have to return to his meagre yet frantic life, full of doubts that he was unable to answer, but also full of purposes that he was unable to abandon.

Given that the transcendental step is natural to us humans, can we avoid absurdity by refusing to take that step and remaining entirely within our sub-lunar lives? Well, we cannot refuse consciously, for to do that we would have to be aware of the viewpoint we were refusing to adopt. The only way to avoid the relevant self-consciousness would be either never to attain it or to forget it—neither of which can be achieved by the will.

On the other hand, it is possible to expend effort on an attempt to destroy the other component of the absurd—abandoning one's earthly, individual, human life in order to identify as completely as possible with that universal viewpoint from which human life seems arbitrary and trivial. (This appears to be the ideal of certain Oriental religions.) If one succeeds, then one will not have to drag the superior awareness through a strenuous mundane life, and absurdity will be diminished.

However, insofar as this self-etiolation is the result of effort, will-power, asceticism, and so forth, it requires that one take oneself seriously as an individual—that one be willing to take considerable trouble to avoid being creaturely and absurd. Thus one may undermine the aim of unworldliness by pursuing it too vigorously. Still, if someone simply allowed his individual, animal nature to drift and respond to impulse, without making the pursuit of its needs a central conscious aim, then he might, at considerable dissociative cost, achieve a life that was less absurd than most. It would not be a meaningful life either, of course; but it would not involve the engagement of a transcendent awareness in the assiduous pursuit of mundane goals. And that is the main condition of absurdity—the dragooning of an unconvinced transcendent consciousness into the service of an immanent, limited enterprise like a human life.

VII

The final escape is suicide; but before adopting any hasty solutions, it would be wise to consider carefully whether the absurdity of our existence truly presents us with a *problem*, to which some solution must be found—a way of dealing with prima facie disaster. That is certainly the attitude with which Camus approaches the issue, and it gains support from the fact that we are all eager to escape from absurd situations on a smaller scale.

Camus—not on uniformly good grounds—rejects suicide and the other solutions he regards as escapist. What he recommends is defiance or scorn.

We can salvage our dignity, he appears to believe, by shaking a fist at the world which is deaf to our pleas, and continuing to live in spite of it. This will not make our lives un-absurd, but it will lend them a certain nobility.[4]

This seems to me romantic and slightly self-pitying. Our absurdity warrants neither that much distress nor that much defiance. At the risk of falling into romanticism by a different route, I would argue that absurdity is one of the most human things about us: a manifestation of our most advanced and interesting characteristics. Like skepticism in epistemology, it is possible only because we possess a certain kind of insight—the capacity to transcend ourselves in thought.

If a sense of the absurd is a way of perceiving our true situation (even though the situation is not absurd until the perception arises), then what reason can we have to resent or escape it? Like the capacity for epistemological skepticism, it results from the ability to understand our human limitations. It need not be a matter for agony unless we make it so. Nor need it evoke a defiant contempt of fate that allows us to feel brave or proud. Such dramatics, even if carried on in private, betray a failure to appreciate the cosmic unimportance of the situation. If *sub specie aeternitatis* there is no reason to believe that anything matters, then that doesn't matter either, and we can approach our absurd lives with irony instead of heroism or despair.

NOTES

1. Cf. Robert Nozick, "Teleology," *Mosaic*, xii, 1 (Spring 1971), 27/8.

2. I am aware that skepticism about the external world is widely thought to have been refuted, but I have remained convinced of its irrefutability since being exposed at Berkeley to Thompson Clarke's largely unpublished ideas on the subject.

3. As Hume says in a famous passage of the *Treatise:* "Most fortunately it happens, that since reason is incapable of dispelling these clouds, nature herself suffices to that purpose, and cures me of this philosophical melancholy and delirium, either by relaxing this bent of mind, or by some avocation, and lively impression of my senses, which obliterate all these chimeras. I dine, I play a game of backgammon, I converse, and am merry with my friends; and when after three or four hours' amusement, I would return to these speculations, they appear so cold, and strain'd, and ridiculous, that I cannot find in my heart to enter into them any farther" (Book 1 Part 4, Section 7; Selby-Bigge, p. 269).

4. "Sisyphus, proletarian of the gods, powerless and rebellious, knows the whole extent of his wretched condition: it is what he thinks of during his descent. The lucidity that was to constitute his torture at the same time crowns his victory. There is no fate that cannot be surmounted by scorn" (*The Myth of Sisyphus,* Vintage edition, p. 90).

CHAPTER 17

E. D. KLEMKE

Living Without Appeal: An Affirmative Philosophy of Life

From time to time, philosophers get together at congresses and symposia in which some philosophers read papers and others criticize and raise questions. To the layman, I am sure, the topics which are discussed seem highly technical and inaccessible, and the vocabulary used is, doubtless, unintelligible. Indeed, if the ordinary man were to drop in on such meetings, he would, I suspect, find the proceedings to be either totally incomprehensible or the occasion for howling laughter. To give some indication of what I am referring to, I shall list the titles of some recent philosophical papers, many of which are acknowledged to be very important works:

The meaning of a word

Performative–constative

Negative existentials

Excluders

Reference and referents

Proper names

On referring

Parenthetical verbs

Bare particulars

Elementarism, independence, and ontology

The problem of counterfactual conditionals

This paper was first read in the Last Lecture Series, at DePauw University, and was repeated, by request, three times. In a revised form, it was read as the Top Prof lecture at Roosevelt University. It was again revised for this volume.

Is existence a predicate?

Etc.

Upon hearing (or reading) papers such as these, the ordinary man would probably exclaim "What's this all got to do with philosophy?" And he would, no doubt, be in agreement with Kierkegaard, who once wrote:

> What the philosophers say about Reality is often as disappointing as a sign you see in a shop window which reads: Pressing Done Here. If you brought your clothes to be pressed, you would be fooled; for the sign is only for sale. (*Either/Or*, v. 1, p. 31)

Now I have no quarrel with what goes on at these professional gatherings. I engage in such activities myself. I believe that most philosophical problems are highly technical and that the making of minute distinctions and the employment of a specialized vocabulary are essential for the solution of such problems. Philosophy here is in the same boat as any other discipline. For this reason, there is (and perhaps always will be) something aristocratic about the pursuit of philosophy, just as there is about the pursuit of theoretical physics or Peruvian excavation. The decriers of philosophy often overlook the fact that any discipline which amounts to more than a type of verbal diarrhea must proceed by making subtle distinctions, introducing technical terminology, and striving for as much rigor and precision as is possible. And the critics fail to see that, in philosophy as in other fields, by the very nature of the discipline, some problems will be somewhat rarified, and of interest mainly to the specialist.

On the other hand, I am inclined to think that the philosopher ought occasionally to leave the study, or the philosophical association lecture hall, or even the classroom, and, having shed his aristocratic garments, speak as a man among other men. For the philosopher is, after all, human too. Like other men, he eats, sleeps, makes love, drinks martinis (or perhaps cognac), gets the flu, files income tax, and even reads the newspapers. On such more democratic occasions, he ought to employ his analytical tools as diligently as ever. But he should select as his topic some issue which is of concern to all men, or at least most men, at some time in their lives. It is my hope that I have chosen such a topic for this essay.

The problem which I wish to discuss has been formulated in a single sentence by Camus (in *The Myth of Sisyphus*), which I take as a kind of "text." The sentence to which I am referring is: "Knowing whether or not one can live *without appeal* is all that interests me."[1] I say that I take this as a *kind* of text because, as so often, Camus overstates the point. Thus I would not—and perhaps most of us would not—say that, knowing whether or not one can live without appeal is *all* that interests me. But I believe that most of us would say that it certainly is one of those crucial problems which each man must confront as he tries to make sense of his life in this wondrously strange existence.

I

Prophets of doom and redemption seem to exist in almost every age, and ours is no exception. It is commonly held by many present-day thinkers, scholars, and poets, that the current state of the world and of many of the individuals within it is one of disintegration and vacuity. As they see it: Men of our age grope for disrupting principles and loyalties, and often reveal a destructive tension, a lack of wholeness, or an acute anxiety. Whether or not this is a unique situation in history, as an account of the present state of things, such disintegration is commonly mentioned. And theorists in almost every discipline and pursuit have given analyses of the current predicament and offered solutions. For example, philosophers and theologians (Jaspers, Marcel, Swenson, Tillich, Schweitzer, Niebuhr), scientists and scientific writers (Einstein, DeNuoy), sociologists (Sorokin), historians (Butterfield), among others, have waved warning signs, sometimes in a last effort to "save civilization from utter destruction." I would like to consider some points which are held in common by many of these writers (and others whom I have not indicated) and then to comment about those views. In this section, I shall state the common core of this position. In the next section, I shall make my comments and show that there is another genuine alternative.

According to many of the above writers (and others whom I have not mentioned), our age is one in which a major catastrophe has taken place. This has been designated as an increasing lack of a determining principle, the severing of a determining bond, the loss of a determining passion, or the rejection of a determining ultimate. What is the nature of this ultimate? It has been described as a principle by which finite forces are held in equilibrium, a bond which relates all horizontally functioning powers vertically to a realm beyond the finite. It is said to be a unifying and controlling power by which the varied inclinations, desires, and aims of an individual may be kept in balance. It is characterized as an agency which removes those oppositions and dichotomies which tend to destroy human selfhood. It has been held, by writers such as the above, to be a *transcendent* and *unconditional ultimate,* the one indispensable factor for the attainment of a *meaningful* and *worthwhile* existence. In their view, in order to prevent the destruction of individuals and cultures, and to provide a sense of direction and wholeness, the awareness of and relationship to such an ultimate are absolutely necessary.

Many of the writers have noted that, not only in intellectual circles, but at a much wider level, many individuals are increasingly refusing to accept the reality of this controlling ultimate. As they see it, such individuals have either remained content with a kind of vacuum in "the dimension of the spiritual," or they have "transvaluated and exalted immanent, finite forces" into a substitute for the transcendent. Men have tried—say these writers—to find equilibrium and unity through "natural," non-authoritative, self-regulating, temporal aims and principles, which they hold to be capable of an innate self-integration which requires no outside aid. According to these writers, this hope is futile, for as soon as reliance upon the transcendent ultimate ceases, disintegration results. Only when finite relationships, processes, and forces are referred back to a transhistorical order can integration, wholeness, meaning, and purpose be achieved. As long as men lack confidence in, or sever the bond to, the transcendent, their accomplishments and goals, no matter how noble or worthy, can have no final consistency or solidity. Rather, their efforts are mere remnants of an "atrophied world," shut up within the realm of immanence, intoxicated with itself, lured by "phantasms and idolatrous forces."

According to this view, the integrity of the individual is today threatened by the loss of belief in the transcendent ultimate and its replacement by a "devitalized" and "perverse" confidence in the all-sufficiency of the finite. The only remedy, we are told, is the recognition of the determining regulation of a dimension beyond the fleeting pace of the temporal world, by which alone existence can have worth and value.

At this point, one might be tempted to ask several questions of these writers:

(1) "Even if the above characterization of the world has some truth, must one look to transcendentalism as the remedy? Cannot a 'natural' philosophy or principle help us?"

The usual answer is: No. All naturalistic views reduce existence to mere finite centers and relationships. But all of these finite agencies are conditioned by others. All are therefore transitory and unstable. None can become a determining ultimate. Only a transcendent ultimate is capable of sustaining the kind of faith which gives human existence meaning and value.

(2) "But isn't this supernaturalism all over again? And doesn't it (as usual) imply either an unbridgeable gulf between the finite and the infinite or an external control or suppression of the finite by the so-called infinite?"

The customary reply is that this view may indeed be called supernaturalism. But (we are told) this does not imply the impossibility of any association of the finite and the infinite. For the ultimate, according to these writers, is not transcendent in the sense of being totally isolated from the finite, but, rather, is operative within the natural world. Furthermore (so the reply goes), the existence of a transcendent order does not entail either external control or suppression of the finite. It merely implies a human receptivity to a non-natural realm. That is, human achievement and value result from the impingement of the infinite upon the finite in moments of *kairos*, providing fullness and meaning but not at the price of denying the human activity which is involved. There always remains the awareness that the human subject is in a personal relation to another subject, a relation of supreme importance.

(3) "And how does one come to this relation?"

Perhaps mainly (say many of these writers) through suffering and sorrow, through a sense of sin and despair. When an individual sees that all finite centers and loyalties are fleeting and incapable of being lasting objects of faith, then he will renounce all previous efforts in despair, repent in humility, and gratefully make *the movement of faith* by which alone his life can become meaningful and worthwhile.

This, then, is the view which I propose to comment on. It is an all-or-nothing position. Its central thesis is that of a transcendent ultimate of absolute supremacy, which reigns over all finite things and powers, and *which alone is capable of providing meaning and worth to human existence.* Finite, historical centers can at best bring temporary assistance. They all wither with time and circumstances. Only when men turn from the finite to the infinite can they find (in the words of Kierkegaard) a hope and anticipation of the eternal which holds together all the "cleavages of existence."

II

I shall refer to the above view (which I have tried to portray justly) as transcendentalism. It contains three component theses. These are:

(1) There *exists* a transcendent being or ultimate with which man can enter into some sort of relation.

(2) Without such a transcendent ultimate, and the relation of faith to it, human life lacks *meaning, purpose,* and *integration.*

(3) Without such meaning or integration, human life is not *worthwhile.*

It is necessary to comment upon all three of these points.

(1) First, the thesis that there *exists* such a transcendent ultimate or power. I assume that those who assert the existence of a transcendent being intend their assertion to be a *cognitive* one. That is, they claim to be saying something which states a fact and which is capable of being either true or false. Thus they would not admit that their claim is merely an expression of feelings or attitudes. I also assume that those who make this assertion intend their statement to be interpreted *literally.* That is, they mean to say that the transcendent *really exists.* The transcendent presumably does not exist in the same sense in which Santa Claus may be said to "exist." These persons would, I assume, hold that the transcendent exists in actuality, although it may not exist in any empirical sense.

I ask: What *reasons* are there for holding that such an entity as the transcendent exists? I take it that I do not have to linger on such an answer as the testimony of a sacred book. The fact that the Bible or any other sacred writing asserts the existence of a transcendent is no more evidential to the existence of such a being than it is to the non-existence. All that a scriptural writing proves is that someone *believed* that a transcendent ultimate exists. And that is not at all the same as showing that such a being actually exists. The same may be said for the testimony of some unusual person—Moses, Jesus, Mohammed, etc. Furthermore, the fact that the testimony is made by a large number of persons does not substantiate the view. An impartial reading of history often shows that, on major issues, the majority is almost always wrong.

I also shall not linger on the traditional arguments for the existence of a god: The ontological, cosmological, teleological arguments, etc. Many theologians themselves now acknowledge that these are not so much arguments for the existence of such a being as they are explications of the affirmation of faith. Therefore, the fact that a certain segment of the universe is orderly, that it exhibits beauty, that it shows an adaptation of means to ends does not in any way provide evidence that there is one who orders, beautifies, and adapts.

Arguments from religious experience are also unconvincing. Due to their lack of intersubjective testability, the most that such arguments can demonstrate is that someone has had an unusual experience. They do not provide any evidence that the *object* of such an experience exists. That object may, of course, exist. But the occurrence of such an experience does not verify the existence of an actual, rather than imaginary, object. Suppose that, while a dentist is drilling my tooth, I have an experience of a blinding light or an unusual voice. I do not take this to be an adequate reason for saying that I *know* that I have now communed with the Absolute. I trust that you do not do so either.

What evidence, then, is there for the existence of a transcendent? I submit that there is *none*. And my reading of religious writings and my conversations with many of those who maintain the existence of the transcendent lead me to affirm that they also would agree that there is none. For they hold that the existence of the transcendent (although a cognitive claim) is apprehended, *not* in a cognitive relationship but in the relationship of *faith.*

Thus in the usual sense of the term "evidence," there seems to be no evidence for the existence of a transcendent ultimate. Why, then, should I accept such a claim? After all, throughout the rest of my philosophical activity *and* throughout my normal, everyday activities, I constantly rely upon criteria of evidence before accepting a cognitive claim. I emphasize that this holds for my *everyday* life and not merely for any philosophical or scientific beliefs which I may entertain. Not only do I accept or reject (say) the Principle of Rectilinear Propagation of Light because of evidence. I also ask for evidence in order to substantiate such simple claims as "The stylus in my stereo tone arm is defective," or "Jones eloped with his secretary."

It is clear that both believers and non-believers share this desire for evidence with me. At least, believers agree up to the point of the transcendent-claim. If I reject this claim because of lack of evidence, I do not think that I can be justly accused of being an extremist. Rather, I should be commended for my consistency!

The transcendentalist will reply: "But the usual criteria do not apply in this case. They work only for natural entities. The transcendent is not a natural being." I answer: Then the only reasonable procedure seems to be that of suspending my judgment, for I do not know of any non-natural criteria. The transcendentalist replies: "No, merely suspending your judgment implies that you think that some evidence might eventually be found. We are in a different dimension here. An act of *faith* is required."

I reply with two points: (a) In its normal usage, the term "faith" still implies evidence and reasons. Why do I have faith in Smith, but not in Jones? Obviously because of *reasons.* I do not have faith in people haphazardly and without evidence. (b) If I am told that faith in the transcendent is not faith in the normal sense, but a special act of commitment, then I can only honestly reply: *I have no need for such faith.* The transcendentalist retorts: "Ah, but you do, for only through faith in the transcendent can life have meaning; and surely you seek a life that is significant and worthwhile." And this leads us to the second thesis.

(2) The transcendentalist claims that without the transcendent and faith in the transcendent, human existence is without *meaning, purpose, integration.* Is this true? And if true in some sense, what follows?

(A) Let us take *meaning* first. Is there any reason to believe that without the existence of the transcendent, life has no meaning? That is, does the existence of meaning presuppose the existence of the transcendent?

It is necessary to distinguish between *objective* meaning and *subjective* meaning. An objective meaning, if there were such, would be one which is either structurally *part of* the universe, apart from human subjective evaluation; or dependent upon some *external agency* other than human evaluation. Two comments are in order: (i) *If* the notion of objective meaning is a plausible one, then I see no reason why it must be tied up with the existence of a transcendent being, for it certainly is not self-contradictory to hold that an objective meaning could conceivably exist even though a transcendent being did not. That is, the two concepts of "transcendent being" and "objective meaning" are not logically related in the way in which the two concepts "three" and "odd" (for example) are related. (ii) But, more fundamental, I find the notion of an objective meaning as difficult to accept as I do the notion of a transcendent being. Therefore I cannot rely upon the acceptance of objective meaning in order to substantiate the existence of the transcendent.

Further comment is needed on this point. It seems to me that there is no shred of evidence for the existence of an objective meaning in the universe. If I were to characterize the universe, attempting to give a complete description, I would do so in terms of matter in motion, or energy, or forces such as gravitation, or events, etc. Such a description is *neutral.* It can have no non-descriptive components. The same holds for a description of any segment of the universe. Kepler, for example, was entitled to say that the paths of the planets are elliptical, etc. But he was not entitled to say that this motion exhibits some fundamental, objective purpose more so than some other type of motion would. From the standpoint of present evidence, evaluational components such as meaning or purpose are not to be found in the universe as objective aspects of it. Such values are the result of human evaluation. With respect to them, we must say that the universe is valueless; it is *we* who evaluate, upon the basis of our subjective preferences. Hence, we do not discover values such as meaning to be inherent within the universe. Rather, we "impose" such values upon the universe.

When the transcendentalist holds that, without the transcendent, no objective meaning for human existence is possible, he assumes that the notion of an objective meaning is an intelligible one. But if one can show, as I believe one can, that the idea of objective meaning is an implausible one, then his argument has no point. In no way does it give even the slightest evidence for the existence of a transcendent ultimate.

However, it is possible that some transcendentalist would want to take a different position here. There are at least two alternatives which he might hold.

(i) The transcendentalist might *agree* that there is no *objective* meaning in the universe, that meaning *is* a function of human subjectivity. His point now is that *subjective* meaning is found if and only if there exists a transcendent. I reply with two points (1) This is a grandiose generalization, which might wow an imbecile but not anyone of normal intelligence, and, like most such generalizations, it is false. (I shall return to this point in connection with the transcendentalist's third thesis.) (2) The meaning which the transcendentalist here affirms cannot be subjective meaning, for it is dependent upon some external, non-human factor, namely, the existence of the transcendent. This sort of meaning is *not* a function of human subjectivity. Thus we are back where we were. The transcendentalist's views about meaning do not provide any evidence at all for the existence of a transcendent ultimate.

(ii) I mentioned that the transcendentalist may take a second alternative. He might want to hold: "Of course, the fact of meaning in human existence does not in any way prove, demonstratively or with probability, that there *is* a transcendent being. Therefore, I won't say that meaning in life is impossible unless the transcendent exists. I will merely say that one cannot find meaning unless *one has faith in* the transcendent. The fact of meaning testifies to the necessity of *faith*."

I reply again with two points. (1) This generalization is also false. I know of many humans who have found a meaningful existence without faith in the transcendent. (2) However, even if this statement were true—even if heretofore not a single human being had found meaning in his life without faith in the transcendent—*I should reject such meaning and search for some other kind.* To me, the price which the transcendentalist pays for his meaning is too dear. If I am to find any meaning in life, I must attempt to find it without the aid of crutches, illusory hopes, and incredulous beliefs and aspirations. I am perfectly willing to admit that *I may not find any meaning at all* (although I think I can, even if it is not of the noble variety of which the transcendentalist speaks). But at least *I must try* to find it on my own. And this much I know: I can strive for a meaning only if it is one which is within the range of my comprehension as an inquiring, rational *man*. A meaning which is tied to some transcendent entity—or to faith in such—is not intelligible to me. Again, I here maintain what I hold throughout the rest of my existence, both philosophically and simply as a living person. I can accept only what is comprehensible to me, i.e., that which is within the province of actual or possible experience, or that for which I find some sound reasons or evidence. Upon these grounds, I must reject any notion of meaning which is bound with the necessity of faith in some mysterious, utterly unknowable entity. If my life should turn out to be less happy thereby, then I shall have to endure it as such. As Shaw once said: "The fact that a believer is happier than a skeptic is no more to the point than the fact that a drunken man is happier than a sober one. The happiness of credulity is a cheap and dangerous quality."

(B) I shall not say much about the transcendentalist's claim that, without the transcendent, or without faith in it, human existence is *purposeless*. For if I were to reply in detail, I should do so in about the same manner as I did with respect to the matter of meaning. An objective purpose is as difficult to detect in the universe as an objective meaning. Hence, again, one cannot argue that there must be a transcendent or that faith in such is necessary.

(C) What about the transcendentalist's claim that, without the transcendent, or, without *faith* in the transcendent, no integration is possible?

(i) In one sense of the term, this assertion, too, is obviously false. There are many persons who have attained what might be called psychological integration, i.e., self-integration, integration of personality, etc., without faith in the transcendent. I know of dozens of people whose lives are integrated in this sense, yet have no transcendental commitments.

(ii) But perhaps the transcendentalist means something much more fundamental than this psychological thesis by his claim. Perhaps he is making some sort of metaphysical assertion—a statement about man and his place in the universe. Thus his assertion must be taken to mean that *metaphysical* integration is not achievable without the transcendent or without faith in it. Like Kierkegaard, he holds that the cleavages of existence cannot be held together without the transcendent. What shall we say to this interpretation?

I am not sure that I understand what such integration is supposed to be. But insofar as I do, it seems to me that it is not possible. I am willing to admit that, if such integration were achievable, it might perhaps be attained only by virtue of something transcendent. But I find no conclusive or even reasonable evidence that such integration has been achieved either by believers in the transcendent or by non-believers. Hence one cannot infer that there is a transcendent ultimate or that faith in such an entity is necessary.

What about the mystics? you ask. It would be silly for me to say that the mystics have not experienced something very unusual which they have *interpreted* as some sort of unity with the universe, or whatever it may be. They may, indeed, have *felt* that, at rare moments, they were "swallowed up in the infinite ocean of being," to quote James. But again, peculiar and non-intersubjectively testable experiences are not reliable evidence for any truth-claim.

Besides, suppose that the mystics *had* occasionally achieved such unity with the universe. Still, this is somewhat irrelevant. For the point is, that I, and many beings like myself (perhaps most of you), have not been favored with such experiences. In fact, it appears that most people who have faith in the transcendent have not had such experiences. This is precisely *why* they have faith. If they had complete certainty, no faith would be needed. Thus faith itself does not seem to be enough for the achievement of integration; and if integration were obtained, faith would be unnecessary. Hence the transcendentalist's view that integration is achieved *via* faith in the transcendent is questionable.

But even if this last thesis were true, it does me no good. Once again, I cannot place my faith in an unknown X, in that which is incomprehensible to me. Hence I must accept the fact that, for me, life will remain without objective meaning, without purpose, and without metaphysical integration. *And I must go on from there.* Rather than crying for the moon, my task must be, as Camus said, to know whether or not one can live *without appeal.*

(3) This leads us to the transcendentalist's third (and most crucial) thesis: That without meaning, purpose, and integration, life is not *worthwhile.* From which he draws the conclusion that without a *transcendent* or *faith* in it, life is not worthwhile. I shall deal only with the claim that without *meaning,* life is not worthwhile. Similar comments could be made regarding purpose and integration.

If the transcendentalist's claim sounds plausible at all, it is only because he continues to confuse objective meaning with subjective meaning. It is true that life has no objective meaning. Let us face it once and for all. But from this it does not follow that life is not *worthwhile,* for it can still be subjectively meaningful. And, really, the latter is the only kind of meaning worth shouting about. An objective meaning—that is, one which is inherent within the universe or dependent upon external agencies—would, frankly, leave me cold. It would not be *mine.* It would be an outer, neutral thing, rather than an inner, dynamic achievement. I, for one, am *glad* that the universe has no meaning, for thereby is *man all the more glorious.* I willingly accept the fact that external meaning is non-existent (or if existent, certainly not apparent), for this leaves me free to *forge my own meaning.* The extent of my creativity and thereby my success in this undertaking depends partly on the richness of my own psyche. There are some persons whose subjectivity is poor and wretched. Once they give up the search for objective meaning, they may perhaps have a difficult time in finding life to be worthwhile. Such is the fate of the impoverished. But those whose subjectivity is enlarged—rationally, esthetically, sensually, passionally—may find life to be worthwhile by means of their creative activity of subjective evaluation, in which a neutral universe takes on color and light, darkness and shadow, becomes now a source of profound joy, now a cause for deep sorrow.

What are some ways by which such worthwhileness can be found? I can speak only for myself. I have found subjective meaning through such things as *knowledge, art, love, and work*. Even though I realize that complete and perfect knowledge of matters of fact is not attainable, this does not lessen my enthusiasm to know and to understand. Such pursuits may have no practical utility; they are not thereby any less significant. To know about the nature of necessary truth or the probable structure of the atom is intrinsically fascinating, to me. And what a wealth of material lies in the arts. A Bach fugue, a Vlaminck painting, a Dostoevsky novel; life is intensely enriched by things such as these. And one must not neglect mention of one's relationships of friendship and love. Fragmentary and imperfect as these often are, they nevertheless provide us with some of our most heightened moments of joy and value. Finally, of all of the ways which I listed, none is more significant and constantly sustaining to me than work. There have been times when I, like many others, no doubt, have suffered some tragedy which seemed unendurable. Every time, it has been my work that has pulled me through.

In short, even if life has no meaning, in an external, objective sense, this does not lead to the conclusion that it is not worth living, as the transcendentalist naively but dogmatically assumes. On the contrary, this fact opens up a greater field of almost infinite possibilities. For as long as I am *conscious*, I shall have the capacity with which to *endow* events, objects, persons, and achievements with value. Ultimately, it is through my *consciousness* and it alone that worth or value are obtained. Through consciousness, the scraping of horses' tails on cats' bowels (to use James' phrase) become the beautiful and melodic lines of a Beethoven string quartet. Through consciousness, a pile of rock can become the memorable Mount Alten which one has climbed and upon which one almost perished. Through consciousness, the arrangements of *P*s and *Q*s on paper can become the symbols of the formal beauty and certain truth of the realm of mathematical logic. Through consciousness, the gift of a carved little piece of wood, left at one's door by a friend, can become a priceless treasure. Yes, it is a *vital* and *sensitive consciousness* that counts. Thus there is a sense in which it is true, as many thinkers and artists have reminded us, that everything begins with my consciousness, and nothing has any worth except through my consciousness.

III

I shall conclude with an ancient story. "Once a man from Syria led a camel through the desert; but when he came to a dark abyss, the camel suddenly, with teeth showing and eyes protruding, pushed the unsuspecting paragon of the camel-driving profession into the pit. The clothes of the Syrian were caught by a rosebush, and he was held suspended over the pit, at the bottom of which an enormous dragon was waiting to swallow him. Moreover, two mice were busily engaged in chewing away the roots of the already sagging plant. Yet, in this desperate condition, the Syrian was thralled to the point of utmost contentment by a rose which adorned the bush and wafted its fragrance into his face."[2]

I find this parable most illuminating. We are all men hanging on the thread of a few rapidly vanishing years over the bottomless pit of death, destruction, and nothingness. Those objective facts are starkly real. Let us not try to disguise them. Yet I find it marvelously interesting that man's *consciousness*, his reason and his passion, can elevate these routine, objective, external events, in a moment of lucidity and feeling, to the status of a personally appropriated ideal—an ideal which does not annual those objective facts, but which *reinterprets* them and clothes them with the apparel of *man's subjectivity*.

It is time, once again, to speak personally. What your situation is, I cannot say. But I know that I am that Syrian, and that I am hanging over the pit. My doom is inevitable and swiftly approaching. If, in these few moments that are yet mine, I can find no rose to respond to, or rather, if I have lost the ability to respond, then I shall moan and curse my fate with a howl of bitter agony. But *if* I can, in these last moments, respond to a rose—or to a philosophical argument or theory of physics, or to a Scarlatti sonata, or to the touch of a human hand—I say, if I can so respond and can thereby transform an external and fatal event into a moment of conscious insight and significance, then I shall go down *without hope or appeal yet passionately triumphant and with joy.*

NOTES

1. A. Camus, *The Myth of Sisyphus*, tr. by J. O'Brien (New York: Vintage Books, 1959), p. 45.
2. R. Hertz, *Chance and Symbol* (Chicago: University of Chicago, 1948), pp. 142–143. Another version of this parable appears in Tolstoy's *My Confession*.

CHAPTER 18

OWEN FLANAGAN

What Makes Life Worth Living?

IDENTITY AND SELF-EXPRESSION

The question "What makes life worth living?" assumes that life is or can be worth living. Perhaps this is an unwarranted assumption. The question "Is life worth living?" comes first. The question is not "Is life lived?" or even "Do people seek to live out their lives?" Nor is it "Do people care about going on—possibly for as long as possible—sometimes even longer than is sensible?" These are easy questions.

We live our lives in the sense that we spend time *not* dead. And by and large people try to go on, to survive. But this proves nothing about worth. Mosquitoes spend time not dead, and they too will do what it takes to live as long as they can. Is it worth anything to live out a mosquito's life? Objectively, the answer is probably yes. It contributes ecologically to the planet that mosquitoes live lives. Does it matter to the individual mosquito? Does it matter subjectively? This is not a question that should worry us since mosquitoes don't worry about it. They can't. But we have minds, and we can ask the question "Is life worth living?" and if it is, "What, or what sorts of things make it so?" And the answers matter to us.

For us, the objective fact that we live out our lives—and even the fact that we have passion to do so (perhaps the result of biological imperatives)—proves nothing. One can do worthless things. I do them all the time. One can even have passion for worthless things. Perhaps a life is one extended worthless thing.

Why entertain this depressing thought? The answer is that it forces reflection on the question "Is life worth living, and if it is, what makes it so?" Why is reflection on this question worthwhile? I'm not sure how to answer. It may well be that a life can be worth living even for an unreflective agent, unreflective generally, or unreflective enough to be befuddled by this two-part question. Asking the question may even move a life that is worth living to fear and trembling, to sickness unto death, to the edge of despair; and not because the life is not worth living. It may be that the person to whom the question is addressed can't see her way to the answer that her life in fact reveals. She cannot articulate value or worth and wrongly thinks value and worth are not there.

On the other side, the question may move us to consider what matters, how it matters, and why it matters. Mattering might, if we are lucky, add up to value, to worth.

The question "Is life worth living and if it is, what makes it so?" is hard enough. It is connected to a more basic and equally bewildering question. "What does it mean to *live* a life?" Again, there is a trivial sense in which we know the answer: To live a life is to spend time *not* dead. Some people choose death quite deliberately while they are alive. Their suicide is partly constitutive of their life. Perhaps the question, intended as it is existentially, can be put this way: Do we *live* our lives? Do we in any sense make ourselves and control our characters and destinies, or are we just puppets, live puppets—whose lives are lived, but not lived or directed by us—the organisms who live these very lives by being, as it were, alive? The question is about living in some stronger sense than simply being alive, and it involves issues of self and agency.

Some philosophers distinguish between things that have some property—for example, value—intrinsically and things that have the property derivatively. Money is worthless until we make it worth something. Happiness is said to have worth in and of itself. Suppose this is true. Would it follow that a life with many happy times in it was worth living? Not necessarily. Properties of parts do not confer the property on the whole. My parts are small, I am large. Happy times, even many of them, might not constitute a worthwhile life. But I am skeptical in any case that a life's meaning could be intrinsic—could come from just being alive or from something that has value, no matter what. Life's meaning must derive from things other than just being alive. Happiness is probably one of the things that confers worth, but it is not enough. After all, one might perversely find happiness in evil things. Perhaps happiness is not necessary even. One might live a life largely devoid of happiness but still live a good and worthwhile life—even as seen from the subjective point of view.

Suppose, however, that happiness is normally a desired component of a life worth living, what else is needed? Having an identity and expressing it. This is the answer that strikes me as most promising: self and self-expression. The idea is romantic, Western, Nietzschean even. But it is also non-romantic, non-Western, Buddhist even. To make myself a "not-self," to work at creating in myself a mode to transcend caring about mundane things is a form of self-expression, as is suicide. But normally in the West and in the East, having a self and expressing it is not a matter of doing things alone, or doing them only your way, or of being Zarathustra-like. Many, probably most, worthwhile forms of self-expression, require others in crucial ways. Even the decision of the cloistered Christian monk or nun or the ascetic Buddhist *arahant* to remove himself or herself from certain dependencies on other people requires that there be social practices in place—certain economies of desire, for example—that are thought to be worth transcending. Sometimes stopping caring about money, fame, and sex are thought to be worthwhile because these things take time and energy away from more worthwhile human things: love, friendship, peace of mind, for example. Other times, the attempt to shift one's orientation from mundane desire is not motivated by the desire to connect with other, more worthwhile, human goods, but with the transcendental—God, or something of that sort.

Wherever one looks, or so I claim, humans seek, and sometimes find worth in possessing an identity and expressing it. This is why I think having a self and expressing it reign when it comes to answering the question of what makes life worth living. Of course, self and self-expression are not sufficient for living well, but they are necessary. If something—if anything, that is—is necessary for a life worth living, it is this: that I develop an identity and that I express it. The idea awaits refinement since, of course, not any identity or form of expressing it will do. But you get the drift.

It is important that I not be understood as promoting a particular conception of self or identity, especially not some controversial individualistic one. Philosophers from Aristotle to the present, as well as anthropologists, have taught us that in every culture, becoming a self capable of expressing anything of worth requires a community, as does self-expression. Furthermore, what an individual is like and what he or she seeks to express may be things of largely communal *or* largely personal value. This will be a matter of great contingency, as will the degree to which a particular individual develops powers of self-authorship and occupies a world in which she can use these powers in creative ways (luck matters—indeed, it matters far too much). What will *not* be contingent, I am claiming, is that there will be individual selves and that if they find meaning and worth, it will be through self-expression. This, I claim, is true of Nietzscheans, Libertarians, Buddhists, and Benedictines. It is as true of Mother Teresa as it is of Madonna.[1]

THE DEATH OF THE SUBJECT

I'll be alone when I die. Or better: Dying is something I will do alone. Or better: My passing from being alive to being dead is something that will happen to me alone. This is true even if loved ones are there for the event. When I die, I'll be nothing. But for the time being, I am something rather than nothing.[2]

One thing that would undermine the idea that *this* subject of experience will die, as well as the ideas about the importance of self and self-expression would be if there were no subjects, no agents. If there were no subjects there would be no selves, and if my self was nothing it could hardly die, and self-expression would be illusory. The very thought I just had, "that for the time being I am something rather than nothing," might be considered to be some sort of mistake. Indeed, there is talk in the air of the "death of the subject." Why think there are no subjects? There are three standard sorts of arguments that one sees in the postmodern literature.

First, there is a metaphysical argument that promotes the idea that I am merely a location at which and through which, like all other locations, certain things happen. The universe just is a complex causal network and what is "me" is just a location, one among an uncountable number of other locations—locations that *sub specie aeternitatis* just nudge each other from place to place.

Second, there is a sociological argument according to which I am just a bunch of roles melded together in the here and now, as differentiated and complex and situation-specific as the various social niches that I occupy require me to be. *Homo sapiens* learns how to be a "self," but a self is no more than a name like "the university," which names nothing in particular, but only a disparate collection that seems to possess, but invariably lacks, any more than nominal unity.

Third, there are developmental, life span sorts of arguments according to which "I" am a series of self-stages. There is no I, no ego, no self, that is *me* over time. "I"—now in raised-eyebrow quotes to indicate that grammar is causing trouble—have a name. It stays the same. But my body changes, my beliefs, my desires, my projects, and commitments, my interpersonal relations change radically over the course of life. Owen Flanagan is the name, but changing is my game. The illusion of identity or sameness is just that: an illusion. Its cause is that all these changes happen incrementally. But just as it does not follow from the fact that 2 is not far from 1, nor 23 from 22, nor 6,000,000 from 5,900,000, that 6,000,000 is not far from 1, so too it does not follow that Owen Flanagan at 45 is remotely close to Owen Flanagan at 1 or even at 20.

Strategically, and ever so briefly, here is how I recommend dealing with all three arguments. First, concede the last argument. There are subjects, they change, some more than others, across a variety of dimensions over the course of a life. The argument proves nothing about the death of the subject, only that subjects are not identical over time. But those philosophers are right who have taught us that self-sameness is not what matters. Continuity and connectedness matter, not strict identity. Second, there is something to the social-role argument. Before and after we gain powers of self-authorship we express ourselves in ways particular situations call upon us to be. But even supposing that I am nothing more than some package of socially responsive roles, I am still something rather than nothing. So the argument hardly establishes the death of the subject; it simply makes the subject a social construction all the way down. But houses are completely constructed, and they exist. Being constructed hardly makes something into nothing. Usually it is the other way round.

Third, regarding the metaphysical argument: It is based upon two tricks at once: one, it evokes the specter of determinism to undermine the idea that there are metaphysically free subjects; two, it paints a picture in which "I" am caused by things, but never cause anything. Even if there are no metaphysically autonomous agents, there still might be agents. A finch may not be metaphysically free, but it expresses its needs and satisfies them when it finds and eats from my bird feeder. Furthermore, even under the deterministic picture, each thing that is an effect is in turn a cause, a something-that-makes-other-things-happen. So the existence of agents, in the sense of systems with beliefs and desires and complex motivational economies, who do things is hardly undermined by the argument. Furthermore, even if nothing matters *sub specie aeternitatis,* the fact remains that evolution has resulted in the existence of organisms that have temporally extended lives and are self-organizing and self-moving in certain well-understood ways.

Death-of-subject arguments, even if interpreted generously, do not show that there are no subjects of experience nor that there are no agents. Depending on the type of argument, they deflate our conception(s) of subjects and agents, but they hardly destroy these conceptions—indeed they presuppose invariably that subjects and agents exist.

The arguments just rehearsed are heard among poststructuralists and postmodernists who are enchanted with human contingency and disenchanted with the idea that a person might be essentially constituted by an immutable soul or transcendental ego. I share the enchantment and disenchantment, respectively, but resist the conclusion. There is another quarter from which worries about self and meaning and worth continue to be heard—the ferment here is caused by the attempt to mix the scientific image of the cosmos and of biological evolution with more traditional pictures of persons. I'll explain a bit.

WHY ME?

Why is there something rather than nothing? Why is there anything at all? And why in particular am *I* among the things that there are? Here are two answers:

1. An omniscient, omnipotent, all-good, and all-loving God decided in his infinite wisdom that the universe and its creatures should exist. He created humans in his own image. He endows us with immortal souls, souls that will join him and all the other saved persons if we use our free will to follow the right path, to worship him, and follow his moral commandments.

2. It is an inexplicable and irrational feature of things that there is something rather than nothing, that there is anything at all, and that there are particular individuals. But once there was something purely natural up and running, the aftermath of the Big Bang perhaps, then we

can give some sketchy accounts of how life emerged on earth, and how natural selection worked to produce *Homo sapiens,* a new kind of animal.

One feature the stories have in common is that they both start by positing an originary force that seems to answer, but does not answer the original question. They both say that there just always was something rather than nothing. To which the original question can then be posed: Why anything at all? And why this, a God who always was, in the first instance, or some set of physical facts, a "singularity" from which the Big Bang emerged, in the second? Both stories stop further questioning and are found satisfying by different groups of people. But this cannot be due to their satisfactoriness as answers. Their appeal must lie elsewhere.

TRANSCENDENT MEANING

One reasonable suspect for where the appeal of the first story lies is in the fact that it provides the possibility that life has transcendent meaning—an omniscient God shows the way, I follow, and I achieve personal immortality. His plan must be the right one; it must make sense and ground a good and meaningful life. He is God, after all.

The second story generates a host of worries. If there is no God, if I am just an animal subject to the same finite fate—becoming nothing when I die as I was before my birth—then of what significance am I? And what basis could there be for thinking that one way of living is better than another? And if my time is limited, why should anything else matter than that I get pleasure, as much and as quickly as I can get it? And why, as I push the thought of my utter contingency to the limit, why think that I am in fact anything at all, rather than some sort of chimera or ephemera, at most a location from which self-expressive and self-generative forces seemingly emerge, but which in fact is simply, like all else, a place where certain things come together in a manner that creates the illusion that I am an agent, a self.

The second image, the scientific image, is thought by many to be deflationary and nihilistic, destroying at once the very idea that *I* am an agent as I conceive of myself, that my life matters, and that being ethical matters in this scheme where nothing matters. There is Dostoevsky's worry that if there is no God then everything is permitted. How could anything be better than anything else if there is no transcendent ground for meaning? But then there is Nietzsche's question: Why should the fact that a certain plan is God's plan assure its meaningfulness? Even if it does assure that the plan is meaningful for God, what makes it meaningful for me? And what assures that the plan is good, or that it grounds meaning, just because it is God's plan. If God always was and always shall be, isn't it the case that he just came with this plan. How could something (two things: God and his plan) so inexplicable, reassure me that the meaning of my life is secure, that it is in good hands, that it is not simply a derivative surd—an offshoot of the originary surd, a God who always was and just had this plan. How is this different from the second picture according to which I am nature's surd?

If it seems like the originary force of all things including this life lies in something personal and spiritual rather than material, then the next philosophical move is to motivate skepticism that God's creation, and God himself are good. I am to be reassured because I was made in *his* image. Why?

William James quotes this poem by James Thomson in his essay "Is Life Worth Living?" The poem makes the worry vivid:[3]

> Who is most wretched in this dolorous place?
> I think myself; yet I would rather be
> My miserable self than He, than He
> Who formed such creatures to his own disgrace.
>
> The vilest thing must be less vile than Thou
> From whom it had its being, God and Lord!
> Creator of all woe and sin! abhorred,
> Malignant and implacable! I vow
>
> That not for all Thy power furled and unfurled,
> For all the temples to Thy glory built,
> Would I assume the ignominious guilt
> Of having made such men in such a world.

MY WAY

It is hard to see why or how either story, the theological one or the naturalistic one, could ground meaning and worth in something instrinsic, timeless, and itself comprehensible. The scientific image seems no worse off at any rate than the theological one.

Perhaps looking for the ground of meaning and worth in origins is the wrong place to be looking. Still, the theological story contains an interesting suggestion. It claims that God needs us as much as we need him for the plan to work. This leads Robert Nozick to ask, "[I]f it were possible for man and God to shore up each other's meaningfulness in this fashion, why could not two people do this for each other as well?"[4]

Or, to put the point more generally: If meaning and worth come with relations of certain sorts, perhaps in the first instance to other selves, but possibly also to nature, to work, to oneself, then perhaps we are wisest to look for grounds of meaning and worth in this life—in relations we can have during this life. Does science say that this life doesn't exist, or that it doesn't matter? I don't see how, any more than I see that "death-of-the subject" arguments in the humanities succeed.

The claim is that it matters a lot that I do what *I* want to do. And it matters at least as much that what I do is something worth doing, something of value. These things of value need not be momentously important—ordinary things matter, eating a tasty meal, throwing a stick for the dog to fetch, shooting a basketball. These are things worth doing. If life was comprised only of such ordinary short-term goods, we might feel that something was missing. Why? Because we think that a person ought to have some long-term projects and plans and these ought to be about things that matter, things that are worth caring about, worth a bit more than the things just mentioned. Love and friendship and work, creative work, are among these things.

What I do and think reflect on me, on who I am. What I think and do also help constitute who I am. Expressing myself, making and modifying myself, and respecting myself all matter, and they are interconnected. Questions of meaning only arise because I am a thinking thing and, in particular, because I am a conscious thinking thing. My conscious thinking abilities stretch to knowing such things as that I will someday be dead. Being dead means once again being nothing at all. For creatures who thrive on self-expression, no longer being able first-personally to express anything thwarts a basic desire. Here is where leaving parts of ourselves in the world, by having changed that world in directions that matter, that are positive, lessens the threat of my demise. This is a kind of naturalistic transcendence, a way each of us, if we are lucky, can leave good-making traces beyond the time between our birth and death. To believe this sort of transcendence is possible is, I guess, to have a kind of religion. It involves believing that there are selves, that we can in self-expression make a difference, and if we use our truth detectors and good detectors well, that difference might be positive, a contribution to the cosmos.

NOTES

1. In this passage, Richard Rorty expresses the sort of picture I want to endorse: "[E]very human life is the working out of a sophisticated idiosyncratic fantasy, and a reminder that no such working out gets completed before death interrupts. It cannot get completed because there is nothing to complete, there is only a web of relations to be rewoven, a web which time lengthens every day.

But if we avoid Nietzsche's inverted Platonism—his suggestion that a life of self-creation can be as complete and as autonomous as Plato thought a life of contemplation might be—then we shall be content to think of any human life as the always incomplete, yet sometimes heroic, reweaving of such a web. We shall see the conscious need of the strong poet to *demonstrate* that he is not a copy or replica as merely a special form of an unconscious need everyone has: the need to come to terms with the blind impress which chance has given him, to make a self for himself by redescribing that impress in terms which are, if only marginally, his own" (Richard Rorty, *Contingency, Irony, and Solidarity* [Cambridge: Cambridge University Press, 1989], 42–43).

2. Robert Nozick, like me, has a relational rather than intrinsic view of how life's meaning must accrue, and he captures nicely the deep psychological urge to avoid becoming totally nothing. "Death wipes you out. Dead, you are no longer around— around *here* at any rate—and if there is nowhere else where you'll be (heaven, hell, with the white light) then all that will be left of you is your effects, leavings, traces.

People do seem to think it important to continue to be around somehow. The root notion seems to be this one: it shouldn't *ever* be as if you had never existed at all. A significant life leaves its mark on the world. A significant life is, in some sense, permanent; it makes a permanent difference to the world—it leaves traces" (*Philosophical Explanations* [Cambridge: Harvard University Press], 1979, 582).

3. William James, "Is Life Worth Living?" In *The Will to Believe and Other Essays in Popular Philosophy* (1897; reprint, New York: Dover, 1956).

4. Nozick, *Philosophical Explanations,* 589.

PART THREE   Questioning the
              Question

CHAPTER 19

ANTONY FLEW

Tolstoi and the Meaning of Life[1]

I

Tolstoi's autobiographical fragment, *A Confession*, marks one of the turning points in his development.[2] It was the first work of the period of his intensive study of the Gospels: the period which begins after the completion of *War and Peace* and *Anna Karenina*, and which continues until the return to fiction in *The Death of Ivan Ilych* and *The Power of Darkness*. In this work Tolstoi recounts his personal search for the meaning of life. It is a powerful revealing document, remarkable in many ways. But on this occasion we propose to use it as the object of a case study. This case study is intended mainly to throw light upon the meaning of the question: "What is the meaning of life?" Once the close examination of Tolstoi's argument is complete there may be room for one or two more general suggestions.

II

A. Tolstoi begins by explaining that he was both baptized and raised in the Orthodox Christian faith. "But when I abandoned the second course at the University at the age of eighteen I no longer believed any of the things I had been taught" (p. 3). Tolstoi's loss of faith came about not as the result of any spiritual struggle but seemed to have been rather a recognition of the fact that he had never really had and lived by any real Christian conviction. In his late teens and for most of his twenties he lived the sort of life that was expected of an aristocrat of his country and period. Then he took up with literature: "faith in the meaning of poetry and in the development of life was a religion, and I was one of its priests" (p. 9). He recognized that his fellow professional writ-

From *Ethics*, Vol. 73, 1963. Used by permission of University of Chicago Press and the author.

ers were a poor lot. Nevertheless: "I naively imagined that I was a poet and artist and could teach everybody without myself knowing what I was teaching" (p. 10). Travel in Europe confirmed him in "the faith of striving after perfection" (p. 12). But in this period he suffered two traumata: he witnessed in Paris an execution by the guillotine; and his brother died young after a long and painful illness "not understanding why he had lived and still less why he had to die" (p. 13). Compare in *Anna Karenina* the impact on Constantine Levin of the death of his brother Nicholas.[3]

Marriage swept all cosmic concerns out of Tolstoi's head, temporarily: "The new conditions of happy family life completely diverted me from all search for the general meaning of life. . . . So another fifteen years passed. . . . But five years ago something very strange began to happen to me. At first I experienced moments of perplexity and arrest of life, as though I did not know what to do or how to live . . . these moments of perplexity began to recur oftener and oftener. . . . They were always expressed by the questions: What is it for? What does it lead to?" (pp. 14–15).

Tolstoi's phrasing is perhaps more apt here than he realized. For interpreted as requests for information the questions he was asking would be rather silly. It is better to construe them as expressions of "arrest of life" formulated in a way which is partly misleading. He explains: "Before occupying myself with my Samara estate, the education of my son, or the writing of a book, I had to know *why* I was doing it?" (p. 16; italics in original). So far of course so good. It is perfectly reasonable to ask why you are doing what you are doing. But Tolstoi in this phase "of perplexity and arrest of life" would not take an answer for an answer. To all the replies which came into his mind he responded again: "What of it? What for?" He asks himself why he is making plans for the education of his son. The obvious reply is that he wants to do his best for the boy. Since this is both what he wants to do and what he ought to do it is hard to see what further or better reason there could be for doing what he is doing. As Hume once said: "It is impossible there can be progress in infinitum, and that one thing can always be a reason why another is desired. Something must be desirable on its own account, and because of its immediate accord or agreement with human sentiment and affection."[4] So to go on, as Tolstoi does, asking "What for?" after you have already seen how your contemplated course of action is rooted in your fundamental sentiments and affections might seem to be just silly, an indication of a failure to appreciate the scope and function of the question "What for?"

But, of course, in Tolstoi there is much more to it than that. The point is that all ordinary desires, affections, and satisfactions have lost their power and appeal: precisely this is that "arrest of life" of which the obsessively reiterated interrogatives are symptomatic. "I could find no reply at all. The questions would not wait, they had to be answered at once, and if I did not answer them it was impossible to live" (p. 17). Compare again *Anna Karenina,* and how "though he was a happy and healthy family man Levin was several times so near to suicide that he hid a cord he had lest he should hang himself, and he feared to carry a gun lest he should shoot himself."[5]

So far it has been suggested only that the interrogative forms here are partly misleading: for it is hard to see what answers, other than those of the kind already rejected, could be given to Tolstoi's symptomatic questionings straightforwardly construed. But they are not wholly misleading: for it is at least quite clearly a genuine question of what would remedy the pervasive disease of which they were expressions, of what would enable him to pick up again after this "arrest of life": "My life came to a standstill" (p. 17).

B. At the beginning of the following section (Section IV) a fresh idea is introduced. It is that what makes Tolstoi's life meaningless, and what apparently should make all human life equally meaningless, is the (presumed) fact that every individual ends in "suffering and real death—complete annihilation" (p. 18). The passage runs: "My life came to a standstill . . . there were no wishes the fulfilment of which I could consider reasonable. . . . The truth was that life is meaningless. . . . It was impossible to . . . avoid seeing that there was nothing ahead but suffering and real death—complete annihilation" (pp. 17–18). As usual there are passages in the great novels where ideas of much the same sort had been expressed. Thus in *War and Peace* Pierre Bezhukov thinks to himself: "All such 'words of honour' are conventional things with no definite meaning, especially if one considers that tomorrow one may be dead. . . ." But there the author adds: "Pierre often indulged in reflections of this sort, nullifying all his decisions and intentions."[6]

In the document which we are considering Tolstoi is speaking in his own person, and there is no similarly astringent comment. Here and now what began as clinical autobiography is developing pretensions to wider insight into the depths of the supposedly universal human situation. Tolstoi is sliding from the merely autobiographical: "there were no wishes the fulfilment of which I could consider reasonable"; to the ostensibly objective conclusion that suffering and mortality really must withdraw all reasonableness from every attempt to satisfy any ordinary human desire. It is the notion of the meaninglessness of life which appears to provide the crucial middle term: if life is meaningless, then there can be no desires the fulfilment of which would be reasonable; but if there is nothing ahead but "suffering and real death," then life must be meaningless. Yet whatever plausibility this argument may have depends on interpreting this crucial middle term ambiguously: the basic sense for Tolstoi is that in which to say that life is meaningless is to say that there are no human desires the fulfilment of which would be reasonable; but sometimes, as in the present argument, the expression is also so construed as in effect simply to mean that life does end in "suffering and real death."

There is a price to be paid even for an unequivocal interpretation of "the meaninglessness of life" as equivalent to "the fact that all our lives end in suffering and real death." If we give the words this meaning then any attempt to press the question "What is the meaning of life?" must amount to a prejudicial insistence that after all we do not really suffer and die—or, at any rate, not finally. Similarly, to lament the meaninglessness of life will not be to lament something which may or may not be the tragic consequence of our mortality and passibility: it will be to express distress over just those very facts of the human condition. But the result of using the expression "the meaningless-ness of life," as Tolstoi does, ambiguously, is to make it seem as if some rea-son had been given for taking it that the only truly deep and adequate response to the facts so labeled is a final decisive arrest of life by suicide. That is the conclusion of Section IV, although it is developed later in Section VII.

C. In Section V Tolstoi tells us how he proceeded to look for answers to his questions in the sciences, but unsuccessfully:"I sought in all the sciences, but far from finding what I wanted, became convinced that all who like myself had sought in knowledge for the meaning of life had found nothing" (p. 23). These questions are all, he thinks, fundamentally the same question, differently formulated. One, considered in IIA above, is: "Why should I live, why wish for anything, or do anything?" This, for reasons elucidated in IIB above, is taken to be the same thing as asking: "Is there any meaning in my life that the inevitable death awaiting me does not destroy?" (p. 24). In Sec-tion VI, by way of Socrates and Schopenhauer Tolstoi reaches *Ecclesiastes* and the story of the Buddha's discovery of disease, death, and decay. For all this, except the reference to the Buddha, compare again the spiritual struggles of Levin in *Anna Karenina*.[7]

In Section VII Tolstoi lists what he regards as the only four possible reac-tions to this supposed fact of the meaninglessness of life. The first, ignorance, is only for the naïvely innocent: it consists in "not understanding that life is an evil and an absurdity." This is out: "one cannot cease to know what one does know" (p. 39). The second, called epicureanism, is substantially that of the author of *Ecclesiastes*. Although "That is the way in which the majority of people of our circle make life possible for themselves," such epicureanism can, in Tolstoi's view, result only from shallowness and lack of imagination. This, again, is out: "I could not imitate these people; not having their dullness of imagination I could not artificially produce it in myself" (p. 40). The third option "is that of strength and energy." This consists in suicide. "I saw that this was the worthiest way of escape and I wished to adopt it" (p. 41). "The fourth way is that of weakness. It consists in seeing the truth of the situation and yet clinging to life, knowing that nothing will come of it" (p. 41). This was Tolstoi's own first response, as well as that of Pierre Bezhukov and Con-stantine Levin.

If these were merely the musings of some character in a novel they might perhaps be allowed to pass. Though even here it is as worthwhile as it is unfashionable to emphasize that if the novel or indeed creative literature generally is to be anything more than a pastime, then men of letters must be prepared for a criticism of content which presses beyond all purely literary and dramatic considerations. Certainly, presented as they are, as in part some contribution to our thinking about the problems of world outlook, Tolstoi's ideas categorically must be challenged. It just will not do at all to offer the facts, or supposed facts, of "suffering and real death" as if they must be, or would have to be, taken as compulsive reasons for deciding "that life is an evil and an absurdity." The fact that all lives contain evils gives no ground sufficient for inferring that all or even any lives are wholly or even predominantly evil. The fact that no life lives forever does not necessarily devalue all the possible activities and achievements of a lifetime.

Apparently Tolstoi was one of those inclined to hold, as if this were a necessary truth, that nothing can matter unless it goes on forever, or at any rate, eventually leads to something else which does. But there really is nothing at all ineluctable, or even especially profound, about this particular value commitment. It is at least no less rational to hold that it is precisely our mortality which makes what we do, or fail to do, so overwhelmingly important. And there is not the slightest warrant for suggesting that this alternative and opposite reaction is possible only for those who are lacking in imagination. Consider the words of another character in another novel: "You don't realize how much more noble it is, how much more tragic and yet exhilarating . . . to have a life ephemeral but infinitely precious, precious *because* it is the only life we have."[8] Or consider the concluding lines of Auden's *Spain:*

> We are left alone with our day, and the time
>   is short, and
>   History to the defeated
> May say Alas but cannot help nor pardon.

D. "Life is a senseless evil, that is certain, said I to myself" (p. 42). Just when he thinks this unsatisfactory conclusion satisfactorily established Tolstoi is struck by a paradoxical observation: "The reasoning showing the vanity of life is not so difficult, and has long been familiar to the very simplest folk; yet they have lived and still live. How is it that they all live and never think of doubting the reasonableness of life?" (p. 43). It is, apparently, because they know the contrary: "from the most distant times . . . people have lived knowing the argument about the vanity of life, which has shown me its senselessness, and yet they lived attributing some meaning to it" (p. 44).

This is a turning point, both of Tolstoi's personal story and of the development of his argument. It is here that he begins to find what he is prepared to call the meaning of life. To appreciate the logic, or the lack of logic, of what is going on, it is essential to bear clearly in mind the various distinctions already drawn. It is one thing to ask what would in fact relieve Tolstoi's disease, the "arrest of life" considered simply as a paralyzing psychological condition. It is quite another to inquire what sense, if any, has been given in this particular and peculiar context to the interrogative sentences the utterance of which is symptomatic of this distressing psychological condition. Again, we must distinguish between the facts of suffering and universal mortality which sometimes are taken as being, and sometimes as showing, the senselessness of life and these evaluative conclusions—about the unreasonableness and the pointlessness of it all—which are sometimes supposed to follow from, and are sometimes equated with, those supposed facts. Certainly, as a matter of biography, the idea of "suffering and real death" presented itself to Tolstoi as if it must involve a devaluation of all values. But, as we have seen, there is no general necessity about this at all, whether logical or psychologi-cal; and there is nothing uniquely deep or dignified about the approved sui-cidal response to these fundamental facts of the human condition.

What at this point struck Tolstoi so forcibly becomes paradoxical only when you take it, as he apparently does, that these simple people must some-how know something which has completely eluded his inquiry. This assumption can be seen in his saying that "there is a whole humanity that lived and lives as if it understood the meaning of its life, *for without under-standing it it could not live*" (p. 43; italics mine). Now, of course, it clearly is true that these people have, in a sense, got something that Tolstoi then had not: for they are clearly not suffering from the condition which he so strikingly dubs "arrest of life." But, as we have seen, this condition is by no means a neces-sary response to, nor a necessary consequence of, a recognition of certain fun-damental facts. He is, therefore, not warranted to assume that the absence of this pathological condition in the simplest folk, combined with the presence of a capacity to appreciate some trite reasonings, provides any sort of indica-tion that they must possess knowledge of life's meaning, in the senses in which he has been employing that expression.

Simply by not suffering from arrests of life, and by being acquainted with such trite arguments, they do not show that they must possess some fount of secret knowledge—philosophical knowledge that and why his ear-lier reasonings are unsound, or metaphysical knowledge that after all we are not really mortal, or that suffering is somehow not what it seems. Neverthe-less Tolstoi was not altogether wrong in thinking that there was something to be learned from the mere existence of such simple folk, unworried by his tor-menting sense of cosmic futility. It might, for instance, lead one to suspect that there are flaws in his questions and in his arguments, which there are. It might also suggest that he could learn from these unsophisticated examples at least one way to escape from his psychological condition, as in fact he did. What we surely need here is Ryle's distinction between knowing *how* and knowing *that*; the peasants may indeed know how to live their lives free of all sophisticated psychological disabilities, but this by no means presupposes the possession of any theoretical knowledge not vouchsafed to their unfortu-nate social superiors.[9]

E. In Section VIII Tolstoi tells how an independent force came to the res-cue in his dissatisfactions: "something else was also working which I can only call a consciousness of life." This force dragged Tolstoi's attention away from "that narrow circle of rich, learned, and leisured people to which I belonged" and toward "the whole life of mankind that surrounded me on all sides" (p. 45). But he does not now want merely to break down what he has come to regard as his unhealthy isolation from the life of ordinary people. He begins to develop a mystique of the masses: "Rational knowledge, presented by the learned and wise, denies the meaning of life, but the enormous masses of men, the whole of mankind, receive that meaning in irrational knowledge. And that irrational knowledge is faith" (p. 47). This mystique later betrays him into some memorably unpersuasive utterances: "All that people sincerely believe in must be true; it may be differently expressed but it cannot be a lie, and therefore if it presents itself to me as a lie, that only means I have not understood it" (p. 68). It would surely be hard to find, even in the prophetic writings of D. H. Lawrence, anything more egregiously grotesque.

Yet Tolstoi was no wilful irrationalist. He was tormented by this apparent contradiction between the deliverances of reason and of faith: "By faith it appears that in order to understand the meaning of life I must renounce my reason, the very thing for which alone a meaning is required" (p. 47). He begins in Section IX to explore as a possible way to the resolution of his antinomy the idea that "rational knowledge" deals only with the finite, whereas "irrational knowledge" is always concerned with a relation between the finite and the infinite. But, like others who have tried to separate two exclusive spheres of influence, he finds difficulty both in determining appropriate territories and in maintaining the necessary barriers. At the end of Section IX, he writes: "I began to understand that in the replies given by faith is stored up the deepest human wisdom and that I had no right to deny them on the ground of reason, and that those answers are the only ones which reply to life's question" (p. 53). Yet at the beginning of Section X Tolstoi, like everybody else, finds himself confronted with rival faiths and rival interpretations; and he in fact resorts to some sort of rational criticism as the only sensible method of attempting to decide between their different claims. It is with an account of the first stages of this process that the rest of *A Confession* is occupied; and in the whole period of his life to which this forms a prologue Tolstoi devoted himself to a strenuous, and radically protestant, study both of the Gospels and of systematical theologies. The upshot was something very far indeed from the uncritical and superstitious faith of a muzhik.

However, we are here concerned with all this only insofar as it bears on his argument about the meaning of life. For present purposes what needs to be underlined once again is that the peasants who seem able to teach Tolstoi a lesson in *how* to live do not thereby and necessarily reveal any knowledge *that* something is the case. There is, therefore, no call, at least on this account, to search for some sphere of the infinite for such "irrational knowledge" to be about. Again, the secret of the peasants is not knowledge *that* the finite and the infinite are thus and thus arranged, but knowledge of *how* to go on living, and to allege that they—along surely with the despised epicureans and others—possess this sort of knowledge is in this case only another way of saying that they all enjoy rude mental health. Even if it were to be established that for some men, or for all men, to hold certain metaphysical beliefs is a condition of full well-being, this suspiciously Jungian fact would still have not the slightest tendency to show that any such therapeutic beliefs are actually true. The antinomy, which was at the end of Section VIII tormenting Tolstoi, thus disappears, not because "rational knowledge" and "irrational knowledge" tell the truth about different spheres, but because no sufficient reason has been provided for believing that the latter tells any truth at all.

Antony Flew

III

A. Tolstoi has told us: "I sought in all the sciences, but far from finding what I wanted, became convinced that all who like myself had sought in knowledge for the meaning of life had found nothing"; and now he confesses: "The solution of all the possible questions of life could evidently not satisfy me" (pp. 23 and 48). Here it is interesting to compare some oracular utterances of a philosopher whom we know to have been deeply influenced by Tolstoi.[10] In the *Tractatus Logico-Philosophicus* Wittgenstein writes:

> We feel that even if all possible scientific questions be answered, the problems of life have still not been touched at all. Of course there is then no question left, and just this is the answer. The solution of the problem of life is seen in the vanishing of this problem. (Is not this the reason why men to whom after long doubting the sense of life became clear, could not then say wherein this sense consisted?)

He then adds, in a vein still more apocalyptic: "There is indeed the inexpressible. This shows itself; it is the mystical."[11]

In her hierophantic exposition of the *Tractatus* Miss Anscombe urges that Wittgenstein cannot be interpreted as saying only the negative thing which he seems to be saying in the first four of the six sentences quoted: quite rightly, for the two following sentences are used to insist that there is after all something to be said, albeit something which unfortunately happens to be unsayable. She goes on to write of Tolstoi, "whose explanations of what he thought he understood are miserable failures; but whose understanding is manifested, and whose preaching comes through, in a story like Hadji Murad."[12] In the light of the whole previous argument it becomes possible to see that and how this is both partly right and partly wrong.

It is right in its suggestion that what Tolstoi was seeking, and preaching, was primarily an attitude to life and a way of life; something combining dignity, realism, and peace of mind. It is wrong in assuming that such a way and such an attitude must be connected necessarily with some mystic truth: no good reason whatsoever has been given for believing that the peace of mind of Platon Karataev, and that eventually achieved by Pierre Bezhukov, by Constantine Levin, or by Hadji Murad either validates or presupposes logically any propositions about some infinite shadow world outside the world.

Indeed what should strike the ideologically minded reader is that although Murad was a Hadji—one, that is, who has made the great pilgrimage to Mecca—his character is not in fact presented as formed by the doctrines of Islam. Again, in *War and Peace*, Pierre Bezhukov's "mental change" is not a conversion to a dogma—not even to an inexpressible dogma—but rather the acquisition of "that tranquillity of mind, that inner harmony, which had so impressed him in the soldiers at the battle of Borodino."[13] His newfound "faith" is a faith wholly devoid of intellectual content; and the "answers" which he now accepts are as empty as the original symptomatic "questions."[14] In *Anna Karenina*, similarly, Constantine Levin is not initiated into any truths necessary to salvation. Yet he too comes to feel that "my whole life, independently of anything that may happen to me, is in every moment no longer meaningless as it was before, but has an unquestionable meaning of goodness with which I have the power to invest it."[15]

The appreciation of this antithesis between the concern about a way of life and the discovery of mystic truth may provide a clue to a constructive understanding of Tolstoi's later religious teaching. We have seen how Tolstoi was "brought to acknowledge that all live humanity has another irrational knowledge—faith which makes it possible to live"; and this, at least in *A Confession*, he mistakes to be a knowledge that something is the case. Thus, though Miss Anscombe dismisses all his attempts to formulate this putative knowledge as "miserable failures", this description scarcely applies to the catechism: "What real result will come of my life?—Eternal torment or eternal bliss. What meaning has life that death does not destroy?—Union with the eternal God: heaven" (p. 50). But later, in such specifically religious works as the studies of the Gospels and *What I Believe,* this traditional doctrine seems to disappear; and the teaching is of a way of life, without benefit of any eschatological threats and promises. Indeed we seem to have there a religion which looks as if it really might be completely analyzable in terms of ethics and psychology only.

In the course of the recent revival of lay interest in the philosophy of religion it has been suggested that traditional Christianity might be analyzed in some such manner. Thus, in the early days, a writer in *Mind* urged: that "God exists" might be interpreted as "some men and women have had, and all may have, experiences called 'meeting God'"; and that "God created the world from nothing" should be construed as "everything which we call 'material' can be used in such a way that it contributes to the well-being of men."[16] More recently the somewhat more sophisticated proposal has been made that a religious assertion is to be taken as "the assertion of an intention to carry out a certain behaviour policy, subsumable under a sufficiently general principle to be a moral one, together with the implicit or explicit statement, but not necessarily the assertion of certain stories."[17] Perhaps the most interesting aspect of this second proposal lies in its emphatic recognition that stories which are not even believed to be literally true may nevertheless have an enormous influence: "Next to the Bible and the Prayer Book the most influential work in English Christian religious life has been a book whose stories are frankly recognized as fictitious—Bunyan's *Pilgrim's Progress;* and some of the most influential works in setting the moral tone of my generation were the novels of Dostoievsky."[18]

Now to proffer anything on these lines as an adequate descriptive analysis of the religion of the Saints and the Fathers would, of course, be quite absurd, not but what it has actually been done. But if we are considering Tolstoi's own rather special interpretation of Christianity, then it is at least not obviously impracticable to attempt an analysis in these terms, or in some variation on or combination of them. And to the extent that this is possible his final goal becomes altogether appropriate to the urge which originally drove him on his religious quest. That quest arose from an intolerable dissatisfaction with his condition. Certainly that "arrest of life" expressed itself in interrogatives. But, as we have seen, these are most charitably to be regarded not as questions requiring an answer but as symptomatic utterances. Similarly in Wittgenstein too we can find suggestions of a religion without reference to any world beyond the world. Thus in the *Notebooks, 1914–1916*, filled while he was working on the *Tractatus*, he writes: "To believe in God means to see that life has a meaning. The world is *given* me, i.e. my will enters into the world completely from the outside as into something that is already there. . . . That is why we have the feeling of being dependent on an alien will. *However this may be*, at any rate we *are* in a certain sense dependent, and what we are dependent on we can call God."[19]

NOTES

1. This article incorporates some material which originally appeared in two papers published in 1959 in *The Humanist* (London). I wish to thank the editor of that journal for his permission to reuse this material here.

2. All references given in parentheses in the text are to the "World's Classics" edition (London and New York: Oxford University Press, 1940).

3. Part III, chap. xxxi.

4. *An Inquiry Concerning the Principles of Morals*, Appendix I.

5. Part VIII, chap. ix.

6. Book I, chap. iii.

7. Part VIII, chaps. viii and ix.

8. Pierre-Henri Simon, Les Raisins Verts, p. 97. (My italics.)

9. See G. Ryle, *The Concept of Mind*, chap. ii.

10. See G. H. von Wright's biographical sketch in the *Philosophical Review*, 1955, p. 534.

11. 6.52, 6.521, and 6.522: I follow, although omitting the italics, the old translation (A.V.) rather than the new (R.V.) because the former seems here to be no less accurate while generally it does more justice to the literary quality of the original.

12. G. E. M. Anscombe, *An Introduction to Wittgenstein's Tractatus*, p. 170.

13. Book XIII, chap. iii.

14. Book XV, chap. v.

15. Part VIII, chap. xix: cf. chaps. x. xi, and xiii.

16. D. Cox, "The Significance of Christianity," *Mind*, 1949, p. 216.

17. R. B. Braithwaite, *An Empiricist's View of the Nature of Religious Belief* (Cambridge: Cambridge University Press, 1955), p. 32.

18. *Ibid.*, p. 27.

19. Oxford: Basil Blackwell, 1961, p. 74; italics in original.

CHAPTER 20

A . J . A Y E R

The Claims of Philosophy

I

Contemporary philosophers may be divided into two classes: the pontiffs and the journeymen. As the names that I have chosen indicate, the basis of this division is not so much a difference of opinion as a difference of attitude. It is not merely that the journeyman denies certain propositions which the pontiff asserts, or that he asserts certain propositions which the pontiff denies. It is rather that he has a radically different conception of the method of philosophy and of the ends that it is fitted to achieve. Thus, it is character-istic of those whom I describe as pontiffs that they think it within the province of philosophy to compete with natural science. They may, indeed, be willing to admit that the scientist achieves valuable results in his own domain, but they insist that he does not, and cannot, attain to the complete and final truth about reality; and they think that it is open to the philosopher to make this deficiency good. In support of this view, they may, for example, argue that every scientific theory is based upon presuppositions which can-not themselves be scientifically proved; and from this they may infer, in the interests of their own "philosophical" brand of irrationality, that science itself is fundamentally irrational; or else they may have recourse to metaphysics to supply the missing proof. Alternatively, they may hold that the scientist deals only with the appearances of things, whereas the philosopher by the use of his special methods penetrates to the reality beyond. In general, the ideal of the pontiff is to construct a metaphysical system. Such a system may actually include some scientific hypotheses, either as premises or, more frequently, as deductions from metaphysical first principles. It may, on the other hand, be

From *Polemic*, March 1947, No. 7, pp. 18–33; reprinted in *Reflections on Our Age: Lectures Delivered at the Opening Session of UNESCO at the Sorbonne University, Paris*, intro. by David Hardman, fore-word by Stephen Spender, London: Allan Wingate, 1948, pp. 51–66. Used by permission of UNESCO and with the approval of the author.

uncompromisingly metaphysical. In either case, the aim is to give a complete and definitive account of "ultimate" reality.

Unfortunately, as the journeymen on their side have been at pains to show, this "ultimate" reality is a fiction, and the ideal of a metaphysical system that is anything other than a scientific encyclopaedia is devoid of any basis in reason. To some extent, indeed, this fact has been borne in upon the pontiffs, and the result is that they now tend to desert reason and even to decry it. This separates them sharply from their philosophical ancestors, who at least professed to reason, even if they did not always reason well. Few men, indeed, can ever have reasoned worse than Hegel, the arch-pontiff of the nineteenth century, but at least he claimed the support of reason for his fantasies. His ground for thinking that a mobile logic is needed to describe a mobile world may have been no better than the principle that "who drives fat oxen must himself be fat"; but at least, if he rejected the "static" Aristotelian logic, he did so in favour of what he, no doubt mistakenly, believed to be a superior logic of his own. Though he misused logic abominably, he did not affect to be above it. But now if we turn to Heidegger, the high priest of the modern school of existentialists, and the leading pontiff of our times, we find ourselves in a country from which the ordinary processes of logic, or indeed reasoning of any kind, appear to have been banished. For what we learn from him is that it is only in the clear light of Nothing that Being has being, and consequently that it is the supreme privilege of the philosopher to concern himself with Nothing.[1] For this he requires no special intellectual discipline. It is sufficient that he experiences anguish, provided always that it is an anguish without any special object. For it is thus, according to Heidegger, that the Nothing reveals itself. This strange thesis is indeed backed by a pretence of argument, but since the argument depends upon the elementary fallacy of treating "nothing" as a name, it is hardly to be taken seriously. Nor does Heidegger himself appear to attach very much weight to it. For it is not by logic that he seeks to convince: nor is his the Socratic method of following an argument wherever it may lead. Like the sermons of Dr. Dodd,[2] his work is addressed to the passions; and it is no doubt for this reason that it has succeeded in becoming fashionable.

Now just as William James thought that all prigs must sooner or later end by becoming Hegelians, so it seems to me that the fate of the contemporary pontiff must be to go the way of Heidegger. I do not mean by this that he will have to subscribe to Heidegger's doctrines. There are other types of "deeply significant nonsense" available. But inasmuch as his quest for ultimate reality cannot be made to prosper by any rational means, he is likely, if he adheres to it, to seek some non-rational source of enlightenment. At this point he devolves into a mystic or a poet. As such he may express an attitude to life which is interesting in itself and even a source of inspiration to others; and perhaps it would be churlish to refuse him the title of philosopher. But it is to be remarked that when philosophy has been brought to this stage then, whatever its emotional value, it has ceased to be, in any ordinary sense, a vehicle of knowledge.

II

The history of philosophy, as it is taught in the textbooks, is largely a parade of pontiffs; and it might be thought that the only course open to the budding philosopher was either to enroll himself under one of their banners, or else to try to become a pontiff in his own right. But in this, as in so many other cases, the textbooks are behind the times. For, at least in England and America, the philosophical scene has been dominated for the last fifty years, not by the pontiffs, but by those whom I describe as journeymen. Unlike the pontiffs, the journeymen do not set out in quest of ultimate reality. Nor do they try to bring philosophy into competition with the natural sciences. Believing, as they do, that the only way to discover what the world is like is to form hypotheses and test them by observation, which is in fact the method of science, they are content to leave the scientist in full possession of the field of speculative knowledge. Consequently they do not try to build systems. The task of the philosopher, as they see it, is rather to deal piecemeal with a special set of problems. Some of these problems are historical, in the sense that they involve the criticism and interpretation of the work of previous philosophers; others are primarily mathematical, as belonging to the specialized field of formal logic; others again are set by the sciences: they involve the analysis of scientific method, the evaluation of scientific theories, the clarification of scientific terms. It is, for example, a philosophical problem to decide what is meant by "probability": and the journeymen have already contributed much towards its solution. Finally, there are a number of problems, such as the problem of perception, the problem of our knowledge of other minds, the question of the significance of moral judgments, that arise out of the common usages and assumptions of everyday life. In a broad sense, all these problems are semantic: that is to say, they can all be represented as concerned with the use of language. But since the term "semantics" is technically applied to a particular formal discipline which does not, even for the journeymen, comprehend the whole of philosophy, I think it better to resume their philosophical activities under the general heading of logical analysis.

Essentially, the journeymen are technicians; and from this point of view the comparison with the pontiffs is very much to their advantage. They suffer, however, from a certain thinness of material. Consider, for example, the so-called philosophers of common-sense, who follow the distinguished leadership of Professor G. E. Moore. In the opinion of this school, it is not sensible for a philosopher to question the truth of such common-sense statements as that this is a sheet of paper or that I am wearing shoes on my feet. And if anyone were to question it they would reply simply that, on the relevant occasions, they knew for certain that statements of this sort were true. Thus, Professor Moore himself has proved, to his own satisfaction, the existence of external objects, a question much canvassed by philosophers, by the simple method of holding up his hands and saying that he knows for certain that they exist,[3] and indeed there is no denying that in its way this is a valid proof. At the same time these philosophers confess to being very doubtful of the correct analysis of the common-sense propositions which they know to be true. The question whether or not this really is a sheet of paper does not puzzle them at all; but the question of what precisely is implied by saying that it is puzzles them a great deal. In technical language, it is a matter of discovering the relationship between the sense-data which are immediately experienced and the physical objects which it is their function to present; and this is a problem which, in the opinion of our common-sense philosophers, has not yet been satisfactorily solved. Now I do not wish to suggest that this is not a difficult problem, or to belittle the ingenuity with which the journeymen have tackled it. But I am afraid that a layman who was told that a question of this sort was of sufficient interest to a modern philosopher to occupy him for a life-time would be inclined to think that modern philosophy was degenerating into scholasticism. If he were told, as he might be by a pontiff, that there was serious doubt of the existence of this piece of paper he would be very properly incredulous, but he might also be impressed: he might even be brought to think that he himself had been excessively naïve in taking such a thing for granted. But once he had been assured that the truth of his common-sense assumption that the paper existed was not after all in doubt, I think it would be difficult to interest him in a meticulous analysis of its implications. He would remark that he understood very well what he meant by saying that this was a piece of paper, and that he did not see what was to be gained by a laborious attempt at further clarification. To this it could, indeed, be objected that he might think very differently if he had been properly educated in philosophy; and that in any case there is no reason why the layman's judgments of value should be binding upon the philosopher. But even so it is difficult not to feel some sympathy for our layman. It is difficult not to suspect that the philosopher of common-sense must sometimes be inclined to say to himself what the poet Clough said when he found himself exclusively engaged in doing up parcels for Florence Nightingale: "This that I see is not all, and this that I do is but little. It is good but there is better than it."

Another prominent set of journeymen are the followers of Ludwig Wittgenstein, who has succeeded G. E. Moore as professor of philosophy at the University of Cambridge. More than twenty years ago, Professor Wittgenstein came to the conclusion, at the end of his remarkable *Tractatus Logico-Philosophicus*, that "the right method of philosophy would be this." "To say nothing except what can be said, i.e. the propositions of natural science, i.e. something that has nothing to do with philosophy: and then always when someone wished to say something metaphysical, to demonstrate to him that he had given no meaning to certain signs in his proposition. This method would be unsatisfying to the other—he would not have the impression that he was learning philosophy—but it would be the only strictly correct method." In other words, the philosopher is reduced, or elevated, to the position of a park keeper whose business it is to see that no one commits an intellectual nuisance; the nuisance in question being that of lapsing into metaphysics. I do not know whether Wittgenstein is still of this opinion; and even if his point of view has remained substantially the same I doubt if he would now express it in such terms as I have quoted. But what I do know is that the effect of his teaching upon his more articulate disciples has been that they tend to treat philosophy as a department of psychoanalysis. In their eyes, the *raison d'être* of the philosopher is the fact that people continually get themselves into states of metaphysical doubt. They are inclined to say, for example, that they can never really be sure of the existence of the material world, or that they can never really know what goes on in another person's mind, or even, more seriously, that he has a mind. Now these, according to the Wittgensteinians, are intellectually neurotic doubts; and it is the business of the philosopher to effect their cure. Admittedly, the people who feel them are usually those who have studied some philosophy: but equally the psychoanalyst finds his most profitable patients among those who have delved a little into psychoanalysis. In both cases, the method of cure is to enter sympathetically into the patient's neurosis and try to talk it out. As Mr. Wisdom puts it,[4] "the treatment is like psychoanalytic treatment in that the treatment is the diagnosis and the diagnosis is the description, the very full description, of the symptoms." That the description is full will hardly be denied by anyone who has read Mr. Wisdom. Whether it is effective is perhaps more doubtful; but, in his hands at any rate, it is a work of fascinating subtlety. Nevertheless one is again tempted to ask: "Is this all that the philosopher is fitted to achieve?"

Not all the contemporary philosophers whom I should classify as journeymen hold the views that I have quoted; but I think it can fairly be said that in the case of nearly all of them there is an unfortunate disparity between the richness of their technique and the increasing poverty of the material on which they are able to exercise it. The principal exceptions are those who, like Bertrand Russell and Professor Whitehead, at least in the days before he became a pontiff, combine a mastery of logic with an understanding of mathematics and natural science. And this suggests that the salvation of the journeymen may be the reunion of philosophy with science, just as the final resource of the pontiff is the passage of philosophy into mysticism, or at least into imaginative literature. In the meantime, however, there remain a number of logical puzzles which the journeyman, who is relatively ignorant of science, may reasonably feel called upon to solve. The importance of his work may not indeed be immediately obvious to the layman; and there may be times when the philosopher himself is reduced to wishing that the field of his achievement were rather more spectacular; but he may perhaps console himself with the words of John Locke that "it is ambition enough to be employed as an under-labourer in clearing the ground a little, and removing some of the rubbish that lies in the way to knowledge."[5]

III

On the side of the pontiffs, imaginative literature. On the side of the journeymen, the re-integration of philosophy with science, or the piecemeal solution of logical or linguistic puzzles. Surely, it will be said, this is not what the public expects of its philosophers. Surely, the business of the philosopher is to make clear the meaning of life, to show people how they ought to live. Call him a pontiff or a journeyman, according to his method of approach; the distinction is not of any great importance. What is important is the message that he has to give. It is wisdom that is needed, not merely scientific knowledge. Of what use to us is the understanding of nature if we do not know the purpose of our existence or how we ought to live? And who is to answer these supremely important questions if not the philosopher?

The reply to this is that there is no true answer to these questions; and since this is so it is no use expecting even the philosopher to provide one. What can be done, however, is to make clear why, and in what sense, these questions are unanswerable; and once this is achieved it will be seen that there is also a sense in which they can be answered. It will be found that the form of answer is not a proposition, which must be either true or false, but the adoption of a rule, which cannot properly be characterized as either true or false, but can nevertheless be judged as more or less acceptable. And with this the problem is solved, so far as reasoning can solve it. The rest is a matter of personal decision, and ultimately of action.

Let us begin then by considering the purpose of our existence. How is it possible for our existence to have a purpose? We know very well what it is for a man to have a purpose. It is a matter of his intending, on the basis of a given situation, to bring about some further situation, which for some reason or other he conceives to be desirable. And in that case it may be said that events have a meaning for him according as they conduce, or fail to conduce, towards the end that he desires. But how can life in general be said to have any meaning? A simple answer is that all events are tending towards a certain specifiable end: so that to understand the meaning of life it is necessary only to discover this end. But, in the first place, there is no good reason whatever for supposing this assumption to be true, and secondly, even if it were true, it would not do the work that is required of it. For what is being sought by those who demand to know the meaning of life is not an explanation of the facts of their existence, but a justification. Consequently a theory which informs them merely that the course of events is so arranged as to lead inevitably to a certain end does nothing to meet their need. For the end in question will not be one that they themselves have chosen. As far as they are concerned it will be entirely arbitrary; and it will be a no less arbitrary fact that their existence is such as necessarily to lead to its fulfilment. In short, from the point of view of justifying one's existence, there is no essential difference between a teleological explanation of events and a mechanical explanation. In either case, it is a matter of brute fact that events succeed one another in the ways that they do and are explicable in the ways that they are. And indeed what is called an explanation is nothing other than a more general description. Thus, an attempt to answer the question why events are as they are must always resolve itself into saying only how they are. But what is required by those who seek the meaning of life is precisely an answer to their question "Why?"

that is something other than an answer to any question "How?" And just because this is so they can never legitimately be satisfied.

But now, it may be objected, suppose that the world is designed by a superior being. In that case the purpose of our existence will be the purpose that it realizes for him; and the meaning of life will be found in our conscious adaptation to his purpose. But here again, the answer is, first, that there is no good reason whatsoever for believing that there is any such superior being; and, secondly, that even if there were, he could not accomplish what is here required of him. For let us assume, for the sake of argument, that everything happens as it does because a superior being has intended that it should. As far as we are concerned, the course of events still remains entirely arbitrary. True, it can now be said to fulfil a purpose; but the purpose is not ours. And just as, on the previous assumption, it merely happened to be the case that the course of events conduced to the end that it did, so, on this assumption, it merely happens to be the case that the deity has the purpose that he has, and not some other purpose, or no purpose at all. Nor does this unwarrantable assumption provide us even with a rule of life. For even those who believe most firmly that the world was designed by a superior being are not in a position to tell us what his purpose can have been. They may indeed claim that it has been mysteriously revealed to them, but how can it be proved that the revelation is genuine? And even if we waive this objection, even if we assume not only the world as we find it is working out the purpose of a superior being, but also that we are capable of discovering what this purpose is, we are still not provided with a rule of life. For either his purpose is sovereign or it is not. If it is sovereign, that is, if everything that happens is necessarily in accordance with it, then this is true also of our behavior. Consequently, there is no point in our deciding to conform to it, for the simple reason that we cannot do otherwise. However we behave, we shall fulfil the purpose of this deity; and if we were to behave differently, we should still be fulfilling it; for if it were possible for us not to fulfil it it would not be sovereign in the requisite sense. But suppose that it is not sovereign, or, in other words, that not all events must necessarily bear it out. In that case, there is no reason why we should try to conform to it, unless we independently judge it to be good. But that means that the significance of our behavior depends finally upon our own judgments of value; and the concurrence of a deity then becomes superfluous.

The point is, in short, that even the invocation of a deity does not enable us to answer the question why things are as they are. At the best it complicates the answer to the question how they are by pushing the level of explanation to a further stage. For even if the ways of the deity were clear to those who believed in him, which they apparently are not, it would still be, even to them, a matter of brute fact that he behaved as he did, just as to those who do not believe in him it is a matter of brute fact that the world is what it is. In either case the question "Why?" remains unanswered, for the very good reason that it is unanswerable. That is to say, it may be answerable at any given level, but the answer is always a matter of describing at a higher level not why things are as they are, but simply how they are. And so, to whatever level our explanations may be carried, the final statement is never an answer to the question "Why?" but necessarily only an answer to the question "How?"

It follows, if my argument is correct, that there is no sense in asking what is the ultimate purpose of our existence, or what is the real meaning of life. For to ask this is to assume that there can be a reason for our living as we do which is somehow more profound than any mere explanation of the facts; and we have seen that this assumption is untenable. Moreover it is untenable in logic and not merely in fact. The position is not that our existence unfortunately lacks a purpose which, if the fates had been kinder, it might conceivably have had. It is rather that those who inquire, in this way, after the meaning of life are raising a question to which it is not logically possible that there should be an answer. Consequently, the fact that they are disappointed is not, as some romanticists would make it, an occasion for cynicism or despair. It is not an occasion for any emotional attitude at all. And the reason why it is not is just that it could not conceivably have been otherwise. If it were logically possible for our existence to have a purpose, in the sense required, then it might be sensible to lament the fact that it had none. But it is not sensible to cry for what is logically impossible. If a question is so framed as to be unanswerable, then it is not a matter for regret that it remains unanswered. It is, therefore, misleading to say that life has no meaning; for that suggests that the statement that life has a meaning is factually significant, but false; whereas the truth is that, in the sense in which it is taken in this context, it is not factually significant.

There is, however, a sense in which it can be said that life does have a meaning. It has for each of us whatever meaning we severally choose to give it. The purpose of a man's existence is constituted by the ends to which he, consciously or unconsciously, devotes himself. Some men have a single overriding purpose to which all their activities are subordinated. If they are at all successful in achieving it, they are probably the happiest, but they are the exceptions. Most men pass from one object to another; and at any one time they may pursue a number of different ends, which may or may not be capable of being harmonized. Philosophers, with a preference for tidiness, have sometimes tried to show that all these apparently diverse objects can really be reduced to one: but the fact is that there is no end that is common to all men, not even happiness. For setting aside the question whether men ought always to pursue happiness, it is not true even that they always do pursue it, unless the word "happiness" is used merely as a description of any end that is in fact pursued. Thus the question what is the meaning of life proves, when it is taken empirically, to be incomplete. For there is no single thing of which it can truly be said that this is the meaning of life. All that can be said is that life has at various times a different meaning for different people, according as they pursue their several ends.

That different people have different purposes is an empirical matter of fact. But what is required by those who seek to know the purpose of their existence is not a factual description of the way that people actually do conduct themselves, but rather a decision as to how they should conduct themselves. Having been taught to believe that not all purposes are of equal value, they require to be guided in their choice. And thus the inquiry into the purpose of our existence dissolves into the question "How ought men to live?"

IV

The question how ought men to live is one that would seem to fall within the province of moral philosophy; but it cannot be said of every moral philosopher that he makes a serious attempt to answer it. Moreover, those who do make a serious attempt to answer it are mostly pontiffs, who approach it wrongly. For having decided, on metaphysical grounds, that reality is of such and such a character they try to deduce from this the superiority of a certain rule of life. But, quite apart from the merits or demerits of their metaphysics, it is a mistake on their part to suppose that a mere description of reality is sufficient to establish any rule of life at all. A familiar instance of this mistake is the claim that men ought to live in such and such a way because such and such is their real nature. But if what is meant by their having such and such a real nature is that they really are of the nature in question, then all that can possibly be established is that they really do behave in the manner indicated. For if they behaved differently, they would thereby show that they had a different nature. Thus in telling men that they ought to live in accordance with their real nature you are telling them to do what they do; and your pretended rule of life dissolves into nothing, since it is equally consistent with any course of conduct whatsoever. If, on the other hand, what is meant by a man's real nature is not the nature that he actually displays but the nature that he ought to display, then the moral rule that the argument is supposed to justify is assumed at the outset, and assumed without proof. As a moral rule, it may be acceptable in itself; but the supposed deduction of it from a non-moral premiss turns out inevitably to be a fraud.

It is not only metaphysicians who commit this fallacy. There is, for example, a brand of "scientific ethics" according to which the right rule of life is that which harmonizes with the course of human evolution. But here again the same ambiguity arises. For if "the course of human evolution" is understood as an actually existent process, then there is no sense in telling people that they ought to adapt themselves to it, for the very good reason that they cannot possibly do otherwise. However they may behave they will be acting rightly, since it is just their behaving as they do that makes the course of evolution what it is. In short, if progress is defined in terms of merely historical development, all conduct is progressive; for every human action necessarily furthers the course of evolution, in the straightforward sense of adding to its history. If on the other hand, it is only some among the many possible developments of human history that are considered to be progressive, then there is some sense in saying that we ought to strive to bring them about; but here again the moral rule which we are invited to adopt is not deduced but simply posited. It is neither itself a scientific statement of fact, nor a logical consequence of any such statement. By scientific methods we can indeed discover that certain events are more or less likely to occur; but the transition from this to deciding that some of these possible developments are more valuable than others carries us outside the domain of science altogether. In saying this, I do not wish to repudiate the humanistic values of those who put forward the claims of scientific ethics, or even to suggest that any other system of values is more securely founded. My objection to these moralists is simply that they fall into the logical error of confusing normative judgments of value with scientific statements of fact. They may have the advantage of the metaphysicians, in that their factual premises are more deserving of belief, but the fundamental mistake of trying to extract normative rules from supposedly factual descriptions is common to them both.

In moral, as in natural, philosophy it is characteristic of the journeymen to have detected the flaw in the method of the pontiffs, but here also they have purchased their freedom from error at the price of a certain aridity. For not only do they not attempt to prove their judgments of value; for the most part they refrain from expressing them at all. What they do instead, apart from criticizing other moral philosophers, is to subject the terminology of ethics to logical analysis. Thus the questions that they discuss are whether the term "good" or the term "right" is to be taken as fundamental, and whether either is definable; whether it is a man's duty to do an action or merely to set himself to do it; whether his duty is to do what is objectively right or merely what he thinks to be right; whether the rightness of an action depends upon its actual consequences, or upon its probable consequences, or upon its consequences as foreseen by the agent, or not upon its consequences at all; whether it is possible to fulfil an obligation unintentionally; whether the moral goodness of an action depends upon its motive; and many other questions of a similar sort. Such questions can be interesting, though they are not always made so, and I do not wish to say that they are not important; but to the practical man they must appear somewhat academic. By taking a course in this kind of moral philosophy a man may learn how to make the expression of his moral judgments secure from formal criticism. What he will not learn is what, in any concrete situation, he actually ought to do.

I think, then, that it can fairly be made a reproach to the journeymen that they have overlooked the Aristotelian principle that the end of moral philosophy is "not knowledge but action."[6] But their excuse is that once the philosopher who wishes to be practical has said this, there is very little more that he can say. Like anyone else, he can make moral recommendations, but he cannot legitimately claim for them the sanction of philosophy. He cannot prove that his judgments of value are correct, for the sufficient reason that no judgment of value is capable of proof. Or rather, if it is capable of proof, it is only by reference to some other judgment of value, which must itself be left unproved. The moral philosopher can sometimes affect men's conduct by drawing their attention to certain matters of fact; he may show, for example, that certain sorts of action have unsuspected consequences, or that the motives for which they are done are different from what they appear to be; and he may then hope that when his audience is fully aware of the circumstances it will assess the situation in the same way as he does himself. Nevertheless there may be some who differ from him, not on any question of fact, but on a question of value, and in that case he has no way of demonstrating that his judgment is superior. He lays down one rule, and they lay down another; and the decision between them is a subject for persuasion and finally a matter of individual choice.

Since judgments of value are not reducible to statements of fact, they are strictly speaking neither true nor false; and it is tempting to infer from this that no course of conduct is better or worse than any other. But this would be a mistake. For the judgment that no course of conduct is better or worse than any other is itself a judgment of value and consequently neither true nor false. And while an attitude of moral indifference is legitimate in itself, it is not easily maintained. For since we are constantly faced with the practical necessity of action, it is natural for most of us to act in accordance with certain principles; and the choice of principles implies the adoption of a positive set of values. That these values should be consistent is a necessary condition of their being fully realized; for it is logically impossible to achieve the complete fulfilment of an inconsistent set of ends. But, once their consistency is established, they can be criticized only on practical grounds, and from the standpoint of the critic's own moral system, which his adversary may or may not accept. No doubt, in practice, many people are content to follow the model rules that are prescribed to them by others; but the decision to submit oneself to authority on such a point is itself a judgment of value. In the last resort, therefore, each individual has the responsibility of choice; and it is a responsibility that is not to be escaped.

V

The same considerations apply to the philosophy of politics. That moral and political philosophy are intimately connected is fairly widely recognized; but the nature of their connection is still a subject of dispute. Thus some philosophers believe that morals can be logically subordinated to politics. They think that if they can establish the proper forms of political association they will be able to deduce from this how men ought to live. But, as we shall see, it is the opposite that is true. A political system may take one form or another; and, in any actual case, there will usually be an historical explanation of its taking the form that it does. But even if its existence can be historically accounted for, there still remains the question whether it is worthy of allegiance. Political institutions are not sacrosanct. It may, in certain circumstances, be beyond the power of a given individual to change them, but it does not follow that he is bound to think them good. That they are what they are is an unmistakable fact, but it does not follow that they are what they ought to be. And the question what they ought to be is ultimately a moral question. It is for the individual to answer it in accordance with the values that he himself adopts.

The confusion of fact with value, which we have seen to be a feature of certain moral systems, is equally a pitfall to political philosophers. Thus Plato seems, in his *Republic,* to look upon his ideal city-state as the unique embodiment of the reality of "justice"; and he seems even to suggest that in depicting the structure of this political community he has answered the moral question how men ought to live. But what he does not appear to have seen is that to assert that true, or real, justice is to be found in such and such a set of institutions is not to make a statement of fact at all, but rather to lay down a standard. It is not a way of describing the institutions in question, but of making a certain claim for them; and the claim is that they ought to be adopted. It may be objected that what is claimed is not merely that they ought to be adopted, but that they ought to be adopted because they are truly just. But the point is that to say that they are truly just is, in this usage, no more than another way of saying that they ought to be adopted: the one statement is not, as it is made to seem, a justification of the other, but simply a repetition of it. Thus, if anyone thinks, as he well may, that Plato's institutions are not the best possible, he may devise a different Utopia; and he too may seek to recommend it by saying that it alone fulfils the true conditions of justice. In saying this he will be disagreeing with Plato, but he will not be formally contradicting him: for neither party is making a statement of fact. What makes this easy to overlook is the occurrence in such a context of words like "true" or "real": for it is assumed that they are being given their ordinary descriptive use. But, in fact, their use in these contexts is not descriptive but persuasive. They serve only to put a little halo round the principles that the speaker wishes to recommend. Accordingly, the question whether one or other of two divergent political systems has the better claim to be considered just, is a question, not of truth or falsehood, in the ordinary sense, but of deciding where to give one's allegiance: and the answer to it will depend upon the system of values of the person who is called upon to judge. Thus, so far from its being the case, as Plato seems to have thought, that the choice of political institutions can determine how men ought to live, it is a previous conception of the way men ought to live that determines the value of the institutions themselves.

For Hegel, the perfect embodiment of justice was not an ideal republic but the contemporary Prussian State: and he based this illiberal view upon the principle that the real was the rational. But this convenient principle turned out to be two-edged. For while it was used by conservatives to prove that whatever happened to exist was best, it occurred to some followers of Hegel to argue that since the contemporary Prussian State was palpably irrational it was not wholly real; and they then conceived it to be their duty to try to put something more real in its place. In so doing they performed a political service: but they also unconsciously rendered a service to logic. For their inversion of Hegel's principle helps us to see how wretchedly ambiguous it is. Thus, if the word "real" is used to mean "existent" and the word "rational" is used, as Hegel seems to have intended, to mean what is in accordance with logic, it will be necessarily true that everything that is real is rational; for what is logically impossible cannot exist. On the other hand, it will not be true that everything that is rational is real; for many states of affairs that do not exist are logically possible. The word "rational," however, can also be used, and is indeed most commonly used, as a term of value. As applied to a political system, it serves to claim that the system is such as to bring about the ends of which the speaker approves; and it carries the implication that the ends in question are such as any reasonable man would share. But if the word "rational" is used in this sense, the statement that the real is the rational is by no means necessarily true. For, whatever may be the set of values that is ascribed to the reasonable man, it is an open question whether they are satisfied. Assuredly much that exists will not come up to them, and very likely nothing exists that does. But, thirdly, the word "real" may itself be used as a term of values; and in that case the principle that the real is the rational becomes entirely verbal. It merely expresses the speaker's intention to use the words "real" and "rational" as equivalent terms of approbation. Thus in the sense in which it is true the principle is trivial, and in the sense in which it is not trivial it is not necessarily true.

The merit of this example is that it again brings out the point that, in politics as in morals, the fact that something is what it is does not by any means entail that it is what it ought to be; nor does the fact that something is considered valuable by any means entail that it exists. Within the domain of fact, the study of politics can yield us fruitful hypotheses about the ways in which political institutions develop. It can enable us to assess the probability that from a given set of circumstances a given situation will result. But over and above this, there remains the question what it is that we desire to bring about. Thus, when Marx said "Philosophers have previously offered various interpretations of the world. Our business is to change it,"[7] he was making a judgment of value. He was implying that the existing state of affairs was not what it ought to be, and consequently that it ought to be changed. He himself, indeed, might not have admitted this, because of his historical determinism. He might have replied that in saying it was "our business" to change the world, he was merely calling upon his contemporaries to fulfil their necessary historical role. But if their role was really determined for them, then they were bound to fulfil it, and there was no sense in urging them to do so. The call to arms was needed to bring about something that Marx wished to happen; it was designed to influence events, not merely to encumber fate with help. That the future will be what it will be is indeed an analytic truth: but it does not prevent its also being true that the future will be what we make it. What changes are possible at any given moment is a subject for scientific inquiry; but the decision, which we then have to make, that one or other of these changes is the most desirable is not itself a scientific hypothesis but a judgment of value. It represents a moral choice.

No more than the scientist is the philosopher specially privileged to lay down the rules of conduct, or to prescribe an ideal form of life. If he has strong opinions on these points, and wishes to convert others to them, his philosophical training may give him a certain advantage in putting them persuasively: but, whether or not the values that he recommends are found to be acceptable, it is not from his philosophy that they can derive their title to acceptance. His professional task is done when he has made the issues clear. For in morals and in politics, at the stage where politics become a matter of morals, there is no repository of truth to which only the learned few have access. The question how men ought to live is one to which there is no authoritative answer. It has to be decided by each man for himself.

NOTES

1. See M. Heidegger, *Was ist Metaphysik?*

2. See Boswell's *Life of Johnson:* "A clergyman (whose name I do not recollect): 'Were not Dodd's sermons addressed to the passions?' Johnson: 'They were nothing, sir, be they addressed to what they may.'" III, 248.

3. See his "Proof of an External World," *Proceedings of the British Academy,* XXV, 1939, 273–300.

4. In the first of his series of articles on "Other Minds," *Mind,* XLIX, 1940, 370.

5. See *An Essay Concerning Human Understanding,* Epistle to the Reader.

6. See *Nicomachean Ethics,* Book I, Section 3.

7. See his *Eleven Theses on Feuerbach.*

CHAPTER 21

KAI NIELSEN

Linguistic Philosophy and "The Meaning of Life"

I

Anglo-Saxon philosophy has in various degrees "gone linguistic." From the faithful attention to the niceties of plain English practiced by John Austin, to the use of descriptive linguistics initiated by Paul Ziff in his *Semantic Analysis,* to the deliberately more impressionistic concern with language typical of Isaiah Berlin and Stuart Hampshire, there is a pervasive emphasis by English-speaking philosophers on what can and cannot be said, on what is intelligible, and on what is nonsensical. When linguistic philosophy was first developing, many things were said to be nonsense which were not nonsense. However, this is something of the past, for linguistic philosophy has for a long time been less truculent and more diffident about what it makes sense to say, but only to become—some would say—unbelievably bland, dull and without a rationale that is of any general interest.[1]

Critics from many quarters have raised their voices to assault linguistic philosophy as useless pedantry remote from the perennial concerns of philosophy or the problems of belief and life that all men encounter when, in Hesse's terms, they feel to the full "the whole riddle of human destiny." Traditionally the philosophical enterprise sought, among other things, to give us some enlightenment about our human condition, but as philosophy "goes linguistic," it has traitorously and irresponsibly become simply talk about the uses of talk. The philosopher has left his "high calling" to traffic in linguistic trivialities.

Criticism of linguistic philosophy has not always been this crude, but there has typically been at least the implied criticism that linguistic philosophy could not really do justice to the profound problems of men with which Plato, Spinoza or Nietzsche struggled.

From *Cross Currents,* Summer 1964. Used by permission of the author.

It is my conviction that such a charge is unfounded. In linguistic philosophy there is a partially new technique but no "abdication of philosophy." Surely most linguistic philosophy is dull, as is most philosophy, as is most anything else. Excellence and insight in any field are rare. But at its best linguistic philosophy is not dull and it is not without point; furthermore, though it often is, it need not be remote from the concerns of men. It is this last claim—the claim that linguistic philosophy can have nothing of importance to say about the perplexities of belief and life that from time to time bedevil us—that I wish to challenge.

With reference to the concepts of human purpose, religion and the problematical notion "the meaning of Life," I want to show how in certain crucial respects linguistic philosophy can be relevant to the perplexities about life and conduct that reflective people actually face. "What is the meaning of Life?" has been a standby of both the pulpiteer and the mystagogue. It has not come in for extended analysis by linguistic philosophers, though Ayer, Wisdom, Baier, Edwards, Flew, Hepburn and Dilman have had some important things to say about this obscure notion which when we are in certain moods perplexes us all and indeed, as it did Tolstoy and Dostoevsky, may even be something that forces itself upon us in thoroughly human terms.[2] I want to show how the use of the analytical techniques of linguistic philosophy can help us in coming to grips with the problems of human purpose and the meaning of Life.

Part of the trouble centers around puzzles about the use of the word "meaning" in "What is the meaning of Life?" Since the turn of the century there has been a lot of talk in philosophical circles about "meanings" or "a meaning criterion" and a good measure of attention has been paid to considerations about the meanings of words and sentences. But the mark (token) "meaning" in "What is the meaning of Life?" has a very different use than it has in "What is the meaning of 'obscurantist'?" "What is the meaning of 'table'?" "What is the meaning of 'good'?" "What is the meaning of 'science'?" and "What is the meaning of 'meaning'?" In these other cases we are asking about the meaning or use of the word or words, and we are requesting either a definition of the word or an elucidation or description of the word's use. But in asking: "What is the meaning of Life?" we are not asking—or at least this is not our central perplexity—about "What is the meaning of the word 'Life'?" What then are we asking?

Indirection is the better course here. Consider some of the uses of the general formula: "What is the meaning of that?" How, in what contexts, and for what purposes does it get used? Sometimes we may simply not know the meaning of a word, as when we come across a word we do not understand and look it up in a dictionary or ask the person using it in conversation what it means. It is not that he is using the word in an odd sense and we want to know what *he means* by it, but that we want to know what is meant by that word as it is employed in the public domain.

There is the quite different situation in which it is not about words that we are puzzled but about someone's non-linguistic behavior. A friend gives us a dark look in the middle of a conversation in which several people are taking part and afterwards we ask him "What was the meaning of those dark looks?" We were aware when we noticed his dark look that he was disapproving of something we were doing but we did not and still do not know what. Our "What was the meaning of that?" serves to try to bring out what is the matter. Note that in a way here we are not even puzzled about the meaning of words. The recipient of the dark look may very well know he is being disapproved of; but he wants to know what for. Here "What is the meaning of that?" is a request for the point or the purpose of the action. In this way, as we shall see, it is closer to the question "What is the meaning of Life?" than questions about the meaning of a word or a sentence.

We also ask "What is the meaning of that?" when we want to know how a particular person on a particular occasion intends something. We want to know what *he means* by that. Thus if I say of some author that he writes "chocolate rabbit stories" you may well ask me what I mean by that. Here you are puzzled both about the meaning of the phrase "chocolate rabbit stories," for as with "the pine cone weeps" or "the rock cogitates" it is a deviant collection of words of indeterminate meanings, and about the point or purpose of making such a remark. After all, the point of making such an utterance may not be evident. Suppose I had said it to a stupid and pompous writer blown up with a false sense of his own importance. I could explain my meaning by saying that I was obliquely giving him to understand that his stories, like chocolate rabbits, were all out of the same mold: change the names and setting and you have the same old thing all over again. And the point of my utterance would also become evidence, i.e., to deflate the pompous windbag. The phrase "chocolate rabbit stories" has no fixed use in human discourse, but language is sufficiently elastic for me to be able to give it a use without generating any linguistic or conceptual shock. To explain my meaning I must make clear the use I am giving it and make evident why I choose to use such an odd phrase.

"What is the meaning of Life?" is in some very significant respects like this last question though it is of course also very different. It is different in being non-deviant and in being a profoundly important question in the way the other question clearly is not. But note the likeness. In the first place when we or other people ask this question we are often not at all sure what we are asking. In this practical context we may in a way even be puzzled about the word "life," though, as I have said, the question does not primarily function as a request for the explanation of the use of a word. There is a sense in which life does and there is a sense in which life does not begin and end in mystery. And when we ask about life here we are not asking Schrodinger's question or J. B. S. Haldane's. We are not in search of some property or set of properties that is common to and distinctive of all those things we call "living things." We are typically concerned with something very different and much vaguer. We are asking: "Is life just one damn thing after another until finally one day we die and start to rot? Or can I sum it up and find or at least give it some point after all? Or is this just a silly illusion born of fear and trembling?"

These are desperately vague, amorphous questions, but—as Wisdom would surely and rightly say—not meaningless for all that. And for some of us, and perhaps for all of us, *sometimes*, they are haunting, edging questions, questions we agonize over, then evade, then again try to come to grips with.

First, I want to say that, like "What is the meaning of calling them chocolate rabbit stories?", "What is the meaning of Life?" does *not* have a clear use; but that it does not have a clear use does not, I repeat, entail or in any way establish that it does not have a use or even that it does not have a supremely important use.[3] Secondly, "What is the meaning of life?" most typically—though not always—functions as a request for the goals *worth* seeking in life though sometimes it may serve to ask if there are *any* goals worth seeking in life.[4] We are asking what (if anything) is the point to our lives? What (if anything) could give our lives purpose or point? In anguish we struggle to find the purpose, point or rationale of our grubby lives. But if this is the nature of the question, what would an answer look like? For this to be a fruitful question, all of us must ask ourselves individually: what would we take as an answer? When we ask this we are apt to come up with a blank; and if we are readers of philosophical literature we may remember that, along with others, a philosopher as persuasive and influential as A. J. Ayer has said that all such questions are unanswerable. But if they are really unanswerable—or so it would seem—then they are hardly genuine questions.

I will concede that *in a sense* such questions are unanswerable, but in a much more important sense they *are* answerable. We can be intelligent about and reason about such questions. Any analysis which does not bring this out and elucidate it is confused and inadequate. In destroying pontifical pseudo-answers the baby has frequently gone down with the bath. In showing what kind of answers could not be answers to this question, the temptation is to stress that there are no answers at all and that indeed no answers are needed. I want to try to show why this is wrong and what an answer would look like.

II

How then is it possible for our life to have a meaning or a purpose? For a while, oddly enough, Ayer in his "The Claims of Philosophy" is a perfectly sound guide.[5] We do know what it is for a man to have a purpose. "It is a matter," Ayer remarks, "of his intending, on the basis of a given situation, to bring about some further situation which for some reason or other he conceives to be desirable."

But, Ayer asks, how is it possible for life *in general* to have a meaning or a purpose?

Well, there is one very simple answer. Life in general has a purpose if all living beings are tending toward a certain specifiable end. To understand the meaning of life or the purpose of existence it is only necessary to discover this end.

As Ayer makes perfectly clear, there are overwhelming difficulties with such an answer. In the first place there is no good reason to believe living beings are tending toward some specifiable end. But even if it were true that they are all tending toward this end such a discovery would not at all answer the question "What is the meaning or purpose of life?" This is so because when we human beings ask this exceedingly vague question we are not just asking for *an explanation* of the facts of existence; we are asking for a *justification* of these facts. In asking this question we are seeking a way of life, trying as suffering, perplexed, and searching creatures to find what the existentialists like to call an "authentic existence." And as Ayer goes on to explain,

> a theory which informs them merely that the course of events is so arranged as to lead inevitably to a certain end does nothing to meet their need. For the end in question will not be one that they themselves have chosen. As far as they are concerned it will be entirely arbitrary; and it will be a no less arbitrary fact that their existence is such as necessarily to lead to its fulfillment. In short, from the point of view of justifying one's existence, there is no essential difference between a teleological explanation of events and a mechanical explanation. In either case, it is a matter of brute fact that events succeed one another in the ways they do and are explicable in the ways they are.

In the last analysis, an attempt to answer a question of why events are as they are must always resolve itself into saying only *how* they are. Every explanation of why people do such and such and why the world is so and so finally depends on a very general description. And even if it is the case, as Charles Taylor powerfully argues, that teleological explanations of human behavior are irreducible, Ayer's point here is not all weakened, for in explaining, teleologically or otherwise, we are still showing how things are; we are not justifying anything.[6]

When we ask: "What is the meaning of life?" we want an answer that is more than *just* an explanation or description of *how* people behave or *how* events are arranged or *how* the world is constituted. We are asking for a *justification* for our existence. We are asking for a justification for why life is as it is, and not even the most complete explanation and/or description of *how* things are ordered can answer this quite different question. The person who demands that some general description of man and his place in nature should entail a statement that man ought to live and die in a certain way is asking for something that can no more be the case than it can be the case that ice can gossip. To ask about the meaning of our lives involves asking how we should live, or whether any decision to live in one way is more *worthy* of acceptance than any other. Both of these questions are clearly questions of value; yet no statement of *fact* about how we in fact do live can by itself be sufficient to answer such questions. No statement of what ought to be the case can be deduced from a statement of what is the case. If we are demanding such an answer, then Ayer is perfectly right in claiming the question is unanswerable.

Let me illustrate. Suppose, perhaps as a result of some personal crisis, I want to take stock of myself. As Kierkegaard would say, I want to appropriate, take to heart, the knowledge I have or can get about myself and my condition in order to arrive at some decision as to what sort of life would be most meaningful for me, would be the sort of life I would truly want to live if I could act rationally and were fully apprised of my true condition. I might say to myself, though certainly not to others, unless I was a bit of an exhibitionist, "Look Nielsen, you're a little bit on the vain side and you're arrogant to boot. And why do you gossip so and spend so much of your time reading science fiction? And why do you always say what you expect other people want you to say? You don't approve of that in others, do you? And why don't you listen more? And weren't you too quick with Jones and too indulgent with Smith?" In such a context I would put these questions and a host of questions like them to myself. And I might come up with some general explanations, good or bad, like "I act this way because I have some fairly pervasive insecurities." And to my further question, "Well, why do you have these insecurities?" I might dig up something out of my past such as "My parents died when I was two and I never had any real home." To explain why this made me insecure I might finally evoke a whole psychological theory and eventually perhaps even a biological and physiological theory, and these explanations about the nature of the human animal would themselves finally rest, in part at least, on various descriptions of how man does behave. In addition, I might, if I could afford it and were sufficiently bedevilled by these questions, find my way to a psychiatrist's couch and there, after the transference had taken place, I would eventually get more quite personalized explanations of my behavior and attitudes. But none of these things, in themselves, could tell me the meaning of life or even the meaning of my life, though they indeed might help me in this search. I might discover that I was insecure because I could never get over the wound of the loss of my father. I might discover that unconsciously I blamed myself. As a child I wished him dead and then he died so somehow I did it, really. And I would, of course, discover how unreasonable this is. I would come to understand that people generally react this way in those situations. In Tolstoy's phrase, we are all part of the "same old river." And, after rehearsing it, turning it over, taking it to heart, I might well gain control over it and eventually gain control over some of my insecurities. I could see and even live through again what *caused* me to be vain, arrogant and lazy. But suppose, that even after all these discoveries I really didn't want to change. After stocktaking, I found that I was willing to settle for the *status quo.* Now I gratefully acknowledge that this is very unlikely, but here we are concerned with the *logical* possibilities. "Yes, there are other ways of doing things," I say to myself, "but after all is said and done I have lived this way a long time and I would rather go on this way than change. This sort of life, is after all, the most meaningful one. This is how I really want to act and this is how I, and others like me, ought to act." What possible facts could anyone appeal to which would prove, in the sense of logically entail, that I was wrong and that the purpose of life or the meaning of life was very different than I thought it was? It is Ayer's contention, and I think he is right, that there are none.

"But you have left out God," someone might say. "You have neglected the possibility that there is a God and that God made man to His image and likeness and that God has a plan for man. Even Sartre, Heidegger and Camus agree that to ask 'What is the Meaning of Life?' or 'What is the purpose of human existence?' is, in effect, to raise the question of God. If there is a God your conclusion would not follow, and, as Father Copleston has said, if there is *no* God human existence can have no end or purpose other than that given by man himself."[7]

I would want to say, that the whole question of God or no God, Jesus or no Jesus, is entirely beside the point. Even if there were a God human existence can, in the relevant sense of "end," "purpose" or "meaning," have no other end, purpose or meaning than what we as human beings give it by our own deliberate choices and decisions.

Let us see how this is so. Let us suppose that everything happens as it does because God intends that it should. Let us even assume, as we in reality cannot, that we can know the purpose or intentions of God. Now, as Ayer points out, either God's "purpose is sovereign or it is not. If it is sovereign, that is, if everything that happens is necessarily in accordance with it, then it is true also of our behavior. Consequently, there is no point in our deciding to conform to it, for the simple reason that we cannot do otherwise." No matter what, we do God's purpose. There is no sense in saying it is *our* purpose, that it is something we have made our own by our own deliberate choice. I have not *discovered* a meaning for my life and other people have not *discovered* a meaning for their lives. If it were possible for us *not* to fulfill it, the purpose would not be God's *sovereign* purpose and if it is His sovereign purpose, it cannot, in the requisite sense, be *our* purpose, for it will not be something of which it would make sense to say that we chose it. It is just something that necessarily happens to us because of God's intentions. If we are compelled to do it, it is not *our* purpose. It is only our purpose if we want to do it and if we could have done otherwise.

On the other hand, if God's purpose is not sovereign and we are not inexorably compelled to do what God wills, we have no reason to conform to God's purpose unless we independently judge it to be *good* or by our own independent decision make it our purpose. We cannot derive the statement "x is good" from "that Being whom people call 'God' says 'x is good'" or from "that Being whom people call 'God' wills x" unless we *independently* judge that whatever this Being *says* is good *is good* or whatever that Being wills *ought* to be done. Again, as Ayer remarks, this "means that the significance of our behavior depends finally upon our own judgments of value; and the concurrence of a diety then becomes superfluous."[8]

The basic difficulty, as Ayer makes clear, is that in trying to answer the questions as we have above, we have really misunderstood the question. "What-is-the-meaning-of-that?" and "What-is-the-purpose-of-that?" questions can be very different. We have already noted some of the differences among "What-is-the-meaning-of-that?" questions, and we have seen that "What is the meaning of Life?" in many contexts at least can well be treated as a "What-is-the-purpose-of-that?" question. But "What is the purpose of life?" is only very superficially like "What is the purpose of a blotter?" "What is the purpose of brain surgery?" or "What is the purpose of the liver?" The first is a question about a human artifact and in terms of certain assumed ends we can say quite explicitly, independently of whether or not we want blotters, what the purpose of blotters is. Similarly brain surgery is a well-known human activity and has a well-known rationale. Even if we are Christian Scientists and disapprove of surgery altogether, we can understand and agree on what the purpose of brain surgery is, just as we all can say Fearless Fosdick is a good safecracker, even though we disapprove of safecrackers. And again, in terms of the total functioning of the human animal we can say what livers are for, even though the liver is not an artifact like a blotter. If there is a God and God made man, we *might* say the question "What is the purpose of human life?" is very like "What is the purpose of umbrellas?" The human animal then becomes a Divine artifact. But, even if all this were so, we would not—as we have already seen—have an answer to the *justificatory* question we started with when we asked, "What is the meaning of life?" If we knew God's purpose for man, we would know what man was made for. But we would not have an answer to our question about the meaning of life, for we would not know if there was purpose *in* our lives or if we could find a point in acting one way rather than another. We would only know that there was something—which may or may not be of value—that we were constructed, "cut out," to be.

Similarly, if an Aristotelian philosophy is correct, "What is the purpose of life?" would become very like "What is the purpose of the liver?" But here again a discovery of what end man is as a matter of fact tending toward would not answer the perplexity we started from, that is to say, it would not answer the question, "What is the meaning of life, how should men live and die?" We would only learn that "What is the purpose of life?" could admit of two very different uses. As far as I can see, there are no good reasons to believe either that there is a God or that the human animal has been ordered for some general end: but even if this were so it would not give us an answer to the question: "What is the meaning of life?"

This is so because the question has been radically misconstrued. When we ask: "What is the meaning of life?" or "What is the purpose of human existence?" we are normally asking, as I have already said, questions of the following types: "What should we seek?" "What ends—if any—are worthy of attainment?" Questions of this sort require a very different answer than any answer to: "What is the meaning of 'obscurantism'?" "What is the purpose of the ink-blotter?" and "What is the purpose of the liver?" Ayer is right when he says: "what is required by those who seek to know the purpose of their existence is not a factual description of the way that people actually do conduct themselves, but rather a decision as to how they *should* conduct themselves." Again he is correct in remarking: "There is—a sense in which it can be said that life does have a meaning. It has for each of us whatever meaning we severally *choose* to give it. The purpose of a man's existence is constituted by the ends to which he, consciously or unconsciously, devotes himself."

Ayer links this with another crucial logical point, a point which the existentialists have dramatized as some kind of worrisome "moral discovery." Ayer points out that "in the last resort . . . each individual has the responsibility of making the choice of how he ought to live and die" and that it is logically impossible that someone else, in some authoritative position, can make that choice for him. If someone gives me moral advice in the nature of the case I must decide whether or not to follow his advice, so again the choice is finally my own. This is true because moral questions are primarily questions about what to do. In asking how I ought to live, I am trying to make up my mind how to act. And to say I deliberately acted in a certain way implies that I decided to do it. There is no avoiding personal choice in considering such questions.

But Ayer, still writing in the tradition of logical empiricism, often writes as if it followed from the truth of what we have said so far, that there could be no reasoning about "How ought man to live?" or "What is the meaning of life?" Thus Ayer says at one point in "The Claims of Philosophy": "He [the moral agent] cannot prove his judgments of value are correct, for the simple reason that no judgment of value is capable of proof." He goes on to argue that people have no way of demonstrating that one judgment of value is superior to another. A decision between people in moral disagreement is a "subject for persuasion and finally a matter of individual choice."

As we have just seen there is a sound point to Ayer's stress on choice vis-a-vis morality, but taken as a whole his remarks are at best misleading. There is reasoning about moral questions and there are arguments and proofs in morality. There are principles in accordance with which we appraise our actions, and there are more general principles, like the principle of utility or the principles of distributive justice in accordance with which we test our lower-level moral rules. And there is a sense of "being reasonable" which, as Hume and Westermarck were well aware, has distinctive application to moral judgments. Thus, if I say, "I ought to be relieved of my duties, I'm just too ill to go on" I not only must believe I am in fact ill, I must also be prepared to say, of any of my colleagues or anyone else similarly placed, that in like circumstances they too ought to be relieved of their duties if they fall ill. There is a certain *generality* about moral discourse and a man is not reasoning morally or "being reasonable" if he will not allow those inferences. Similarly, if I say "I want x" or "I prefer x" I need not, though I may, be prepared to give reason why I want it or prefer it, but if I say "x is the right thing to do" or "x is good" or "I ought to do x" or "x is worthy of attainment," I must—perhaps with the exception of judgments of intrinsic goodness—be prepared to give *reasons* for saying "x is the right thing to do," "x is good," "I ought to do x" and the like. (Note, this remark has the status of what Wittgenstein would call a grammatical remark.)

It is indeed true in morals and in reasoning about human conduct generally that justification must come to an end; but this is also true in logic, science and in common sense empirical reasoning about matters of fact; but it is also true that the end point in reasoning over good and evil is different than in science and the like, for in reasoning about how to act, our judgment finally terminates in a choice—a decision of principle. And here is the truth in Ayer's remark that moral judgments are "*finally* a matter of individual choice." But, unless we are to mislead, we must put the emphasis on "finally," for a dispassioned, neutral analysis of the uses of the language of human conduct will show, as I have indicated, that there is reasoning, and in a relevant sense, "objective reasoning," about moral questions. It is not at all a matter of pure persuasion or goading someone into sharing your attitudes.

I cannot, of course, even begin to display the full range of the reasoning which has sought to establish this point. But I hope I have said enough to block the misleading implications of Ayer's otherwise very fine analysis. Early linguistic philosophy was primarily interested in (1) the descriptive and explanatory discourse of the sciences, and (2) in logico-mathematico discourse; the rest was rather carelessly labelled, "expressive or emotive discourse." But the thrust of the work of linguistic philosophers since the Second World War has corrected that mistaken emphasis, as recent analytical writing in ethics makes evident. Here I commend to you R. M. Hare's *The Language of Morals,* and his *Freedom and Reason,* Stephen Toulmin's *An Examination of the Place of Reason in Ethics,* Kurt Baier's *The Moral Point of View,* Marcus Singer's *Generalization in Ethics,* P. H. Nowell-Smith's *Ethics,* Bernard Mayo's *Ethics and the Moral Life,* or George von Wright's *The Varieties of Goodness.* They would also reinforce the point I tried briefly to make against Ayer, as would an examination of the essays of Philippa Foot or John Rawls.[9]

III

There are, however, other considerations that may be in our minds when we ask "What is the meaning of life?" or "Does life have a meaning?" In asking such questions, we may *not* be asking "What should we seek?" or "What goals are worth seeking really?" Instead we may be asking "Is *anything* worth seeking?" "Does it matter finally what we do?" Here, some may feel, we finally meet the real tormenting "riddle of human existence."

Such a question is not simply a moral question: it is a question concerning human conduct, a question about how to live one's life or about whether to continue to live one's life. Yet when we consider what an answer would look like here we draw a blank. If someone says "Is anything worthwhile?" we gape. We want to reply: "Why, sitting in the sunshine in the mornings, seeing the full moon rise, meeting a close friend one hasn't seen in a long time, sleeping comfortably after a tiring day, all these things and a million more are most assuredly worthwhile. Any life devoid of experiences of this sort would most certainly be impoverished."

Yet this reply is so obvious we feel that something different must be intended by the questioner. The questioner knows that we, and most probably he, ordinarily regard such things as worthwhile, but he is asking if these things or *anything* is worthwhile *really*? These things *seem* worthwhile but are they in reality? And here we indeed do not know what to say. If someone queries whether it is really worthwhile leaving New York and going to the beach in August we have some idea of what to say; there are some criteria which will enable us to make at least a controversial answer to this question. But when it is asked, in a philosophical manner, *if anything, ever* is really worthwhile, it is not clear that we have a genuine question before us. The question borrows its form from more garden-variety questions but when we ask it in this general way do we actually know what we mean? If someone draws a line on the blackboard, a question over the line's straightness can arise only if some criterion for a line's being straight is accepted. Similarly only if some criterion of worthiness is accepted can we intelligibly ask if a specific thing or anything is worthy of attainment.

But if a sensitive and reflective person asks, "Is anything worthwhile, really?" could he not be asking this because, (1) he has a certain vision of human excellence, and (2) his austere criteria for what is worthwhile have developed in terms of that vision? Armed with such criteria, he might find nothing that man can in fact attain under his present and foreseeable circumstances *worthy* of attainment. Considerations of this sort seem to be the sort of considerations that led Tolstoy and Schopenhauer to come to such pessimistic views about life. Such a person would be one of those few people, who as one of Hesse's characters remarks, "demand the utmost of life and yet cannot come to terms with its stupidity and crudeness." In terms of his ideal of human excellence nothing is worthy of attainment.

To this, it is natural to respond, "If this is our major problem about the meaning of life, then this is indeed no intellectual or philosophical riddle about human destiny. We need not like Steppenwolf return to our lodging lonely and disconsolate because life's 'glassy essence' remains forever hidden, for we can well envisage, in making such a judgment, what would be worthwhile. We can say what a meaningful life would look like even though we can't attain it. If such is the question, there is no 'riddle of human existence,' though there is a pathos to human life and there is the social-political pattern problem of how to bring the requisite human order into existence. Yet only if we have a conception of what human life should be can we feel such pathos."

If it is said in response to this that what would really be worthwhile could not possibly be attained, an absurdity has been uttered. To say something is worthy of attainment implies that, everything else being equal, it ought to be attained. But to say that something ought to be attained implies that it *can* be attained. Thus we *cannot* intelligibly say that something is worthy of attainment but that it cannot possibly be attained. So in asking "Is anything worthy of attainment?" we must acknowledge that there are evaluative criteria operative which guarantee that what is sincerely said to be worthy of attainment is at least in principle attainable. And as we have seen in speaking of morality, "x is worthy of attainment" does not mean "x is preferred," though again, in asserting that something is worthy of attainment, or worth-while, we imply that we would choose it, everything else being equal, in pref-erence to something else. But we cannot intelligibly speak of a choice if there is no possibility of doing one thing rather than another.

Life is often hard and, practically speaking, the ideals we set our hearts on, those to which we most deeply commit ourselves, may in actual fact be impossible to achieve. A sensitive person may have an ideal of conduct, an ideal of life, that he assents to without reservation. But the facts of human liv-ing being what they are, he knows full well that this ideal cannot be realized. His ideals are intelligible enough, logically their achievement is quite possi-ble, but as a matter of *brute fact* his ideals are beyond his attainment. If this is so, is it worthwhile for him and others like him to go on living or to strive for anything at all? Can life, under such circumstances, be anything more than an ugly habit? For such a man, "What is the meaning of life?" has the force of "What *point* can a life such as mine have under these circumstances?" And in asking whether such a life has a point he is asking the very question we put above, viz. can life be worth living under such conditions.

Again such a question is perfectly intelligible and is in no way unan-swerable any more than any other question about how to act, though here too we must realize that the facts of human living *cannot* be sufficient for a man simply to read off an answer without it in any way affecting his life. Here, too, *any* answer will require a decision or some kind of effective involvement on the part of the person involved. A philosopher can be of help here in showing what kind of answers we cannot give, but it is far less obvious that he can provide us with a set of principles that together with empirical facts about his condition and prospects, will enable the perplexed man to know what he ought to do. The philosopher or any thoughtful person who sees just what is involved in the question can give some helpful advice. Still the person involved must work out an answer in anguish and soreness of heart.

However, I should remind him that no matter how bad his own life was, there would always remain something he could do to help alleviate the sum total of human suffering. This certainly has value and if he so oriented his life, he could not say that his life was without point. I would also argue that in nor-mal circumstances he could not be sure that his ideals of life would perma-nently be frustrated, and if he held ideals that would be badly frustrated under almost any circumstances, I would get him to look again at his ideals. Could such ideals really be adequate? Surely man's reach must exceed his grasp, but how far should we go? Should not any ideal worth its salt come into some closer involvement with the realities of human living? And if one deliberately and with self-understanding plays the role of a Don Quixote can one justifi-ably complain that one's ideals are not realized? Finally, it does not seem to me reasonable to expect that *all* circumstances can have sufficient meaning to make them worthwhile. Under certain circumstances life is not worth living. As a philosopher, I would point out this possibility and block those philo-sophical-religious claims that would try to show that this could not possibly be.

Many men who feel the barbs of constant frustration, come to feel that their ideals have turned out to be impossible, and ask in anguish—as a consequence—"Does life really have any meaning?" To a man in such anguish I would say all I have said above and much more, though I am painfully aware that such an approach may seem cold and unfeeling. I know that these matters deeply affect us; indeed they can even come to obsess us, and when we are so involved it is hard to be patient with talk about what can and cannot be said. But we need to understand these matters as well; and, after all, what more can be done along this line than to make quite plain what is involved in his question and try to exhibit a range of rational attitudes that could be taken toward it, perhaps stressing the point that though Dr. Rieux lost his wife and his best friend, his life, as he fought the plague, was certainly not without point either for him or for others. But I would also try to make clear that finally an answer to such a question must involve a decision or the having or adopting of a certain attitude on the part of the person involved. This certainly should be stressed and it should be stressed that the question "Is such a life meaningful?" is a sensible question, which admits of a non-obscurantist, non-metaphysical treatment.

IV

There are many choices we must make in our lives and some choices are more worthwhile than others, though the criteria for what is worthwhile are in large measure at least context-dependent. "It's worthwhile going to Leningrad to see the Hermitage" is perfectly intelligible to someone who knows and cares about art. Whether such a trip to Leningrad is worthwhile for such people can be determined by these people by a visit to the Museum. "It's worthwhile fishing the upper Mainistee" is in exactly the same category, though the criteria for worthwhileness are not the same. Such statements are most assuredly perfectly intelligible; and no adequate grounds have been given to give us reason to think that we should philosophically tinker with the ordinary criteria of "good art museum" or "good trout fishing." And why should we deny that these and other things are really worthwhile? To say "Nothing is worthwhile since all pales and worse still, all is vain because man must die" is to mistakenly assume that because an eternity of even the best trout fishing would be not just a bore but a real chore, that trout fishing is therefore not worthwhile. Death and the fact (if it is a fact) that there is nothing new under the sun need not make all vanity. That something must come to an end can make it all the more precious: to know that love is an old tale does not take the bloom from your beloved's cheek.

Yet some crave a more general answer to "Is anything worthwhile?" This some would say, is what they are after when they ask about the meaning of life.

As I indicated, the criteria for what is worthwhile are surely in large measure context-dependent, but let us see what more we can say about this need for a more general answer.

In asking "Why is anything worthwhile?" if the "why" is a request for *causes*, a more general answer can be given. The answer is that people have preferences, enjoy, admire and approve of certain things and they can and sometimes do reflect. Because of this they find some things worthwhile. This, of course, is not what "being worthwhile" *means*, but if people did not have these capacities they would not find anything worthwhile. But *reasons* why certain things are worthwhile are dependent on the thing in question.

If people find x worthwhile they generally prefer x, approve of x, enjoy x, or admire x on reflection. If people did not prefer, approve of, enjoy or admire things then nothing would be found to be worthwhile. If they did not have these feelings the notion of "being worthwhile" would have no role to play in human life; but it does have a role to play and, as in morality, justification of what is worthwhile must finally come to an end with the reflective choices we make.

Moral principles, indeed, have a special onerousness about them. If something is a moral obligation, it is something we ought to do through and through. It for most people at least and from a moral point of view for everyone overrides (but does not exhaust) all non-moral considerations about what is worthwhile. If we are moral agents and we are faced with the necessity of choosing either A or B, where A, though very worthwhile, is a non-moral end and where B is a moral one, we must choose B. The force of the "must" here is logical. From a moral point of view there is no alternative but to choose B. Yet we do not escape the necessity of decision for we still must *agree* to *adopt* a moral point of view, to *try* to act as moral agents. Here, too, we must finally make a decision of principle.[10] There are good Hobbesian reasons for adopting the moral point of view but if one finally would really prefer "a state of nature" in which all were turned against all, rather than a life in which there was a freedom from this and at least a minimum of cooperation between human beings, then these reasons for adopting the moral point of view would not be compelling to such a person. There is, in the last analysis, no escape from making a choice.

In asking "What is the meaning of Life?" we have seen how this question is in reality a question concerning human conduct. It asks either "What should we seek?" or "What ends (if any) are really worthwhile?" I have tried to show in what general ways such questions are answerable. We can give reasons for our moral judgments and moral principles and the whole activity of morality can be seen to have a point, but not all questions concerning what is worthwhile are moral questions. Where moral questions do not enter we must make a decision about what, on reflection, we are going to seek. We must ascertain what—all things considered—really answers to our interests or, where there is no question of anything answering to our interests or failing to answer to our interests, we should decide what on reflection we prefer. What do we really want, wish to approve of, or admire? To ask "Is anything worthwhile?" involves our asking "Is there nothing that we, on reflection, upon knowledge of ourselves and others, want, approve of, or admire?" When we say "So-and-so is worthwhile" we are making a normative judgment that cannot be derived from determining what we desire, admire or approve of. That is to say, these statements do not entail statements to the effect that so and so is worthwhile. But in determining what is worthwhile this is finally all we have to go on. In saying something is worthwhile, we (1) *express* our preference, admiration or approval; (2) in some sense imply that we are prepared to defend our choice with *reasons;* and (3) in effect, indicate our belief that others like us in the relevant respects and similarly placed, will find it worthwhile too. And the answer to our question is that, of course, there are things we humans desire, prefer, approve of, or admire. This being so, our question is not unanswerable. Again we need not fly to a metaphysical enchanter.

As I said, "Is anything really worthwhile, really worth seeking?" makes us gape. And "atomistic analyses," like the one I have just given, often leave us with a vague but persistent feeling of dissatisfaction, even when we cannot clearly articulate the grounds of our dissatisfaction. "The real question," we want to say, "has slipped away from us amidst the host of distinctions and analogies. We've not touched the deep heart of the matter at all."

Surely, I have not exhausted the question for, literally speaking, it is not one question but a cluster of loosely related questions all concerning "the human condition"—how man is to act and how he is to live his life even in the face of the bitterest trials and disappointments. Questions here are diverse, and a philosopher, or anyone else, becomes merely pretentious and silly when he tries to come up with some formula that will solve, resolve or dissolve the perplexities of human living. But I have indicated in skeletal fashion how we can approach general questions about "What (if anything) is worth seeking?" And I have tried to show how such questions are neither meaningless nor questions calling for esoteric answers.

V

We are not out of the woods yet. Suppose someone were to say: "Okay, you've convinced me. Some things are worthwhile and there is a more or less distinct mode of reasoning called moral reasoning and there are canons of validity distinctive of this *sui generis* type reasoning. People do reason in the ways that you have described, but it still remains the case that here one's attitudes and final choices are relevant in a way that it isn't necessarily the case in science or an arguments over plain matters of fact. But when I ask: 'How ought men act?' 'What is the meaning of life?' and 'What is the meaning of *my* life?, how should I live and die?' I want an answer that is logically independent of any human choice or any pro-attitude toward any course of action or any state of affairs. Only if I can have that kind of warrant for my moral judgments and ways-of-life will I be satisfied."

If a man demands this and continues to demand this after dialectical examination we must finally leave him unsatisfied. As linguistic philosophers there is nothing further we can say to him. In dialectical examination we can again point out to him that he is asking for the logically impossible, but if he recognizes this and persists in asking for that which is impossible there are no further rational arguments that we can use to establish our point. But, prior to this last-ditch stand, there are still some things that we can say. We can, in detail and with care, point out to him, describe fully for him, the rationale of the moral distinctions we do make and the functions of moral discourse. A full description here will usually break this kind of obsessive perplexity. Furthermore, we can make the move Stephen Toulmin makes in the last part of his *The Place of Reason in Ethics*. We can describe for him another use of "Why" that Toulmin has well described as a "limiting question."[11]

Let me briefly explain what this is and how it could be relevant. When we ask a "limiting question" we are not really asking a question at all. We are in a kind of "land of shadows" where there are no clear-cut uses of discourse. If we just look at their grammatical form, "limiting questions" do not appear to be extra-rational in form, but in their depth grammar—their actual function—they clearly are. "What holds the universe up?" looks very much like "What holds the Christmas tree up?" but the former, in common sense contexts at least, is a limiting question while the latter usually admits of a perfectly obvious answer. As Toulmin himself puts it, limiting questions are "questions expressed in a form borrowed from a familiar mode of reasoning, but not doing the job which they normally do within that mode of reasoning."[12] A direct answer to a limiting question never satisfies the questioners. Attempted "answers" only regenerate the question, though often a small change in the questions themselves or their context will make them straightforward questions. Furthermore, there is no standard interpretation for limiting questions sanctioned in our language. And limiting questions do not present us with any genuine alternatives from which to choose.

Now "limiting questions" get used in two main contexts. Sometimes, they merely express what Ryle, rather misleadingly, called a "category mistake." Thus someone who was learning English might ask: "How hot is blue?" or "Where is anywhere?" And, even a native speaker of English might ask as a *moral* agent, "Why ought I to do what is right?" We "answer" such questions by pointing out that blue cannot be hot, anywhere is not a particular place, and that if something is indeed right, this entails that it ought to be done. Our remarks here are grammatical remarks, though our speaking in the material mode may hide this. And if the questioner's "limiting question" merely signifies that a category mistake has been made, when this is pointed out to the questioner, there is an end to the matter. But more typically and more interestingly, limiting questions do not *just* or at all indicate category mistakes but express, as well or independently, a *personal predicament*. Limiting questions may express anxiety, fear, hysterical apprehensiveness about the future, hope, despair, and any number of attitudes. Toulmin beautifully illustrates from the writings of Dostoevsky an actual, on-the-spot use, of limiting questions:

> He was driving somewhere in the steppes. . . . Not far off was a village, he could see the black huts, and half the huts were burnt down, there were only the charred beams sticking out. As they drove in, there were peasant women drawn up along the road . . .
>
> "Why are they crying? Why are they crying?" Mitya [Dmitri] asked, as they dashed gaily by.
>
> "It's the babe," answered the driver, "the babe is weeping."
>
> And Mitya was struck by his saying, in his peasant way, "the babe," and he liked the peasant's calling it a "babe." There seemed more pity in it.
>
> "But why is it weeping?" Mitya persisted stupidly. "Why are its little arms bare? Why don't they wrap it up?"
>
> "The babe's cold, its little clothes are frozen and don't warm it."
>
> "But why is it? Why?" foolish Mitya still persisted.
>
> "Why, they're poor people, burnt out. They've no bread. They're begging because they've been burnt out."
>
> "No, no," Mitya, as it were still did not understand. "Tell me why it is those poor mothers stand there? Why are people poor? Why is the babe poor? Why is the steppe barren? Why don't they hug each other and kiss? Why don't they sing songs of joy? Why are they so dark from black misery? Why don't they feed the babe?"
>
> And he felt that, though his questions were unreasonable, and senseless, yet he wanted to ask just that, and he had to ask it just in that way. And he felt that a passion of pity, such as he had never known before, was rising in his heart, that he wanted to cry, that he wanted to do something for them all, so that the babe should weep no more, so that the dark-faced, dried-up mother should not weep, that no one should shed tears again from that moment . . .
>
> "I've had a good dream, gentlemen," he said in a strange voice, with a new light, as of joy, in his face.[13]

It is clear that we need not, may not, from the point of view of analysis, condemn these uses of language as illicit. We can point out that it is a muddle to confuse such questions with literal questions, and that such questions have no fixed *literal* meaning, and that as a result there are and can be no fixed literal ways of answering them, but they are indeed, genuine uses of language, and not the harum-scarum dreams of undisciplined metaphysics. When existentialist philosophers and theologians state them as profound questions about an alleged ontological realm there is room for complaint, but as we see them operating in the passage I quoted from *The Brothers Karamazov,* they seem to be not only linguistically proper but also an extremely important form of discourse. It is a shame and a fraud when philosophers "sing songs" as a substitute for the hard work of philosophizing, but only a damn fool would exclude song-singing, literal or metaphorical, from the life of reason, or look down on it as a somehow inferior activity. Non-literal "answers" to these non-literal, figurative questions, when they actually express personal predicaments or indeed more general human predicaments may, in a motivational sense, *goad* people to do one thing or another that they *know* they ought to do or they may comfort them or give them hope in time of turmoil and anxiety. I am not saying this is their only use or that they have no other respectable rationale. I do not at all think that; but I am saying that here is a rationale that even the most hard nosed positivist should acknowledge.

The man who demands "a more objective answer" to his question, "How ought men to live?" or "What is the meaning of Life?" may not be just muddled. If he is *just* making a "category mistake" and this is pointed out to him, he will desist, but if he persists, his limiting question probably expresses some anxiety. In demanding an answer to an evaluative question that can be answered independently of any attitudes he might have or choices he might make, he may be unconsciously expressing his fear of making decisions, his insecurity and confusion about what he really wants, and his desperate desire to have a Father who would make all these decisions for him. And it is well in such a context to bring Weston LaBarre's astute psychological observation to mind. "Values," LaBarre said, "must from emotional necessity be viewed as absolute by those who use values as compulsive defenses against reality, rather than properly as tools for the exploration of reality."[14] This remark, coming from a Freudian anthropologist, has unfortunately a rather metaphysical ring, but it can be easily enough de-mythologized. The point is, that someone who persists in these questions, persists in a demand for a totally different and "deeper" justification or answer to the question "What is the meaning of Life?" than the answer that such a question admits of, may be just expressing his own insecurity. The heart of rationalism is often irrational. At such a point the only reasoning that will be effective with him, if indeed any reasoning will be effective with him, may be psychoanalytic reasoning. And by then, of course you have left the philosopher and indeed all questions of justification far behind. But again the philosopher can describe the kinds of questions we can ask and the point of these questions. Without advocating anything at all he can make clearer to us the structure of "the life of reason" and the goals we human beings do prize.

VI

There is another move that might be made in asking about this haunting question: "What is the meaning of Life?" Suppose someone were to say: "Yes I see about these 'limiting questions' and I see that moral reasoning and reasoning about human conduct generally are limited modes of reasoning with distinctive criteria of their own. If I am willing to be guided by reason and I can be reasonable there are some answers I can find to the question: 'What is the meaning of Life?' I'm aware that they are not cut and dried and that they are not simple and that they are not even by any means altogether the same for all men, but there are some reasonable answers and touchstones all the same. You and I are in perfect accord on that. But there is one thing I don't see at all, 'Why ought I to be guided by reason anyway?' and if you cannot answer this for me I don't see why I should think that your answer—or rather your schema for an answer—about the meaning of Life is, after all, really any good. It all depends on how you *feel*, finally. There are really no answers here."

But again we have a muddle; let me very briefly indicate why. If someone asks: "Why ought I to be guided by reason anyway?" or "Is it really good to be reasonable?" one is tempted to take such a question as a paradigm case of a "limiting question," and a very silly one at that. But as some people like to remind us—without any very clear sense of what they are reminding us of—reason has been challenged. It is something we should return to, be wary of, realize the limits of, or avoid, as the case may be. It will hardly do to take such a short way with the question and rack it up as a category mistake.

In some particular contexts, with some particular people, it is (to be paradoxical, for a moment) reasonable to question whether we ought to follow reason. Thus, if I am a stubborn, penny-pinching old compulsive and I finally take my wife to the "big-city" for a holiday, it might be well to say to me: "Go on, forget how much the damn tickets cost, buy them anyway. Go on, take a cab even if you can't afford it." But to give or heed such advice clearly is not, in any fundamental sense, to fly in the face of reason, for on a deeper level— the facts of human living being what they are—we are being guided by reason.

It also makes sense to ask, as people like D. H. Lawrence press us to ask, if it really pays to be reasonable. Is the reasonable, clear-thinking, clear-visioned, intellectual animal really the happiest, in the long run? And can his life be as rich, as intense, as creative as the life of Lawrence's sort of man? From Socrates to Freud it has been assumed, for the most part, that self-knowledge, knowledge of our world, and rationality will bring happiness, if anything will. But is this really so? The whole Socratic tradition may be wrong at this point. Nor is it obviously true that the reasonable man, the man who sees life clearly and without evasion, will be able to live the richest, the most intense or the most creative life. I hope these things are compatible but they may not be. A too clear understanding may dull emotional involvement. Clear-sightedness may work against the kind of creative intensity that we find in a Lawrence, a Wolfe or a Dylan Thomas.

But to ask such questions is not in a large sense to refuse to be guided by reason. Theoretically, further knowledge could give us at least some vague answers to such unsettling questions; and, depending on what we learned and what decisions we would be willing to make, we would then know what to do. But clearly, we are not yet flying in the face of reason, refusing to be guided by reason at all. We are still playing the game according to the ground rules of reason.

What is this question, "Why should I be guided by reason?" or "Why be reasonable?" if it isn't any of these questions we have just discussed? If we ask this question and take it in a very general way, the question is a limiting one and it does involve a category mistake. What could be *meant* by asking:

"Why ought we *ever* use reason at all?" That to ask this question is to commit a logical blunder, is well brought out by Paul Taylor when he says:

> ... it is a question which would never be asked by anyone who thought about what he was saying, since the question, to speak loosely, answers itself. It is admitted that no amount of arguing in the world can make a person who does not want to be reasonable want to be. For to argue would be to give reasons, and to give reasons already assumes that the person to whom you give them is *seeking* reasons. That is it assumes he is reasonable. A person who did not want to be reasonable in any sense would never ask the question, "Why be reasonable?" For in asking the question, Why? he is seeking reasons, that is, he is being reasonable in asking the question. The question calls for the use of reason to justify *any* use of reason, including the use of reason to answer the question.[15]

In other words, to ask the question, as well as answer it, commits one to the use of reason. To ask: "Why be guided by reason at all?" is to ask "Why be reasonable, ever?" As Taylor puts it, "The questioner is thus seeking good reasons for seeking good reasons," and this surely is an absurdity. Anything that would be a satisfactory answer would be a "tautology to the effect that it is reasonable to be reasonable. A negative answer to the question, Is it reasonable to be reasonable? would express a self-contradiction."

If all this is pointed out to someone and he still persists in asking the question in this logically senseless way there is nothing a philosopher *qua* philosopher can do for him, though a recognition of the use of limiting questions in discourse may make this behavior less surprising to the philosopher himself. He might give him all five volumes of *The Life of Reason* or *Vanity Fair* and say, "Here, read this, maybe you will come to see things differently." The philosopher himself might even sing a little song in praise of reason, but there would be nothing further that he could say to him, philosophically: but by now we have come a very long way.

VII

Ronald Hepburn is perceptive in speaking of the conceptual "darkness around the meaning-of-life questions."[16] We have already seen some of the reasons for this; most generally, we should remark here that people are not always asking the same question and are not always satisfied by answers of the same scope when they wrestle with meaning-of-life questions. And often, of course, the questioner has no tolerably clear idea of what he is trying to ask. He may have a strong gut reaction about the quality and character of his own life and the life around him without the understanding or ability to conceptualize why he feels the way he does. Faced with this situation, I have tried to chart some of the contexts in which "What is the meaning of Life?" is a coherent question and some of the contexts in which it is not. But there are some further contexts in which "meaning-of-life questions" get asked which I have not examined.

There are philosophers who will agree with me that in a world of people with needs and wants already formed, it can be shown that life in a certain "subjective sense" has meaning, but they will retort that this is not really the central consideration. What is of crucial importance is whether we can show that the universe is better with human life than without it. If this cannot be established then we cannot have good reason to believe that life really has meaning, though in the subjective senses we have discussed, we can still continue to say it has meaning.[17]

If we try to answer this question, we are indeed brought up short, for we are utterly at a loss about what it would be like to ascertain whether it is better for the universe to have human life than no life at all. We may have certain attitudes here but no idea of what it would be like to know or have any reason at all to believe that "It is better that there is life" is either true or false or reasonably asserted or denied. It is quite unlike "It is better to be dead than to live with such a tumor." Concerning this last example, people may disagree about its correctness, but they have some idea of what considerations are relevant to settling the dispute. But with "It is better that there be life" we are at a loss.

We will naturally be led into believing that "What is the meaning of Life?" is an unanswerable question reflecting "the mystery of existence," if we believe that to answer that question satisfactorily we will have to be able to establish that it is better that there is life on earth than no life at all. What needs to be resisted is the very acceptance of that way of posing the problem. We do not need to establish that it is better that the universe contains human life than not in order to establish that there is a meaning to life. A life without purpose, a life devoid of satisfaction and an alienated life in which people are not being true to themselves is a meaningless life. The opposite sort of life is a meaningful or significant life. We have some idea of the conditions which must obtain for this to be so, i.e. for a man's life to have significance. We are not lost in an imponderable mystery here and we do not have to answer the question of whether it is better that there be human life at all to answer that question. Moreover, this standard non-metaphysical reading of "What is the meaning of Life?" is no less objective than the metaphysical reading we have been considering. There are no good grounds at all for claiming that this metaphysical "question" is the real and objective consideration in "What is the meaning of Life?" and that the more terrestrial interpretations I have been considering are more subjective. This transcendental metaphysical way of stating the problem utilizes unwittingly and without justification arbitrary *persuasive* definitions of "subjective" and "objective." And no other grounds have been given for *not* sticking with the terrestrial readings.

A deeper criticism of the account I have given of purpose and the meaning of life is given by Ronald Hepburn.[18] It is indeed true that life cannot be meaningful without being purposeful in the quite terrestrial sense I have set out, but, as Hepburn shows, it can be purposeful and still be meaningless.

> One may fill one's days with honest, useful and charitable deeds, not doubting them to be of value, but without feeling that these give one's life meaning or purpose. It may be profoundly boring. To seek meaning is not just a matter of seeking justification for one's policies, but of trying to discover how to organise one's vital resources and energies around these policies. To find meaning is not a matter of judging these to be worthy, but of seeing their pursuit as in some sense a fulfillment, as involving self-realisation as opposed to self-violation, and as no less opposed to the performance of a dreary task.[19]

A person's life can have significance even when he does not realize it and even when it is an almost intolerable drudge to him, though for human life generally to have significance this could not almost invariably be true for the human animal. But one's own life could not have significance *for oneself* if it were such a burden to one. To be meaningful to one, one's life must be purposive *and* it must be a life that the liver of that life finds satisfactory in the living of it. These conditions sometimes obtain and when it is also true that some reasonable measure of an individual's purposive activity adds to the enhancement of human life, we can say that his life is not only meaningful to him but meaningful *sans phrase*.[20]

This is still not the end of the matter in the struggle to gain a sense of the meaning of life, for, as Hepburn also points out, some will not be satisfied with a purely terrestrial and non-metaphysical account of the type I have given of "the meaning of Life."[21] They will claim "that life could be thought of as having meaning only so long as that meaning was believed to be a matter for discovery, not for creation and value-decision."[22] They will go on to claim that "to be meaningful, life would have to be *comprehensively* meaningful and its meaning invulnerable to assault. Worthwhile objectives must be ultimately realisable despite appearances."[23]

However, even if they are not satisfied with my more piecemeal and terrestrial facing of questions concerning the meaning of life, it does not follow that life can only have meaning if it has meaning in the more comprehensive and less contingent way they seek. It may be true that life will only have meaning *for them* if these conditions are met, but this does not establish that life will thus lack meaning unless these conditions are met. That is to say, it may be found significant by the vast majority of people, including most non-evasive and reflective people, when such conditions are met and it may be the case that everyone *should* find life meaningful under such conditions.

It is not the case that there is some general formula in virtue of which we can say what the meaning of life is, but it still remains true that men can through their purposive activity give their lives meaning and indeed find meaning in life in the living of it. The man with a metaphysical or theological craving will seek "higher standards" than the terrestrial standards I have utilized.

Is it rational to assent to that craving, to demand such "higher standards," if life is really to be meaningful? I want to say both "Yes" and "No."

On the one hand, the answer should be "No," if the claim remains that for life to be meaningful at all it must be comprehensively meaningful. Even without such a comprehensive conception of things there can be joy in life, morally, aesthetically and technically worthwhile activity and a sense of human purpose and community. This is sufficient to give meaning to life. And as Ayer perceptively argues and as I argued earlier in the essay, and as Hepburn argues himself, the man with a metaphysical craving of the transcendental sort will not be able to succeed in finding justification or rationale for claims concerning the significance of life that is any more *authoritative* and any more certain or invulnerable to assault than the non-metaphysical type rationale I have adumbrated. In actuality, as we have seen, such a comprehensive account, committed, as it must be, to problematic transcendental metaphysical and/or theological conceptions, is more vulnerable than my purely humanistic reading of this conception.

On the other hand, the answer should be "Yes" if the claim is reduced to one asserting that to try to articulate a comprehensive picture of human life is a desirable thing. However, it should be noted that this is quite a reduction in claim. In attempting to make such an articulation, the most crucial thing is not to wrestle with theological considerations about the contingency of the world or eternal life, but to articulate a comprehensive normative social and political philosophy in accordance with which we could set forth at least some of the conditions of a non-alienated life not simply for a privileged few but for mankind generally. We need to show in some general manner what such a life would look like and we need to attempt again, and with a reference to contemporary conditions, what Marx so profoundly attempted, namely, to set out the conditions that could transform our inegalitarian, unjust, vulgar and—as in countries such as South Africa and the United States—brutal capitalist societies into truly human societies.[24] Linguistic philosophers and bourgeois philosophers generally have been of little help here, though the clarity they have inculcated into philosophical work and into political and moral argument will be a vital tool in this crucial and yet to be done task.[25] When this task is done, if it is done, then we will have the appropriate comprehensive picture we need, and it is something to be done without any involvement with theology, speculative cosmology or transcendental metaphysics at all.[26]

NOTES

1. John Passmore remarks in his brief but thoroughly reliable and judicious *Philosophy in the Last Decade* (Sydney University Press: 1969) "Philosophy is once again cultivating areas it had declared wasteland, or had transferred without compunction to other owners," p. 5.

2. A. J. Ayer, "The Claims of Philosophy" in M. Natanson (ed.), *Philosophy of the Social Sciences* (Random House, 1963).

3. John Wisdom has driven home this point with force. In particular see his "The Modes of Thought and the Logic of 'God'" in his *Paradox and Discovery* (California, 1965).

4. Ronald Hepburn has correctly stressed that this for some people may not be what is uppermost in their minds when they ask that question. See Hepburn's essay in this

volume. See also Ilham Dilman's remarks about Hepburn's analysis in "Life and Meaning," *Philosophy*, 40 (October 1965).

5. See Ayer, *op cit*. The rest of the references to Ayer in the text are from this essay. His brief remarks in his "What I Believe" in *What I Believe* (London: 1966), pp. 15–16 and in his introduction to *The Humanist Outlook*, A. J. Ayer (ed.) (London: 1968), pp. 6–7 are also relevant as further brief statements of his central claims about the meaning of life.

6. Charles Taylor, *The Explanation of Behavior* (Routledge and Kegan Paul, 1964).

7. See his discussion of existentialism in his *Contemporary Philosophy*.

8. While I completely agree with the central thrust of Ayer's argument here, he has, I believe, overstated his case. Even if our behaviour finally depends on our own standards of value, it does not follow that the concurrence of the deity, if there is one, is superfluous, for we could still find crucial moral guidance from our grasp of something of God's wisdom.

9. I have discussed these issues in my "Problems of Ethics" and "History of Contemporary Ethics," both in Vol. 3 of *The Encyclopedia of Philosophy*, Paul Edwards, ed. (Macmillan, 1967).

10. I have discussed the central issues involved here at length in my "Why Should I Be Moral?" *Methods*, 15 (1963).

11. Stephen Toulmin, *An Examination of the Place of Reason in Ethics* (Cambridge University Press, 1950).

12. *Ibid.*, p. 205.

13. *Ibid.*, p. 210.

14. Weston LaBarre, *The Human Animal* (University of Chicago, 1954).

15. Paul Taylor, "Four Types of Relativism," *Philosophical Review* (1956).

16. Ronald W. Hepburn, "Questions about the Meaning of Life."

17. See in this context Hans Reiner, *Der Sinn unseres Daseins* (Tubingen; 1960). This view has been effectively criticized by Paul Edwards, "Meaning and Value of Life," *The Encyclopedia of Philosophy*, Paul Edwards, ed. (Macmillan, 1967), Vol. 4, pp. 474–476.

18. Hepburn's criticisms are directed toward an earlier version of this essay, "Linguistic Philosophy and 'The Meaning of Life'," *Cross-Currents*, 14 (Summer 1964).

19. *Ibid.*

20. *Ibid.*

21. "Questions about the Meaning of Life." For arguments of this type see F. C. Copleston, "Man and Metaphysics I," *The Heythrop Journal*, I, 2 (January 1960), p. 16. See in addition his continuation of this article in successive issues of *The Heythrop Review* and his *Positivism and Metaphysics* (Lisbon: 1965).

22. "Questions about the Meaning of Life."

23. *Ibid.*

24. For a contemporary Marxist account see Adam Schaff, *A Philosophy of Man* (London: 1963). But also note the criticism of Schaff's views by Christopher Hollis in "What is the Purpose of Life?" *The Listener*, 70 (1961), pp. 133–136.

25. The strength and limitations here of linguistic analysis as it has been practiced are well exhibited in Ayer's little essay "Philosophy and Politics."

26. If what I have argued above is so, many of the esoteric issues raised by Milton Munitz in his *The Mystery of Existence* and in his contribution to *Language, Belief, and Metaphysics*, Kiefer and Munitz, eds. (New York: 1970) can be bypassed.

CHAPTER 22   JOHN WISDOM

The Meanings of the Questions of Life

When one asks "What is the meaning of life?" one begins to wonder whether this large, hazy and bewildering question itself has any meaning. Some people indeed have said boldly that the question has no meaning. I believe this is a mistake. But it is a mistake which is not without excuse. And I hope that by examining the excuse we may begin to remedy the mistake, and so come to see that whether or not life has a meaning it is not senseless to enquire whether it has or not. First, then, what has led some people to think that the whole enquiry is senseless?

There is an old story which runs something like this: A child asked an old man "What holds up the world? What holds up all things?" The old man answered "A giant." The child asked "And what holds up the giant? You must tell me what holds up the giant." The old man answered "An elephant." The child said, "And what holds up the elephant?" The old man answered "A tortoise." The child said "You still have not told me what holds up all things. For what holds up the tortoise?" The old man answered "Run away and don't ask me so many questions."

From this story we can see how it may happen that a question which looks very like sensible meaningful questions may turn out to be a senseless, meaningless one. Again and again when we ask "What supports this?" it is possible to give a sensible answer. For instance what supports the top-most card in a house of cards? The cards beneath it which are in their turn supported by the cards beneath them. What supports all the cards? The table. What supports the table? The floor and the earth. But the question "What supports all things, absolutely all things?" is different. It is absurd, it is senseless, like the question "What is bigger than the largest thing in the world?" And it is easy to see why the question "What supports all things?" is absurd. Whenever we ask, "What supports thing A or these things A, B, C," then we can answer this question only by mentioning some thing other than the thing A or things A, B, C about which we asked "What supports it or them." We must if we are to answer the question mention something D other than those things which form the subject of our question, and we must say that this thing is what supports them. If we mean by the phrase "all things" absolutely all things which exist then obviously there is nothing outside that about which we are now asked "What supports all this?" Consequently any answer to the question will be self-contradictory just as any answer to the question "What is bigger than the biggest of all things" must be self-contradictory. Such questions are absurd, or, if you like, silly and senseless.

In a like way again and again when we ask "What is the meaning of this?" we answer in terms of something other than this. For instance imagine that there has been a quarrel in the street. One man is hitting another man on the jaw. A policeman hurries up. "Now then" he says, "what is the meaning of all this?" He wants to know what led up to the quarrel, what caused it. It is no good saying to the policeman "It's a quarrel." He knows there is a quarrel. What he wants to know is what went before the quarrel, what led up to it. To answer him we must mention something other than the quarrel itself. Again suppose a man is driving a motor car and sees in front of him a road sign, perhaps a red flag, perhaps a skull and cross bones. "What does this mean?" he asks and when he asks this he wants to know what the sign points to. To answer we must mention something other than the sign itself, such as a dangerous corner in the road. Imagine a doctor sees an extraordinary rash on the face of his patient. He is astonished and murmurs to himself "What is the meaning of this?" He wants to know what caused the strange symptoms, or what they will lead to, or both. In any case in order to answer his question he must find something which went before or comes after and lies outside that about which he asks "What does this mean?" This need to look before or after in order to answer a question of the sort "What is the meaning of this?" is so common, so characteristic, a feature of such questions that it is natural to think that when it is impossible to answer such a question in this way then the question has no sense. Now what happens when we ask "What is the meaning of life?"

Perhaps someone here replies, the meaning, the significance of this present life, this life on earth, lies in a life hereafter, a life in heaven. All right. But imagine that some persistent enquirer asks, "But what I am asking is what is the meaning of all life, life here and life beyond, life now and life hereafter? What is the meaning of all things in earth and heaven?" Are we to say that this question is absurd because there cannot be anything beyond all things while at the same time any answer to "What is the meaning of all things?" must point to some thing beyond all things?

Imagine that we come into a theatre after a play has started and are obliged to leave before it ends. We may then be puzzled by the part of the play that we are able to see. We may ask "What does it mean?" In this case we want to know what went before and what came after in order to understand the part we saw. But sometimes even when we have seen and heard a play from the beginning to the end we are still puzzled and still ask what does the whole thing mean. In this case we are not asking what came before or what came after, we are not asking about anything outside the play itself. We are, if you like, asking a very different sort of question from that we usually put with the words "What does this mean?" But we are still asking a real question, we are still asking a question which has sense and is not absurd. For our words express a wish to grasp the character, the significance of the whole play. They are a confession that we have not yet done this and they are a request for help in doing it. Is the play a tragedy, a comedy or a tale told by an idiot? The pattern of it is so complex, so bewildering, our grasp of it still so inadequate, that we don't know what to say, still less whether to call it good or bad. But this question is not senseless.

In the same way when we ask "What is the meaning of all things?" we are not asking a senseless question. In this case, of course, we have not witnessed the whole play, we have only an idea in outline of what went before and what will come after that small part of history which we witness. But with the words "What is the meaning of it all?" we are trying to find the order in the drama of Time. The question may be beyond us. A child may be able to understand, to grasp a simple play and be unable to understand and grasp a play more complex and more subtle. We do not say on this account that when he asks of the larger more complex play "What does it mean?" then his question is senseless, nor even that it is senseless for him. He has asked and even answered such a question in simpler cases, he knows the sort of effort, the sort of movement of the mind which such a question calls for, and we do not say that a question is meaningless to him merely because he is not yet able to carry out quite successfully the movement of that sort which is needed in order to answer a complex question of that sort. We do not say that a question in mathematics which is at present rather beyond us is meaningless to us. We know the type of procedure it calls for and may make efforts which bring us nearer and nearer to an answer. We are able to find the meaning which lies not outside but within very complex but still limited wholes whether these are dramas of art or of real life. When we ask "What is the meaning of all things?" we are bewildered and have not that grasp of the order of things the desire for which we express when we ask that question. But this does not render the question senseless nor make it impossible for us to move towards an answer.

We must however remember that what one calls answering such a question is not giving an answer. I mean we cannot answer such a question in the form: "The meaning is this."

Such an idea about what form answering a question must take may lead to a new despair in which we feel we cannot do anything in the way of answering such a question as "What is the meaning in it all?" merely because we are not able to sum up our results in a phrase or formula.

When we ask what is the meaning of this play or this picture we cannot express the understanding which this question may lead to in the form of a list of just those things in the play or the picture which give it its meaning. No.

The meaning eludes such a list. This does not mean that words quite fail us. They may yet help us provided that we do not expect of them more than they can do.

A person who is asked what he finds so hateful or so lovable in another may with words help himself and us in grasping what it is that so moves him. But he will only mislead us and himself if he pretends that his words are a complete account of all that there is in the matter.

It is the same when we ask what is it in all things that makes it all so good, so bad, so grand, so contemptible. We must not anticipate that the answer can be given in a word or in a neat list. But this does not mean that we can do nothing towards answering these questions nor even that words will not help us. Indeed surely the historians, the scientists, the prophets, the dramatists and the poets have said much which will help any man who asks himself: Is the drama of time meaningless as a tale told by an idiot? Or is it not meaningless? And if it is not meaningless is it a comedy or a tragedy, a triumph or a disaster, or is it a mixture in which sweet and bitter are for ever mixed?

CHAPTER 23

R . W . H E P B U R N

Questions about the Meaning of Life

Claims about "the meaning of life" have tended to be made and discussed in conjunction with bold metaphysical and theological affirmations. For life to have meaning, there must (it is assumed) be a comprehensive divine plan to give it meaning, or there must be an intelligible cosmic process with a "telos" that a man needs to know if his life is to be meaningfully orientated. Or, it is thought to be a condition of the meaningfulness of life, that values should be ultimately "conserved" in some way, that no evil should be unredeemable and irrational. And it may be claimed that if death were to end our experience, meaninglessness would triumph.

Because of this rich metaphysical background, the agnostic or naturalist faces a problem when he asks himself, "Does life have meaning, for me?": or more formally, "Can the vocabulary of life as 'meaningful' or 'meaningless' still play a role in my naturalistic interpretation of things?" The answer is not simple; for the informal logic of the vocabulary itself is not simple. This is a situation in which the naturalistic philosopher is tempted in one of two directions: either to renounce the vocabulary—as too deeply entangled with unacceptable beliefs, or to radically redefine the terms "meaning," "meaningful" and their cognates, thereby giving them work to do, but misleadingly different from their traditional work. The task for such a philosopher may be to mediate delicately between these poles, and in the course of trying to do that a good many complexities in the language of "meaning" may come to light—complexities of interest perhaps not only to the naturalistic philosopher himself.

In the last few years some analytical philosophers have in fact written on the expression "the meaning of life"; for instance, Kurt Baier, Inaugural Lecture, "The Meaning of Life" (Canberra, 1957), Antony Flew, "Tolstoi and the Meaning of Life," *Ethics* (Jan. 1963), Kai Nielsen, "Linguistic Philosophy and 'The Meaning of Life'," *Cross-Currents* (Summer, 1964). Their analyses over-

From *Religious Studies*, Vol. 1, 1965. Used by permission of Cambridge University Press.

lap at many points, though not completely. I shall first of all offer a very brief, compressed and somewhat schematised account of these analyses, conflating them where they overlap, and then discuss some of the issues they raise.[1]

According to the interpretations being now worked out, questions about the meaning of life are, very often, conceptually obscure and confused. They are amalgams of logically diverse questions, some coherent and answerable, some neither. A life is not a statement, and cannot therefore have linguistic meaning. But admittedly we do use the word "meaning" outside linguistic contexts. We speak of the meaning of a gesture, of a transaction, of a disposition of troops; and in such cases we are speaking of the point or purpose or end of an act or set of acts. This usage suggests an equation between meaningfulness and purposiveness. For a life to be meaningful, it must be purposeful: or—to make life meaningful is to pursue valuable ends.

To adopt this schema, however, already involves a shift from traditional ways of speaking about life as meaningful. Meaning is not now something to be found, as awaiting discovery, but is imparted to it by the subject himself. A person looks in vain for meaning and is needlessly frustrated when he cannot find it—if he conceives it as somehow existing prior to his decisions about what policies to pursue.

To say that "making life meaningful" is a matter of "pursuing valuable, worthwhile ends" is to say that it is an activity that indispensably involves value judgments. The description of cosmic patterns, tendencies or trends does not obviate the need to make autonomous judgments about the worthwhileness or otherwise of following, or promoting or opposing any of these. This is true no less of statements about God or a hereafter. Since claims about God and hereafter are ultimately claims about what is the case, not what ought to be, no conclusion will follow deductively from them about values. Even in the religious context, the question (as now analysed) still arises, "What ends are *worthy* of pursuit?" Religious propositions cannot guarantee meaningfulness. Conversely, it is argued, loss of religious or metaphysical belief does not entail the denial of meaningfulness.

If we concentrate on the question "What is the purpose of life?" rather than on "What is its meaning?" we are still dealing with the questions "What ends shall I choose?" "What purposes shall I hold to?" The analytical philosopher characteristically and quite intentionally changes the question from singular to plural, from "purpose" to "purposes." He will claim that the original question contains a presupposition that must be rejected, the presupposition that life, if purposeful, can have only a single purpose, that only a single policy is worthwhile. Why may not a purposeful existence be a network of many purposes, with trajectories of varying reach, scope and seriousness? "We are not and cannot always be doing or caring about one big thing."[2]

The phrase, "the purpose of human life," can be offensive on a second count, because it may suggest an analogy with the purpose of an instrument, utensil, tool or organ in a living body. The theist, who does take this analogy seriously, sees human life (with its help) as subordinated to the intentions, activities of another being, who "assigns" (Baier) tasks and roles to men, and thereby imbues his life with purpose. Two senses of "purpose" must be contrasted: the first, the sense in which one has a purpose if one "purposes" or plans to do something, perhaps with the help of an artefact, an instrument, or other means: the second is the sense in which an artefact itself has a purpose, that is, a function. Only the first of these senses is compatible with moral autonomy, with being an autonomous purposer. To subordinate oneself wholly to the purposes of another is to forfeit moral status. This amounts to a moral argument against the manner in which theism seeks to secure purpose for human life. We must resist the temptation to translate "What is the purpose of life?" into "What are people *for*?"

We have seen two ways in which recent analyses of questions about the meaning of life seek to disconnect those questions from metaphysical and religious claims, or at least try to deprive such claims of any unique, privileged importance in the handling of the questions. Religious and metaphysical statements are still statements of fact, and therefore logically cannot in themselves be answers to questions about meaning. Second: if human life is given purpose by virtue of man's fulfilling the task assigned him by God, it will be "purpose" in the autonomy-denying, dignity-destroying sense. Two further arguments tend to the same general conclusion.

Consider the familiar claim that life is meaningless if death ends all, that a necessary condition of life being meaningful is immortality or resurrection. Against this it is argued that there is no entailment between temporal finiteness and disvalue, futility. We can and do love flowers that fade; and the knowledge that they will fade may even enhance their preciousness. To be everlasting, that is, is no necessary or sufficient condition of value and worthwhileness, nor therefore of meaningfulness. An eternity of futility is not logically impossible.

Again, the quest for the meaning of life is very often thought of, but thought of confusedly, as a quest for *esoteric wisdom*, metaphysical or theological. On this, Flew's discussion of Tolstoi is interesting and relevant. First, we find in Tolstoi's *A Confession* (Oxford University Press ed., 1940) an account of a period of "arrest of life," the loss of a sense that life has any meaning or purpose, an inner deadness and disorientation. Tolstoi asked, "What is it for?" "What does it lead to?" His reflection took various pessimistic turns, including notably a refusal to account anything worthwhile, if death ends all. It struck him eventually, however, that the vanity and brevity of life were well enough known to very simple and unreflective people: yet in their cases there was seldom any "arrest of life." Tolstoi concluded that these people must know the meaning of life, the meaning that eluded the learned Tolstoi himself: it must be, not a piece of rational knowledge, but some non-rational or supra-rational knowledge to which they somehow had access. Flew now contests the assumption that these people necessarily had any esoteric, mystical knowledge that Tolstoi lacked. "What we surely need here is Ryle's distinction between knowing *how* and knowing *that*; the peasants may indeed know how to live their lives free of all sophisticated psychological disabilities, but this by no means presupposes the possession of any theoretical knowledge" hidden from such a man as Tolstoi. In fact, the characters in Tolstoi's novels know better. In *War and Peace* Pierre's "mental change" is a coming to have (a learning how to have) peace of mind, not a matter of acquiring new information, new dogma. The same is true of Levin and Hadji Murad. In so far as this kind of discovery of meaning is religious, it is so in a way that may be "analysable in terms of ethics and psychology only." Crucially, to know the meaning of life is to know how to live, as at one stage Tolstoi did not.

If we continue thus and develop these last themes, it becomes clear that the first-mentioned schematic account of the meaning of life is quite misleadingly oversimple. To give life meaning cannot be just a matter of pursuing worthy projects, for that account fails to cope with phenomena like Tolstoi's arrest of life—or John Stuart Mill's during his mental crisis of 1826. More generally, it is quite possible to make various value-judgments in cold blood, while yet suffering from a sense of meaninglessness. One may fill one's days with honest, useful and charitable deeds, not doubting them to be of value, but without feeling that these give one's life meaning or purpose. It may be profoundly boring. To seek meaning is not just a matter of seeking justification for one's policies, but of trying to discover how to organise one's vital resources and energies around these policies. To find meaning is not a matter of judging these to be worthy, but of seeing their pursuit as in some sense a fulfilment, as involving self-realisation as opposed to self-violation, and as no less opposed to the performance of a dreary task. Baier's account of "meaning" includes reference to the pursuit of worthwhile projects, both in the sense of "projects that affords satisfaction to the pursuer," and in the sense of "morally worthwhile projects"—concerning, for instance, the well-being of others. Questions of the meaning of life, I suggest, are typically questions of how these two sorts of pursuit can be *fused*. I do not think that the use of such words as "fulfilment" and "self-realisation" need force one into a refined form of egoism, nor that the price of avoiding such is to empty the words of all sense. It need not be claimed that the values, duties, etc. involved *derive their force* from their ability to gratify the agent. If a particular agent fails to see the pursuit of moral and social goals as conferring meaning on his life, he need not be lamenting that he has failed to envisage how their pursuit could yield gratification for him. Nor is he necessarily revealing *Akrasia*. He may actually rise to his duty, but he rises to it as one rises from a warm bed to a chill morning's tasks. If he is asking how his duties (and other pursuits) can be represented as of "interest" to him; it need not be in the sense of "interest" that egoism requires, but in the sense *"of concern"* to him. What one often finds, on reading the reflective autobiographies and semi-autobiographies that are undoubtedly our best source-books here, is that in asking questions about the meaning of his life, the author is asking how he can relate the pursuit of various valuable ends to the realising of a certain kind or form of life, the thought of which evokes in him the response: "The pursuit of these goals really concerns me, matters to me!" He may achieve this by way of an imaginative vivifying of the objectives (moral, social, religious . . .) of his policies and pursuits, by summoning up and dwelling upon a vision of the ideal that facilitates self-identification with it. The writer may be helped in this by some extant public myth (compare R. B. Braithwaite on religious belief), or he may elaborate a private myth in which he casts himself in the role of a person dedicated to the pursuit of the valuable ends, whatever they are.[3]

I have kept the plural—"goals," "ends"—following the tendency (noted above) to repudiate "monolithic" accounts of the good life. But it needs to be remarked that there are perfectly intelligible occurrences of the singulars in many contexts; occurrences that do not stem from bad metaphysics or bad moral philosophy. A life may be said to acquire "new meaning" through the rallying and ordering of resources that have hitherto been dispersed and conflicting in disunity. This is a sort of "integrating" that is independent of any claims about all goods being ultimately one. Vronsky, in love with Anna Karenina, "felt that all his powers, hitherto dissipated and scattered, were now concentrated and directed with terrible energy toward one blissful aim . . . He knew that . . . all the happiness of life and the only meaning of life for him now was in seeing and hearing her" (I, ch. xxxi). In the same novel, Levin, having seen Kitty passing in a coach, reflects: "in the whole world there was only one being able to unite in itself the universe and the meaning of life for him. It was Kitty" (III, ch. xii).

All these complexities are reflected in the complexity of the criteria we are likely to use in commenting upon or appraising discourse about the meaning a person's life has for him. Where we are moved to disapproval, our criticism may certainly be in part a *moral* criticism: one may disapprove, for instance, of a person's commitment to the Don Juan pattern of life, its goals and priorities. But such criticism may involve other factors besides the moral. Suppose someone does take the Don Juan pattern as fitting his life as lived at present and as setting "tasks" for his future. But suppose also that in this particular case, the life as it is being lived is totally ineffectual in the relevant respects. We shall want to say, "*This* meaning cannot be given to *this* life"; and the cost of trying to impose it is a falsification of the course the life is taking in fact. The effect of such blunders in self-commitment to a pattern of life may be grotesque or pathetic, or, as in the case of the other Don—Don Quixote— it may be richly comic. Or again, although we might not wish to speak of falsification, of events and pattern at loggerheads, we might detect that there is a self-conscious, self-dramatising and only half-sincere playing-out of a role. Whereas, on the other hand, we should count integrity, the refusal of stereotyped, paste-board *personae*, as pre-eminent among grounds for approval in this domain. The agent himself may come to see, in a dawning self-knowledge, that some attempt to give meaning or purpose has been proceeding on the wrong lines. Once more, in *Anna Karenina* (Part II, ch. xxxv), Kitty's attempt to find meaning through adopting Varenka's religious way of life ends unhappily. She decides it has not risen above the level of an imitation, and has involved pretence and self-deception. Some pages later, Anna reflects on her efforts to love Karenin: "Have I not tried, . . . with all my might, to find a purpose in my life? Have I not tried to love him . . . ? But the time came when I could no longer deceive myself . . ." (Part III, ch. xvi). Where we can estimate them, the ease or difficulty, "slickness" or strenuousness involved in the quest for meaning may figure in criticism. We sometimes say that someone has found meaning in too facile or superficial a way, or that an autobiography discloses a "lack of probing," "a relaxed mood" or a cock-sureness that replaces the tension of real self-exploration.[4]

The pursuit of meaning, in the senses we have been examining, is a sophisticated activity, involving a discipline of attention and imagination. Is this true of *all* relevant senses? The case of Tolstoi and the peasants, as discussed by Flew, suggests otherwise. To look back at that may help to plot further ramifications.

What makes it plausible to say that the peasants knew the meaning of life, and in what sense, if any, did they *not* know it? On Flew's Rylean account (*ibid.* p. 116) "the secret of the peasants . . . [is] knowledge of *how* to go on living, [and this is] only another way of saying that they . . . enjoy rude mental health." This "no nonsense" analysis relies on a very weak sense of "knowing how." It is not being claimed that the peasants had mastered techniques for banishing depression—for they did not suffer from it; nor even rules, skills by which to steer their lives round the hazards of depression and mental arrests. They could hardly know of such states of mind as Tolstoi's or J. S. Mill's or Coleridge's in "dejection." They are unaware of the perils they have missed. If for the peasants "knowing the meaning of life" equals "knowing how to live," it amounts to no more than this: that as a matter of fact the peasants were not vulnerable to the malaise that Tolstoi suffered. One might want to say, "This is surely not a 'knowing' *at all*," but just a fortunate combination of circumstances *happening* to produce "rude mental health." It is true, however, that ordinary language allows this weak sense of "knowing how," a sense that is consistent with Flew's account of the peasants. It is applicable, for instance, to the baby who "knows how to cry," even to the bird who "knows how to build a nest."

On the other hand, if one's aim is (like Flew's) "to throw light upon the meaning of the question: 'What is the meaning of life?'" (*ibid.* p. 110), one must keep in mind that a quite important element of meaning is not covered by this weak sense of "knowing how . . . ," "knowing how to live," etc. Tolstoi may well have been mistaken in thinking that the peasants had an esoteric knowledge that he lacked, a knowledge that gave a key to the problem of life's meaning. But, in thinking so, he was testifying to that side of the logic of "the meaning of life" that has to drop out in the case of the peasants: namely, that questions about the meaning of life involve a problem, see life as a problem, and involve a search for an answer. This is so frequently presupposed in discourse about the meaning of life, that such discourse is felt as curiously attenuated, if it is thought away. If we do take the problematic context as built in to the logic, then the sense of "knowing how to live" that is correlative with solving the problem and coming to know that meaning, will be a stronger sense than can be used of the peasants. It will involve awareness of the hurdles, the threats of futility, and the devising of tactics to overcome them.

Could a man's life have or fail to have meaning, without his knowing that it did or did not have meaning? This question could be answered either way, according to the interpretation given to "the meaning of life." We can answer Yes: his own awareness of his life's meaning is not a necessary condition for its being meaningful. This is so, if "having meaning" is equated with "contributing to valuable projects," "achieving useful results." But it may be felt, again, that such an answer goes against the grain of language: that it is too odd to say, for instance, "White did not himself find the meaning of his life: but Black (White's biographer, writing after White's death) did find it." Finding the meaning of White's life may be deemed to be something only White is logically able to do. The giving of meaning to life is seen as essentially a task for the liver of it. Conversely, in the case of people who have not worked at it, seen it as a task, who have been unreflectively happy or unhappy, it would be most natural to say that they have neither found nor failed to find the meaning of life.

It must, of course, be admitted that the peasants had something Tolstoi wanted to have but did not have. In the sense we have been elucidating, if Tolstoi succeeded in getting it, he could be said to have found the meaning of life, but we should not say the same of the peasants, since they had never been conscious of a problem. If this is logically curious, it is not unintelligible. Were life never problematic, were people never subject to arrests of life, it is unlikely that we should ever have acquired the expressions we are discussing. But having once acquired them in the problematic context, they can be extended to other and non-problematic contexts. The former seem to remain primary, however, and it distorts the logic of "the meaning of life" if we take as paradigmatic instances of success in discovering meaning, people who have never been troubled by the problematic aspects of life, its limits, contingency and the like.

(Two smaller, related points may be mentioned in passing. Flew's statement that the characters in Tolstoi's novels know better than Tolstoi is contestable. In the case of Levin there is a good deal about the revelation of "a knowledge unattainable by reasoning." The knowledge of "what we should live for . . . cannot be explained by reason" (Part VIII, chs. xix, xii, etc.). Again, Tolstoi does permit himself to use the expression, "the meaning of life" in a remarkably different sense from that on which our discussion, and Flew's, has centred. When Anna, just before her suicide, discerned the hopelessness of her position, "she saw it clearly in the piercing light which now revealed to her the meaning of life and of human relations" (Part VII, ch. xxx)—a diabolical, not a benign, pattern being revealed. To have seen this "meaning" was not to be enabled to live, but was to judge, on the contrary, that a continuance of life was unendurable. This is an eccentric but noteworthy usage.)

On the highly particularised problems of giving meaning to an individual life, philosophy may not have much to say: but it is certainly concerned with what seem to be general threats to meaningfulness arising out of the human situation as such. For the non-theist, the chief threat may well appear to come from the realisation of mortality. The relation between meaning and mortality is, as we have noted, a focus of attention in current discussions. On the one side are writers (Tolstoi is again among them—as Flew brings out) who in some contexts virtually identify the question of meaningfulness with the question of immortality: deny immortality and you necessarily deny meaningfulness. This account plainly distorts the logic of the question about the meaning of life, not least by reducing its complexity to a single issue of fact. On the other side, a naturalistic account oversimplifies and dogmatises if it claims that "death is irrelevant" (Baier) to questions of value, worthwhileness—and hence to meaningfulness. The argument that values are not devalued by mortality, although unassailable on grounds of logic, may be used to express a naturalism that is more optimistic and brash than it is entitled to be. For a person may heed the argument that mortality and value are compatible, and yet may be burdened with a sense of futility that the argument cannot dispel. His malaise may range from occasional vague misgivings over the worthwhileness of his activities, to a thoroughgoing arrest of life.

We can most usefully consider this sort of malaise at a still more general level. A complaint of meaninglessness can be a complaint about a felt disproportion between preparation and performance; between effort expended and the effect of effort, actual or possible. Yeats expressed the complaint in well-known words: "When I think of all the books I have read, wise words heard, anxieties given to parents, . . . of hopes I have had, all life weighed in the balance of my own life seems to me *a preparation for something that never happens.*" (Compare again, Tolstoi's question, "What does it *lead* to?")

A useful vocabulary in which to discuss this can be borrowed from aesthetics. In Monroe Beardsley's book, *Aesthetics* (New York, 1958, pp. 196 f.), he distinguishes, in a musical composition, passages that have "Introduction quality" and passages that have "Exhibition quality": the one is felt as leading up to the other, the first as preparation and the second as fulfilment. He quotes, *apropos*, an amusing criticism by Tovey of Liszt's tone poem, *Ce qu'on Entend sur La Montagne.* The work consists of "an introduction to an introduction to a connecting link to another introduction . . . ," etc. Beardsley adds: "When [the tone poem] stops it is still promising something that never arrives."

In music this sort of disappointment can be due to more causes than one. It may be the listener's expectations, not the music, that are at fault. He may be simply misinformed about the programme he is to hear; expecting a symphony, but getting only a concert overture. A musical idiom may disappoint him: he awaits a fully-fashioned melody in the style of Brahms, but—since the music happens to be in the style of Webern—it provides none. In different cases, different kinds of correction are required: to study the programme, to familiarise himself with musical development after Brahms. What sounded prefatory can come to sound performatory. But, as in the Liszt-Tovey case, the fault may lie with the music, and nothing the listener can do can give it an exhibition quality.

How far can the analogy be applied? To draw first its limits: a piece of music is "given" to a listener in a way that his life, being partly shaped by his choices, is not given. The nearest to a given in the latter case is an awareness of the general conditions and scope of human existence, of what is it open for men to do and to be, of what they can reasonably count on doing and being. Suppose a person who has lost belief in immortality has a sense of futility due to the feeling that life is all prefatory, has no exhibition quality. An analytical philosopher points out to him that things can be valuable although not eternal, and so on. This is rather like pointing out that a symphony was never on the programme, but that other valuable things were. The implication is that just as a satisfactory short piece of music can be heard as having exhibition quality, so can life within the limits of earthly existence be perceived as having it.

This suggestion may dispel the sense of futility, or it may not. It may dispel it, because to some considerable extent it does lie within our power to take a particular experience either in a prefatory or exhibitory way, although how this is done we cannot inquire here in any detail. In general, and very obviously, many activities can be understood both as leading to anticipated worthwhile ends, and as worthwhile in themselves also. A person may sometimes successfully counsel himself to dwell less upon the possible future effects of his various activities, and relish the present activities themselves. (To do so, there must, admittedly, be something relishable about the activities.)

Suppose, then, the suggestion does not dispel the sense of futility. To follow the analogy a step further: life may be found recalcitrant in the way that Liszt's tone-poem was recalcitrant to Tovey. Clearly there are experiences, of prolonged and unrelievable ill-health, for instance, that can be regarded as valuable, in the sense of disciplinary, only so long as death is not believed to be the end. Lacking such belief, a person cannot simply be counselled to endow a life pervaded by pain with exhibition quality. It is of such suffering that people tend to use words like "pointless" and "senseless." If this experience is followed by no "exhibition-section," it is unredeemably futile.

What follows? The existence of unsuccessful musical compositions exposed to the Tovey criticism does not devalue those that are not exposed. Must one say any more, in the case of lives, than that some lives are without meaning, in the present sense; but that others are meaningful? Or, in terms of the earlier discussion, that some people are confronted with a stiffer problem than others in giving meaning to their lives, and that the task may sometimes be impossible for them. This would be enough to qualify an over-optimistic naturalism that implies that (where meaning is concerned) everything remains as it was in the days of belief in immortality and Providence.[5] As an index of the difficulty of nicely proportioning prefatory and exhibitory quality in a life, one may instance an aesthetic theory like John Dewey's, according to which the distinctiveness of art is its capacity to provide just such completeness and balance in experience—in contrast to the ordinary experience of life, which seldom can maximise these qualities and can never *guarantee* them.[6]

If it is a condition for life-in-general to be meaningful that these qualities *should* be guaranteed, then life-in-general is without meaning to the naturalist or agnostic—though individual lives may happen to attain it, by practical wisdom and good fortune.

Judgments about the value or futility of human projects are problematic in yet another way. Our appraisal of the value of our activities tends to vary according to the "backcloth" against which they are viewed. To the naturalist, human endeavour viewed *sub specie aeternitatis,* may seem to shrivel, frighteningly. (Compare Sartre's troubled musings on the heat-death of the sun, in his autobiographical essay, *Les Mots,* p. 208.) He may nonetheless judge as entirely worthwhile some social reform, viewed against the backcloth of a dozen years, or months, of social abuse. Yet it is not only a vestigial romanticism that prompts one to give privileged importance to the widest and broadest backcloth. For the more fully synoptic one's view, the more confident one becomes that one is reckoning with all possible threats of vilification. The movement is towards the discarding of blinkers and frames that artificially confine attention to a narrow context and which might equally artificially boost a sense of importance and worthwhileness. Only: on naturalist assumptions, the *sub specie aeternitatis* view must at least seem to vilify, by revealing human history in an ocean of emptiness before and after. Some of the logical darkness around the meaning-of-life questions comes from the uneasy awareness that there *are* alternative views, perspectives, more or less synoptic or selective in different ways, giving very different answers to questions of value, importance, futility. From this bewildering diversity the questioner seeks some release.

He may come to the problem with the belief or half-belief that there must be an authoritative view; and that if life is to be shown to be meaningful, this authoritative view will also be a value-confirming, value-enhancing view. On authoritativeness, however, I think he is asking for what cannot be given. Either a "view" is a sheer psychological fact about how someone sees human activity, in which case it has nothing that can properly be called "authority"—though it may have strikingness and imaginative force. Or, if we judge that a particular view does have authority, this is to make a judgment of value and not simply to describe one's imaginings. Now, the estimate of the importance of human life implied in the "authoritative" view may or may not conflict with the estimate one makes on other bases. If it does not conflict, there is no further problem: if it does conflict, then we must ask, Which has to yield, the judgment that the perspective is authoritative, or the independent (perhaps workaday) estimate of worthwhileness? The criteria for authoritativeness, crucially, are no less challengeable than the independent value-judgment: only by the agent weighing up, arbitrating between, or oscillating between, the two clashing sets of evaluations, can he deal with his dilemma. If he resolves the dilemma, it is resolved by his own autonomous value-judgments: and therefore the promise of having it resolved for him by some self-evident authoritativeness is not fulfilled.

Despite this argument, the naturalist ought to admit a substantial difference between his position and that of the Christian theist. There must in fact remain, with the naturalist, an uncomfortable tension or conflict between the "close-up," anthropocentric view or perspective that can sustain his sense of meaningfulness and worthwhileness, and on the other hand his sense of intellectual obligation to the objective, scientific and anti-anthropocentric view—which tends to vilify, if not logically, then psychologically. The Christian is not exposed to this tension in the same way or to the same extent. The doctrines of divine creation and of incarnation combine to rule out the judgment that, in leaving the arena of the human, one is leaving simultaneously the theatre of mind and purpose and value. For the theist, that is, there is the implicit promise of a *harmony* of perspectives. To challenge that is to challenge the ultimate coherence of theism.

Once again, the meaning-of-life vocabulary may be so used (with exacting criteria of application), that only where such a harmony is promised can human life be properly called meaningful. Or at least the reluctance of a theist to concede that life can be meaningful to the unbeliever may reflect this, perhaps unanalysed but sensed, difference between their views of the world.

In the greater part of this discussion we have been assuming that the paradigm case of a satisfactory answer to problems about the meaning of life is contained in Christian theism, and that the question for the non-Christian is whether anything at all can be rescued from a collapse of meaning. This assumption, however, may be questioned in various ways. Two of these must be briefly mentioned.

That Christianity is able to provide a satisfactory answer is implicitly denied by those critics who claim that no hereafter, even of endless beatitude, could compensate for some of the evils actually endured by men here and now.[7] To revert to the musical analogy: in a "meaningful" work, the exhibition passages fulfil and complete the anticipatory passages, which are unsatisfying by themselves. We can conceive of an anticipatory passage, however, which is so atrocious musically that nothing that followed it, even of high quality, could be said to fulfil or complete it. It may be argued that some "passages" in some people's lives are so evil that nothing could conceivably justify them. As with a *privatio* theory of evil, so with analysis in terms of "introductory quality": it makes out evil to be what we cannot by any means always see it to be, as able to be supplemented so as to become an ingredient in an aesthetically and morally valuable whole. Here, therefore, the meaning-of-life problem runs into the problem of evil. To the extent that one is baffled by the problem of evil, to the same extent one must be baffled by the meaning of life. We cannot open up that problem here.

Secondly, in his aggressively anti-theistic argument, Kurt Baier claims that theism seeks to give meaning and purpose to human life in a morally objectionable way. Understanding one's life as given purpose by God involves a thoroughgoing self-abasement or self-annulment quite incompatible with the stance of a moral agent. This self-abasement is a correlative of the recognition of God's holiness (on current accounts), the realisation in numinous dread that God is "wholly other."

The objection is impressive and serious, and certainly effective against some forms and formulations of theism. If the "otherness" of God and the *tremendum* side of the mystery are one-sidedly stressed, then human moral judgment and divine purpose are bound to be seen as incommensurable. An attitude of worshipfulness will involve an abrogating of moral autonomy.

It seems equally clear, however, that this is not the only posture a theist can adopt. Worship is by no means a simple, single-stranded concept. To worship is not only to yield to an overwhelming of the intellect or engage in unthinking, undiscerning adulation. Something very different from this is expressed, for instance, in the *B Minor Mass* or Stravinsky's *Symphony of Psalms*. An act of worship need not be a submitting of oneself, without insight, to the wholly inscrutable. Moral perfection and beauty, fused in an intensifying strangeness, are being celebrated, as these are believed to inhere in God. Evaluative reflection is being exercised: it is very far from abdicating. The worshipper is not passively, heteronomously, accepting claims about divine greatness: he is actively and autonomously recognising and relishing them. His worship is not a preface to a life of submission to commands *ab extra*. The very ingredients of his worship itself—in attitude and feeling—become part of his own inner life, the stillness of soul, the wonderment and solemnity.

The element of strangeness, of *mysterium*, has however a further role to play. Without cancelling the values, moral and aesthetic, that are celebrated in the act of worship, it powerfully intimates that they are nonetheless open to further transformation. It forbids thinking that the human vision of the good is precisely congruent with the nature of divine goodness. There is both recognition of affinity and awareness of disparity. But the latter need not be taken as a command to surrender autonomy: rather to extend progressively the zone of "recognition."

If it is true that a worshipful stance does not involve abrogating moral autonomy, neither need an acceptance of a divine purpose or meaning to the worshipper's life. This would indeed involve a regulating of one's life, a limiting of one's projects to what, rightly or wrongly, one judged to be compatible with God's will and intention. But such a limiting or circumscribing is a common feature of familiar moral situations, where one acts say, as a member of a trust, or has a special status in a group, a status that prescribes special obligations. In many, if not all such cases—and the case of divine purpose is no exception—the regulating of action is necessary, if some good or goods is to be realised. A rational person will make it his business to understand how the relevant moral institution does bring about that good. In the theistic case one needs reasons for believing that God's wisdom, goodness and power are such that the following of his will is a surer way to achieving goods in general than by carving out patterns of life that ignore or transgress his will.

Nevertheless, this sort of language quickly brings one to difficulties more stubborn than the original problem of autonomy. The fact that some worshipful activity expresses morally and aesthetically valuable states of mind does nothing to guarantee the existence of the God who is the primary object of the worship. It cannot show that God, if he exists, has the qualities celebrated in the act of worship, that these qualities are mutually compatible in a single being or that God can have these qualities and the world be the sort of world it is. And we confront the problem of how one can meaningfully speak of God, an infinite being, as having such features of finite person-hood as willing, intending, purposing. In a word, there remain difficulties enough in the theistic conception of the meaning and purpose of life, but they are the general difficulties of theism itself. The objection that the theist must abdicate his moral status is by no means decisive against all forms of theism, although valid against some.[8]

At the start of this article I mentioned one terse and gruff dismissal of the whole topic, the meaning of life: "Life is not a statement, is not a linguistic entity, so cannot strictly be said to have or lack meaning." We evaded this objection by way of a part-equating of "meaning," in this context, with "point" or "purpose." Yet it is worth asking whether, in discussing the meaning of life, some analogy with linguistic meaning may not often be operative—either in the background or the foreground of attention, helpfully or misleadingly. In what ways could it operate?

The words in a meaningful sentence "cohere." Words in a random list do not: like the events of a "meaningless" life, they merely succeed each other discretely and atomistically, and are no more. The "past" of a piece of discourse to which one is listening is felt as active and as bearing upon the presently uttered words. It is not a "lost" past. Neither is it an obsessively dominant past, that imposes a static and completed pattern in place of the developing and novel pattern that the piece of discourse builds up. Certainly life is not a piece of discourse, and the motifs that supply coherence and continuity to it are very different from a rule-governed syntax. But if not pressed to breaking-point, the analogy may have a regulative function in the managing of our relation to our own past. Extreme cases of *failure* in this task can be seen in schizophrenics to whom every day is "a separate island with no past or future," and who lack all sense of continuity, coherence; and, at the other pole, those who feel "nailed" to their past, unable to distance it at all.[9]

The vocabulary of"meaning," however, can obviously do no detailed regulating or managing by itself. If it appears to do much more than hold the bare form of the task before the attention, it may be spellbinding its user into illusion. It may suggest that the pattern of our life as a whole has a unity, and an availability to recollection *in* its unity, beyond what is in fact possible. We may say of apparent unity and coherence in life what Proust said of "the total value of our spiritual nature": "At whatever moment we estimate it, . . . it is more or less fictitious; . . . notwithstanding the long inventory of its treasures, . . . now one, now another of these is unrealisable . . . It is an illusion that our inward wealth is perpetually in our possession."[10]

The linguistic analogy may lure one on still further. The words of a sentence are uttered as the clock ticks, and the events of a life occur as the clock ticks: but the meaning of the sentence is not an episode in time—and the meaning of the life . . . ? To yield to the suggestion, and to say "timeless" of the patterns of continuities, overlapping motifs of a life would be no more illegitimate than to say the same thing of logical relations and patterns. Nevertheless, one cannot use the language of "timelessness," in respect of life, without evoking a whole syndrome of distinctive aspirations, for "deliverance from time," for experience as a *"totum simul,"* for "eternal life": and, seductive though these are, would they not surely be out of place in such reflections?

Yet some writers might not hurry to exorcise them. Santayana, for instance, argued that eternal life cannot be satisfactorily conceived as an endless succession of events, nor, coherently, as a *totum simul;* and concluded that eternity is experienced only in the contemplating of timeless objects and structures.[11] To contemplate the web of one's life's aims, its themes and articulating images, might count, on such a view, as affording as much fulfilment of the longing for eternity as the nature of things affords, everything beyond that being ultimately delusory.

It is natural and not at all absurd for a naturalistic philosopher to seek some (inevitably limited and provisional) substitute for a metaphysical or religious doctrine of eternal life. If he judges that doctrine to be logically incoherent anyway, there is all the less reason to protest if he chooses to savour those facets of experience that give a *partial* backing to the doctrines. The important thing is that he should himself be under no illusions. When he uses the vocabulary of timelessness, the "metaphysical pathos" of his discourse must be appropriate to his real beliefs and must not borrow illegitimate splendour from the theism and mysticism he rejects.

It is possible (and we have remarked on this briefly already) to take note of all the senses we have been discussing, senses in which life may be held to have meaning within a non-theistic philosophy, to share, at least in outline, the value-theory of the philosophers with whom we started, and yet to insist that life and individual lives are without meaning—"really." What is a person doing who insists on this answer?

He may be claiming that life could be thought of as having meaning only so long as that meaning was believed to be a matter for discovery, not for creation and value-decision. He may be claiming that, to be meaningful, life would have to be *comprehensively* meaningful and its meaning invulnerable to assault. Worthwhile objectives must be ultimately realisable, despite appearances. If the Kantian postulates cannot be made, meaningfulness goes: it is for him an all-or-nothing matter. Otherwise expressed, the question about meaning can be put as a question about contingency and fortuitousness. If our attempts to impose or discover coherence and purpose in a life can operate only within the narrow *Spielraum* left by an unplanned and patternless "facticity," in the end by accidents of birth and death, then the language of meaning is far more misleading (sardonically so) than it is useful.[12] If Nietzsche speaks of how desirable it is to "die at the right time," of the "free death" that "consummates," he succeeds only in throwing into stronger relief the impossibility of guaranteeing anything of the sort, and we recall his own lingering ("meaningless") end as a case in point.

The vocabulary of meaning can thus be rejected *en bloc,* as for instance atheist existentialists have tended to reject it. In criticism, perhaps only this can be said: that it is a pity to expend in one rhetorical gesture a piece of discourse that can be used to express important distinctions between and within individual human lives. The gesture, though impressive, is extravagant and linguistically wasteful. But, so far as the rejection is a piece of (negative) verbal stipulation, one is free to opt for it: the language of the meaning of life is not indispensable. Alternatively, as we saw, one may prune and rationalise and redefine the vocabulary, restricting it to judgments about purposefulness or knowledge how to live. Perhaps there is most to be said for the third option, an elucidatory and conservative tracing of senses of "the meaning of life" in literature and philosophy, and an attempt to see how differently the tasks of a life can look when they are viewed in the light of the many analogies of meaning.

Our sample of these analogies in this article, if not random, is certainly not complete.[13]

NOTES

1. I had completed this article before seeing relevant studies by John Wisdom—*Paradox and Discovery* (1966), Ch. IV, and by Ilham Dilman—*Philosophy,* October 1965.

2. H. D. Aiken, *Reason and Conduct* (New York, 1962), p. 374. See chapter xvi as a whole.

3. Obviously relevant autobiographical quarries include *The Prelude, Dichtung und Wahrheit,* Chesterton's *Autobiography* and Berdyaev's *Dream and Reality.* I have discussed some other aspects of these topics in "Vision and Choice in Morality," *Proc. Arist. Soc. Suppl.* vol. 1956, reprinted in *Christian Ethics and Contemporary Philosophy,* ed. I. T. Ramsey (S.C.M. 1966). The present article is generally complementary to that paper.

4. Roy Pascal, *Design and Truth in Autobiography* (1960), pp. 181, 191.

5. In the studies from which this discussion started, Baier and Nielsen, e.g., acknowledge that, on their analysis, particular lives may, in particular extreme situations, be "meaningless."

6. For instance: "Art celebrates with peculiar intensity the moments in which the past reënforces the present and in which the future is a quickening of what now is" (Dewey, *Art as Experience* [1934], p. 18).

7. Dostoevsky's is the classic statement: see *The Brothers Karamazov,* Book V, chap. 4.

8. Further arguments on this topic can be found in C. C. J. Webb's criticism of N. Hartmann, *Religion and Theism* (1934), pp. 69–86, 87, 144 to end.

9. On these forms of schizophrenia, see R. May, *Existence* (1958), pp. 66 (quoting Minkowski), 68.

10. *Sodome et Gomorrhe*, vol. 1, p. 213 (Eng. tr., (*Cities of the Plain*, vol. 1, p. 218).

11. *The Philosophy of Santayana*, ed. I. Edman (1953), pp. 206–211.

12. Sartre: "All existing things are born for no reason, continue through weakness and die by accident. . . . It is meaningless that we are born; it is meaningless that we die."

13. A version of this study was included in my Stanton Lectures, at the University of Cambridge, Lent Term 1966.

CHAPTER 24

R. M. HARE

"Nothing Matters"

Is "the Annihilation of Values" Something That Could Happen?

I

I want to start by telling you a story about something which once happened in my house in Oxford—I cannot remember now all the exact details, but will do my best to be accurate. It was about nine years ago, and we had staying with us a Swiss boy from Lausanne; he was about 18 years old and had just left school. He came of a Protestant family and was both sincerely religious and full of the best ideals. My wife and I do not read French very well, and so we had few French books in the house; but those we had we put by his bedside; they included one or two anthologies of French poetry, the works of Villon, the confessions of Rousseau and, lastly, *L'Etranger* by Camus. After our friend had been with us for about a week, and we thought we were getting to know him as a cheerful, vigourous, enthusiastic young man of a sort that anybody is glad to know, he surprised us one morning by asking for cigarettes—he had not smoked at all up till then—and retiring to his room, where he smoked them one after the other, coming down hurriedly to meals, during which he would say nothing at all. After dinner in the evening, at which he ate little, he said he would go for a walk. So he went out and spent the next three hours—as we learnt from him later—tramping round and round Port Meadow (which is an enormous, rather damp field beside the river Thames on the outskirts of Oxford). Since we were by this time rather worried about what could be on his mind, when he came back at about eleven o'clock we sat him down in an armchair and asked him what the trouble was. It appeared that he had been reading Camus's novel, and had become convinced that *nothing matters*. I do not remember the novel very well; but at the end of it, I think, the hero, who is about to be executed for a murder in which he saw no particular point even when he committed it, shouts, with intense conviction, to the priest who is trying to get him to confess and receive absolution, "Nothing matters." It was this proposition of the truth of which our friend had become convinced: *Rien, rien n'avait d'importance.*

Now this was to me in many ways an extraordinary experience. I have known a great many students at Oxford, and not only have I never known one of them affected in this way, but when I have told this story to English people they have thought that I was exaggerating, or that our Swiss friend must have been an abnormal, peculiar sort of person. Yet he was not; he was about as well-balanced a young man as you could find. There was, however, no doubt at all about the violence with which he had been affected by what he had read. And as he sat there, it occurred to me that as a moral philosopher I ought to have something to say to him that would be relevant to his situation.

Now in Oxford, moral philosophy is thought of primarily as the study of the concepts and the language that we use when we are discussing moral questions: we are concerned with such problems as "What does it mean to say that something *matters,* or *does not matter?*" We are often accused of occupying ourselves with trivial questions about words; but this sort of question is not really trivial; if it were, philosophy itself would be a trivial subject. For philosophy as we know it began when Socrates refused to answer questions about, for example, what *was* right or wrong before he had discussed the question "*What is it to be* right or wrong?"; and it does not really make any difference if this question is put in the form "What is rightness?" or "What is the meaning of the word 'right'?" or "What is its use in our language?" So, like Socrates, I thought that the correct way to start my discussion with my Swiss friend was to ask what was the meaning or function of the word "matters" in our language; what is it to be important?

He very soon agreed that when we say something matters or is important what we are doing, in saying this, is to express concern about that something. If a person is concerned about something and wishes to give expression in language to this concern, two ways of doing this are to say "This is important" or "It matters very much that so and so should happen and not so and so." Here, however, I must utter a warning lest I be misunderstood. The word "express" has been used recently as a technical term by a certain school of moral philosophers known as the Emotivists. The idea has therefore gained currency that if a philosopher says that a certain form of expression is used to *express* something, there must be something a bit shady or suspicious about that form of expression. I am not an emotivist, and I am using the word "express" as it is normally used outside philosophical circles, in a perfectly neutral sense. When I say that the words "matters" and "important" are used to express concern, I am no more committed to an emotivist view of the meaning of those words than I would be if I said "The word 'not' is used in English to express negation" or "Mathematicians use the symbol '+' to express the operation of addition."

Having secured my friend's agreement on this point, I then pointed out to him something that followed immediately from it. This is that when some-body says that something matters or does not matter, we want to know *whose* concern is being expressed or otherwise referred to. If the function of the expression "matters" is to express concern, and if concern is always *some-body's* concern, we can always ask, when it is said that something matters or does not matter, "Whose concern?" The answer to these questions is in most cases obvious from the context. In the simplest cases it is the speaker who is expressing his own concern. If we did not know what it meant in these sim-ple cases to say that something matters, we should not be able to understand what is meant by more complicated, indirect uses of the expression. We know what it is to be concerned about something and to express this concern by saying that it matters. So we understand when anybody else says the same thing; he is then expressing his own concern. But sometimes we say things like "It matters (or doesn't matter) to *him* whether so and so happens." Here we are not expressing our own concern; we are referring indirectly to the con-cern of the person about whom we are speaking. In such cases, in contrast to the more simple cases, it is usual to give a clear indication of the person whose concern is being referred to. Thus we say, "It doesn't matter *to him.*" If we said "It doesn't matter," and left out the words "to him," it could be assumed in ordinary speech, in the absence of any indication to the contrary, that the speaker was expressing his *own* unconcern.

II

With these explanations made, my friend and I then returned to the remark at the end of Camus's novel, and asked whether we really understood it. "Noth-ing matters" is printed on the page. So somebody's unconcern for absolutely everything is presumably being expressed or referred to. But whose? As soon as we ask this question we see that there is something funny, not indeed about the remark as made by the character in the novel, in the context in which he is described as making it (though there is something funny even about that, as we shall see), but about the effect of this remark upon my friend. If we ask whose unconcern is being expressed, there are three people to be considered, one imaginary and two real: the character in the novel, the writer of the novel, and its reader, my Swiss friend. The idea that Camus was expressing his *own* unconcern about everything can be quickly dismissed. For to produce a work of art as good as this novel is something which cannot be done by someone who is not most deeply concerned, not only with the form of the work, but with its content. It is quite obvious that it mattered very much to Camus to say as clearly and tellingly as possible what he had to say; and this argues a concern not only for the work, but for its readers.

As for the character in the novel, who thus expresses his unconcern, a writer of a novel can put what sentiments he pleases in the mouths of his characters—subject to the limits of verisimilitude. By the time we have read this particular novel, it seems to us not inappropriate that the character who is the hero of it should express unconcern about absolutely everything. In fact, it has been pretty clear right from the beginning of the novel that he has not for a long time been deeply concerned about anything; that is the sort of person he is. And indeed there are such people. I do not mean to say that there has ever been anybody who has literally been concerned about *nothing*. For what we are concerned about comes out in what we choose to *do*; to be concerned about something is to be disposed to make certain choices, certain efforts, in the attempt to affect in some way that about which we are concerned. I do not think that anybody has ever been *completely* unconcerned about *everything*, because everybody is always doing something, choosing one thing rather than another; and these choices reveal what it is he thinks matters, even if he is not able to express this in words. And the character in Camus's novel, though throughout the book he is depicted as a person who is rather given to unconcern, is depicted at the end of it, when he says these words, as one who is spurred by something—it is not clear what: a sense of conviction, or revelation, or merely irritation—to seize the priest by the collar of his cassock with such violence, while saying this to him, that they had to be separated by the warders. There is something of a contradiction in being so violently concerned to express unconcern; if nothing *really* mattered to him, one feels, he would have been too bored to make this rather dramatic scene.

Still, one must allow writers to portray their characters as their art seems to require, with all their inconsistencies. But why, because an imaginary Algerian prisoner expressed unconcern for the world which he was shortly to leave, should my friend, a young Swiss student with the world before him, come to share the same sentiments? I therefore asked him whether it was really true that nothing mattered to him. And of course it was not true. He was not in the position of the prisoner but in the position of most of us; he was concerned not about nothing, but about many things. His problem was not to find something to be concerned about—something that mattered—but to reduce to some sort of order those things that were matters of concern to him; to decide which mattered most; which he thought worth pursuing even at the expense of some of the others—in short, to decide what he really wanted.

III

The values of most of us come from two main sources; our own wants and our imitation of other people. If it be true that to imitate other people is, especially in the young, one of the strongest desires, these two sources of our values can be seen to have a common head. What is so difficult about growing up is the integration into one stream of these two kinds of values. In the end, if we are to be able sincerely to say that something matters for *us*, we must ourselves be concerned about it; other people's concern is not enough, however much in general we may want to be like them. Thus, to take an aesthetic example, my parents may like the music of Bach, and I may want to be like my parents; but this does not mean that I can say sincerely that I like the music of Bach. What often happens in such cases is that I *pretend* to like Bach's music; this is of course in fact *mauvaise foi*—hypocrisy; but none the less it is quite often by this means that I come in the end to like the music. Pretending to like something, if one does it in the right spirit, is one of the best ways of getting really to like it. It is in this way that nearly all of us get to like alcohol. Most developed art is so complex and remote from what people like at the first experience, that it would be altogether impossible for new generations to get to enjoy the developed art of their time, or even that of earlier generations, without at least some initial dishonesty.

Nevertheless, we also often rebel against the values of our elders. A young man may say, "My parents think it matters enormously to go to church every Sunday; but *I* can't feel at all concerned about it." Or he may say, "Most of the older generation think it a disgrace not to fight for one's country in time of war; but isn't it more of a disgrace not to make a stand against the whole murderous business by becoming a pacifist?" It is by reactions such as these that people's values get altered from generation to generation.

Now to return to my Swiss friend. I had by this time convinced him that many things did matter for him, and that the expression "Nothing matters" in his mouth could only be (if he understood it) a piece of playacting. Of course he didn't actually understand it. It is very easy to assume that all words work in the same way; to show the differences is one of the chief ways in which philosophers can be of service to mankind. My friend had not understood that the function of the word "matters" is to express concern; he had thought mattering was something (some activity or process) that things did, rather like chattering; as if the sentence "My wife matters to me" were similar in logical function to the sentence "My wife chatters to me." If one thinks that, one may begin to wonder what this activity is, called mattering; and one may begin to observe the world closely (aided perhaps by the clear cold descriptions of a novel like that of Camus) to see if one can catch anything doing something that could be called mattering; and when we can observe nothing going on which seems to correspond to this name, it is easy for the novelist to persuade us that after all *nothing matters*. To which the answer is, "'Matters' isn't that sort of word; it isn't intended to *describe* something that things do, but to express our concern about what they do; so of course we can't *observe* things mattering; but that doesn't mean that they don't matter (as we can be readily assured if, as I told my friend to do, we follow Hume's advice and 'turn our reflexion into our own breast'[1])."

There are real struggles and perplexities about what matters most; but alleged worries about whether anything matters at all are in most cases best dispelled by Hume's other well-known remedy for similar doubts about the possibility of causal reasoning—a good game of backgammon.[2] For people who (understanding the words) say that nothing matters are, it can safely be declared, giving but one example of that hypocrisy or *mauvaise foi* which Existentialists are fond of castigating.

I am not saying that no *philosophical* problem arises for the person who is perplexed by the peculiar logical character of the word "matters": there is one, and it is a real problem. There are no pseudo-problems in philosophy; if anything causes philosophical perplexity, it is the philosopher's task to find the cause of this perplexity and so remove it. My Swiss friend was not a hypocrite. His trouble was that, through philosophical naïveté, he took for a real moral problem what was not a moral problem at all, but a philosophical one—a problem to be solved, not by an agonising struggle with his soul, but by an attempt to understand what he was saying.

I am not denying, either, that there may be people who can sincerely say that very little matters to them, or even almost nothing. We should say that they are psychologically abnormal. But for the majority of us to become like this is a contingency so remote as to excite neither fear nor attraction; we just are not made like that. We are creatures who feel concern for things—creatures who think one course of action better than another and act accordingly. And I easily convinced my Swiss friend that he was no exception.

So then, the first thing I want to say in this talk is that you cannot annihilate values—not values as a whole. As a matter of empirical fact, a man is a valuing creature, and is likely to remain so. What may happen is that one set of values may get discarded and another set substituted; for indeed our scales of values are always changing, sometimes gradually, sometimes catastrophically. The suggestion that *nothing* matters naturally arises at times of perplexity like the present, when the claims upon our concern are so many and conflicting that we might indeed wish to be delivered from all of them at once. But this we are unable to do. The suggestion may have one of two opposite effects, one good and one bad. On the one hand, it may make us scrutinise more closely values to which we have given habitual allegiance, and decide whether we really prize them as much as we have been pretending to ourselves that we do. On the other, it may make us stop thinking seriously about our values at all, in the belief that nothing is to be preferred to anything else. The effect of this is not, as might be thought, to overthrow our values altogether (that, as I have said, is impossible); it merely introduces a shallow stagnation into our thought about values. We content ourselves with the appreciation of those things, like eating, which most people can appreciate without effort, and never learn to prize those things whose true value is apparent only to those who have fought hard to reach it. . . .

NOTES

1. *Treatise,* III 1 i.
2. *Treatise,* I 4 vii.

CHAPTER 25

W. D. JOSKE

Philosophy and the Meaning of Life

Most intelligent and educated people take it for granted that philosophers concern themselves with the meaning of life, telling us whether or not life has a meaning, and, if it has, what that meaning is. In this sense questions about the meaning of life are thought to be the direct concern of the philosopher. Philosophy is also believed to concern itself indirectly with the meaning of life, for it is thought that many purely philosophical disputes, about such topics as the existence of God, the truth or falsity of determinism, and the nature of moral judgments, can render certain attitudes to life more or less appropriate. In particular, many people are afraid of philosophy precisely because they dread being forced to the horrifying conclusion that life is meaningless, so that human activities are ultimately insignificant, absurd and inconsequential.

Although philosophy has had its great pessimists the prevailing mood among linguistic philosophers is one of qualified optimism. The mood is optimistic in so far as it is widely argued that philosophical positions cannot demonstrate the insignificance of life; but it is qualified by a caveat reminding us that if philosophical views cannot justify pessimism, they are equally incapable of providing a secure foundation for optimism. Life, it is claimed, cannot be shown to be either significant or insignificant by philosophy. In this paper I wish to argue that the contemporary attempt to establish the bland neutrality of philosophical views is not successful; philosophy is indeed dangerous stuff, and it is fitting that it should be approached with fear.

Of course the question "What is the meaning of Life?" is notoriously vague, and its utterance may be little more than an expression of bewilderment and anxiety or a shy request for help and illumination. In addition to being vague it is ambiguous. The questioner may be seeking or doubting the significance of life in general, of human life or of his own particular life. In this paper I will restrict myself to considering the significance of human life,

From *Australasian Journal of Philosophy*, Vol. 52, No. 2, 1974. Used by permission of the journal.

and will not raise the questions concerning the significance of biological life or of individualistic and idiosyncratic life styles.

However, even if we restrict our concern to human life we have not removed all ambiguity. Many philosophers who have written about the meaning of human life have dealt with the significance of the course of history or the totality of human deeds, and sought to discover whether or not there was some goal which unified and made sense of all the individual and social strivings of mankind. They investigated the significance of the existence of *homo sapiens*. Yet others have wanted not the purpose of history, but a justification of the typical features of human existence, of what is fashionably called the human condition. They have asked whether or not the typical human life style can be given significance, and it is this question that I shall be concerned with. This is not to deny that there may well be connections between the two senses of the question "What is the meaning of human life?" for it may be argued that the human life style derives its significance by enabling the totality of human deeds to bring into being some valuable end. Scholastic philosophers thus see a life lived in accordance with human nature as deriving its meaning from the part which such a life will play in the fulfilment of eternal law.

If the ambiguity of our question stems from different meanings of the word "life," the vagueness grows out of the obscurity of the word "meaning." It is the vagueness of "meaning" which has enabled contemporary philosophers to dismiss pessimistic fears as unwarranted. Aware of the confusion and uncertainty that surrounds the word, they attempt to give the question "What is the meaning of life?" respectability by reading "meaning" in a precise sense borrowed from some context in which it is used with comparatively rigorous propriety. It is then discovered that the question makes no sense when interpreted in this way, so that our worries about life's meaning are shown to be pseudo-worries. The fact that somebody asks the question shows that he has not thought seriously about the meanings of the words which make it up. Nobody need live in dread of discovering that life is meaningless, just as a prudish person need not fear the vulgarity of a fraction.

The simplest and crudest example of this rejection of the legitimacy of the question is given by those philosophers who insist that only words, sentences or other conventional symbols can have meaning. Life is not a conventional symbol and is therefore neither meaningful or meaningless. Pessimism is inappropriate, and so too is optimism, but we should be cured of the desire for optimism when we realise the conceptual absurdity which it presupposes.

I do not think that any contemporary philosopher would be guilty of such a crude dismissal of the question. Intellectual fashion has changed, and in addition, we are considerably more subtle about our theories of language than we used to be. However, there is a currently popular view which, although more sophisticated and less condescending in its willingness to admit that people who puzzle about the meaning of life may be puzzling about something real, is ultimately as disparaging of the intelligence of the questioner and the seriousness of his problem as the crude argument of the past.

It is nowadays conceded that "meaning" when it occurs in the phrase "the meaning of life" is not used in the sense of conventional meaning. Things other than conventional signs may have meaning—things such as activities. A contemporary philosopher is therefore prepared to grant that a questioner may be asking if human life is meaningful in the way in which activities can be meaningful.

What is it that makes activities meaningful? It is argued that a meaningful activity is one which has significance or importance, and that the significance of an activity may either be *intrinsic*, coming from the value of a performance in itself, or *derivative*, stemming from the part which it plays in the achievement of some worthwhile end. Now it does not require much reflection to discover that people who ask about the meaning of life are not simply asking whether the standard pattern of human life is worth following for its own sake, for they are asking a question which relates both to the world and to life. They wish to know whether the world is the sort of place which justifies and gives significance to what might otherwise seem to be the drudgery of a typical human existence. In other words, they are asking whether or not the world confers derivative meaning upon life.

At this point it is easy to argue that an activity can only possess derivative value if it can be seen as bringing nearer some end which is itself worthwhile. If, as Kurt Vonnegut speculates in *The Sirens of Titan*,[1] the ultimate end of human activity is the delivery of a small piece of steel to a wrecked space ship wanting to continue a journey of no importance whatsoever, the end would be too trivial to justify the means. It is therefore appropriate to ask how the end from which life might derive its value gains its own value, and the answer which is commonly given is that even the value of this ultimate end, must, if it is to be effective, be given to it by human agents. Even if there are objective and non-natural value facts, the most worthwhile end will not satisfy an agent unless he subscribes to the value of the end, unless he commits himself to it and makes it *his* end. Even the purposes of God are useless until a man makes them his own.

It follows from this that one cannot seek the fundamental justification of human life from the nature of the world. We fail to understand the nature of meaning if we attempt to do so. The world is neutral and cannot give meaning to men. If someone wants life to be meaningful he cannot discover that meaning but must provide it himself. How we go about giving meaning to life seems to depend upon the society we accept as our own; a Frenchman might leap into the dark, an American go to a psycho-analyst, and an Englishman cease asking embarrassing questions.

The seeker after the meaning of life is thus shown to be confused, even if his confusion about the relation between fact and value is excusable. He is not however left without consolation, for if the world cannot produce meaning it cannot produce triviality. In addition, the diagnosis of his confusion directs him to the way out of his bewilderment. He must examine his own life and undertake his own commitments, even if, in order to commit himself, he may have to turn himself into a different kind of person.

An interesting variant of this contemporary optimism is proposed by Kurt Baier in his *The Meaning of Life*.[2] Baier attempts to demonstrate that any attempt to show that life is intrinsically worthless must be false, for it will depend upon criteria that are both unreasonably high and inappropriate to the evaluation of life. He argues that a worthwhile life is simply one that is above the average of the kind in respect to such things as "the balance of happiness over unhappiness, pleasure over pain, and bliss over suffering." The mere fact of its being human cannot make a life worthless, for it is necessarily true that we cannot all be below average.

It should be noted that Baier's dissolution of utter pessimism tells against the popular view that life is itself intrinsically valuable, for we cannot all be above average any more than we can all be below it. If we can assume a normal distribution of hedonic values among mankind, Baier's criteria condemn approximately half of us to lives that are not worthwhile. I would not accuse a man of undue concern if he deplored this state of affairs. However, Baier's account of the criteria of evaluation is clearly implausible. We should not describe as intrinsically worthwhile a life in which unhappiness, pain and suffering outweighed happiness, pleasure and bliss if it turned out to be the case that such a life was above the average of our kind. Again, Baier's account of evaluation has the paradoxical consequence that a man can raise himself above the average and so make his life worthwhile, not only by improving himself, but also by increasing the balance of misery in the lives of other people. Clearly, the value of a life cannot be measured simply by comparing it to the average of its kind.

In spite of the plausibility of contemporary optimism I think that most of those people who question the meaning of life would not be happy with the diagnosis they have been offered. They would feel that it belittled their perplexity. All that agonising about a conceptual muddle! Perhaps their dissatisfaction is no more than pique. A neurotic who requested psychotherapy and was promptly and successfully treated with pills might well feel chagrin. He wanted to be cured, but he also wanted the adventure and discovery and struggle that are part and parcel of the sort of cure he had anticipated. He would feel less of a human being because he and his troubles were not considered worthy of analysis. Yet I do not think that the questioner's dissatisfaction is so completely unjustified. The diagnosis which he had been offered is too simple, so that the therapy suggested is not suited to the affliction from which he suffers.

I want to argue that life may be meaningless for reasons other than that it does not contribute to a worthwhile goal, so that the failure to find meaning in life can be due to the nature of the world and not simply to failure of adequate commitment by an agent. Discoveries about the world can force us to the conclusion that a committed life spent in pursuing worthwhile ends lacks meaning.

Our contemporary optimists are correct in taking the meaning of life to be analogous to the meaning of an activity, but their account of activities has been too simple. I want to argue that the significance of an activity can be challenged on grounds other than that the activity lacks intrinsic or derivative worth. To be precise, I shall claim that there are at least four elements of the meaningless, which I shall label worthlessness, pointlessness, triviality, and futility. To forestall unnecessary criticism, I must emphasise that I am not attempting to analyse the meanings of these terms as they occur in everyday discourse; I am, rather, stipulating uses of these terms which will I believe help clarify our problem.

I shall call an activity "worthless" if it lacks intrinsic merit, so that its performance needs justification by reference to some external purpose. An activity which is mere drudgery would thus be a worthless activity. Most of us would find the practice of parsing and analysing sentences worthless, and would need some extra reason for indulging in its exercise. We find ourselves bewildered by the school master in Guthrie Wilson's[3] novel, *The Incorruptibles* who devotes his life to parsing and analysing every sentence of *Paradise Lost*.

An activity can, of course, be meaningful even if worthless provided it is performed for some worthwhile end. An activity which is not directed towards the fulfilment of an end I shall call "pointless." A person who hits a ball against a wall without hoping to improve his health or to earn money would thus be indulging in a pointless activity. If the activity is not worthless, there is nothing absurd about it. Indeed, the very pointlessness of an activity can contribute to its pleasure, making it more truly play.

In contrast to worthless and pointless activities, an activity is trivial if, although it has a point, the purpose lacks sufficient worth to justify its performance. These are cases where the end fails to justify the means.

If lack of worth, pointlessness, and triviality were the only shortcomings which could be used to support the claim that a certain activity lacked meaning, we might indeed find it difficult to see how states of affairs outside the values of the agent could make an activity meaningless. The contemporary optimist has, however, neglected the category of the futile. This is surprising in view of the fact that so many existentialists have exalted futility into a paradigm of their beloved absurdity.

I shall call an activity "futile" if, although it has a point or needs a point in order to make it fully meaningful, the world prevents the achievement of the required end. One extreme type of futility would be an attempt to achieve some goal which is necessarily unobtainable. When we try to square the circle or solve Euler's puzzle we are guilty of such extreme futility. At the other extreme, accidental features of the world can happen to produce futility. Normally we can find uses for estimates of future population based upon current statistics and life tables, yet the task could be made futile by the unexpected disaster. In between these two extremes we find cases where the futility is neither necessary nor unpredictable. Thomas Nagel gives us the example of the man who delivers a brilliant and persuasive speech in support of a motion which has already been passed. Another case from Nagel is that of the impassioned declaration of love to a recorded announcement.[4]

The examples given above are all cases in which the world prevents the actor from realising his consciously intended end. In other cases an action may be futile although it has no consciously intended end, provided that it is the sort of activity which normally requires an end if it is to be considered worthwhile. The classical example of this sort of futility is that of Sisyphus—condemned to spend eternity pushing his stone to the top of a hill in order that it might roll down so that it could again be pushed to the top. A parallel case is found in the alleged practice of military prisons. A prisoner is given a small spoon and a large heap of sand. He is instructed to move the heap from one place to another, and when the task is completed to move it back again. In both these cases the punishment is peculiarly degrading because the actor is aware of the futility of the performance, and is compelled to act in accordance with desires which he cannot make his own.

We have then four different elements of the meaningful, four different ways in which we can criticise an activity for lacking in meaning.

I shall say that an activity is *fully meaningful* if it suffers from none of these defects, so that it is valuable in itself, directed towards an end which is not trivial, and is not futile. Many people who seek a short answer to the question "What is the meaning of life?" are, I suspect, looking for some simple fact or vision which will enable a human being who knows the secret to so organise his life that all of his activities will be fully meaningful. The meaning of life is thought to be the fact which makes such re-direction possible. However, few of us have such high expectations, and we are content to perform tasks that are not fully meaningful. We will endure drudgery if we can accomplish something worthwhile, and we are happy playing pointless games.

At the other extreme, I shall say that an action is *valueless* if it lacks all four elements of the meaningful, so that, from the point of view of the agent, there is no internal reason why it should be undertaken. The performance of a valueless activity is rational only if the agent is compelled to undertake it.

In between the valueless and the fully meaningful, we have those activities which are worth performing even though they fall short of the fully meaningful, such activities I shall call *valuable*.

How do our four elements of the meaningful determine the value of an action? I do not wish to explore this problem fully, but merely to make a few points. In the first place, it is clearly a tautology that if an action has worth then it is valuable. Even the performance of a futile task is justified if it is fun, and Sisyphus would have defeated the intentions of the Gods if he had happened to like rolling rocks up hills. However, it is not unnatural to hold that worth alone does not make an action completely satisfying. Many people have an incurable desire to cast a shadow across the future and affect the world so that it is forever modified by their intentions. They would find an activity which possessed only worth not nearly as rewarding as one which possessed some additional value. Those who protest concerning the irrationality of such desires should remember how we expect the activities of parents, politicians and public servants to be, in part at least, directed toward the production of benefits which will be enjoyed only by people yet unborn.

In the second place, while it is clear that triviality prevents an activity which has point gaining any additional value from that point, it is not so clear that this is the case with futility. Does an activity which is directed towards a non-trivial end, gain significance from that end if the activity is futile so that the goal can never be reached? My tentative answer is that we are each of us justified in striving for an unattainable end, provided we do not realise that the end is unattainable. However, when we do become aware of the futility of an activity, the goal loses its power to add meaning to the performance.

That is why the fear of futility is peculiarly haunting. We can never rid ourselves of the possibility of discovering that the world has doomed us to frustration. The altruistic project which is intended to increase the well-being of mankind may produce effects that run counter to our intentions. Subjectively, it seems that ignorance is at least near to bliss, for the ignorant man can gain satisfaction from the pursuit of the impossible, and he can derive that satisfaction only because he is ignorant.

I want now to show that certain commonly held and rationally defendable philosophical views can be seen as threatening human life with futility. I have said that I would use the phrase "human life" to refer to "the typical human life style," and this vague phrase now needs elucidation.

We expect a member of a biological species to develop in a manner which is both typical of and distinctive to the species to which it belongs. The life style of a species is the pattern of behaviour which an animal follows because it is a member of the species. When we say that cats are predatory and carnivorous we are claiming that certain types of behaviour are part of the life style of the cat. Unfortunately, if we treat human beings as a biological species, we encounter difficulties when we seek the human life style. The physiological phases of our development are clear enough, the human being will inevitably develop from childhood through adolescence to maturity and senescence, but in contrast to other animals human behaviour is pliable. There are no fixed courting rituals, no common habits of nest building, and not even any common practices of child rearing. Moreover, the variety of human practices is not akin to the variety of life styles which would be found in a collection of many different kinds of animals. *Homo sapiens* is not an assortment of species. We each of us know that if we had chosen otherwise or been brought up differently we might be enjoying or enduring a way of life very different from that which we are now living. We might have had more or fewer spouses, have left school earlier, be working in a different profession or be aiming at some achievement towards which we at present have no sympathy whatsoever.

Yet it is the very diversity of individual lives which enables us to sketch in the fundamentals of the human life style. The peculiarity of the human animal is that he can rationalise, reflect and criticise, so that he is not like a bird which cannot help but build a nest instead of a cocoon. We are creatures who pursue very general ends imposed upon us by the brute facts of physiology, and who must choose patterns of life in accordance with these general ends. The human life style thus involves critical and reflective activity, and requires the use of practical and theoretical reason directed, among other things, towards the discovery and achievement of ends which will not be seen to be futile when we learn more about our own natures and the world.

How strong is the analogy between the human life style and straight-forward activities? Is there any point in assessing that life style by criteria derived from the assessment of action? It might seem not, for we do not choose either our fundamental drives or our intellectual pretensions. We find ourselves with them, rather than adopt them. A man criticising the human life style might seem as absurd as a caterpillar speculating about the value of building cocoons. We do not undertake living in the way in which we deliberately decide to do something.

Nevertheless, there is point in evaluating human life as if it were an activity. In the first place, we are not as helpless as nesting birds or metamorphosing insects. Even if the fundamentals of human life are given, there is always the choice of not living, which is why philosophers who have worried about the meaning of life have so often been obsessed by the thought of suicide. In the second place it is by no means clear that human nature cannot be changed through the interference of man. Koestler, who finds certain elements of our nature anachronistic, looks for chemicals to alter this nature.[5] Finally, even if we are only playing a game of let's pretend when we construe human life as if it were a deliberately chosen activity, many people find satisfaction in playing the game. They would find intellectual or aesthetic delight in discovering that if human life were a voluntary activity it could justifiably be chosen by a rational creature.

Having argued that there is sufficient analogy between human life and an activity to warrant our assessing them by common criteria, I want to show how philosophical views about the world may give us reason for believing in the futility of that life.

CASE 1. THE NAKED APE

If the speculations of some popularisers of biological theories are correct, there is good reason for holding that human life possesses the anachronistic futility exemplified by the speaker who declaims brilliantly after the motion has been passed.[6] They claim that many bewildering human activities such as our common aversion and hostility towards members of out groups, and our propensity to become violent and quarrelsome when huddled too close to our fellows, represent biological survivals which, although they once served our needs, are inappropriate to the modern environment. If our lives are necessarily an accommodation to these primitive leftovers there is a good deal of pointless struggle and torment; but the salt has yet to be rubbed into the wound.

If we see people as naked apes, we cannot but be cynical concerning the superstructure of justification associated with many of the most memorable human enterprises. Once we accept that many of our political and military endeavours are the working out of a primitive instinct of territoriality, we can no longer regard as fully meaningful the gloss of reasoning and argument which men use in an attempt to show that their undertakings are reasonable. The words of debate become mere persiflage; the talk a mere epiphenomenon of creatures ignorant of the true springs of their actions. We begin to undermine our faith in the capacity of human beings to know the truth, discover what causes what, and learn, through self-examination, about the integrity of their own motives.

CASE 2. MORAL SUBJECTIVISM

I do not believe that moral subjectivism necessarily produces a lack of accord between the world and our activities. If we were lucky, the universe and a man's attitudes could be in harmony. However, it seems that, in fact, the moral stances which people take are often of such a kind that they are futile in the face of the world. People not uncommonly sacrifice their happiness, and even their lives, for hopeless causes. Even odder than this is the fact that men who do not share a martyr's attitudes frequently admire him for standing up for truth, and the integrity of his personality. Good motives do not provide complete absolution, but the man who suffers in vain for his morality is commonly admired.

If we hold that ultimate value judgments can possess objective truth or falsity, and that this truth or falsity is not determined by the desires and attitudes of man, we can lend sense both to the act of self-sacrifice and to our reverence for it. The martyr is a martyr not simply for integrity but also for truth. Yet if relativistic subjectivism is true, the self-sacrifice is vain, for truth is not at stake. The martyr for the lost cause becomes, not silly, but pitiful. He accomplishes nothing and is simply a person who would have been better off had his ultimate desires been other than they were.

It will undoubtedly be said that I have missed the point of relativism. A man can have no better reason, it will be argued, for acting in a certain way than the excellent reason that what he does accords with his innermost being. It may well be the case that no reason could be better, but if this is so it is an ironic misfortune. The best reason a man has may fail to fit the nature of the universe, so that the rational act is futile.

CASE 3. ULTIMATE CONTINGENCY

I think it is still true that, among professional philosophers, the orthodox view concerning the explanation of natural phenomena is modified Humeanism. It is believed that our ability to discover the laws of nature, and to utilise them in order to both explain and cope with the world about us, depends upon the occurrence of ultimate regularities which are contingent and inexplicable. They are not inexplicable because we lack the intellectual capacity to explain, rather they are inexplicable because they have no explanation. Of course, the regularities which we encounter and recognise in our everyday dealings with the world are almost certainly not inexplicable, for we can justify our reliance upon them if we can show that they are the products of more fundamental regularities, but ultimately, it is held, the edifice of science rests upon brute and inexplicable regularities—the fundamental laws of nature.

Yet here we have a paradox. In ordinary life when we come to accept that a regularity has no explanation we regard it as a mere coincidence. If, for example, we find that all the books on a particular shelf are between 200 and 250 pages long, and we cannot discover any causal connection between their being on the shelf and their having that length, we dismiss the regularity as a mere coincidence. When we do this we acknowledge that we have no right to make any inference concerning the number of pages of the next book that might be put upon the shelf. Yet according to Humeanism, the basic regularities which we hold to be laws of nature have no explanation. If we were to be consistent it seems that we should dismiss them as merely coincidental. Yet of course we label them laws of nature precisely because we do not wish to surrender our right to make inductive inferences concerning natural phenomena. If the world view of the Humean is correct, it seems we cannot be consistent in our attempt to construct rational models of the world. Yet reason demands consistency, so that science becomes futile; a game which cannot be won unless the rules are broken.

CASE 4. ATHEISM

The relationship between belief in God and the meaning of life is notoriously complex. Traditionally God has been used as a guarantee of objective values to provide justification for holding that certain activities are worthwhile in themselves, and also, in his capacity as designer of the universe, to justify our hope that there is point to our lives, the point deriving from the part which human existence plays in the fulfilment of the divine purpose. Unfortunately for the theist, I do not believe that anyone has been able to adequately ground objective values in the nature of God. The question which Plato asked in "The Euthyphro," "Why do the Gods value what is just?" cannot be evaded. Similarly, the attempt to give indirect value to human life by deriving that value from the purpose of God is open to the argument already mentioned, that the purposes of God are irrelevant unless we accept them as valuable in themselves and adopt them as our own. In addition, many philosophers find degrading the very idea of our lives being ordered by a superior being for the production of an end determined by the nature of that being. Thus, Kurt

Baier has written, "To attribute to a human being a purpose in that sense is not neutral, let alone complimentary: it is offensive. It is degrading for a man to be regarded as merely serving a purpose."[7]

In spite of this, many people do feel that without God human life becomes meaningless. In part, the explanation of this is obvious. In most societies it is common to indoctrinate children with the belief that everything that matters derives from God. Yet what is surprising is that the view that unless there is a God life has no meaning is still proclaimed not just by children but by the sophisticated. Thus, Paul Ramsey, Professor of Religion at Princeton, is still able to claim in his *Modern Moralists* that "suicide is an inner logical consequence of *vital* atheism."[8] If Ramsey is correct I and many others have started people along the road to suicide. Of course he is not correct, and shows a surprising lack of awareness of the traditional arguments concerning the relation between God and morality. Nevertheless, although it does not follow from atheism that a person has no reason to continue living or to regard any activity as worthwhile, I think that atheism does open the possibility of discovering that human life possesses an extra element of absurdity. The traditional religions do claim that because the world is designed, and because a rational nature plays a part in this design, human activities cannot be futile. Although we cannot know how our desires accord with the nature of the world, the theist claims that it would be contrary to the nature of a perfect and omnipotent being to have given us desires that were not in principle capable of being acted upon and fulfilled, or to have imposed upon us life-patterns which could not be held consistent and justifiable. In this sense, I believe that although atheism does not render life meaningless, it *opens* for us the possibility of discovering that it is futile. Perhaps Descartes should not be lightly dismissed when he claims that only the theist has reason to trust his intellectual powers.

I have used these four cases to demonstrate that philosophical positions are not neutral in the conflict between pessimism and optimism, and in particular I have argued that certain widely held views lend strength to the claim that there are strong analogies between human life and a futile activity. I have not of course established that life is futile, but merely that there are *prima facie* analogies between pointless activities and many of the goal-directed undertakings that are part of the human life style. What are the practical consequences which we should draw?

In the first place, we are not justified in rejecting a philosophical view simply because if that view is true, valued life styles can no longer be uncritically accepted. We are not entitled, for example, to believe in God simply to protect our species against the charge that its activities are futile. On the other hand, views which demonstrate the fuility of the procedures of reasoning which we rely upon in order to establish that futility may be queried. Perhaps the scepticism which follows from Humeanism is a ground for holding that Humeanism must be false.

In the second place, the futility of human life does not warrant too profound a pessimism. An activity may be valuable even though not fully meaningful, and we have seen that Sisyphus would have frustrated the Gods if he could have given worth to his eternal task. We, too, can value life even if we believe that it is futile, and an active life may be fruitful in that it is productive of unexpectedly valuable consequences.[9] In addition, the pessimist is not by his pessimism exempted from all responsibility for his individual decisions; he is still faced with choices, and with giving meaning to the life which is the outcome of those choices.

Yet in spite of these consolations, it seems to me that it would be a matter of regret if we did discover that the basic capacities which make us human were incapable of being fulfilled. Human life would be flawed, tarnished and ultimately unreasonable; a second-best existence. When we remember that we do not choose to be human, the analogy between our lot and that of Sisyphus, the eternal prisoner, becomes grim. A philosopher, even though he enjoys living, is entitled to feel some resentment towards a world in which the goals that he must seek are forever unattainable.

NOTES

1. K. Vonnegut: *The Sirens of Titan* (1962).

2. K. Baier: *The Meaning of Life* (1957) esp. pp. 25–27.

3. Guthrie Wilson: *The Incorruptibles* (1960).

4. T. Nagel: "The Absurd," *Journal of Philosophy* LXVIII No. 20 (October 4 1971), pp. 716–727.

5. A. Koestler: *The Ghost in the Machine* (1968).

6. See, for example, K. Lorenz: *On Aggression* (1967); Desmond Morris: *The Naked Ape: A Zoologist's Study of the Human Animal* (1967); and Robert Ardrey: *The Territorial Imperative: A Personal Inquiry into the Animal Origins of Property and Nations* (1967).

7. K. Baier: *The Meaning of Life* (1957), p. 20.

8. P. Ramsey: *Modern Moralists* (1970), p. 26.

9. I owe this suggestion to Professor D. A. T. Gasking.

EPILOGUE

Love, Knowledge, and Pity

Bertrand Russell

Three passions, simple but overwhelmingly strong, have governed my life: the longing for love, the search for knowledge, and unbearable pity for the suffering of mankind. These passions, like great winds, have blown me hither and thither, in a wayward course, over a deep ocean of anguish, reaching to the very verge of despair.

I have sought love, first, because it brings ecstasy—ecstasy so great that I would often have sacrificed all the rest of life for a few hours of this joy. I have sought it, next, because it relieves loneliness—that terrible loneliness in which one shivering consciousness looks over the rim of the world into the cold unfathomable lifeless abyss. I have sought it, finally, because in the union of love I have seen, in a mystic miniature, the prefiguring vision of the heaven that saints and poets have imagined. This is what I sought, and though it might seem too good for human life, this is what—at last—I have found.

With equal passion I have sought knowledge. I have wished to understand the hearts of men. I have wished to know why the stars shine. And I have tried to apprehend the Pythagorean power by which number holds sway above the flux. A little of this, but not much, I have achieved.

Love and knowledge, so far as they were possible, led upward toward the heavens. But always pity brought me back to earth. Echoes of cries of pain reverberate in my heart. Children in famine, victims tortured by oppressors, helpless old people a hated burden to their sons, and the whole world of loneliness, poverty, and pain make a mockery of what human life should be. I long to alleviate the evil, but I cannot, and I too suffer.

This has been my life. I have found it worth living, and would gladly live it again if the chance were offered me.

Bibliography

Althaus, Paul. "The Meaning and Purpose of History in the Christian View." *Universitas,* Vol. 7 (1965), pp. 197–204.

Baier, Kurt. "Meaning and Morals." In Paul Kurtz (ed.), *Moral Problems in Contemporary Society.* Englewood Cliffs, NJ: Prentice-Hall, 1969.

Black, Algernon. "Our Quest for Faith: Is Humanism Enough?" In P. Kurtz (ed.), *The Humanist Alternative.* Buffalo: Prometheus Books, 1973.

Blackham, H. J. "The Human Programme." In J. Huxley (ed.), *The Humanist Frame.* London: G. Allen and Unwin, 1961.

Blackham, H. J. "The Pointlessness of it All." In H. J. Blackham (ed.), *Objections to Humanism.* Philadelphia: Lippincott, 1963.

Britton, Karl. *Philosophy and the Meaning of Life.* Cambridge: Cambridge University Press, 1969.

Brown, Delwin. "God's Reality and Life's Meaning." *Encounter,* Vol. 28, No. 3 (1968), pp. 252–262.

Brown, Delwin. "Process Philosophy and the Question of Life's Meaning." *Religious Studies,* Vol. 7 (1971), pp. 13–29.

Clark, C. H. D. *Christianity and Bertrand Russell.* London, 1958. de Saint Exupery, Antoine. *Wind, Sand, and Stars,* Chap. 9. New York: Harcourt, Brace and World, 1939.

Dilman, Ilham. "Professor Hepburn on Meaning in Life." *Religious Studies,* Vol. III (1937), pp. 547–554.

Dilman, Ilham. "Life and Meaning." *Philosophy,* Vol. 40 (1965), pp. 320–333.

Durant, Will (ed.) *On the Meaning of Life.* New York, 1932.

Edwards, Paul. "Why?" In P. Edwards (ed.), *The Encyclopedia of Philosophy,* Vol. 8, pp. 296–302. New York: Macmillan, 1967.

Fackenheim, E. L. "Judaism and the Meaning of Life." *Commentary,* Vol. 39 (1965), pp. 49–55.

Flew, Anatony. "Tolstoi and The Meaning of Life." *Ethics,* Vol. 73 (1963), pp. 110–118.

Frankl, Victor. *Man's Search for Meaning.* New York: Beacon, 1963

Fromm, Erich. *Man For Himself.* New York: Holt, Rinehart, & Winston, 1947.

Greene, T. M. "Man Out of Darkness." *Atlantic Monthly,* April 1949.

Heschel, Abraham. *Man Is Not Alone.* New York: Farrar, Strauss, and Giroux, 1951.

Heschel, Abraham. *Who Is Man?,* pp. 50–80. Stanford: Stanford University Press, 1965.

Hocking, W. E. "Meanings of Life." *Journal of Religion,* Vol. 16 (1936).

Hollis, Christopher. "What Is the Purpose of Life?" *The Listener,* Vol. 70 (1961), pp. 133–136.

James, William. "Is Life Worth Living?" In *The Will to Believe and Other Essays in Popular Philosophy.* New York, 1897.

Ketcham, Charles B. *The Search for Meaningful Existence.* New York: Weybright and Talley, 1968.

Kurtz, Paul. *The Fullness of Life.* New York: Horizon, 1974.

Lachs, John. "To Have and to Be." *The Personalist,* Vol. 45, No. 1 (1964), pp. 540–547.

Lamont, Corliss. "The Philosophy of Humanism." In C. Lamont (ed.), *The Philosophy of Humanism.* New York: Frederich Ungar, 1949.

Lewis, C. S. "De Futilitate." *In Christian Reflections.* London: Geoffrey Bles, 1967.

Maguire, J. J. "The Illogical Dr. Stace." *Catholic World*, Vol. 168 (1948), pp. 102–105.

Marcel, Gabriel. *The Mystery of Being*, Vol. I, pp. 199–215. Chicago: Henry Regnery, 1960.

May, Rollo. *Man's Search for Meaning*. New York: W. W. Norton, 1953.

McGee, C. D. *The Recovery of Meaning—An Essay on the Good Life*, Chap. 1. New York, 1966.

Mohl, Oscar. "Man's Search for Significance in Recent Literature." *Journal of Critical Analysis*, Vol. 2 (1970), pp. 21–27.

Moreland, J. P. "God and the Meaning of Life." In J. P. Moreland (ed.), *Sealing the Secular City; A Defense of Christianity*, pp. 105–132. Grand Rapids: Baker Book House, 1987.

Munitz, Milton K. *The Mystery of Existence*. New York: Appleton-Century-Crofts, 1965.

Nielsen, Kai. "Ethics without Religion." *The Ohio University Review*, Vol. VI (1964), pp. 48–62.

Nielsen, Kai. *Ethics without God*. Buffalo: Prometheus Books, 1973.

Nielsen, Kai. "Death and the Meaning of Life." In *The Search for Absolute Values in a Changing World*. Proceedings of the Sixth International Conference on the Unity of Sciences, pp. 483–490. New York: International Cultural Foundation, 1978.

Norton, David L. *Personal Destinies*. Princeton: Princeton University Press, 1976.

Popper, Sir Karl. *The Open Society and Its Enemies*, 5th edition, Vol. 2, Chap. 25. Princeton: Princeton University Press, 1966.

Robinson, Richard. *An Atheist's Values*, pp. 54–57, 155–157. Oxford: Oxford University Press, 1964.

Rosen, Stanley. *Nihilism: A Philosophical Essay*. New Haven: Yale University Press, 1969.

Russell, L. J. "The Meaning of Life." *Philosophy*, Vol. 28 (1953), pp. 30–40.

Sanders, Steven, and Cheney, David R. *The Meaning of Life: Questions, Answers, and Analysis*. Englewood Cliffs, NJ: Prentice-Hall, 1980.

Sartre, Jean-Paul. "Existentialism." *In Existentialism and Human Emotions*. New York: Philosophical Library, 1948.

Schopenhauer, Arthur. "On the Sufferings of the World." Trans. by T. B. Saunders. In Richard Taylor (ed.), *The Will to Live: Selected Writings of Arthur Schopenhauer*. New York, 1962.

Smart, Ninian. "On Understanding the Meaning of Life." In *The Philosophy of Religion*, pp. 75–98. New York: Random House, 1970.

Stern, Alfred. *The Search for Meaning: Philosophical Vistas*. Memphis, 1971.

Tolstoy, Leo. *The Death of Ivan Ilych*. Trans. by A. Maude. New York: New American Library, 1960.

Toynbee, Arnold. "The Meaning of History for the Soul." In A. Toynbee (ed.), *Civilization on Trial*, pp. 253–263. New York: Oxford University Press, 1948.

Troubetzkoy, Eugene. "The Meaning of Life." *The Hibbert Journal*, Vol. 16 (1918).

Warnock, G. J. *The Object of Morality*. London: Metheun, 1971.

Wittgenstein, Ludwig. *Tractatus Logico-Philosophicus*, Sections 6, 4–7. Trans. by D. F. Pears and B. F. McGuinness. London: Rutledge and Kegan Paul, 1961.

Wittgenstein, Ludwig. *Notebooks, 1914–16*, pp. 72e–75e. Oxford: Basil Blackwell, 1961, 1979.